Rosa Luxemburg

Paul Frölich

Rosa Luxemburg
Ideas in Action

Translated by Johanna Hoornweg

Haymarket Books
Chicago, Illinois

First published in Paris in August 1939.
Published in English by the Left Book Club in London in 1940.
This translation first published in 1972 © Pluto Press.

This edition published in 2010 by
Haymarket Books
P.O. Box 180165
Chicago, IL 60618
773-583-7884
info@haymarketbooks.org
www.haymarketbooks.org

Trade distribution:
In the U.S., Consortium Book Sales and Distribution, www.cbsd.com
In Canada, Publishers Group Canada, www.pgcbooks.ca
In the UK, Turnaround Publisher Services, www.turnaround-uk.com
In Australia, Palgrave Macmillan, www.palgravemacmillan.com.au
All other countries, Publishers Group Worldwide, www.pgw.com

ISBN: 978-1-60846-074-8

Cover design by Josh On and Melanie Cervantes.
Cover image by Melanie Cervantes.

Special discounts are available for bulk purchases by organizations and
institutions. Please contact Haymarket Books for more information at
773-583-7884 or info@haymarketbooks.org.

This book was published with the generous support
of Lannan Foundation and the Wallace Action Fund.

Library of Congress CIP Data is available.

Contents

Translator's Note   vii

Introduction to the English edition by Tony Cliff   ix

Preface to the second German edition   xiii

1   Youth   1
At home 1; The struggle begins 5

2   The fate of Poland   10
Zürich 10; Leo Jogiches 12; The *Proletariat* party 15; Against Blanquism 18; The national question as a strategic problem 21; The founding of Polish Social Democracy 32

3   In defense of Marxism   38
In the ranks of German Social Democracy 38; Reformism thrusts forward 43; A world-view 48; Reform and revolution 51; Capitalism tamed 54; The labour of Sisyphus 58

4   The conquest of political power   61
The limitations of parliamentarism 61; An experiment in government 62; Ultima ratio 67; A fighting spirit 70; Skirmishes 72

5   The Russian Revolution of 1905   77
Russia awakens 77; The organisation of the party 80; Lenin and Luxemburg 86; The character of the 1905 revolution 89; Skirmishing in the rear 94

6   In the line of fire   100
Warsaw 100; The problems of armed uprising 102; Polish Social Democracy and the Polish Socialist Party 108; in Prison 113; Criticism of the revolution 118

7   A new weapon   124
Disappointment 124; The political mass strike 127; *The mass strike, the party, and the trade unions* 132; Leaders without vocation 138; A theory of spontaneity 140

8   Concerning the end of capitalism   146
The party school 146; Introduction to economics 148; The accumulation of capital 150; Imperialism and the theory of capital accumulation 156; The epigoni attack 158

9   The struggle against imperialism   164
The political problem 164; Against the danger of war 166; The struggle for equal suffrage 169; The courts step into action 176;

10 Like a candle burning at both ends   181
The woman 181; The fighter 188; The writer 193; The
orator 196

11 War   199
The fourth of August 199; Under the banner of revolt 205;
Die Internationale 209; A year in a women's prison 214; The
Juniusbroschüre 217; Spartakus 222; Barnimstrasse, Wronke,
Breslau 227

12 Russia 1917   232
The first triumph 232; The October Revolution 238; Criticism
of the Bolsheviks 243

13 The German revolution   253
Prelude 253; November 257; The gathering of forces 261; The
programme of the revolution 265; The counter-revolution strikes
back 271; The founding of the German Communist Party 279

14 The road to death   284
The January struggle 284; Spartakus and the January
uprising 289; The man-hunt 293; The murders 297;
Afterwards 300

Postscript by Iring Fetscher   304
References   313
Bibliography   319
Index   325

Translator's Note

This translation is based on the 3rd revised German edition of Paul Frölich's *Rosa Luxemburg. Gedanke und Tat*, which was published in Frankfurt am Main in 1967. It leans heavily on Edward Fitzgerald's translation which was published by Victor Gollancz, in a Left Book Club Edition, in 1940. For reasons associated with the conditions under which this earlier English translation was produced–in slightly abridged form without the author having access to the original source material–the author's widow Rose Frölich felt that a new definitive edition of the work should appear in English, a thorough re-translation, incorporating all the revisions and changes of the 3rd German edition.

Information which appears in square brackets has been added by the translator to elucidate the text. Material in round brackets generally occurs in the German original. Footnotes are taken from the German edition except where otherwise indicated.

A number of abbreviations have been used throughout the text and they are appended here with full English titles for the convenience of the reader:

The *Bund*   Jewish Workers' League (*Algemener Yiddisher Arbeter Bund*)
PPS   Polish Socialist Party
SDKPiL   Social Democratic Party of the Kingdom of Poland and Lithuania
SPD   Social Democratic Party of Germany
USPD   Independent Social Democratic Party of Germany
KPD   Communist Party of Germany

Introduction

It has been a great honour to be asked by Rose Frölich, the widow of Paul Frölich, to write an introduction to the present edition of *Rosa Luxemburg*. It is good to have a new and fuller edition of a magnificent book, which has been a rarity for a whole generation. Frölich's book is written in the spirit of its heroine. Frölich shows clearly that above all Rosa Luxemburg was a giant of thought and action; she dared to think because she dared to act; her will matched her reason.

Franz Mehring, the biographer of Marx, did not exaggerate when he called Rosa Luxemburg the best brain after Marx. But she did not contribute her brain alone to the working-class movement; she gave everything she had–her heart, her passion, her strong will, her very life.

Above all else, Rosa Luxemburg was a revolutionary socialist. And among the great revolutionary socialist leaders and teachers she has a special historical place of her own.

When reformism degraded the socialist movements by aspiring purely for the 'welfare state', by tinkering with capitalism, it became of first importance to make a revolutionary criticism of this hand-maiden of capitalism. It is true that other Marxists besides Rosa Luxemburg–Lenin, Trotsky, Bukharin and others–conducted a revolutionary fight against reformism. But they had a limited front to fight against. In their country, Russia, the roots of this weed were so weak and thin, that a mere tug was sufficient to uproot it. Where Siberia or the gallows stared every socialist or democrat in the face, who in principle could oppose the use of violence by the labour movement? Who in Tsarist Russia would have dreamed of a parliamentary road to socialism? Who could advocate a policy of coalition government, for with whom could coalitions be made? Where trade unions scarcely existed, who could think of considering them the panacea of the labour movement? Lenin, Trotsky and the other Russian Bolshevik leaders did not need to counter the arguments of reformism with a painstaking and exact analysis. All they needed was a broom to sweep it onto the dungheap of history.

In Central and Western Europe conservative reformism had much deeper roots, a much more embracing influence on the thoughts and moods of the workers. The arguments of the reformists had to be answered by superior ones, and here Rosa Luxemburg excelled. In these countries her scalpel was a much more powerful weapon than Lenin's sledgehammer.

In Tsarist Russia the mass of the workers were not organised in parties or trade unions. There was no great threat of powerful empires being built by a bureaucracy rising from the working class as in the well-organised workers' movement of Germany; and it was natural that Rosa Luxemburg had a much earlier and clearer view of the role of the labour bureaucracy than Lenin or Trotsky. She understood long before they did that the only power that could break through bureaucratic chains is the initiative of the workers. Her writings on this subject can still serve as an inspiration to workers in the advanced industrial countries, and are a more valuable contribution to the struggle to liberate the workers from the pernicious ideology of bourgeois reformism than those of any other Marxist.

Rosa Luxemburg's blend of revolutionary spirit and clear understanding of the nature of the labour movement in Western and Central Europe is in some way connected with her particular background of birth in the Tsarist Empire, long residence in Germany, and full activity in both the Polish and the German labour movements. Anyone of smaller stature would have been assimilated into one of the two environments, but not Rosa Luxemburg. To Germany she brought the 'Russian' spirit, the spirit of revolutionary action. To Poland and Russia she brought the 'Western' spirit of workers' self-reliance, democracy and self-emancipation.

Her *Accumulation of Capital* is an invaluable contribution to Marxism. In dealing with the mutual relations between the industrially advanced countries and the backward agrarian ones she brought out the most important idea that imperialism, while stabilising capitalism over a long period, at the same time threatens to bury humanity under its ruins.

Being vital, energetic and non-fatalistic in her approach to history, which she conceived of as the fruit of human activity, and at the same time laying bare the deep contradictions of capitalism, Rosa Luxemburg did not consider that the victory of socialism was inevitable. Capitalism she thought, could be either the prelude to socialism or the brink of barbarism.

A passion for truth made Rosa Luxemburg recoil from any dogmatic thought. Nothing was more intolerable to her than bowing down to 'infallible authorities'. As a real disciple of Marx she was able to think and act independently of her master. Though grasping the spirit of his teaching, she did not lose her critical faculties in a simple repetition of his words, whether these fitted the changed situation or not, whether they were right or wrong. Rosa Luxemburg's independence of thought is the greatest inspiration to socialists everywhere and always.

During a period when so many who consider themselves Marxists sap Marxism of its deep humanistic content, no one can do more to release us from the chains of lifeless mechanistic materialism than Rosa Luxemburg. For Marx communism (or socialism) was 'real humanism', 'a society in which the full and free development of every individual is the ruling principle'. (*Capital*, Vol 1) Rosa Luxemburg was the embodiment of these humanistic passions. Sympathy with the lowly and oppressed were central motives of her life. Her deep emotion and feeling for the suffering of people and all living things expressed themselves in everything she did or wrote, whether in her letters from prison or in the deepest writings of her theoretical research.

Rosa Luxemburg, however, well knew that where human tragedy is on an epic scale, tears won't help. Her motto, like that of Spinoza, might have been: 'Do not cry, do not laugh, but understand', even though she herself had her full share of tears and laughter. Her method was to reveal the trends of development in social life in order to help the working class to use its potentialities in the best possible way in conjunction with objective development. She appealed to man's reason rather than to his emotions.

Deep human sympathy and an earnest desire for truth, unbounded courage and a magnificent brain united in Rosa Luxemburg to make her a great revolutionary socialist. As her closest friend, Clara Zetkin, wrote in her obituary: 'In Rosa Luxemburg the socialist idea was a dominating and powerful passion of both heart and brain, a truly creative passion which burned ceaselessly. The great task and the overpowering ambition of this astonishing woman was to prepare the way for social revolution, to clear the path of history for socialism. To experience the revolution, to fight its battles, that was the highest happiness for her. With a will, determination, selflessness and devotion for which words are too weak, she consecrated her whole life and her whole being to socialism. She gave herself completely to the cause of socialism, not only in her tragic death, but throughout her whole life, daily and hourly, through the struggles of many years. She was the sharp sword, the living flame of the revolution.'

TONY CLIFF
September 1971

Preface

The first edition of this book was published in Paris at the end of August 1939, a few days before the outbreak of the Second World War. The book is a child of the German Emigration and bears the marks of its origins. The author left Germany at the beginning of 1934 after his release from a concentration camp. At the time he thought that the material which he had been gathering for many years to prepare for the *Collected Works (Gesammelte Werke) of Rosa Luxemburg* was in safe hands. Somehow, however, it got lost or fell into hands which would not let go of it. Among these papers were manuscripts and letters of Rosa Luxemburg; almost all of her works published in German, Polish and French; Volume v of the *Gesammelte Werke*, already typeset and ready to be printed, which contained her writings on imperialist politics; political and private letters to Rosa; a number of notes and many other items. Outside Germany only a part of the losses could be made good, and it became necessary to do without many papers which would have been useful in describing background details and personalities.

Despite these unfavourable circumstances, however, the book had to be written. Rosa Luxemburg's name has become a symbol in the international working-class movement. Yet little is known of her work today, and even those who are generally well-versed in socialist literature are acquainted with mere fragments of her writings. The publishing of her literary remains ran into frequent obstacles and–because of the factional fighting within the Communist International –into determined (even if never openly admitted) opposition. It could therefore not be completed. Thus whole areas of her work, a knowledge of which would have been of great significance in assessing her views, were forgotten. In the disputes of the various parties and tendencies in the working-class movement many teachings of the master were misconstrued, and many maliciously distorted. It seemed that if any socialist literature could be salvaged and brought out of hiding in a post-Nazi period, it would prove to be only rubble. There was a danger that only a faded memory or a deceptive legend of Rosa Luxemburg's historical achievements would be left.

The biographical works published about her either served a limited purpose, such as the one by Luise Kautsky, or they disregarded essential sectors of Rosa's life-work, such as the one by Henriette Roland-Holst. Both authors were very close to Rosa, and depicted her personality with much warmth and understanding. However, because both of them after all advocated views decidedly different from Rosa's, they could not succeed in presenting her ideas correctly and in doing justice to her political work.

One person would have been eminently qualified to revive Rosa Luxemburg's life and work: Clara Zetkin. The two of them had worked together for decades. Each was a strong person in the light of her own development and worth. They came from different backgrounds and each was influenced by other experiences. Nevertheless, in the intellectual disputes and political battles they had arrived at the same views and decisions. Of the leading socialists who survived Rosa, no one knew Luxemburg, the person and the fighter, better than Clara Zetkin; no one was more familiar with the battlefield, the historical circumstances, and with the identity of friend and foe in the skirmishes. Moreover, she knew the specific motives behind many of the decisions, motives which would have remained hidden to a researcher forced to make a judgment based on documents alone. What a biography of Rosa by Clara Zetkin would have provided can be surmised from the essays and pamphlets she wrote to commemorate her friend. Until her death on 20 June 1933, however, Clara Zetkin devoted herself completely to the tasks of the daily struggle, and declared again and again that she was thereby fulfilling the obligation she felt for her fallen comrade-in-arms.

The victory of fascism in Germany and the resulting effort to analyse the causes of the severe defeat of the proletariat led not only German socialists to make a more thorough study of the teachings of Rosa Luxemburg. Indeed, one could speak of a Luxemburg-Renaissance in the international working-class movement. The more the interest in her work grew, the deeper the gaps in the available material were felt to be. However, it was evident that it would not suffice merely to republish the lost writings insofar as they were at all accessible. The attempt now had to be made to provide an overall presentation of her ideas and actions using her own views as a starting-point. To define and work out as clearly as possible the ideas of Rosa Luxemburg was the chief task which the author set for himself. He therefore had carefully to consider his presentation and to let Rosa herself speak whenever the opportunity arose, even if the narrative flow might suffer from the break. He was thereby hoping to serve those readers whom he kept constantly in mind while working on the book–active socialists interested in theoretical and tactical problems.

That the book could be written at all was due above all to the efforts of the distinguished publisher and tireless defender of the deprived and the downtrodden, Victor Gollancz. It was his publishing company which, in the spring of 1940, brought out the English edition of the book in Edward Fitzgerald's excellent translation. It had an astonishing success in wartime England.

The book puts the reader back into a time that is past. In the three decades since Rosa Luxemburg's death the world has undergone cruel changes. Those January days of 1919 when the German Revolution was dealt a decisive blow marked, in fact, the end of an epoch of the working-class movement, a period which had begun with the repeal of the Anti-Socialist Laws and had been characterised by an almost uninterrupted socialist advance. Even in times of serious internal upheaval, such as the years of the First World War, this advance had continued, for, as the new experiences and problems were worked out intellectually, new heights of knowledge and insight were reached, and new moral strengths acquired in the more bitter struggles. Since then the conditions under which socialists have had to work have become increasingly more complicated and more difficult. It is true that working-class organisations everywhere grew impressively in size and that significant successes were obtained in individual struggles. However, the working-class movement remained divided by a deep rift; it became crippled by violent internal struggles, and its fighting morale weakened. The general development went from failure to defeat, finally ending in the terrible catastrophe for the whole proletariat brought on by German fascism. In this period of decline the old comrades-in-arms of Rosa Luxemburg felt more and more keenly how sorely the movement lacked her advice, her leadership, and her example. Today anyone trying to assess the difficulties facing the working class in all countries and particularly in Germany, and to grasp the dangers currently confronting all of mankind, becomes aware of the need of our times for a person with Rosa Luxemburg's clarity and boldness.

An attempt should be made to investigate how, under the cataclysmically changed conditions of today, Rosa Luxemburg's ideas, and particularly her tactical teachings, might be used in a fruitful way. However, this is not possible in a preface, even in bare outline form. The first prerequisite for such an undertaking would be a thorough analysis of all the characteristic social and political phenomena of our times. But it should be emphasised that Rosa Luxemburg never looked upon the results of her theoretical work as ultimate truths or as tactical models to be pressed to fit changed conditions. In a speech delivered to trade-union members in Hagen (October 1910) she herself said:

> The modern proletarian class does not conduct its struggle according to a schema laid down in a book or in a theory. The modern

workers' struggle is a fragment of history, a fragment of social development. And it is in the midst of history, in the midst of struggle, that we learn how we must fight. . . . The first commandment of a political fighter is to go with the development of the times and to account always for any changes in the world as well as for any changes in our fighting strategy.

For her there was no dogma or authority which commanded blind obedience. Even the mere thought that her own ideas should not be subject to criticism would have taken her aback and roused her indignation. Ever alert and critical thinking was for her the life-blood of the socialist movement, the first prerequisite for common action. Without constant and conscientious examination of the teachings which were handed down, without thorough analysis of the facts, without recognition of the new tendencies of development, it would be impossible for the movement to keep abreast of history and to master the tasks of the present. And, it should be added–because many years of experience have shown its importance–Rosa was well aware of the unavoidability of compromises in both organisational life and practical politics if unanimity in action towards a common aim was to be achieved. Where knowledge and recognition of the facts were concerned, however, she knew no compromise, and especially no submission to alien will. To stand up for her convictions to the bitter end was a moral principle, something she deemed a matter of course for any socialist; behind this was her unbroken urge to get to the bottom of things.

In her work there are enough scientific observations and tactical principles which stand up to every test, as well as conclusions which were not only valid in the particular circumstances of her time but could also stimulate and guide us in the solution of present-day problems. There remain, of course, those views of Rosa which are still the object of intellectual controversy. However, to make a critical evaluation of every word of the master would be to acquire her legacy, to take possession of it.

After the experience of the last decades objections were raised to certain of Rosa Luxemburg's ideas even by Marxists. It is necessary to make a more exact sketch of Rosa's standpoint in these questions and to test its justification. Marxist teaching culminates in the assertion that, in capitalism, production assumes a progressively social character, although private property remains linked to the means of production. Capitalist society must, according to this theory, inevitably perish because of this and other contradictions, i.e. because of the effects of its own laws of development. Rosa Luxemburg was deeply convinced of this historical necessity, and expressed this view in many of her works. Her chief work, *The Accumulation of Capital*, was concerned with proving that the decay of the capitalist social order was inevitable. Her conviction has been confirmed by history, for all the things we have been experiencing in the last several decades–this whirlpool of crises, wars, revolutions, and counter-revolutions, with all their frightful effects–are the convulsions of a disintegrating society. Here contradictions are operating which have always been at work in capitalist society, but they have now gelled into an explosive mixture of such force and of such proportions that it seems as if the whole world were being ravaged by a continuous series of earthquakes.

Marxists, including Rosa Luxemburg, have assumed that this process of decay would lead directly to socialism, for the development of the contradictions of capitalism would be accompanied, of course, by the growth of the chief contradiction, the one between the bourgeoisie and the proletariat. As Marx put it, 'As the mass of misery, oppression, servitude, degeneration, and exploitation grows, so, too, does the indignation of the ever swelling working class, trained, united and organised by the mechanism of the capitalist production-process itself'. The fact of the matter was that in the epoch when the capitalist economic mode was developing and bringing the techniques of production to an ever higher level, the working-class movement also grew in size and strength. The generation to which Rosa Luxemburg belonged observed that this process was happening consistently, almost as if it were following certain laws. For this reason Rosa Luxemburg did not doubt that in the coming catastrophes the working class would have the will and the drive to fulfil its historic task.

During the First World War, however, when she experienced the collapse of the International and the crossing of the socialist parties into the imperialist camp, when the working masses were making one sacrifice after the other for the capitalist order, and the German proletarians in uniform were letting themselves be misused even against the Russian Revolution, Rosa repeated the warning more and more loudly: the catastrophes into which capitalist society will be plunged do not by themselves offer the certainty that capitalism will be superseded by socialism. If the working class itself does not find the strength for its own liberation, then the whole of society, including the working class, could be consumed in internecine struggles. Mankind now stands before the alternatives: either socialism or descent into barbarism! And she maintained this either-or view when the Central Powers collapsed and the revolution in Central Europe was making more powerful progress every day. In the *Spartakus* programme she wrote: 'Either the continuation of capitalism, new wars and a very early decline into chaos and anarchy, or the abolition of capitalist exploitation.'

The self-assertion of the Russian Revolution and the long-drawn-out revolutionary tremblings in Europe and in the colonial countries provided new nourishment for the optimism of the most active cadres of the socialist movement. Even if the path of development had to go through violent struggles with occasional reverses, it seemed to be leading inexorably to a socialist transformation of society. Although Rosa Luxemburg's warning of the dangers of sinking into barbarism was often repeated in both speeches and writings, its whole earnestness was not grasped. People had no idea what sinking into barbarism could mean at all—not until the victory of Hitler and his barbarians showed with brutally clear force that Rosa Luxemburg's warning cry had been no mere rhetorical phrase. The destruction of the working-class movement, the atomisation of the different social strata, the book-burnings, the strangulation of intellectual life, the horrors of the concentration camps, the extermination of whole sectors of the population, the total control of society by the state apparatus, and total war with its inevitable total defeat and terrible consequences—all this was the reality of barbarism.

The socialist working-class movement which had developed so powerfully alongside the capitalist mode of production was drawn into the catastrophe because it was incapable of halting its onset. The overturning of the socialist hopes of the broad masses was perhaps the most dangerous feature of the descent into barbarism. The course of events in Russia, whose revolution would at one time have lent new strength to these hopes, now had an especially shattering effect on the international socialist movement. The stunting of democratic organs in Russia, the control of the people by an almighty bureaucracy, the murder of Lenin's comrades-in-arms, and finally the pact with Hitler, left any remaining faith in the socialist politics of the Russian state only to those who were prepared to sacrifice all their critical faculties. Thus new problems arose for those who clung unswervingly to the aims of socialism. Discussions dealt no longer with the means and ways of achieving socialism, but with the question of whether or not the development towards socialism was at all secure. What is historical necessity? This now became the burning political question.

According to the Marxist analysis of capitalism, the ever greater socialisation of the production process, the growth of cartels and trusts, the development in the direction of state capitalism is historically necessary. This, however, means the formation of the prerequisites for a socialist organisation of the economy. Historical necessity is the dissolution of the capitalist social order in violent economic and political crises in which the class struggle is intensified and the working class obtains the possibility of gaining political power and bringing about socialism. The relative strength of the proletariat in the class struggles is to a great extent historically conditioned. In recent decades certain phenomena have had a disastrous effect on this strength, for example, the strong differentiation within the working class, its political split into different parties, the wearing down of the petit-bourgeoisie by the Great Depression and its swing to fascism, the ruthless use of state power in the class struggle, and finally the general effects of the whole complex of world-political conflicts with its confusing abundance of contradictory phenomena.

The intervention of a class and of its different strata and organisations in the historical process is not only the fruit of knowledge and will. It is heavily conditioned by social and political factors affecting the class from outside. However, classes and parties are themselves factors in the multifarious assortment of forces. Their commissions and omissions react continuously on the conditions under which they themselves have to fight. The knowledge and will of individuals, of the organisations and thereby of the class itself are of weighty significance in this process; they are decisive for the final victory when other conditions have also ripened, and they are decisive for the course taken by history at its turning points. This is part and parcel of the Marxist concept of history, which becomes bowdlerised if viewed as fatalism. Rosa Luxemburg often explained the relation between objective facts and tendencies of development on the one hand and the conscious action of men on the other, as, for example, in the compact sentences of her *Junius-broschüre*:

> (The) victory of the socialist proletariat . . . is tied to the iron laws of history, to the thousand rungs of the previous tortured and all too slow development. But it can never be brought about unless the igniting spark of the conscious will of the great mass of the people springs up out of all the elements of the material prerequisites collected from this development.

This conscious will arises from a long process of experience, of training and struggle, a development of knowledge and morale. Here the teachings and the example of Rosa Luxemburg should and could be made fruitful. It is not given to everyone to recognise, with her scientific insight and visionary power, the great historic tendencies at work amid the chance phenomena of the day. However, everyone can, as she did, fearlessly and without shirking the consequences, look reality in the eye and strive to recognise the essential features in the events of the day, and thereby find the road that needs to be taken. One would always have to examine one's own views again and again in order to gain the confidence and the strength to stand up for one's own convictions. For Rosa Luxemburg loyalty to oneself was the natural prerequisite for loyalty to the cause of the oppressed. Her whole life bears witness to this.

But what did socialism mean to her? This question is being asked in a period when political concepts have become ambiguous and many have been used deliberately to deceive people. Again and again Rosa Luxemburg emphasised that the strategic aim of the working-class struggle, the aim which was supposed to determine all tactical measures, was the conquest of political power. This is the aim of struggle in class society. But it is only the method of transferring all the means of production into the hands of the general public and of organising production in a socialist way. But even this latter step is only the means to an end. The goal of socialism is man, i.e. a society without class differences in which men working in community, without tutelage, forge their own fate. It is – in Marx's words – 'an association where the free development of each individual is the condition for the free development of all'. It is not socialism if the means of production are socialised and set into motion according to a plan, but a class or a social stratum autocratically controls the means of production, regiments and oppresses the working masses, and deprives them of their rights. No socialism can be realised in a country where the state power breaks in and gets rid of the old ruling classes and property relations but at the same time subjects the whole nation to a ruthless dictatorship which prevents the working class from being conscious of its particular role and tasks and acting accordingly. As Rosa Luxemburg expressed it in the *Spartakus* programme: 'The essence of socialist society is in the fact that the great working mass ceases to be a ruled mass, and that it itself lives and directs the whole of political and economic life in free and conscious self-determination.' Socialism is democracy completed, the free unfolding of the individual personality through working together with all for the well-being of all. Wherever state power still has to be applied to suppress the working masses, the socialist struggle has not yet achieved its aim.

The historical process has become more confusing and more cruel than the experiences of earlier times would have led one to expect. Never have the conditions of living and struggle of the German working class been so severe as they are at present, and there is no magic way of avoiding all the convulsions resulting from the greatest social crisis of mankind. However, the socialist movement can shorten the period of decline and of internecine warfare and can direct the course of history to new heights. Rosa Luxemburg's legacy will help the movement to gain the strength, self-confidence, and courage for this task.

PAUL FRÖLICH
New York, autumn 1948

1
Youth

At home

Zamość is a little Polish town in the Lublin district, close to the old Polish-Russian border. It was a poverty-stricken place, and the cultural level of the populace was low. Even after the great agrarian reform introduced by Tsarism (after the suppression of the insurrection led by the Polish nobles in 1863) in order to play off the peasants against the *szlachta* or gentry, the dependence, sufferings, and difficulties of the lower strata of the population from the days of serfdom lingered on. The penetration of the monetary system into this district, remote as it was from the industrial centres, brought only the hardships attendant on the destruction of an old order of society, and not the advantages of the new.

Fate placed a particularly heavy burden on the large Jewish population. They shared all the oppression and all the miseries of their fellows, the harsh despotism and absolutism of the imperial Russian regime, the foreign domination in Poland; and the general impoverishment of the country. In addition, theirs was the misery of the outcast. In this empire, where each was the slave of his master or of those in the next social rank, the Jew was the slave of the lowest of the low, and the kicks distributed at all levels of the social pyramid from the top downwards finally landed on him with a vengeance. He was dogged at every turn, intimidated and maltreated by a malicious anti-Semitism. No Jew enjoyed even the few civil rights which Russian absolutism had allotted to the rest of the population. The great mass of the Jewish people was tightly restricted by special laws, cooped up in ghettos, excluded from most professions, and exposed to the arbitrariness and blackmail of the almighty bureaucracy. Against all odds they struggled to eke out an existence. In the face of persecution they withdrew behind the walls of their religion, where they stoically sought to assert themselves with either a messianic faith in a better future or a stifling fanaticism. It was an out-of-the-way, backward world, a world of resignation and want.

A small upper stratum of wholesale merchants and intellectuals managed to raise themselves from this material and spiritual misery. In the decade of reforms (1856-1865) which followed the salutary defeat in the Crimean War they were just about the only Jews freed from the worst special laws. The young generation belonging to this class strove to free itself from the oppressive narrowness of Hebrew scholasticism. Voraciously it reached out for the forbidden fruits of Western culture. It raved about freedom of thought, Darwinism and socialism, and sought contact with the Russian freedom movement, which sprung up with great force in the 1860s and whose teachers and exponents were Chernyshevski, Lavrov and Herzen. In Poland these young people had plunged wholeheartedly into the revolt of 1863; in spite of the reservations of the leaders of the Polish insurrection, they had swept along considerable portions of the Jewish population and had shouldered the heavy sacrifices of defeat. These young intellectuals of the 60s were the first of the great militant forces offered by the Russian Jews to the liberal and particularly to the socialist movement in the Tsarist empire.

Both cultural strata existed also in the large Jewish population of the little town of Zamość in the second half of the nineteenth century. In this community several families were conspicuous for their acceptance of Western culture and progressive thought. The writer Leon Peretz, one of the first supporters of the *Haskala* (enlightenment) among the Polish Jews, had flourished here in the 1870s. His early stories were a strong protest against the tyranny of the ancestral tradition and, at the same time, an exposé of the social abuses, the exploitation of the workers, and the terrible privations of the poor in the Polish provinces. The Luxemburg family probably had close ties with Peretz, for it was in Zamość that Rosa Luxemburg was born on 5 March 1871,* and the Luxemburg house was one of the cultural oases of the town.

Rosa's grandfather had succeeded in raising his family to a certain level of prosperity. The timber trade in which he was engaged not only brought him in contact with the *szlachta*, but took him to Germany, and that lifted him out of the narrow confines of Zamość. He gave his children a modern education, and sent his sons to commercial schools in Berlin and Bromberg (Bydgoszcz). From Germany Rosa's father brought back liberal ideas, an interest in world affairs and also particularly in West European literature. He was alienated from the strictness of the ghetto and from Jewish orthodoxy, but he served his people in his own way by furthering

---

* In the previous editions of this book PF gave her birthdate as 5 March 1870. He had reached this conclusion after consulting the material published by close friends of Rosa Luxemburg. However, according to the *curriculum vitae* she herself submitted to the University of Zürich the year of birth is 1871 (Staatsarchiv, Zürich, U 105 h 4).

their cultural aspirations. Hostility to Tsarism, democratic convictions, and a love of Polish literature gave him all his father may have
lacked to complete his Polish assimilation. He was certainly sympathetic towards the national-revolutionary movements amongst the
Poles, but he was not politically active himself and devoted his attention to cultural problems, in particular to the Polish school system.
He was a man of considerable energy; material well-being and education had given him self-reliance, and he felt himself called upon to
work for the public welfare beyond the horizon of his family and his
profession. He belonged to that social stratum from which emerged
the Jewish intellectual type, best represented by the great Jewish
artists, men of science, and fighters for a better world.

There is very little material available concerning Rosa's childhood. She herself hardly spoke about it, as she was generally reticent
in all personal matters. Only in prison, when memories crowded in
on her, and she sought to break the leaden stillness by writing
letters, did she sometimes mention her childhood experiences. These
are incidents artistically recreated with great feeling, but they are
usually too insignificant to give us a picture of the outward circumstances of her childhood; and it is often difficult to distinguish, in
these observations of concrete events, what has its origin in the ideas
and emotions of the child, and what belongs to the literary art of
the mature writer. Such an episode occurs in a letter written to
Luise Kautsky in the autumn of 1904 from Zwickau Prison. She
describes how as a child she crept to the window very early one
morning and, looking out, watched the big yard awaken, and 'Long
Antoni', the servant, begin his work, after loud yawning and half-
sleepy ruminations:

> The solemn stillness of the morning hour lay over the triviality of
> the pavement; above in the window panes the early gold of the
> young sun glistened, and high above swam little roseate fragrant
> clouds which then dissolved into the gray city sky. At that time I
> firmly believed that "life", "real" life, was somewhere far away,
> beyond the roofs. Since then I have been travelling after it. But it
> is still hidden away behind roofs somewhere. . . . In the end it was
> all a cruel game with me, and life, real life, stayed there in the
> yard.[1]*

Who can tell whether the belief of the child that real life was
somewhere beyond the roofs was anything more than the interest in
the unknown outside world which moves every child, or whether it
contained the seed of that unrest, that longing and that urge which
drove the grown-up Rosa Luxemburg beyond the daily humdrum

* Numbered footnotes will be found at the end of the text. They consist
essentially of references and source material. Footnotes which elucidate the text
are asterisked and placed on the pages where they occur.

and the petty things of this world, and was always a spur to action? Observations such as hers, full of refined self-irony, can easily tempt the psychologist to undertake adventurous excursions. We are therefore almost exclusively dependent on the material provided by her brothers and her sister. On the whole, her youth was a happy one. Her parents occasionally experienced straitened circumstances, and once Rosa lit the lamp with a piece of paper which then turned out to be the only money left in the house. But otherwise life was comfortable and secure, marked by that intense intimacy characteristic of Jewish families.

Rosa was the youngest of five children. A hip disease in early life kept her in bed for a whole year. It was wrongly treated as tuberculosis of the bone and caused irreparable damage. Small wonder that she became the centre of everyone's love. Moreover, she had a cheery disposition, and was an unusually bright and active child who quickly won the affection of people. At five she could already read and write. Following the urge to imitate her elders, she began to write letters to her parents and to her brothers and sister about everything which preoccupied her mind, and she insisted on receiving answers which showed that her game was being taken seriously. She sent her first 'literary efforts' to a children's magazine. Her pedagogical streak showed itself early too. She herself had hardly learnt to read, when she made the household servants into her pupils.

The mother exercised considerable influence on the intellectual development of the children, and particularly on Rosa's. Her education and interests were far above those of the average Jewish woman. She was an eager reader not only of the Bible, but also of German and Polish classical literature. There was a real cult of Schiller in the house, but Rosa obviously deserted him very early and learned to appreciate him only very much later in life, under the influence of Franz Mehring. In line with Freudian theory, this rejection has been interpreted as an unconscious protest against her mother. But disaffection towards the classical 'poet of aphorisms' occurs very frequently amongst young Germans; and it was precisely Schiller's pathos, his idealistic and very airy worship of freedom, which touched related chords in the Luxemburg family, but which must have revolted the critical Rosa, whose political ideas ripened early. On the other hand, her devotion to the classical Polish authors, especially to Mickiewicz [1798-1855], whom at one time she placed even above Goethe, remained unshaken. We do not know when she found her way to Russian literature, but she later spoke of it with great enthusiasm.

In any case, the atmosphere of the Luxemburg home was filled with Polish and German culture and a love of their literatures.

These Rosa avidly devoured. The magic of verse and rhyme seized her when she was still a child, and she spouted forth poems of her own. Her early intellectual development naturally made Rosa the pride of her parents, who were unable to resist the temptation to show off the infant prodigy to visitors. However, an instinctive aversion to pose and affectation guarded the young Rosa against the dangers of such experiments. She would then often react with a certain obstinacy, and utilise her natural gifts for satire and for quickly uncovering the weaknesses of others. Thus she loved to tease visitors who came from out of town and who did not display too much intelligence with a poem, the moral of which ran like this: even on journeys the fool does not become any the wiser!

The struggle begins

When Rosa was about three years old her family moved to Warsaw. Her father wished to secure for his children a better education than Zamość could offer. School presented few difficulties to the lively and confident girl who found it easy to learn; she was naturally always at the top of her class. But the school regime of oppressed Poland certainly helped to thrust her into the course of struggle which gave purpose to her life. The Russianisation tendencies of Tsarism were carried through with particular ruthlessness in the schools. The first High School in Warsaw, both for boys and girls, was reserved almost exclusively for Russians, the children of officials and officers. Only a few Poles belonging to respectable Russianised families were admitted here, and Jews not at all. Even in the second girls' High School – the one which Rosa attended – there was a rigid quota for Jews.

The use of the native Polish language, even among the pupils themselves, was strictly forbidden, and the Russian teachers even stooped to becoming informers in order to enforce the prohibition. Such narrow-minded repressive measures did not fail to awaken the spirit of resistance amongst the pupils. They opposed their teachers in open hostility which occasionally erupted in rebellious demonstrations, especially when some political clash occurred in the world outside the school. The secondary schools were hotbeds of political conspiracy; though the conspiracies were mostly of a child-like and romantic character, they nonetheless had connections with political organisations outside. Thus what began as Polish national opposition to the Russianisation attempts in the schools often led into the revolutionary socialist movement, whose supporters in those days were almost exclusively the intellectual youth.

The liberal spirit and the Polish national consciousness of her family, her early kindled hatred of absolutism and her defiantly independent spirit, drove young Rosa into this school opposition. Indeed, she did not stand merely on the edge, but was at the head of it. This is attested to by an eloquent fact which also leads one to conjecture that by her last school years Rosa was already in touch with the revolutionary movement outside: the gold medal to which her attainments would certainly have entitled her on leaving the school–in all subjects she received the marks 'excellent' or 'very good'–was withheld from her 'on account of her rebellious attitude towards the authorities'. Even if we can now no longer ascertain to what extent this opposition was consciously socialist or connected with an illegal organisation, it is nevertheless certain, however, that soon after leaving the High School in 1887 Rosa Luxemburg was active in the 'Revolutionary-Socialist Party *Proletariat*' and that she worked closely together with the then leader of the Warsaw group of this party, the workingman Martin Kasprzak.

At that time the revolutionary movement in Russia and in Poland was going through a severe crisis and had just reached the nadir of a depression. She herself describes the then-prevailing conditions in her *Accumulation of Capital*:

> In Russia . . . the seventies and eighties represent in every respect a transitional period, a period of internal crisis with all its agonies. Large-scale industry was only just now celebrating its advent under the effect of the period of high protective tariffs. . . . "Primitive accumulation" of capital was flourishing splendidly in Russia, favoured by all kinds of state subsidies, guarantees, premiums and government orders, and was reaping profits such as already belonged to the realm of fable in the West at that time. The internal conditions of Russia, however, presented anything but an attractive or hopeful picture. On the plains, the decline and disintegration of peasant economy under the pressure of fiscal exploitation and the monetary system resulted in horrifying conditions, periodic famines and periodic peasant unrest. On the other hand, the factory proletariat in the towns had not yet consolidated, either socially or intellectually, into a modern working class . . . primitive forms of exploitation provoked primitive methods of defence. Not until the early eighties did the spontaneous factory outbreaks in the Moscow district, marked by the smashing of machinery, provide the impetus for the first rudiments of factory legislation in the Tsarist empire.

> If the economic side of public life in Russia exhibited at every turn the shrill discords of a transitional period, there was a corresponding crisis in intellectual life. "Populism"*, the indigenous Russian socialism theoretically based on the peculiarities of the

---

* The Populists (*Narodniki*) were socialists who rejected Marxism and advocated the idea of peasant revolution and utopian agrarian socialism. In this way they hoped that Russia would be spared the preliminary experience of capitalism. The later party of the Social-Revolutionaries arose from this group.

Russian agrarian constitution, was politically bankrupt following the fiasco of its extreme revolutionary exponent, the terrorist party of *Narodnaya Volya* (the People's Will), after the successful attempt on the life of Alexander II in 1881. On the other hand, the first writings of Georgii Plekhanov, which were intended to introduce Marxist trains of thought into Russia, did not appear until 1883 and 1885, and even then, for about a decade, they had seemingly little influence. During the eighties and into the nineties, the intellectual life of the Russian intelligentsia, particularly the oppositional socialist intelligentsia, was dominated by a peculiar mixture of "indigenous" remnants of populism and snapped-up elements of Marxist theory, a mixture whose salient feature was a scepticism regarding the possibilities of capitalist development in Russia. . . .[2]

The frame of mind of the Russian intelligentsia of that day has been described by Rosa Luxemburg in her introduction to Wladimir Korolenko's *History of My Contemporary:*

> In the eighties, after the assassination of Alexander II, a period of numb despair descended on Russia. The liberal reforms of the sixties with respect to the judiciary and rural self-government were thoroughly revised everywhere. Under the leaden sway of Alexander III's government the silence of the graveyard prevailed. Russian society, equally discouraged by the collapse of all hopes for peaceable reforms and by the apparent ineffectiveness of the revolutionary movement, was in the grip of a mood of depression and resignation.

> In this atmosphere of apathy and despondency, metaphysical and mystical tendencies became fashionable amongst the Russian intelligentsia. . . . The influence of Nietzsche could be clearly felt; the belles-lettres were dominated by the hopeless, pessimistic tone of Garshin's short stories and Nadson's poetry. However, the spirit of the day was reflected above all in Dostoevsky's mysticism, as expressed in *The Brothers Karamazov*, and particularly in Tolstoy's asceticism. The propaganda of "non-resistance to evil", the condemnation of all violence in the struggle against the ruling reaction (which was to be opposed only by the "inner purification" of the individual)–these theories of social passivity in the atmosphere of the eighties became a serious danger for the Russian intelligentsia, especially since they could avail themselves of such powerful supports as the pen and moral authority of Leo Tolstoy.[3]

Poland was economically more highly developed than Russia and intellectually closer to the West. Yet the leaden heaviness of general depression weighed her down too. The national-revolutionary movement led by the Polish gentry, the *szlachta*, was dead. The bourgeoisie danced around the Golden Calf, rejected all ideas which could not be turned into immediate profits, and submitted with calculated slavishness to the sway of absolutism. The *Proletariat* party, the hopeful forerunner of the modern socialist movement in Poland, had been involved in the defeat of *Narodnaya Volya*. It was almost decimated by the incarceration of its leaders in the Schlüsselburg fortress and by the mass arrests of its members; intellectually, too, it was on the decline. After its first great strike actions the Polish working class had crept back into its old torpor. The young intelligentsia was intimidated. For some years the stream of new blood into the revolutionary movement from this source had ebbed away almost completely. But just around the time when Rosa Luxemburg left the High School, a revival began, paving the way for a regeneration of the movement, which was to become manifest about five years later.

The step from rebellious behaviour at school to revolutionary socialism was fatefully laid down for Rosa. The yoke of Russian conditions weighed on her threefold: she belonged to the Russian people enchained by Tsarism, to the Polish people suppressed by foreign rule, and to the downtrodden Jewish minority. She was always ready to take up the cause of the suffering and the oppressed; she felt doubly every blow that fell on others. The deepest sympathy with all those who were humiliated or wronged was the mainspring of her active life and was vibrant in her every word, even her loftiest theoretical abstraction. But this sympathy could not be content with individual assistance or palliative measures. Her overly powerful sensitivity was bridled early on by a keen intellect. She had already recognised what she was to write to her friend Hans Diefenbach much later, after the outbreak of the World War–that when the growing dimensions of a misfortune make it a world-historic drama, then objective, historical judgment prevails, and all other considerations must give way before it. And, to her, historical judgment meant the search for a common source of all individual phenomena, for the motive-forces of development, and for a synthesis which would resolve conflicts.

The small circles of the *Proletariat* party must have vigorously encouraged Rosa Luxemburg's inquiring disposition. Here she came together with a small elite of enlightened workers who tended the theoretical heritage of the *Proletariat*. She came to know the underground literature; this certainly included the writings of Marx and Engels, which were to become the basis of her conception of life. Towards the end of her stay in Warsaw a breath of fresh air stirred the working-class movement. New circles were formed in the factories. Rosa Luxemburg probably took part in the founding of a new organisation, the Polish Workers League; in any case, she was very closely connected with it from its beginnings in 1889.

It was in this year, however, that she had to leave Poland. Her activity in revolutionary circles had been discovered by the police.

The threat of imprisonment, and perhaps banishment to Siberia, hung over her. She was at all times prepared to bear the consequences of her actions. Nevertheless, her comrades thought that, rather than living in exile in Siberia, it would be better for her to go abroad to study and, from that vantage point, to continue to serve the movement. Martin Kasprzak organised her flight. Smugglers were supposed to lead Rosa Luxemburg over the Russian-German border. In the frontier village difficulties arose about carrying out the plan. Kasprzak then resorted to a stratagem. He sought out the local Catholic priest and explained to him that a Jewish girl had a burning desire to become a Christian, but could only do so abroad because of the vehement resistance of her relatives. Rosa Luxemburg played her part in the pious deception so adroitly that the priest rendered the necessary assistance. Hidden under straw in a peasant's cart, Rosa Luxemburg crossed the border to freedom.

2
The fate of Poland

Zürich

From Warsaw to Zürich, that was the way out of the dungeon of absolutism into the freest country in Europe, from the misty, stifling lowlands to the fresh air and the commanding view of the heights. Zürich was the most important centre of Polish and Russian emigration; its University was the alma mater of young revolutionaries. These were mostly people who, in spite of their youth, had already experienced the serious side of life; they had been in prison, had suffered in exile, and had been torn away from their families and out of the social milieu into which they had been born. They lived apart from the young bourgeois students whose aim in life was a career and security. These young emigrés worked seriously at their chosen studies, but they thought less of their bread and butter in the future than of the future of humanity. In their colony men and women were deemed equal. Free thought prevailed and at the same time a strict, ascetic morality. There was much privation as well as a natural, unsentimental solidarity.

These students did not squander their time in drinking bouts. Their discussions were tireless and never-ending: about philosophy; Darwinism; the emancipation of women; Marx; Tolstoy; the fate of the *obshchina*, the last remnant of Russian agrarian communism; the prospects and the historical significance of capitalist development in Russia; the upshot of the terrorism of *Narodnaya Volya*; Bakunin, Blanqui and the methods of revolutionary struggle; the demoralisation of the Western bourgeoisie; Bismarck's fall and the victorious struggle of German Social Democracy against the Anti-Socialist Laws (*Ausnahmegesetz*); the liberation of Poland; the teachings of Lavrov and Chernyshevsky, and the 'treachery' committed by Turgenev in his novel *Fathers and Sons*; Spielhagen and Zola; a thousand 'questions' and always the same theme—Revolution.

Little bread and much tea, cold garrets full of cigarette smoke, faces absorbed in heated argument, excited gestures, exuberance and romanticism. Many of these young people were fated to rot away in the prisons of the Tsar or in the wastelands of Siberia.

Others were destined, after the exhilaration of Swiss emigration, to become props of the state as factory-owners, lawyers, doctors, teachers or journalists in some nook of Russia. Only a few were to experience as activists the revolutionary storms which they all dreamt about.

Rosa Luxemburg only brushed against the fringes of this emigré bohemia. Its endless debates, leading nowhere, provoked her ironic amusement. A voracious desire for work absorbed her. She took up quarters with the family of Lübeck, a German social democrat expatriated under the Anti-Socialist Laws. Lübeck scraped a living as a writer. He furthered her knowledge of the German working-class movement, and she helped him with his literary work, now and then even writing an article in his stead. Soon she was managing the somewhat neglected Lübeck household.

At the University of Zürich Rosa Luxemburg first enrolled in the faculty of philosophy and took courses in the natural sciences and in mathematics. What she felt for the world of plants and animals was more than an interest; it was almost a passion, and this world remained a refuge whenever she sought relaxation away from political struggles. However, her vocation was politics, and in 1892 she therefore switched over to the study of the political sciences. The official curriculum of the University probably did not offer her much. Economics is too closely tied to class interests to enable it to be an objective science even to the extent that other fields of inquiry can be. And German economics, having begun only after the fading away of classical theories, came already crippled into the world, and fear of the social consequences of ultimate scientific conclusions kept its luminaries always in the nether regions of vulgar economics.

Julius Wolf occupied the chair of economics in Zürich. He was the type of German professor who works through mountains of detailed material with untiring industry, but who always remains eclectic, and never manages to achieve a complete, coherent view and picture of society. Rosa Luxemburg, however, was always driven to seek just such a synthesis, the ultimate conclusion of reason. She made an intensive study of the classical economic writers, Adam Smith, Ricardo, and Marx, and thereby developed a deep contempt for the typically German professor, the 'theorising bureaucrat who plucks apart the living material of social reality into the most minute fibres and particles, rearranges and categorises them according to bureaucratic procedure, and delivers them in this mangled state as scientific material for the administrative and legislative activity of Privy Councillors'.[4]

She was unable to refrain from letting the good professor feel her quickly-won superiority. Her friend and fellow-student Julian

Marchlewski has described in his memoirs (unfortunately unpublished) how the satire of the young students made life difficult for Professor Wolf. They used to hatch little plots before the seminar classes. Predetermined questions were submitted to the master in all innocence. Then when Wolf had hopelessly entangled himself, Rosa Luxemburg would get up and demonstrate his professorial incompetence point by point. Apparently Julius Wolf took the malicious game with the necessary sense of humour; in an autobiographical sketch he paid great tribute to his best pupil.[5]

Alongside her studies Rosa Luxemburg was active in the Zürich working-class movement and took part in the intense intellectual life of the leaders of the political emigration. She came into contact with the leading Russian Marxists: with Pavel Akselrod, the Nestor of Russian Social Democracy, though at that time it existed only as an idea; with Vera Zasulich, and Georgii Plekhanov, the most brilliant Marxist of his day. She looked up to the latter with admiration, but even with him she was careful to preserve her own personality. She met Parvus-Helphand, who was studying in Basel and whose lively, productive fantasy, grasp of practical politics, and great activism made him seem a kindred spirit to her. She was even more closely connected with several fellow-students who had already won their spurs in the Polish socialist movement, including in particular Julian Marchlewski-Karski and Adolf Warszawski-Warski.

Leo Jogiches

The friendship of Leo Jogiches, who came to Zürich in 1890, was to prove of the greatest importance for her intellectual and political development and for her personal life. Little is known about the life of this unusual man, who played a prominent role in the Russian and Polish working-class movements and in the German Spartakus League, and who was fated to become the victim of a political murder only a few months after his great friend, in March 1919 in Berlin. A reserved man, he never spoke of his past. What little is known of his youth comes almost exclusively from Z Rejzin, who interviewed Jogiches's childhood companions about his early political life.

Leo Jogiches, born in 1867 in Vilna, came from a rich Jewish family. His grandfather had been considered a great Talmud scholar, but his father was enlightened and quite Russianised. Yiddish was hardly ever spoken in the family. Whilst still in high school Leo began to make revolutionary propaganda among his school-fellows. He left school prematurely in order to devote himself entirely to political work. Around the year 1885 he founded the first revolutionary circles in Vilna. Gordon of the *Bund* [*Algemener Yiddisher Arbeter Bund*–Jewish Workers' League, founded 1897] regards him as the first leader and real founder of the working-class movement in Vilna. Of course the groups were still very weak, for there were not many workers, and the decline of *Narodnaya Volya* had dampened oppositional stirrings among the intellectual youth. And yet a host of well-known leaders came out of this small Vilna movement. Among them was Charles Rappaport, who made a name for himself as a theoretician in the French Socialist Party; also Pilsudski, later the Polish dictator. Lenin's brother, who was hanged in 1891 as a member of the Russian terrorist organisation *Narodnaya Volya*, had contact in St Petersburg with Jogiches's student circles.

Jogiches enjoyed a tremendous reputation among his followers. One of them has said: 'He was a very clever and able debater. In his presence one felt that this was no commonplace man. He devoted his whole existence to his work as a socialist, and his followers idolised him.' He disciplined himself very rigorously to do what he regarded as necessary for revolutionary work, sleeping on the hard floor in order to be prepared for the prison cot. Once he worked as a locksmith at the bench–not with that deliberate self-abasement of the previous generation of revolutionaries who 'went among the people', but in order to understand the workers better and to influence them more strongly. At the same time he sought to make contact with the army, and actually managed to organise a circle of Russian officers. Very early he developed a bent for the strictest conspiratorial activity which was to govern his whole life. He also learnt engraving and typesetting. He imposed the greatest discipline on himself, compelled his fellow-comrades to do likewise, and demanded that they obey the rules of conspiratorial secrecy. He acquired a wide-ranging knowledge becoming the teacher of his comrades and demanding of them an equally zealous pursuit of learning. Karl Radek later recalled how, in the midst of the turmoil of the 1905 Revolution, Leo forced him to wade through the works of some old writers whose names were hardly known.

Soon the police became suspicious of his activities; he was arrested for the first time in the autumn of 1888 and imprisoned in the Vilna Citadel. From May to September 1889 he was again locked up, and even after his release he remained under police surveillance. He was then supposed to do military service. He reflected that as a political suspect he would not stand a chance of being politically effective in the army. Also he feared his own temperament in such circumstances. At the assembly-point for conscripts he decided to escape. The story goes that he was brought out of the town in a wagon, covered with a layer of clay. In the winter of 1890 he came to Zürich with papers identifying him as Leon Grosowski.

Politically he affiliated himself with the group of Russian Marxists which had formed in exile around Akselrod and Plekhanov.

He had considerable financial resources at his disposal, which he used for the socialist propaganda cause. He proposed the founding of a journal to Plekhanov, who joyfully accepted the offer in the hope that this publication might be able to provide the leverage for a real social-democratic movement in Russia. Besides, Plekhanov himself would finally be freed from the wretched drudgery of earning his own bread–he kept body and soul together by addressing letters–and could develop his great talents as a theoretician and a propagandist. They negotiated an agreement, but it collapsed on the question of who was to be the political director of the venture. Plekhanov had his full share of imperiousness, and anyway how could he leave this important weapon to a rich stripling who had yet to win his spurs? However Leo Jogiches knew his own worth, and he was unwilling to give away his own creation or to subordinate himself; he himself was domineering to the point of tyranny. He therefore left the Pan-Russian movement and threw himself wholly into the Polish movement, where he very quickly became the undisputed organiser and leader, a personality the equal of the great Russian working-class leaders.

In the political emigré circles of Zürich he met Rosa Luxemburg, and common activities soon led to a lifelong union. At first glance this match seems odd: Rosa with her cheerful disposition and stormy temperament, and the rich talents of a genius which she was ready to lavish on all sides; and this man Leo, whose very being was hardness and discipline, who lived only for duty–duty to the point of pedantry–and demanded the same of others, who was prepared coldbloodedly to sacrifice himself and others for the sake of the cause, and who only in rare, fleeting moments showed the depths of feeling of which he was capable. For both of them in their life-work this contrast in temperament and character actually proved to be the greatest support, and it testifies to the strength of character of both of them that their union could endure without them tearing each other apart; indeed it rather enhanced their capabilities. Clara Zetkin, who knew them both intimately, bears witness that Leo Jogiches was the incorruptible critic and judge of Rosa Luxemburg and her work, and her theoretical and practical conscience as well; at times he was the more farsighted and the initiator, while Rosa Luxemburg retained a more penetrating, creative vision. And what Clara Zetkin has said about Jogiches is deeply true: 'He was one of those very masculine personalities–an extremely rare phenomenon these days–who can tolerate a great female personality in loyal and happy comradeship, without feeling her growth and development to be fetters on his own ego.' This comradeship lost nothing of its lasting strength even in those later years when their feelings for each other had subsided.

The *Proletariat* Party

Much of the best in Jogiches was certainly incorporated in Rosa Luxemburg's life-work. But it is impossible to mark off the limits of this contribution. We also do not know which of the two took the decisive first steps and gave the impetus to the political world-view which they now created and which was to determine their future activity. But even considering the fact that Leo deliberately kept himself in the background, thereby waiving public recognition of the part he played, Rosa's self-assuredness in scientific and theoretical questions is nevertheless proof that in this field at least she was the stronger one, who contributed and created the most.

It was just around the time of their initial encounter that a revision of socialist thought and the establishment of a definite point of view became necessary. International socialism stood on the threshold of a new phase of development. The founding of the new International in 1889 in Paris was the outward expression of the internal consolidation of the socialist movement. In France the period of confusion which followed the defeat of the Commune was coming to an end, though half-a-dozen different tendencies still wrestled with each other. In England, alongside of the old hidebound trade unions, new ones were rising which took in the unskilled workers, rejecting the Lib-Lab tradition of economic collaboration and resuming the class struggle. In Germany the Anti-Socialist Laws had been repealed. The working-class movement was granted a bourgeois legal basis. The barriers to its organisational expansion fell, and two extremist tendencies attacked the traditional party policy: the radical 'Youths' (*Jungen*), with their semi-anarchist leanings, on the Left, and the reformists on the Right. At the same time the trade-union movement, which was gaining strength, raised new questions and tasks.

Socialism in Poland had also entered into a period of crisis. The Polish socialist movement had originated in 1877, at a time when Polish capitalism, mollycoddled by Tsarism, was seized by the intoxication of a boom; profits amounting to 100% of the share-capital were not unusual, and the average rate reached was between 45% and 50%. These orgies of 'primitive accumulation' were celebrated on the backs of a proletariat harnessed for fourteen and fifteen hours a day to the treadmill, with no state protection whatsoever against even the most unrestrained exploitation, and lacking all means of self-defence.

In this situation young students raised the socialist banner. Their leader was Ludwik Waryński, a man of boldness, political far-sightedness, and organisational talent. Next to him stood, above all others, Kasimir Dluski, Stanislaus Mendelsohn, and Simon Dickstein. They were active among the workers, creating small circles, founding resistance funds as the start of illegal trade unions, organising the first strikes, and spreading the socialist message among a vanguard of the working class. The difficulties were enormous. The little groups were broken up again and again. Waves of arrests were followed by mass trials. During the first four years 120 members were imprisoned or exiled – a serious drain for an illegal organisation working under the conditions of Russian absolutism.

Nevertheless the movement made headway. In 1882 the different circles and workers' committees combined to form the 'Revolutionary Socialist Party *Proletariat*.' In 1883 the party was the life and soul of a real mass movement occasioned by an insolent decree of the Warsaw police-chief, placing women factory-workers on a par with prostitutes by forcing them to subject themselves to humiliating examinations. An appeal issued by the *Proletariat* stirred up the working masses. In the weaving mill at Zyradow 6,000 workers went on strike. Although they were bloodily suppressed by the military, nevertheless the opprobrious decree had to be withdrawn, and the workers gained the consciousness of their first success against the absolutist regime.

Waryński now established relations with *Narodnaya Volya* in St Petersburg, which led to a formal, militant alliance in March 1884. However, Waryński himself had already been arrested beforehand [1883], and a continuous chain of mass arrests broke the backbone of the *Proletariat* party. In December 1885 the party was tried before a court-martial. Waryński outlined his programme in an inspiringly forceful and bold speech for the defence. Four of the accused were sentenced to death, 23 to long terms of hard labour; about 200 were banished by administrative fiat. On 28 January 1886 the first martyrs of the Polish socialist movement – Bardowski, Kunicki, Ossowski, and Pietrusiński – were hanged. Waryński, who had been sentenced to 16 years hard labour, died a slow death in the Schlüsselburg fortress [1889]. His party fell to pieces. When Rosa Luxemburg joined a group of the *Proletariat* about a year after the great Warsaw trial, only remnants of the organisation still existed.

However, from the very beginning the 'Revolutionary Socialist Party *Proletariat*' was a long step ahead of the revolutionary movement in Russia, both in its principles and its programme. It originated during the period when *Narodnaya Volya* was making its greatest efforts and experiencing its most triumphant progress, which awakened such fantastic hopes that even Marx expected it would overthrow Tsarism. But *Narodnaya Volya* was not the party of the proletariat–neither in its political actions nor in its consciousness. The Russian revolutionary movement was still engaged in the dispute as to whether Russia would have to tread the same path to socialism via capitalism as the 'degenerate and corrupt' West, or whether the old peasant community, already in a state of advanced decay, would furnish a native basis for a socialist organisation of Russian society. As Rosa Luxemburg once put it, 'the very physical existence of the Russian working class still had to be extracted from the dry language of official industrial statistics; every mathematical proletarian, so to speak, had to be fought over in heated polemics'.

Thus *Narodnaya Volya* was a movement of intellectuals, without any support among the popular masses, without any insight into the social process, and without even a clear programme concerning the future shape of Russian society. It was a small band of men and women who entered the lists against absolutism with high-minded audacity, thinking they could fight for freedom on behalf of a hundred million souls with nothing but revolvers and bombs. All the idealism, devotion, self-sacrifice, and fortitude that are vital forces in humanity were concentrated with luminous purity in Zheliabov, Kilbalshitch, Sophie Perovskaya, Vera Figner, and their fellow-militants. However, just as Kilbalshitch blew himself up in killing the Tsar [Alexander II, on 1 March 1881], so the day of triumph for *Narodnaya Volya* turned into the day of its decisive defeat. The method proved itself false. The highest levels of individual heroism cannot achieve what only the mass of the people itself can struggle for–liberation.

In its perception of social reality and the prerequisites of the struggle for liberation the *Proletariat* party was just as much superior to *Narodnaya Volya* as the social development of Poland was superior to that of central Russia. It acknowledged capitalism as a fact and declared itself to be the party of the working class, both in name and in its basic ideas. It wanted to wage the liberation struggle as a struggle of the working masses. It strongly emphasised its international character, broke with the traditions of the old Polish revolutionary movement, and rejected the independence of Poland as a political aim: 'We want neither a *Szlachta*-Poland nor a democratic Poland. And not only do we not want it [independence], but we are convinced that this demand is an absurdity.' In the view of the *Proletariat*'s leader, Polish patriotism would inevitably render the working class an appendage of the other classes. However, the problem was in fact to sever it from the other classes, to awaken its consciousness of its own mission. According to a programmatic appeal of November 1882,

The interests of the exploited cannot be reconciled with those of the exploiters, and under no circumstances can they travel the same road of fictitious national unity; on the other hand, the urban workers do share common interests with the workers in the country-side. Thus the Polish proletariat is completely separate from the privileged classes and enters the struggle as an independent class, distinct in its economic, political, and moral undertakings.

The closest comrades-in-arms of the working classes were not to be found in Polish society, but in the revolutionary movement in Russia. And the Polish national question would be solved within the framework of the international socialist revolution. This revolution would overthrow Tsarism and the bourgeois rule, and would bring to power the proletariat, which would put socialism into practice. The party thus ignored the bourgeois revolution in Russia as a stage on the way to socialism. Only Waryński, by far and away its best thinker, gropingly comprehended the necessity of fighting for demo-cratic liberties in order that the working class might better be able to develop itself culturally and organisationally.

The *Proletariat* party was active among the working class for about five years. It created educational circles and workers' commit-tees in various parts of Poland; it led strikes, including the big textile workers' strike of February 1883, and created the beginnings of a trade-union movement. The Polish workers were already capable of dealing isolated hard blows, but they were still too backward for an all-embracing organisation. The party could attract only a narrowly-based elite. And then came the repeated blows of the police, which deprived the party of its leadership, and not only disorganised it, but also disoriented it. The alliance with *Narodnaya Volya* became a fatal burden. The fundamental views of the *Proletariat* were in ir-reconcilable contradiction with the terrorist tactics of *Narodnaya Volya*. But if the alliance was not to remain a dead letter, the *Pro-letariat* would have to accept terrorist methods and a Blanquist tactic which implied that the revolution could be achieved through a con-spiracy on behalf of the working class and not through mass actions by the working class itself. The party degenerated into a conspira-torial organisation, plotting terrorist activities together with *Narod-naya Volya*, but without ever carrying them out. At the same time it was drawn into the debacle of *Narodnaya Volya*, and all that could be saved were those small circles in which Rosa Luxemburg spent her years of political apprenticeship.

Against Blanquism

In 1888 the Polish working-class movement again began to make pro-gress. The *Proletariat* party was reorganised. Once more it turned its attention to the working masses. Resistance funds for factory-workers were founded as a new start towards the formation of trade unions. Another result of these efforts was the founding of the Polish Workers League. This organisation limited its activities to furthering the economic interests of the working class, and on occasion even rejected political action altogether. It was analogous to that 'economistic' tendency which sprang up in the young socialist movement of Russia a decade later. The *Proletariat* and the League carried out concerted militant actions–above all, the May-Day celebration of 1892, when 8,000 workers struck in Warsaw and as many as 60,000 in Lodz. The strike in Lodz came to a bloody end. A massacre by the Cossacks left 46 victims dead and over 200 wounded. Both groups suffered from persecutions by the police, and finally, in 1893, a programmatic rapprochement led to the fusion of the *Proletariat* party, the Polish Workers League, and two smaller groups into the Polish Socialist Party (PPS). The organ of this party was the *Sprawa Robotnicza* (The Workers' Cause), founded in 1893 and published in Paris. Its founder was Leo Jogiches, its editor Adolf Warski, and its intellectual head the young Rosa Luxemburg.

The founding of the new party urgently demanded a revision of the ideas inherited from its predecessors. With characteristic passion and persistence Rosa Luxemburg, while in Zürich, had studied the history of Poland, its national-revolutionary and socialist movements, as well as the theoretical foundations of the international working-class movement. She formulated the results of this work for the Polish working-class movement in the first significant document that we have from her pen–a comprehensive report written on behalf of the PPS and presented to the Third Congress of the Socialist International, which met in Zürich in 1893.

The document first dealt with the establishment of a 'social-democratic',* i.e. Marxist policy for the Polish working-class movement. To this end Rosa Luxemburg had to take up the cudgels on two fronts: against Blanquist-anarchism and against reformism, against the traditions of the *Proletariat* and against the economistic tendencies which had appeared in the Polish Workers League. She opposed the Blanquist idea that the overthrow of Tsarism would be identical with the socialist revolution, and was against a tactic which sought to undermine absolutism by means of a conspiracy, a tactic which intended to rely on the masses if the need should arise, but

---

* Before the outbreak of the First World War and the collapse of the Second International, the term social-democratic meant quite simply 'revolutionary socialist'. It was only after the founding of the Third (Communist) International that 'social democracy' finally became totally identified and equated with reformism.–Tr.

which in fact would replace the masses with the leadership of an elite group. The masses themselves had to lead the struggle. But how could they be won for the struggle? Obviously generalising unduly from her own perceptions, Rosa Luxemburg wrote:

> People finally understood that the role of the social-democratic party rests on its conscious leadership of the mass struggle against the existing society, a struggle that must reckon with the vital, necessary conditions of capitalist society. People understood that the economic struggles for the daily interests of the working class, and the struggle for a democratic form of government, are a school through which the proletariat must necessarily pass before becoming capable of overthrowing the present social order.

She explained how, in its struggle for better wages, against inhumanly long working-hours, and against the shameful punishment system in the factories, the working class came up against the restraints and the opposition of the absolutist regime, and how it would have to lead the struggle for democratic liberties. At the same time she gave a strictly objective account of the actual condition of the working class. When Polish social democrats asserted that it was not possible to form trade unions in Prussian Poland, but only a political party of Poles, she wrote on 27 September 1893 to her Russian friend Krichevskii: 'Can you imagine? And that's in a country where the masses are completely indifferent and silent, and where they can be brought into movement only by appealing to their immediate interests–by wage struggles!' And she complained that even Bebel was succumbing to such false ideas. She refused to accept aspirations as reality. She was always ready to use the smallest beginnings for a movement. But she did not want the party to become absorbed in the daily struggle; instead, it should bear in mind that the whole course of its future development would be the result of its perception of history and that every step of its practical activity should be dictated by the thought of its final aim. Not only did the bourgeois revolution seem to her to be an objectively unavoidable stage in the total development of Russia, but also the democratic rights to be won in this revolution and the very struggle for these rights were to her the means by which the working class would mature intellectually, morally, and organisationally in preparation for the struggle for political power.

Today such a view may appear self-evident. But not in those days. Even years later Rosa Luxemburg's opponents in the Polish movement (whom she termed 'social-patriots') considered the idea of an organised trade-union struggle in Poland to be a pure utopia; such a venture they believed would break any party. They themselves, however, were the real utopians. The significance of Luxemburg's conception of that period can been seen in the fact that even in our own day the working-class movement has to wrestle again and again with the problem of the importance of the small-scale, day-to-day struggles and their relationship to the final objective. Yet in the nineties already, Rosa Luxemburg produced nothing less than the theoretical foundation of a militant socialist strategy. Such a theory might have been constructed at a pinch from occasional, generally ignored hints left by Marx and Engels. In fact, however, the whole trade-union and parliamentary activity of social democracy in Western Europe rested on a purely empirical base, and the dangers of this were to become evident very soon in the revisionist movement. This was an astonishing achievement for such a young woman, who fought against absolutism as a political emigré, in circumstances where romantic ideas luxuriated like weeds. The achievement was the fruit of a serious study of revolutionary theories and of history, but at the same time it was also the expression of a sound political instinct.

The national question as a strategic problem

A second test of strength faced her. The working-class revolutionary movement had to find some solution to the Polish national question. The *Proletariat* party had rejected the independence of Poland as an immediate aim of the socialist struggle. But in the crisis experienced by the Polish working-class movement in those years the old comrades-in-arms of Waryński–Mendelsohn, Mrs Jankowska, Daszyński, and others–were the ones who once again raised the banner of Polish independence. Without a doubt the *Proletariat* party had not sufficiently substantiated its attitude; its conception rested more on a cosmopolitan than on a Marxist international base. Rosa Luxemburg had already condemned the notion that the Polish national question would be solved as a matter of course in the imminent socialist revolution, because she perceived the bourgeois revolution as an unavoidable intermediate stage. Thus the problem was now to examine whether it would be correct for the Polish socialist movement to reject altogether the idea of making the country's national independence the object of its strivings. If this principled tactic proved to be correct, then, the result would be a break with the policy which Marx and Engels–the old masters of scientific socialism, whom Rosa Luxemburg regarded as the highest authorities–had upheld until Marx's death, which Friedrich Engels was still defending (1893), and which had become a dogma of Western European social democracy.

In the previously mentioned report to the Zürich Congress Rosa Luxemburg set forth in a few sentences a standpoint which contained elements of her general ideas on the Polish national question. But she took up the problem again and again, examining ever new aspects of the relation between the proletarian struggle and the struggle for national liberation, and defending her conclusions in innumerable and comprehensive polemical works. In pursuit of this problem she made wide-ranging studies. For decades she worked on a history of Poland, which she probably completed during the World War in her prison cell. However, the manuscript was lost, together with other important works, in the storms of the German Revolution; perhaps it was even destroyed by marauding soldiery. Only the skeleton of this work is extant. Franz Mehring used Luxemburg's manuscript for the explanatory notes to his edition of the essays by Marx and Engels from the years 1848-49,[6] and it is not difficult to distinguish the intellectual influence of Rosa Luxemburg in his work. There also exists a study by her on capitalism in Poland,[7] which has become the basis of all subsequent research in Polish economic history. With this work she obtained a doctorate in political science at the University of Zürich. These historical investigations were all-important in enabling Rosa Luxemburg to work out her own standpoint on the Polish national question.

Since the Polish insurrection of 1830-31, support for the Polish struggle for national independence had been a matter of course for Western European democracy–that is, so long as a progressive, militant democracy actually existed. And until Rosa Luxemburg appeared on the scene, for the social-democratic movement the restoration of Poland had had the force of dogma, in opposition to which the attitude of Waryński and his friends seemed an incomprehensible heresy. This dogma was based on the policy which Marx and Engels had consistently maintained since the 1840s. For them the national-revolutionary movement of Poland had been the battering-ram against the bulwark of European reaction, Tsarist Russia.

Tsarism had been the nucleus of the Holy Alliance, which for decades had smothered every stirring towards freedom on the continent. It was the prop of all the ruling feudal powers in Central Europe. The revolutionary waves of 1848 were broken on the frontiers of the Tsarist empire. The Tsarist power incited the Prussian King to his counter-revolutionary actions, its reactionary pressure going so far as to bring even a man like Humboldt to demand in 1844 that the Guizot government deport Karl Marx from France. With the suppression of the Hungarian freedom armies in 1849 Russian troops finally liquidated the revolution. In the following year the Tsar himself intervened in German domestic affairs by compelling Friedrich Wilhelm IV under threat of violence to sign the Treaty of Olmütz and thereby give up his attempt to unify Germany.

Any major democratic reform on the European continent seemed impossible so long as this power existed in the East, ever ready to strike with its Cossack armies.

For this reason Marx and Engels had concentrated their attention on Russia. They regarded its defeat and weakening as the prerequisite for any decisive political progress in the West. In 1848 they called for war against Russia as the only guarantee for the victory of the revolution; to them the victory of the Polish national idea was synonymous with the victory of democracy in Germany. After the defeat of the revolution the restoration of Poland remained for them a prerequisite of any democratic and proletarian policy. In a memorandum to the delegates to the Provisional Central Council of the First Congress of the International in 1866 in Geneva, Marx replied to the question as to why the workers of Europe should take up the Polish question:

a /... First of all, because the writers and agitators of the bourgeoisie have agreed to hush it up, although they champion all sorts of other nationalities on the continent, even Ireland. Whence this conspiracy of silence? Because both aristocrats and bourgeois look upon the sinister Asiatic power in the background as a last refuge against the advancing tide of the working class. This power can only really be broken by the restoration of Poland on a democratic basis.
b / In view of the present-day changed situation in Central Europe, especially in Germany, it is more than ever necessary to have a democratic Poland. Without it Germany will become the outpost of the Holy Alliance; with it, an ally of republican France. The working-class movement will be continually interrupted, checked, and retarded as long as this great European question remains unsolved.
c / It is the special duty of the German working class to seize the initiative in this question because Germany is an accomplice in the partitions of Poland.[8]

Marx was certainly of the opinion that no nation which oppresses other nations can itself be free. But it was not general national ideas which actuated him to adopt his attitude on the Polish question. Like Engels he was very sceptical about the right of self-determination of peoples and he saw in the Czech national movemen an expression of reactionary Pan-Slavism. His advocacy of an independent democratic Poland was determined by his political strategy.

Rosa Luxemburg also approached the solution of the question from the standpoint of political strategy. She overturned the foreign-policy postulates of Marx and Engels; these in the meantime had become firmly anchored in the minds of Marxists, who accepted them as determinations of natural law without bothering to examine them at all. But shifting alignments and the development of society in general in Europe had thoroughly altered the assumptions of Marxist policy. During those very years when Rosa Luxemburg was acquainting herself with this question, an alliance was forming between the French Republic and Russian absolutism. This already indicated that France was no longer an altar keeping the sacred flame of the revolution alive and that Russia was no longer the stronghold of reaction in the old sense.

It was true that all the reactionary forces in Europe still sought to lean upon Russia. However, it was no longer the direct threat of bayonets which accounted for Russia's influence, but diplomacy, and no buffer state was a help against that. It could be broken only by the overthrow of Tsarism. The Russian rouble no longer rolled into European chancelleries; on the contrary, the French franc and the German mark rolled into Russia to finance its armaments. The mainstay of reaction now had to be propped up on all sides. Just when Tsarism was being threatened most dangerously by *Narodnaya Volya*, Bismarck concluded the 'Reinsurance' Treaty [1887], which offered backing to Russian diplomacy in international politics. When it was not renewed three years later, the alliance with France took its place. Thus Tsarism reinvigorated itself at the energy-giving springs of France and Germany in preparation for the struggle against the revolution threatening at home.

The deepest reason for Marx's policy was the apparent entrenchment of absolutism in Russia, where social relations had seemed static for centuries. Tsarism was based chiefly on a primitive agricultural economy and the serfdom connected with it. As long as this primitive economy remained untouched, violent peasant uprisings were bound to fail. However, because of its power politics, Tsarism had to do its best to promote capitalist development in Russia. Russian society was disintegrating, and the inevitable consequence was the emancipation of the serfs in 1861. The peasant was pushed into the commodity economy. At the same time he was ruined by fiscal burdens. Then, in addition, when American competition began to make itself felt on the European grain market, bringing with it the first international agrarian crisis, the already precarious state of the large-scale landed property system became worse than ever. The terrible famine and the plague outbreak of 1891-93 were symptomatic of the process of decay afflicting the absolutist regime. The citadel of oppression and reaction was crumbling. And a new class was developing in Russia, the proletariat, a class which was not yet active, but which would—as Marxists like Rosa Luxemburg recognised—smash the walls of absolutism. In Western Europe there were no longer any bourgeois-democratic powers willing to cast off the yoke of Russian reaction. But in Russia itself those forces were astir which were to give this sinister power the *coup de grâce*. For these reasons revolutionary political strategy needed to be reoriented.

Not only had Marx's strategy lost its validity, but also the decisive means by which he hoped to carry it out—the national revolutionary movement in Poland—no longer existed. The standard-bearer of national insurrections was the nobility. The Polish lesser nobility in particular had been deeply impressed by the democratic ideas of the West, and its most progressive representatives fought as the most competent officers in all the arenas of revolutionary struggle throughout the nineteenth century up to the days of the Paris Commune. However, the class itself is not identical with its individual representatives. It cannot jump over its own shadow. The aim of the nobility lay not in the future, but in the past—as was the case with the aristocratic Sickingens and Huttens in the age of the German Reformation. As a class it was anti-capitalist, because basically it wanted to restore the old feudal rule of the nobility, and this was why its insurrections failed. They could have been successful only if the nobility had been able to win the enthusiastic loyalty of the peasants, and only an agrarian revolution could have achieved that.

Since 1846 the democratic leaders of the aristocratic party had again and again proclaimed the principle of agrarian reform, but nothing was ever done about it. In the end it was Tsarism itself which carried it through, after the insurrection of 1863, by abolishing the last vestiges of serfdom in Poland. With this the primitive agricultural system was destroyed in Poland too. The nobility was deposed from its position of social hegemony. Capitalism began to flourish, as in a hotbed.

The new bourgeoisie took over the leadership of Polish society. It also took over the national programme as a heritage—in order first to devitalise it and then hurriedly to bury the remains. This bourgeoisie owed its existence to the fact that Tsarism greatly encouraged the development of capitalism. In the Tsarist empire the Polish bourgeoisie found the large market it needed. Separation from Russia or the restoration of an independent Poland would have been the death sentence for this class. Thus its aim was not—unlike that of the bourgeoisie in other countries—national unity and independence. By subjugating itself it endeavoured to use absolutism for its own ends. It is true that thousands of individual Polish bourgeois were opponents of the Russianisation of Poland, but the bourgeoisie as a class was not. The higher its profits rose and the more energetically the Polish working class acted, the more loyal the bourgeoisie became to the oppressor of its own nation. Only in one stratum of the population did the national idea survive—in the intelligentsia. However, the latter represented no real social force; at best, it provided officers, but no troops, and in the end its impotence plunged it into pure adventurism.

And the Polish working class? How could it take over the nationalist heritage, if it regarded the 'leader of the nation', the bourgeoisie, as its mortal enemy against whom it had to struggle for every inch of living space? And how was the Polish working class supposed to create a bourgeois Polish national state against the vital interests of the bourgeoisie itself–particularly in a Poland that was dismembered into three parts and subject threefold to foreign domination?

> In order to win independence for Poland, the Polish proletariat would not only have to break the grip of the three most powerful governments in Europe, but would also have to be strong enough to overcome the material conditions of existence of its own bourgeoisie. In other words, despite its position as an enslaved class, it would have to take the position of a ruling class at the same time and to use its rule to create a new class state, which, in turn, would be the instrument of its further oppression.[9]

If the Polish proletariat had sufficient strength for this task, then surely it could also carry out the socialist revolution itself, and only the socialist revolution offered those prerequisites for the solution of the Polish national question acceptable to the working class.

Thus, in the view of Rosa Luxemburg, national independence could not be the immediate aim of the Polish proletariat. The working class should set up goals which were not merely desirable, but which corresponded to the objective course of social development and for which the material prerequisites existed. The working class should not pursue utopias, but should adopt a hard-line policy (Realpolitik)–not realist politics in the traditionally narrow-minded and cowardly sense of petit-bourgeois politics, but a policy which strives for the final revolutionary aim with the utmost determination.

When Rosa Luxemburg first set forth these ideas publicly, she encountered above all the furious resistance of both the nationalist elements among the Poles and all those elements in the working-class movement which held fast to what was regarded as the Marxist tradition. Karl Kautsky, who was considered the greatest Marxist authority of his day, agreed with the basic points of her argument, but not with its essence. In particular, he countered that the anti-nationalist tendencies of the Polish bourgeoisie observed by Rosa Luxemburg were only a temporary phenomenon: in those very years of the 1890s a fierce struggle had broken out between Russian and Polish industry, and the Tsarist state was using all the means of economic policy at its disposal against the interests of Polish industry. As a result of this struggle, according to Kautsky, the bourgeoisie would be forced to take up again the cause of national independence, and would rally around itself the petit-bourgeoisie, the peasants, and the intelligentsia. 'On the grave of the old feudal movement for the restoration of Poland a new national Polish movement will begin to rise up after a short interlude, a movement with modern origins, vigorous and promising.'[10]

Rosa Luxemburg subjected this expectation to a thorough examination in her doctoral dissertation, and exposed it as an illusion. She pointed out that Russian and Polish capitalism were bound to each other by a strong solidarity of interests, that they depended on each other and profited from each other. To be sure, the *bellum omnium contra omnes* (war of all against all) prevailed here, as it did in every capitalist economy. A part of this general war was the dispute between the fustian barons of Lodz and the calico kings of Moscow, in which of course the attempt was made to 'wrap the trivial woolly object of their dispute in an ideological veil of nationalism'.[11] However, those Tsarist measures adduced as evidence of anti-Polish economic policies all aimed in reality at prodding Polish industry into purchasing Russian, rather than foreign, raw materials. And, finally, Russian expansionist policies led Tsarism to form stronger ties with Polish, than with native Russian, industry, because Polish industry was better equipped to take advantage of the expanding market. With this, the last hopes for a regeneration of the national idea in Poland had to disappear.

There was, however, one means which could change the idea of the restoration of Poland from a utopia into a political reality—and that was war. But for Rosa Luxemburg's political purposes this means was out of the question. It was not pacifism which moved her to exclude the factor of war from her political calculations. She knew only too well that wars are inevitable so long as class rule exists. But she explained at that time that because the alignment of forces in a future war could not be anticipated, certain expectations might well determine the tactics to be adopted during the war itself, but not the programme intended for the daily struggle in peace-time. Later on, in the period of the imperialist conflicts of the great powers, she regarded reliance on war as the most dangerous political adventurism, which would eventually turn the Polish proletariat into a mercenary army of one of the imperialist fronts.

The fact that for all these reasons Rosa Luxemburg spoke out against the idea of the restoration of Poland might easily lead to the seemingly logical conclusion that she did not care at all about the national freedom of the Polish people and that she quietly put up with the national oppression of the Polish people. Such a reproach was actually made and seemed indeed to be supported by certain strongly-worded statements made in the heat of debate. But how could this be imputed to one, whose rebellious spirit had been awakened by the Russification policy of Tsarism? Rosa never tired of fighting against the national oppression of the Poles, both in the Russian empire as well as in Germany and Austria. But when she recognised that the Polish national revolution had become a utopia, she nevertheless saw the liberation of the Polish nation included in a higher aim. Now the task was not to wrench Poland from Russia, but to overthrow Russian absolutism itself. This was not only a more all-embracing aim: it raised revolutionary sights from the national to the international and social level. By 1905 it became obvious that the higher task of overcoming Tsarism was endangered by the narrower objective of restoring Poland. Rosa confronted the apparent, but in reality impossible, unity of the proletariat and bourgeoisie in Poland with the unity of the proletariats of all the nations within Russia. The realisation of freedom for the Poles needed to be sought in a Russian democratic republic, in their voluntary incorporation into an all-Russian community of liberated peoples. To all the peoples still oppressed by Russia the victorious revolution would bring cultural autonomy and the right of broad self-government. For Poland this would mean Polish-language schools, the recognition of Polish as an official language, Polish jurisdiction over its affairs, i.e. the removal of every discrimination against the Polish people by foreign rule and the safeguarding of the free development of Polish culture. The solution of the Polish national question was thus included in the large strategic aim which Rosa Luxemburg set for the Polish working class, and in the course of time this strategic aim was acknowledged by almost all the important Marxist theoreticians.

An absolute contrast to this 'repudiation of Polish national interests' was a further revision of Marxist tradition which Rosa Luxemburg also undertook in the nineties, as a result of which she was now all the more decried as a blind enemy of the Polish people. When the insurrection of the Greeks on the island of Crete in 1896 raised the Turkish question once again, she took a determined stand in favour of the national liberation of the various peoples subjugated by the Turks–the Greeks, Serbians, Bulgarians, Armenians. An odd contradiction indeed to her attitude on the Polish question. How could these be reconciled?

It was the reversal of exactly the same contradiction contained in the policy of Marx and Engels, a contradiction which found its solution then, as now, in a consistent political strategy. As in the case of Poland, the creation or the maintenance of a bulwark against Russian absolutism in the Balkans and on the Russian frontiers in Asia Minor was fundamental for Marx's policy and his judgment of national questions. In the southeast corner of Europe and the Near East Turkey stood guard against Russia. Her own vital interests compelled her to oppose any Russian advance. Therefore, in Marx's view, the general interests of European democracy demanded the preservation of the Ottoman empire, particularly as the nationalist currents in the Balkans had been poisoned by the reactionary ideas of Pan-Slavism and the existing small states were nothing but outposts and weak-willed tools of Tsarist power. Thus, during the Crimean War, Marx resolutely supported the Turks against Russia and denounced the feeble conduct of the war by France and England. In 1878 he again championed the territorial integrity of Turkey 'because a Russian defeat would greatly accelerate that social upheaval whose elements are present on a massive scale in Russia and thereby also accelerate the revolution in the whole of Europe'. [In a letter of advice sent to Liebknecht on 4 February 1878–Tr (Fitzgerald)]

In the opinion of Rosa Luxemburg, however, there was no further need for foreign powers to act as midwives to the Russian revolution. She relied on the revolutionary forces within Russia itself, and these only needed time to develop. Turkey, on the other hand, was increasingly becoming the storm-centre of Europe. Her very existence as an oppressor power kept alive the rotten Austro-Hungarian empire. Turkish foreign rule shackled the development of the culturally superior and economically advanced peoples of the Balkans, and the bourgeoisie of these peoples really represented their national aspirations for independence. But what about the influence of Tsarism in the Balkans? Rosa Luxemburg was sure that the throwing off of the Turkish yoke would not further it. On the contrary! Russian influence would be strong only so long as the Balkan peoples were oppressed; as soon as they could form free national states, however, their own national and state interests would drive them into a front against Russia.

Thus Rosa Luxemburg did not accept any dogma or universally applicable formula for the solution of national questions. As she later stated it: 'National states and nationalism are innately empty shells into which each historical epoch and the class relations in each country pour their particular material content.'[12] In her opinion all national movements in the period of bourgeois revolutions, whether in Germany or Italy, in Poland, the Balkans, Ireland or India, had to be carefully and individually analysed. Such national movements could be historically progressive or reactionary, depending on existing social relations and international conditions as well as the character and interests of the class or classes supporting them. As a result, the attitude of the socialist parties to national tendencies might well change. In any case, however, the interests of the proletarian revolution had to be placed above all other considerations. For these reasons Rosa Luxemburg refused to regard the right of self-determination as a general formula for all the peoples in the capitalist world.

At a later date Rosa Luxemburg clashed violently with Lenin over this question of self-determination, and for a long time the conflict prevented the fulfilment of one of her hopes in the struggle against Tsarism: the organisational affiliation of the Polish party to Russian Social Democracy. Their opposing views basically derived from the fact that circumstances had placed the two great working-class leaders in different positions. Rosa Luxemburg was active on behalf of the working class of an oppressed people: she had to guard against the proletarian class struggle being misrepresented and swamped by nationalist tendencies and therefore she had to attach the greatest importance to a fighting alliance of the Polish and the Russian working classes. In contrast, Lenin was active in the Pan-Russian milieu, as a member of a people which oppressed a 'hundred peoples'. In order to unite the revolutionary forces of all these peoples against absolutism, he had to recognise unequivocally the national interests of the peoples oppressed by the Pan-Russians, including the right of complete political separation from Russia. For this reason he insisted emphatically on the formula of the right of self-determination for all peoples, a right which Marx and Engels never recognised and which Rosa Luxemburg showed with cogent arguments to be inapplicable to the given situation, though it was to become an important psychological factor indeed for Russian Social Democracy. Rosa Luxemburg failed to recognise the psychological aspect of this question. In her anxiety to maintain the general line of socialist strategy in Poland, she also underestimated the role which the national question could play in large popular movements.

How far Lenin agreed with Luxemburg in her solution of the strategic problem for Poland can be seen from the big discussion which took place in 1916 between him and several opponents of the right of self-determination (Karl Radek, Hermann Gorter, Henriette Roland-Holst). Referring to the Polish question, he wrote:

> To favour a European war purely and simply for the sake of re-establishing Poland would be nationalism of the worst sort; it would place the interests of the small number of Poles above the interests of the hundreds of millions of people who would suffer in such a war. Examples of such nationalists are the supporters of the right wing of the PPS, who are socialists only in words; compared to them the Polish social democrats are a hundred times more correct in their attitude. To put forward the slogan of Polish independence now, in the present state of relations among the imperialist neighbour countries, would be, in reality, to chase utopias, to lapse into the most petty nationalism, and to forget the prerequisites of the European revolution—and even those of the Russian and the German revolutions. . . .

It is not a paradox, but a simple fact that the Polish proletariat as such can serve the cause of socialism and freedom, including also Polish socialism and Polish freedom, only if it wages a joint struggle with the proletariat of the neighbouring countries against the narrow-minded Polish nationalists. We must not deny the great historical services rendered by the Polish social democrats in the struggle against these people. . . .

The situation is undoubtedly very confused, but there is a way out which would permit all those involved to remain internationalists, and that is if the Russian and German social democrats would demand the unconditional "freedom of separation" for Poland, and the Polish social democrats would fight for the unity of the proletarian struggle in both the small and the large countries without putting forward the slogan of Polish independence in the given epoch.[13]

Despite some reservations which ought to be expressed about certain arguments put forward by Lenin in the discussions on the right of self-determination, his overall judgment was correct, namely that the nationalist opponents of Rosa Luxemburg in Poland merely reiterated the words of Marx without comprehending their spirit, and that Rosa herself was quite correct in her Polish policy, but that she tended too much to generalise elsewhere her correct solution of the national question in Poland. This is a fate which pioneers of theory can avoid only with difficulty.

But was her solution correct after all? Has not history disproved it? Rosa Luxemburg had declared that the independence of Poland under capitalist conditions was utopian, and yet an independent Poland was founded. Nevertheless, she was right. It was in fact the idea of wanting to realise an independent Poland by revolutionary means which seemed to her utopian and fatal for the Polish working class. It was hardly possible for her to foresee what new territorial relations would arise out of [a war bringing about] the collapse of half of Europe, and she of course rejected this solution on principle as well as the means required to realise it. She was correct in predicting that the nationalist current in the Polish socialist movement would inevitably be demoralised by its political attitude. That was demonstrated in the Russian Revolution of 1905, and it revealed itself again in the reactionary dictatorship of Pilsudski and his 'Colonels' after 1921. And she was right in saying that international revolutionary strategy should not adopt any aim which would make Poland a bulwark of capitalist Europe against revolution in the East. She was 'refuted' by history just as the radical democrats of 1848 who strove for a Greater-German republic including Austria were 'refuted' by Bismarck's creation of a semi-absolutist Prussian Germany, which barred the way to historical progress in Central Europe for half a century and finally led to the World War and the German defeat.

With her solution of the national question of Poland and of the peoples subjugated by the Turks Rosa Luxemburg overthrew the postulates of Marx's foreign policy. In doing so she proved herself a true pupil of Marx. This is what in fact distinguishes the epigoni from the creative successors of great thinkers. The former piously take over the finished products of the mind-work of their masters as rigid formulae and defend them in spite of transformed conditions; the latter grasp the real spirit of their great models by retaining a freely critical attitude towards them, and as masters themselves apply their own masters' methods to changed conditions. Essential aspects of the method in Rosa's case were a rejection of all mere wishes and hopes, an understanding of the objective historical process, and the active influence of the working class in shaping this process in the same way as the physicist seeks to master Nature: by studying her laws and subordinating himself to them.

This first great political achievement of Rosa Luxemburg was all the more significant because she not only hated Russian absolutism from the bottom of her heart, but she was also closely associated with every fibre of her being to the culture of the Polish people. She was an internationalist *par excellence*, and if her Polish patriotism burst forth time and again, it was, however, never in the narrow-minded nationalistic sense. Her revision of Marxist tactics in the Polish question was therefore the triumph of an incorruptible critical intellect over strong personal feelings.

The founding of Polish Social Democracy

Rosa Luxemburg was well aware of her own intellectual strength. Her letters at the beginning of the 1890s already reveal that self-confidence which later took many people aback, and aroused and aggravated political enmities. However, she very much needed this unlimited self-reliance, which was prepared to make no concessions whatever in matters of principle, in order to maintain her ground in the violent disputes into which she was plunged immediately after her first public appearance on the political scene.

The unification of all Polish socialists in the PPS was short-lived. In the autumn of 1892 an 'Association of Polish Socialists Abroad' had been formed in Paris. The old leaders of the *Proletariat* party belonged to it, and they now adopted the slogan of the restoration of Poland, which they had up to then rejected. They did not succeed in putting across their new views to the cadres inside Poland. The contrast in political outlook and in the tactical attitude it determined was so great that common membership in the same party was no longer possible. Nevertheless, the fight was not settled by any objective discussion of the points at issue. Even after the opposing views had become irreconcilable because of the complete organisational separation of the social-democratic group of Rosa Luxemburg from the 'social-patriots', no thorough discussion took place.

The views of the opposing side on the national question were not internally coherent; they had not been thought out very much and were based almost exclusively on emotion. At first these people contented themselves with repeating the arguments of Marx and Engels, but in the long run they proved to have no effect either on the advanced workers in Poland or on the International. Searching for a better theoretical position, some of them represented the restoration of Poland as a slogan which would be realised by the victory of the socialist revolution. They thereby came very close to Rosa Luxemburg's own position, but the slogan completely lost its character as the central focus of the actual day-to-day struggle in Poland. Others asserted that the weakness of the Russian working-class movement made any hope of gaining political liberty in Russia illusory; therefore the idea of an alliance with Russian Social Democracy was completely worthless: the Polish proletariat could become strong only on a purely national basis. Still others resorted to highly confused interpretations of the historical perspective and the tactics to be adopted. Almost all of them looked down with nationalist arrogance on the Russians and on the other oppressed peoples of Russia. With such poor arms it was difficult to enter the arena against a fighter like Rosa Luxemburg.

The struggle against the young social-democratic group was therefore waged along the low lines of intrigue, insinuations, and backbiting. It began in 1893 with a baiting campaign against Kasprzak, the first mentor of Rosa Luxemburg. For years he had shuttled back and forth among various German and Russian prisons, and in consequence his health had been ruined, but he was nevertheless smeared as an agent of the Okhrana [the Tsarist Russian secret police] by the Galician leader Daszyński and his friends. For decades he was practically ostracised because of this accusation, and the fact that he was completely rehabilitated by committees of investigation set up by the International did not put an end to it until his death on the gallows placed his loyalty to the revolutionary socialist cause beyond all doubt.*

This method of fighting reached a high point at the Third

---

* In the summer of 1905 Kasprzak was discovered in a secret printing-office by the Warsaw police. Having resisted arrest with his own pistol, he was sentenced to death and executed in November 1905.

Congress of the Socialist International in Zürich in 1893. The 'Association of Polish Socialists Abroad'–i.e. an organisation of fugitives, students, etc.–was represented by ten delegates, including Mendelsohn, Jankowska, Perl, and Daszyński, who already had some reputation internationally and close connections with the leading figures of the International. The members of the social-democratic delegation belonged to the younger generation; they were almost unknown in international socialist circles and therefore in a weak position from the outset. Karski's mandate was quashed, although it was the only one put forward by the real organisation in Russian Poland. Rosa Luxemburg was a delegate from *Sprawa Robotnicza*, under the name of Kruszyńska. Her opponents made covert insinuations against her and in particular against the editor of the paper, Warski (Michalkowski). A stifling atmosphere of lies and allegations was created.

Rosa Luxemburg cut right through it. Without showing the least bit of self-consciousness in the presence of the illustrious heads of the world's socialist parties, this young unknown woman defended her cause by taking the offensive. With a wave of the hand she brushed aside all the petty intriguing on the question of mandates, and went straight to the heart of the political differences, achieving an initial moral success. Emile Vandervelde [Belgian socialist leader, 1866–1938] later recollected his impressions of her speech:

> Rosa, 23 years old at the time, was quite unknown except in a few socialist circles in Germany and Poland. . . . Her opponents had a great deal of trouble in holding their ground against her. I can see her now: how she sprang to her feet out of the sea of delegates and jumped onto a chair to make herself better heard. Small, delicate and dainty in a summer dress which cleverly concealed her physical defects, she advocated her cause with such magnetism in her eyes and with such fiery words that she enthralled and won over the great majority of the congress, who raised their hands in favour of the acceptance of her mandate.

The general impression given by Vandervelde from memory forty years later is probably correct. However, in one point he is wrong: it was not this enthusiastic plenum who decided on her mandate, but a commission which afterwards rejected it by nine votes to seven. The decision becomes intelligible once we learn the fact that at the Congress two very powerful figures came to the aid of the Polish 'social-patriots': Georgii Plekhanov and Friedrich Engels. Plekhanov greatly mistrusted Luxemburg's group, for one reason because of his old conflict with Leo Jogiches, but especially because her group had emerged from the *Proletariat* party. This was an old matter which one would have thought had been long settled. Plekhanov had dissociated himself in 1877 from *Narodnaya Volya* when the latter resorted to terrorist action against Tsarism, and he had fought against this party ever since. The *Proletariat* party, however, had later formed an alliance with *Narodnaya Volya* and had thereby become opponents of Plekhanov's Group for the 'Liberation of Labour', which was the forerunner of Russian Social Democracy. Engels, who participated in the Congress, set great store by Plekhanov's judgment, and was naturally mistrustful of a political line which disavowed the aim of national independence for Poland, an aim which he still resolutely pursued.

The intolerance of the old Polish leaders at the Congress, and in particular the rejection of Karski's mandate, led to the break-up of the Polish Socialist Party. The whole organisation in Poland broke away from the PPS and created the 'Social Democratic Party of the Kingdom of Poland', which thereafter was under the leadership of Rosa Luxemburg and Leo Jogiches. The failure of their party did not discourage the leaders of the now social-patriotic PPS; indeed it intensified their rage. At the London Congress in 1896 they again tried to have their opponents' mandates quashed, and by the same methods. Although in the meantime the accusations against Warski had been refuted by a committee of investigation under the chairmanship of the old Russian revolutionary Peter Lavrov, these were raised once more. Also a story was spread that Rosa Luxemburg was in special favour with the Commandant of the Warsaw Gendarmerie, Colonel Markgravski. At the Congress Daszyński thundered in blind fury against the leaders of the new party:

> We cannot tolerate our movement being compromised by such scoundrels as Rosa Luxemburg, Urbach, etc. We shall use every possible means to fight against this disgrace, and shall unmask and defeat all those who are smearing our movement with their ink. We must liberate our international army from a band of publicist-brigands who are out to destroy our struggle for freedom.[14]

However, on this occasion not even such round abuse proved effective any more. Rosa Luxemburg had the satisfaction of seeing a resolution proposed by the PPS leaders on the restoration of Poland rejected by the Congress, and in its stead a resolution on the right of self-determination adopted—a resolution which was so formulated that the Polish social democrats were able to accept it. Again in 1900 an attempt was made to eject Luxemburg from the Fifth Congress of the International in Paris, a venture which can only be described as pitiful, because Rosa Luxemburg held not only mandates from Posen [Poznan] and Upper Silesia, but also one from the workers of Warsaw, bearing 218 signatures including those of 27 political prisoners; she had also been entrusted by the Congress organisers with the drawing up of the important report on militarism.

Slanderous, fabricated insinuations and coarse abuse directed at that 'ambitious intriguing woman' and that 'hysterical female' formed the loud accompaniment to Rosa Luxemburg's Polish policy – the expression of the wounded national feelings of her opponents, who were only too conscious of their intellectual inferiority. When Luxemburg published her articles on the Oriental question, even old Wilhelm Liebknecht set upon her with a letter which failed to refute any of her arguments, but which let fly at her a whole quiver of choice invectives, going so far as to make the scarcely veiled accusation that she had been bought by the Russian Okhrana – an action which, somewhat later, the old man admitted to be wrong and regretted.

All this merely glanced off Rosa Luxemburg. In political argument she could be extremely trenchant, and her irony was often caustic, but she always stuck to the point. The mud thrown at her was so ineffective that not even a trace of an effort to ward it off appears in her writings. She would have agreed with Goethe:

Wirbelwind und trocknen Kot,

Lass sie drehn und stäuben!

Gusts of wind and dried-up dung,

Let them swirl into dust!

Toward her friends she was sensitive and forbearing; with her enemies, however, she engaged in battle, and then her only concern was always to fight as skilfully as possible.

Other experiences were more bitter. The Polish working-class movement, at whose head she stood, developed quite favourably in the beginning, but it soon had to suffer all the hardships which beset illegal parties. Arrests followed one after the other on such a large-scale that by 1896 only scanty remnants of the organisation were left, and even the newspaper *Sprawa Robotnicza* had to suspend publication. Not until around 1899 did the movement flower afresh, which was in particular to provide the opportunity for the young Dzierzyński* to develop his energies and organisational capacities. He managed to win the acceptance of Rosa Luxemburg's ideas by the Lithuanian movement and to unite Lithuanian with Polish Social Democracy in the 'Social Democratic Party of the Kingdom of Poland and Lithuania' (SDKPiL).

Rosa Luxemburg used the difficult years of stagnation in Poland above all to continue her studies and complete her doctoral dissertation on 'The Industrial Development of Poland'. At the same time she was active in the Swiss working-class movement and

* Feliks Dzierzyński, later a prominent Bolshevik and head of the Cheka (the Soviet security police). – Tr.

appeared as a contributor, especially on Polish questions, in the socialist press. In the theoretical journal edited by Kautsky, *Neue Zeit*, she published some of her more important articles: 'New Tendencies in the Polish Socialist Movement in Germany and Austria' (1896), 'Social Patriotism in Poland' (1896), and 'Step by Step: The History of the Bourgeois Classes in Poland' (1897). These attracted a lot of attention, both because of their rich subject-matter and their brilliant form. This debut in the most respected socialist periodical brought her not only early fame, but also a new wave of slanders and invectives on the part of the PPS. [In 1897] she spent several months in France, where she established close contact with the Marxist leaders of the French working-class movement–Jules Guesde, Edouard Vaillant, Allemane, and others. She developed an especially close friendship with Vaillant, the Communard, who had studied in Germany and who had led the French Blanquist movement into the Marxist camp.

3
In defense of Marxism

In the ranks of German Social Democracy

Rosa Luxemburg's apprentice years were at an end. She had now
completed her studies by obtaining a doctorate at the University of
Zürich. Directing the illegal SDKPiL from Switzerland may have contented an organiser like Jogiches, but she was driven to tackle new
tasks and to establish herself independently. Her political friends
probably agreed with her about the great importance of propagating
their views in Germany. The impetus to engage in such work probably came from those friends who were already leading activist lives
there: Parvus, Warski, Karski, etc.

Germany of the 1890s was the land of a powerfully developing
working-class movement, a land where the interest in theoretical and
tactical questions was extremely lively; the German Social Democratic Party (SPD) and the German trade unions by virtue of the
strength and the respect which they commanded were the most
significant pillars of the international working-class movement. In
the East, Germany enclosed vast, formerly Polish areas with an overwhelmingly Polish-speaking population; in these areas, namely in
Upper Silesia and Posen province, legal social-democratic organisations and trade unions existed, with their own press, etc. Here were
tasks to justify the highest concentration of effort: to represent and
to defend on this soil the views of the Polish social democrats, and
thereby to gain influence in the leading circles of the SPD and thus
in the International; to create bases and, wherever possible, to establish contacts here with the illegal party in Russian Poland. To
embark on such a course seemed all the more inviting, because
Polish social-patriots were actively bustling about in Germany, making use of every opportunity to seek and find recognition and support even at the highest committee levels of the party.

As a foreigner, however, Rosa Luxemburg could not have performed this task. Foreigners were strictly forbidden to engage in any
political activity, particularly in Prussia, and all the more so in the
border areas. For appearance's sake, she therefore married Gustav

Lübeck, the son of her old friends Karl and Olympia [on 19 April 1898]. She thus acquired Prussian citizenship and was somewhat better protected from the Prussian police, who customarily acted as Tsarist henchmen.

Rosa Luxemburg arrived in Berlin in May 1898. It was an election year: the whole attention of Social Democracy was concentrated on the approaching Reichstag election–the second one since the lapse of the Anti-Socialist Laws [1890]. She immediately got in touch with the party executive and offered her services as an agitator among the Poles in Upper Silesia during the election campaign. Because of her appearances at international congresses and her articles on Polish issues in *Neue Zeit*, the *Sächsische Arbeiterzeitung*, and *Vorwärts* she was not unknown. Her proposal was accepted, and shortly thereafter she was making her debut 'in the darkest pits' of Upper Silesia. She was severely frustrated at first, for in Switzerland she and Leo had dreamt that, with her speaking talents, she would create a sensation at huge mass meetings in the larger German cities and bring her particular views directly to a very wide audience. But this first agitation-tour among the Polish-speaking miners and metal-workers in Königshütte, Katscher, Gleiwitz, etc. in fact proved to be a great success. Her listeners, who were certainly not easy to stir up, brought flowers to her and did not want to let her go again. Happy, she reported to Jogiches about the good contact, and how it had refreshed her and made her more sure of herself. His reaction was one of anger, however, because he feared he might lose her.

On returning to Berlin, she retired completely at first, to devote herself to working on the articles she contributed to the social-democratic press. She set high standards for her work. To her Zürich-friends Robert and Mathilde Seidel she wrote very graphically about it (23 June 1898):

> Do you know what keeps bothering me now? I'm not satisfied with the way in which people in the party usually write articles. They are all so conventional, so wooden, so cut-and-dry. By comparison, the words of [Ludwig] Börne sound as if they came from another world. I know–the world is different now, and other times want to have other lyrics (*Lieder*). But at least these were real "lyrics". Our scribblings are usually not lyrics, but whirrings, without colour or resonance, like the tone of an engine-wheel. I believe that the cause lies in the fact that when people write, they forget for the most part to dig deeply into themselves and to feel the whole import and truth of what they are writing. I believe that every time, every day, in every article you must live through the thing again, you must feel your way through it, and then fresh words–coming from the heart and going to the heart–would occur to express the old familiar thing. But you get so used to a truth that you rattle off the deepest and greatest things as if they were the "Our Father". I

firmly intend, when I write, never to forget to be enthusiastic about what I write and to commune with myself. And that is why from time to time I read old man Börne: he reminds me faithfully of my pledge. . . .[15]

This strength of purpose doubtless also explains how she managed within a short time to win a place for herself in the social-democratic movement. Through her literary work she was already in touch with Karl Kautsky, the 'Pope of Marxism', in Zürich, and this association grew into an enduring friendship with him and his family, in particular with his wife, Luise. She was soon at home in the circle of August Bebel, Paul Singer, and Franz Mehring.

She was attracted to Clara Zetkin, whom she knew from international congresses, because they shared the same intellectual interests and temperament. Clara joined the movement as a young teacher, even before the Anti-Socialist Laws were passed [1878]. When Ossip Zetkin was expelled for violating these laws, she followed him to exile in Paris. She was especially interested in the problems of women in general and of working-class women in particular. In a report to the Founding Congress of the Second International in Paris in 1889 she was the first to give the women's question a Marxist interpretation, which determined the socialist standpoint for a long time. After she returned to Germany in 1891, she was given the editorship of the socialist women's paper *Die Gleichheit* (Equality), which she made into a leading periodical. Rosa and Clara developed a bond of friendship which endured throughout all their political struggles.

Only in the case of her relationship with old Liebknecht did a long-standing grudge keep them apart, but she finally managed to win even his recognition and sympathy. Parvus, as editor of the *Sächsische Arbeiterzeitung* in Dresden, opened the way for her into the daily press of the German party. Common intellectual interests, militancy, and temperament created a strong bond, above all, between her and Bruno Schönlank, the founder of the *Leipziger Volkszeitung*, who had liberated the social-democratic press from the confines of a mere party mouthpiece and raised its cultural level considerably. Well-read in both economics and history, vigorously active, and very sensitive to all the phenomena of social life, Schönlank was a born journalist. But Rosa Luxemburg was on firmer ground theoretically and had a surer grasp in making tactical decisions. She could direct her attention beyond day-to-day events to their relation to the context of society as a whole and the general tendencies of development. For these very reasons Schönlank sought to win her for his paper.

With her lively temperament (unusual by German standards), sharp tongue, and ideas which removed the dust of routine from people's eyes, and brightened and widened the horizon, Rosa Luxemburg probably aroused mistrust rather than the confidence of the 'Fathers of the Party', as she somewhat ironically referred to the party leaders. But it was soon clear that she was no mere dazzling light or suddenly flashing meteor, but a personality imbued with an earnest sense of responsibility and devoted to the cause of the working class with every fibre of her being. Before long, her strong influence on most of the party leaders was undisputable. In working with others she gave more than she took. Mehring occasionally changed a rashly made political judgment once Rosa Luxemburg had published her opinion of the matter. She spurred Kautsky on to climb into the arena to defend party principles; from him we know, for example, that his pro-Bolshevik views on the great issues of the Russian Revolution of 1905 were essentially formed in discussions with her. In earlier times Schönlank had sometimes moved out of line, but Rosa Luxemburg reined him in again. She reaped recognition and admiration. Schönlank was only voicing the opinion of all who came into close contact and exchanged ideas with her, when he declared that, young though she was, Rosa had at all times shown accurate political judgment and an ability to see through the tricks and subterfuges of opponents. Such an ability was usually acquired only after long political experience and was all the more astonishing because, up to that time, Rosa had hardly ventured outside Russo-Polish emigré circles; she was scarcely familiar with the workings of a large party, with all its internal struggles, and was only now beginning to be active in practical politics. Her political acumen was inborn and instinctive.

Her reputation as an extraordinary speaker had spread rapidly. Requests came from everywhere. More than one local organiser must have pulled a long face (to her private amusement), already estimating the extent of the certain failure ahead when he met this frail little woman at the railway station. But every speech was a triumph. Not that she was an agitator in the usual sense: she avoided pathos and appealed more to the reason of her listeners than to their emotions. But she led them out of the limited circle of their usual ideas into wider perspectives and swept them along with her fieriness and her whole forceful personality. Of every such speaking tour she could have said: *veni, vidi, vici!*

But amid this joy there were also bitter moments. A few years later, after she had again gone through a disagreeable experience of petty intrigues, she wrote to Bebel[16] complaining that from the very beginning she had been given a 'peculiar reception' in the German social-democratic camp–and not only by those who opposed her views. She attributed it to her being a foreigner, an outsider ('*nicht de la maison*'). The real reason was probably even more malicious:

it was important to resist her above all because she was a woman–a woman who dared to interfere in the masculine business of politics. Not only that: she did not content herself with asking modestly for the opinions of the 'practical politicians' (*Praktiker*), but was 'cheeky' enough to develop her own views, and–what was worst of all–put forth such convincing arguments that the others had grudgingly to capitulate. It was not long before this pettiness of spirit brought about her first defeat.

In September 1898 Parvus and Marchlewski were expelled from Saxony, and they made their further contributions to the *Sächsische Arbeiterzeitung* conditional on Rosa Luxemburg's being handed over the running of the paper. She found her inheritance in a messy state. Tired of the many conflicts with his colleagues, Parvus in the end had confined himself to writing his daily leading articles and had let the editorial staff do as they pleased. Rosa, however, wanted to give the paper a uniform policy. As editor-in-chief, she intervened in the various departments and made innovations: for example, she created an Economic-Review feature. The old humdrum way of doing things was supposed to make way for a lively, intellectual and activist approach. As if this were not 'monstrous' enough, Georg Gradnauer had launched a vehemently worded, but lamentably argued polemic against Rosa Luxemburg in *Vorwärts* (published in Berlin). To this, she dared to make an objective, if not exactly gentle reply in the *Sächsische Arbeiterzeitung*. Gradnauer happened to be the Reichstag's deputy for Dresden, and therefore criticism of him was taboo, at least in the local party paper. The affair developed into an editorial-staff rebellion against the troublesome chief. The party leaders who controlled the paper allowed Rosa's colleagues to censure her and even denied her the right to defend herself under her own name against attacks. The gallant comrades were rather astonished when she flung her resignation at them.

Gradnauer could not conceal his triumph. In *Vorwärts* he sneered at the fact that Rosa Luxemburg's attempt to direct a party paper had ended in her beating a hasty retreat. To this she replied in plain language in the *Leipziger Volkszeitung* (26 September 1899): *Vorwärts* was not capable of expressing opinions, because it had no opinions, and none of its editors would leave the job of his own free will. 'There are two sorts of living organisms: namely those who have a backbone and therefore also walk, at times even run, and others who don't have one, and therefore only creep and cling.' Rosa could not stand spineless creepy-crawlies in politics.

She then moved to Berlin, where she edited the *Wirtschaftliche und sozialpolitische Rundschau* (Economic and Social Review) as a news service, writing under the pseudonym 'ego'. Mainly she worked for the theoretical journal *Neue Zeit* and the *Leipziger Volkszeitung*. Around the latter paper Schönlank had gathered a brilliant body of contributors. However, it was Rosa Luxemburg in particular who gave the paper its Marxist character and enhanced its reputation among socialist newspapers.

Reformism thrusts forward

The period when Rosa Luxemburg began to be active in the Polish working-class movement was characterised by the rising tide of international socialism. This transition to a new phase had impelled her to make her first independent investigations. At the same time a transformation was taking place in the structure and politics of the big capitalist states, and its characteristic features were clearly visible towards the end of the 1890s. Later, in her *Juniusbroschüre* (Junius Pamphlet), written in prison [in 1915], Rosa Luxemburg described the situation as follows:

> The upswing of capitalism, which established itself in a newly constructed Europe after the war period of the 60s and 70s, and which —particularly in the period of recovery after the long depression that had followed the feverish years of reckless financial speculation and the panic of 1873—reached an unprecedented zenith in the prosperity of the 90s, opened up a new period of *Sturm und Drang* (Storm and Stress) for the states of Europe: a period of rivalry in their expansion towards the non-capitalist countries and zones of the world. As early as the 80s a new and particularly forceful drive towards colonial conquests was making itself felt. England got control of Egypt and created for herself a powerful colonial empire in South Africa; France occupied Tunis in North Africa and Tonkin in the Far East; Italy gained a foothold in Abyssinia; Russia concluded her conquests in Central Asia and pushed forward into Manchuria; Germany acquired her first colonies in Africa and in the South Seas; and finally the USA joined the circle and acquired "interests" in the Far East by taking possession of the Philippine Islands. This period of feverishly plucking Africa and Asia to pieces unleashed an almost uninterrupted chain of bloody wars, beginning with the Sino-Japanese War in 1895, culminating in the great Chinese expedition, and winding up with the Russo-Japanese War of 1904.
>
> All these events, occurring in rapid succession, created new antagonisms in all directions outside Europe: between Italy and France in North Africa, between France and England in Egypt, between England and Russia in Central Asia, between Russia and Japan in the Far East, between Japan and England in China, between the USA and Japan in the Pacific. It was an agitated ocean,

a tossing and turning of sharp antagonisms and temporary alliances, of strained relations and détentes. And every few years war threatened to break out among the European powers, but it was put off again and again ...

In Germany one can observe the rise of imperialism, crowded as it was into a very short period of time, in its purest form. There the unexampled upswing of large-scale industry and commerce since the founding of the Reich [1871] produced two characteristic and peculiar forms of capitalist accumulation in the 80s: the most vigorous growth of cartels in Europe, and the best-developed as well as the most concentrated banking system in the whole world. The cartels have organised heavy industry—i.e. that branch of capitalist endeavour with a direct interest in government contracts, in armaments as well as in imperialist undertakings (railway construction, the working of mines, etc.)—into the most influential factor in the state. The banks have compressed finance capital into a firmly organised power always bursting with the greatest energy— a power that autocratically directs and rules the industry, trade and credit system of the country; equally decisive in private as well as in public enterprise; unbounded and erratic in its powers of expansion; ever hungry for profit and activity; impersonal, and therefore generous, reckless and unscrupulous; international by its very nature; and, because of these predisposing factors, cut out to use the world-stage as the setting for its actions.

If one added to these the strongest personal regime with the most erratic initiative and the weakest kind of parliamentarism, incapable of opposition; together with all the bourgeois strata united in absolute opposition to the working class and entrenched behind the government—then it was a foregone conclusion that this young, robust, and uninhibited imperialism, stepping with a prodigious appetite onto the world-stage, at a time when the world was already practically divided up, was bound to become an incalculable factor of general unrest.

This was already prefigured by the radical upheaval in the military policies of the Reich. In 1898 and 1899 two naval bills, one right after the other, signalled in an unprecedented way a sudden doubling of the battle-fleet, with a tremendous naval-armaments building programme calculated to cover almost two decades. This meant not only an extensive transformation of the financial and trade policies of the Reich—the customs duty introduced in 1902 was only the shadow which followed the two naval bills. A further logical consequence was the transformation of its social policies and of the whole internal system of class and party relationships. The naval bills above all meant a demonstrative change in the foreign-policy course which had prevailed since the founding of the Reich. Bismarck's policy had been based on the principle that the Reich was and had to remain a land power ... but now a whole new policy was drawn up: Germany was supposed to become the first power on land and on sea. This marked the turning-point from

Bismarck's continental policies to *Weltpolitik* (world politics), from the defensive to the offensive as the aim of armaments.[17]

This later description of the period is naturally more rounded off than the picture of the 1890s must have seemed to contemporaries. But the essential features of the new epoch were perceived even then. The naval armaments build-up, the Sino-Japanese War, the Spanish-American War, the Boer War, and the invasion of China by the European powers demanded a re-examination of the whole social and political situation. In the German social-democratic movement, the works of Kautsky, the investigations of Parvus, the agitational writings of Wilhelm Liebknecht, and the numerous speeches of Clara Zetkin exposed with considerable clarity the new phenomena and their underlying forces, and it was proclaimed that the capitalist world had entered into a new period of political catastrophes, both domestic and foreign, and that a world war was brewing.

There were others, however, who were unwilling to heed the approaching storm-clouds. To them the sunshine seemed warm, and they painted an idyllic picture of future social development. According to them, capitalism had left its mad rapacious years of youth behind and had become tame and reasonable. For over two decades –except for rather mild convulsions–there had been none of the crises which, according to Marx, were supposed to ravage the economy every ten years. A period of ever growing prosperity was under way. Since 1870 no wars had taken place on European soil, except in that storm-centre, the Balkans. The working-class movement was no longer outlawed. Young Wilhelm II had promised a 'social monarchy' of social and protective-labour legislation. Democracy was making progress everywhere. German Social Democracy was winning bigger successes at the polls. The trade unions were growing in strength, and wages were rising. Workers' co-operative societies were gaining ground as 'socialist islands' within the capitalist economy. These phenomena brought forth a new tendency inside the Marxist working-class movement: reformism developed into a conscious theoretical concept.

In the German working-class movement, as in the movements elsewhere, radical and reformist views existed side by side. But German Social Democracy was a special sort of movement. It originated a decade and a half after the semi-revolution of 1848, and was therefore without any revolutionary experience. Its whole activity was directed to obtaining those bourgeois reforms which had been abandoned by the bourgeois opposition, and this practice, even more than its socialist creed, determined its real character. At the same time, however, it had to contend with a semi-absolutist state which was merely masked by democratic forms and which persecuted the working-class movement with brutal police methods. Social

Democracy was in irreconcilable antagonism to this state, but its political struggles were directed more against the Junkers than against the bourgeoisie. And, finally, numerous radical bourgeois elements streamed into the social-democratic movement, because they had found no opportunity to effect their ideas in the bourgeois parties; they tended to strengthen the reformist wing of the SPD. This contradictory situation determined the character of the party: apparently radical in its political behaviour, but essentially reformist in principles. In time its outward radicalism became more marked. The Anti-Socialist Laws had intensified the antagonisms towards the existing state, and Marxist ideas gained more and more ground in the party, that is, as far as the general situation allowed, i.e. without the revolutionary character of these conceptions being grasped. There was a pre-condition underlying the party's very existence: because of the fact that in the given political situation any agreement with the state would have meant capitulating to it, Social Democracy had to preserve the character of a radical opposition party. Therefore it watched zealously to ensure that it would not be compromised by an open avowal of reformist views.

Friedrich Engels, the adviser of international socialism and the devoted guardian of Marxist ideas died in 1895. His death removed a strong obstacle to the advance of opportunism; indeed, the 'mature and mellow' Engels now became the sworn witness of reformist policy. His last work was an Introduction to Marx's book on the French revolution of 1848, *Class Struggles in France*. This Introduction is one of the most important documents on Marxist strategy. 'The General', as Engels was called because of his knowledge of military affairs, argued that the old barricade tactics, based on a defensive strategy of attrition, i.e. of wearing down the enemy army, had been rendered inoperable by the development of modern military technique and modern town-planning. Future insurrections would have to take on a very different character, and be carried out by large masses of the people in a stormy offensive against the military forces of the enemy. This would demand a much more intensive programme of enlightenment and a firmer organisation of the working class than had been achieved up to then. Any toying with the idea of insurrection had to be condemned. For quite a long time international Social Democracy would have to confine itself to utilising all its legal possibilities; it should follow the example of the SPD, which had made the franchise into an instrument of emancipation.

The SPD Executive regarded this Introduction, because of its revolutionary trenchancy, as a document which might offer the reaction in Germany a new excuse for repressive measures, especially since at that very time a bill against subversive activities (*Umsturzgesetz*), aimed at crushing Social Democracy, was pending in the

Reichstag. It therefore cut out all those sentences and words in the manuscript which referred to future armed struggles. At first Engels protested against the emasculation of his Introduction, but then he submitted to the tactical considerations of the moment. Thus it was this bowdlerised Introduction to *Class Struggles* which went into history as the 'Testament of Friedrich Engels': a condemnation of all forms of violence and of all future revolutions, and a glorification of legality, under which working-class parties would 'develop strong muscles and ruddy cheeks, and have life everlasting'.[18] Not until 1924 did Ryazanov [head of the Marx-Engels-Lenin Institute in Moscow] rediscover the manuscript and publish the original text.

Books have their destinies, and they become destiny itself. Engels's 'Testament' in its published form plainly cried out for a revision of the Marxist conception of history, and as the party executive obstinately concealed its manipulation of the manuscript, the 'Introduction' became a telling argument in the hands of the reformists. Even the radicals were strongly impressed by it. Although Kautsky knew from Engels that something was wrong with the text, he did not know the full truth. Even Parvus adopted the 'Testament', with its condemnation of violence, as the basis of his attempts to radicalise social-democratic policy. Rosa Luxemburg alone never accepted the falsified meaning of the document, and she steadfastly refused to regard it as representing Engels's real opinions.

It was a man from Engels's immediate circle who carried out the 'Revision of Marxism': Eduard Bernstein. Born in Berlin in 1850, he joined the social-democratic movement in his youth even before the passage of the Anti-Socialist Laws, and rendered it great services during the period of persecution. As editor of the *Sozialdemokrat*, published during those years in London, he had changed, under Engels's influence, from an ethical petit-bourgeois socialist into a radical socialist. At the same time, however, he had been influenced by conditions prevailing in England: the broad democratic base, the policy of economic collaboration pursued by the trade unions, and the social-reformist views of the Fabians. A study of the French revolution of 1848 shocked his fundamentally petit-bourgeois nature, and he recognised with horror that the policy of the Radical Clubs (Auguste Blanqui) agreed in essential points with that of Marx. And it was in this revolutionary policy that he saw the eventual defeat of the revolution. From 1896 to 1898 he wrote a series of articles in *Neue Zeit* on 'Problems of Socialism', attacking with increasing determination the fundamental principles of Marxism. At first the import of his essays was not realised, and no opposition arose until an English socialist, Belfort Bax, gave out the call to battle: 'Bernstein has completely abandoned the final aim of the socialist movement in favour of the ideas of present-day bourgeois liberalism and radicalism.' Rumblings were heard in the German social-democratic movement, but Bernstein was still being defended by Wilhelm Liebknecht, Kautsky, and Schönlank. But then Bernstein uttered the fatal sentence: "The final aim of socialism, whatever it may be, means nothing to me; it is the movement itself which is everything" (*Das Endziel, was immer es sei, ist mir nichts, die Bewegung alles*), Parvus sounded the alarm in the *Sächsische Arbeiterzeitung*. Thus arose the great Bernstein controversy, which preoccupied German Social Democracy for years. It was just at this time that Rosa Luxemburg began her activity in the German party.

The Bernstein controversy ushered in the most difficult and most protracted crisis in the history of pre-war international social democracy. It called out all the Marxist theoreticians and practical politicians onto the battle-field. Parvus, Kautsky, Mehring, Bebel, Clara Zetkin, and Rosa Luxemburg in Germany; Plekhanov, who defended historical materialism above all in the field of philosophy, in Russia; Antonio Labriola in Italy; Jules Guesde and even Jean Jaurès in France. The stormy temperament of Jaurès, fired by the traditions of the great French Revolution, led him to reject the sober and pedantic views of Bernstein, although they were actually closely related to his own.

A world-view

In these intellectual battles Rosa Luxemburg stood at the fore. Though she was the youngest, she outdid all her fellow comrades in her high-spirited militancy, in her self-assurance in the use of polemical weapons, and in the depth of her ideas. She outshone even the famous Kautsky, who was considered the administrator of the Marxist inheritance after Engels's death, and at one blow she became a central figure in the international working-class movement. Even from her opponents she commanded admiration. A certain Max Schippel [one of Bernstein's supporters] had received such a drubbing at her hands in economic and military questions that, in his utter confusion, he got more and more entangled in his own cloudy thinking. Nevertheless, he declared that he valued her works for their 'lively militant spirit, honest convictions and stimulating dialectics' and that he followed 'with astonishment the ever increasing momentum in the development of her arguments to their logical conclusion'. And, indeed, her strength lay in the fact that she thought all questions through to their logical end and was prepared to accept the final consequences. Against her opponents she had a trump card which she played out again and again: facts have their own logic, even if human beings lack it! She regarded it as her chief task to make people conscious of the logic of facts rather than to develop any formal system of logic.

She had a characteristic method of approaching all theoretical and political discussions: she never proceeded from fixed propositions for which she then sought proofs. Only very seldom did she invoke the views of the recognised experts, for it went against her whole intellectual grain to develop her ideas by dogmatically quoting the great masters. Proceeding from the given realities of society, she strove on the whole to examine its tendencies of development in order to use the resources of the working-class movement to the greatest advantage in the historical process.

At the same time Rosa Luxemburg was a decided opponent of all empiricism, both in political convictions and in political action. All her politics and all the politics of the party, at least insofar as she had any influence, were determined by scientific analysis. Her instrument was the Marxist method of investigation. Like Marx, she regarded history as a process in which class forces struggled against each other for their own interests, the shaping of which was the result of the development of objective economic relationships. For her, Marxism was not a theoretical model solving all questions once and for all. She preferred to set herself the task of examining the process of economic upheaval at every new phase of its development, with its effects on the interests, views, aims, and political activities of the various groups in society. The purpose of this task was to enable her to maintain intellectual mastery of the total social process and to make the right political decisions for every situation that arose. In her opinion, even the moral and political attitude of the working class in each individual situation was substantially determined by this total social process. She was unshakeable in her conviction that scientific Marxism had established the inevitability and the historical necessity of socialism, and that it was possible to speak of scientific socialism precisely because Marx had proved that the certain collapse of capitalism was the result of a 'natural law' of society.

Certain critics of Rosa Luxemburg have charged her with 'objectivism' for these views, i.e. with viewing history as a process in which objective forces assert themselves with a kind of fatalistic violence, leaving no room for the will of individuals or social classes to operate. This is not only false, but it was precisely in this respect that Rosa Luxemburg went decisively beyond the usual conceptions held by the epigoni of Marx and Engels in her day. These people had made 'economic relationships' into an almost mystical, supernatural power, which ploughed its way forward in a blindly fatalistic way irrespective of human will. They quite forgot that economic

relationships are nothing but the relationships into which human beings enter in the production process and that they are therefore the
result of human activities and human struggles. They interpreted
Marx's following statement in a dull and mechanical way: 'Men
make their own history, but they make it neither of their own free
will nor under conditions chosen by themselves, but under conditions already present and given and directly handed down from the
past.'[19] Rosa Luxemburg preferred to invert the statement:

> Men do not make history of their own free will, but they do make
> it themselves. The proletariat is dependent in its action on the given
> degree of maturity in social development, but social development
> does not proceed independent of and apart from the proletariat:
> the proletariat is as much its mainspring and cause as it is its pro-
> duct and consequence. The very action of the proletariat is a deter-
> mining factor in history. And although we can no more jump over
> the stages of historical development than a man can jump over his
> shadow, nevertheless we can accelerate or retard that develop-
> ment.[20]

Marx had formulated his words against the systematisers and
will-o'-the-wisps in politics. Rosa Luxemburg turned the statement
around and emphasised the fact that men indeed make their own
history themselves. She was trying to counteract the complacent and
passive optimism which lay behind the indolent policy of noninter-
ference in social development by confronting the working class, its
party and its leaders with the responsibilities they all had before history for their own fate. She demanded of politicians that they should
strive like natural scientists to investigate the laws of nature in order
to comply with them and thereby learn to master the forces of
nature. As the protagonists of history, they should have the motto:
in the beginning was the deed! But the deed must be determined by
knowledge of the historical process. Writing about Marx on one occasion (*Die Internationale* 1915), she sketched in passing her own
views, life principle, and character:

> Just as in Marx himself the keen historical analyst was inseparably
> bound up with the daring revolutionary, the man of thought with
> the man of action, supporting and complementing each other, so—
> for the first time in the history of the modern working-class move-
> ment—did Marxism, as the theory of socialism, pair theoretical
> knowledge with the revolutionary energy of the proletariat, the one
> illuminated and fructified by the other. Both aspects belong equally
> to the inner core of Marxism; separated from each other, each
> transforms Marxism into a sad caricature of itself.

She also kept herself free of that crude vulgar Marxism, which
arrogates to itself the task of explaining the richly varied social life
of a people from a table of economic statistics and of drawing pre-

REFORM AND REVOLUTION | 51

cipitate conclusions from it about future social developments. She knew 'that, besides purely economic factors, political and historical factors, too, have had such a conspicuous influence on the rate of bourgeois development that they could throw to the winds any contrived theory about the duration of the capitalist order of society'.[21] With visionary force she was able to grasp the whole great historical process, in which technique, the organisation of production and distribution, historical traditions, scientific achievements, juridical conceptions and regulations, government measures, etc. interact to hinder or to further the mammoth struggle of the classes, but in which, in the long run, economic factors prevail and determine the organisation of society. She therefore never accepted uncritically the surface phenomena of everyday social life, and investigated the motive forces below the surface, often arriving at conclusions which seemed nothing but wild speculations to her contemporaries, but which were afterwards brilliantly proved by the actual course of history.

Reform and revolution

This method of looking at history shines forth with particular clarity in her pamphlet *Social Reform or Revolution*. It appeared in two series of articles in the *Leipziger Volkszeitung*, the first in September 1898 in answer to Bernstein's articles in *Neue Zeit*, the second in April 1899 attacking his book *Die Voraussetzungen des Sozialismus und die Aufgaben der Sozialdemokratie* [lit. 'The Prerequisites of Socialism and the Tasks of Social Democracy', published in Stuttgart 1899; in English under the title *Evolutionary Socialism*, New York 1909].

The Bernstein controversy revolved around the fundamental character of the socialist working-class movement. Disputes on this point had existed since the very beginning of the movement and were finally the reason for its disintegration into two camps. Bernstein's book ended in the advice to Social Democracy to summon up the courage 'to emancipate itself from an outworn phraseology and to display its true colours as a democratic-socialist reform party'. That raised the question: reform or revolution? Or more correctly, the question of the relationship between reform and revolution. That is the theme not only of the little pamphlet with which Rosa Luxemburg made her debut in the German social-democratic movement, but of all her more important works for half a decade of intellectual struggle. The reformists praised the policy of striving to achieve more and more reforms by legal means as realist politics, as the slow but certain method by which society gradually grew towards socialism, whereas they regarded revolution as a means which was perhaps necessary under absolutism, but which, under democratic rule, was likely to be preached only by dangerous fanatics. Against this view Rosa Luxemburg posed her own: both reform and revolution! And she handled this fundamental problem in a way which forcefully brought out her dialectical and polemical abilities:

> Legal reform and revolution are not simply different methods of obtaining historical progress that can be chosen at pleasure from the buffet of history, like hot or cold sausages; they are different *moments* in the development of class society, factors which both condition and complement each other, but at the same time are mutually exclusive, like the South Pole and the North Pole, or like the bourgeoisie and the proletariat.
>
> In fact, the existing legal constitution is nothing but the *product* of a revolution. Revolution is the act of political creation in the history of classes, while constitutional legislation is the expression of the continual political vegetation of a society. The work for legal reform does not have its own inherent motive power, independent of revolution. In every historical period, such work takes place only along the lines laid down by the last revolution, and only so long as the impetus given to it by that last upheaval continues to make itself felt. To put it in concrete terms, work for legal reform takes place only within the *framework* of the social form created by the last revolution. Herein lies the heart of the question.
>
> It is fundamentally false and completely ahistorical to regard the work for legal reform merely as a long drawn-out revolution, and the revolution as reform condensed into a short period of time. A social revolution and a legal reform are different *moments*, not in the *space of time* they take up, but in their *essential characteristics*. The whole secret of historical revolutions brought about by the use of political power lies precisely in the sudden turning of the merely quantitative changes into a new quality, or, to put it concretely: in the transition from one historical period, from one social order, to another.
>
> Therefore, whoever opts for the path of legal reform, *in place of* and in contradistinction to the conquest of political power, actually chooses not a calmer and slower road to the *same* aim, but a *different* aim altogether. . . .
>
> In other words, democracy is indispensable, not because it renders *superfluous* the conquest of political power by the proletariat, but, on the contrary, because it makes this seizure of power both *necessary* and possible. When Engels, in his preface to the *Class Struggles in France*, revised the tactics of the working-class movement and set forth the legal struggle as opposed to the barricades, he was not —*as every line of the preface makes clear*—dealing with the question of the final conquest of political power, but with the question of the present daily struggle; not with the attitude of the proletariat towards the capitalist state at the moment of its seizure of state power,

but with its attitude within the framework of the capitalist state. In other words, Engels was giving guidance to the proletariat *oppressed* and not to the proletariat victorious. . . .

The necessity of the seizure of political power by the proletariat was never at any time in doubt for either Marx or Engels. It was left to Bernstein to consider the bourgeois parliamentary hen-house as the instrument qualified to carry out the mightiest revolution in the history of the world; the transformation of society from *capitalist into socialist* forms.[22]

Rosa Luxemburg was thus by no means an opponent of reforms. She regarded the struggle for reforms – for the improvement of living standards, for the protection of labour, and for the extension of democratic rights within the framework of the bourgeois state – as the very means of preparing the working class for the revolution, of educating and organising it, and of making it realise through practical experience that the capitalist state had to be overthrown if the proletariat were ever to be freed from the bonds of wage-slavery:

> Only on the high seas of political life, only in the broadly based struggle with the present state and in adapting itself to the whole variety of situations in real life can the proletariat be educated and guided in a social-democratic direction. And everyday life itself will urge it in this direction with compelling force.[23]

According to her, however, socialism would not, by any means ensue automatically and under all circumstances from the daily struggle for reforms. She agreed with Lenin's evaluation of 'spontaneity' – i.e. the direct struggle of the workers against the effects of capitalism, a struggle not guided by any socialist theories – as he was expounding it during that same period in his fight against 'economism' [the subordination of political activity to the trade-union struggle] in Russia. For example, she criticised the policy of the English trade unions: in her opinion, not only did it lack any conscious and consistent striving towards socialism, but it was an aimless road straying away from socialism. And this was her judgment of reformism in general, that is, of the attempt to replace revolution with an endless series of reforms. The trade-union struggle for improved working-class conditions and for social reforms, and the parliamentary struggle for democratic reforms took on a fundamentally socialist character only if their final aim was socialism.

As early as 1893, in her report to the Third Congress of the Socialist International in Zürich, she gave a theoretical basis to the relation between daily struggle and the aim of socialism, and defended the necessity of daily activity for very modest aims against the Blanquist elements in the Polish socialist movement. Now she formulated her old ideas in an even more trenchant way: she established the strategic principle that the daily struggle of the proletariat must be organically connected with its final aim. Every solution of a daily task must be such that it leads to the final aim, not away from it. 'And by *final aim* I do not mean, as [Wolfgang] Heine has said, this or that conception of some future state, but *that which must precede the establishment of any future society, namely the conquest of political power.*'[24]

Rosa Luxemburg made this fundamental principle the basis of proletarian political activity as a whole as well as of her own tactical decisions. She often used it as a touchstone to prove the unsuitability of certain practical suggestions and measures. Just at that time, in 1898, the deputy Wolfgang Heine had been seeking to demonstrate the practical value of Bernstein's politics by pointing to what the working class might gain if it were ready to vote in favour of granting cannons to the government in exchange for civil liberties. If such a policy were pursued by a bourgeois party, there would not be the slightest objection. But as far as the eventual conquest of power by Social Democracy was concerned, a 'logrolling policy' (*Kompensationspolitik*) had to be condemned. This was because every tactical gain or momentary success resulting from such a policy would necessarily turn out to be a dubious victory which would prevent or at least hinder the attainment of final victory. The enemy would have the cannons with which it could mow down every democratic achievement. But even if it could be said that the state did not need to depend on the SPD for its armaments, any support by the working class and its party would inevitably dim their consciousness of their fundamental antagonism to this state, to militarism, and to the expansionist policies of capitalism; it would sap the class and the party intellectually and render them incapable of carrying on the decisive struggles. This strategic principle of Rosa Luxemburg's has been confirmed again and again by experience, including, of course, the many setbacks which occurred when it was ignored.

The question of reform or revolution must have appeared as a purely theoretical problem at the end of the 1890s, for the prospects of revolution in Western Europe in the foreseeable future were very faint. Nevertheless, Rosa Luxemburg's analysis of the relation between reform and revolution led to one practical conclusion which has proved of decisive importance for the content and character of the proletarian daily struggle: it saved the struggle from the confusion of empirical trials and experiments, and gave it a direction and an aim.

Capitalism tamed

Bernstein had attacked Marxism as a whole. In particular, he had asserted that the idea of the inevitable collapse of the capitalist economic system had been refuted by experience. Capitalism had proved itself very adaptable: economic crises had already been reduced to mild fluctuations in the general trend of prosperity. The anarchy of the capitalist mode of production was being increasingly overcome by the credit system and by cartels and trusts. The formation of limited-liability companies was bringing about a democratisation of the ownership of capital, exemplified particularly in the small-share system prevailing in the English economy. Finally–according to Konrad Schmidt, a well-known socialist economist, adding to Bernstein's views–because of trade unions and social reforms the owners of capital were being reduced more and more to the role of mere administrators: in the end the capitalists would be worn down and the management of the factories taken out of their hands.

Such opinions aimed directly at the core of Rosa Luxemburg's ideas. If the contradictions of capitalism were not intensifying, and if, indeed, capitalism was 'progressively adapting itself to its own conditions of existence', then socialism ceased to be objectively necessary, for it would no longer have a scientific base, but only an ethical one, and the working class would no longer have even that vital interest which, according to Marxism, drives it to overthrow the capitalist social order. In short, socialism would revert to what it was before Marx's time–utopianism.

On examining the question, Rosa Luxemburg found that Bernstein looked at economic phenomena from the standpoint of vulgar political economy (*Vulgärökonomie*), i.e. from the standpoint of the individual capitalist in his business. It was quite true that under certain circumstances credit might tide the individual capitalist over critical situations. But the effects of the credit system on capitalism as a whole were different. Economic crises arose out of the contradiction between the capitalists' permanent tendency to expand production and the market's limited capacity to consume goods. Credit, however, had the effect of enormously increasing the expansive capacity of production, and therefore of providing the motive power ceaselessly urging production beyond the limits of the capitalist market. But, at the first sign of economic stagnation, credit dried up and proved itself ineffective and useless when it was most urgently needed; it called in the money it had put into circulation and thus intensified the crisis. Far from serving as a means to enhance the adaptability of capitalism, it aggravated the internal contradictions of capitalism by furthering the concentration of capital in the form of joint-stock companies and commercial credit, by weakening the competitive capacities of small companies and thus helping to destroy them, and by separating production from property and accentuating more and more the contradiction between the social

character of production and the private-property basis of capitalism.
'The first way to increase the adaptability of capitalism . . . should
therefore be to *abolish* credit, to undo it. As credit exists today, it is
not a means of adaptation, but a means of destruction, and its effect
is highly revolutionary.'[25]

And what about cartels and trusts? Rosa Luxemburg admitted
that far too little research had been done on these phenomena–it
was only towards the end of the 19th century that they had captured
their powerful position in large-scale industry. However, it was already clear that they could substantially reduce capitalist anarchy
only if they virtually became the general capitalist productive form.
Meanwhile, their function consisted in raising the rate of profit in
one branch of industry at the expense of others. But even in this
they were successful only in the domestic market; in the world
market they intensified competition and anarchy. Moreover, cartels
and trusts brought about an increase in the rate of their profits only
by a desperate expedient–namely by letting a part of the accumulated capital lie fallow, a phenomenon usually restricted to times of
economic crisis. As Rosa Luxemburg pointed out, 'Such a remedy
resembles the illness as one egg resembles another'. Her argument
came to a head in an idea that she dealt with later in her book *The
Accumulation of Capital:*

> If the capitalist market begins to shrink because of the utmost
> development and exhaustion of the world market by the competing
> capitalist countries–and it obviously cannot be denied that such a
> situation is bound to arise sooner or later–then the forced partial
> idleness of capital will reach such dimensions that the medicine
> will suddenly change into the illness itself, and the capital, already
> heavily socialised (*vergesellschaftet*) through regulation, will revert
> to its private form . . . (Cartels and trusts) exacerbate the con-
> tradiction between the international character of the capitalist
> world-economy and the national character of the capitalist state be-
> cause they are accompanied by a general tariff war, which carries to
> extremes the antagonisms among the individual capitalist states.[26]

Rosa Luxemburg then examined the history of economic crises.
She established that all the crises up to 1873 were the effects of
erratic extensions of production on the world market, and came to
the conclusion that they did not yet represent the type of economic
crisis Marx had in mind when elaborating his theories:

> As a whole, this scheme applies rather to a fully developed capital-
> ist economy, in which the world market is presupposed as some-
> thing already existing. Only then are crises liable to recur, as a result
> of the internal movement of the process of production and exchange,
> in that mechanical way supposed by Marx, i.e. without the necessity
> of an external cause such as a sudden convulsion in productive and

market relations. When we bring to mind the present economic situation, we are compelled to admit that we have not yet entered that phase of full capitalist maturity which is postulated in the Marxist scheme of periodically recurring crises. The world market is still being developed. . . . Therefore, although, on the one hand, we have already experienced the sudden opening up, by leaps and bounds, of new areas to the capitalist economic system, such as took place periodically up to the 70s, and the resulting crises–the crises of youth, so to speak–on the other hand, we have not yet advanced to that stage of development and exhaustion of the world market which would produce those dreadful periodic crashes of the productive forces against the limits of the capitalist market–i.e. the old-age crises of capitalism. . . .

However, it follows precisely from those same conditions which are causing the current, temporary absence of crises that we are inevitably approaching the beginning of the end, the beginning of the period of capitalism's final crises. One day, when the world market is more or less fully developed and can no longer be suddenly enlarged, and if labour productivity continues to advance, then sooner or later the periodic clashes between productive forces and market barriers will begin, and, because of their recurrence, these will naturally become increasingly rough and stormy. Now if there is anything very likely to bring us nearer to this phase, to establish the world market quickly and to exhaust it equally quickly, then it is precisely those phenomena which Bernstein regards as capitalism's "means of adaptation"–the credit system and the big-business organisations (cartels and trusts).[27]

These words were written in 1898. Two years later a crisis broke out whose effects were most devastating in precisely those industries–e.g. in the electrical industry–in which the credit system and the cartels were most highly developed. Bernstein was refuted. Only in one respect did history proceed differently: the reversion of cartel (*kartelliert*) capital into private capital in times of crisis was just a temporary phenomenon which, in the long run, actually forced the building of even more trusts. Nevertheless, thirty years later her bold prediction came to pass in the first of those terrible 'old-age crises', which led to the dismemberment of the world market, permanent tariff warfare, autarky, and the armoured march of the great powers racing to redistribute markets and raw-material resources. Here was proof of Luxemburg's genius–a combination of profound scientific analysis and prophetic intuition.

We should note here that in the second edition of her pamphlet *Social Reform or Revolution* (1908) Rosa Luxemburg struck out the passages referring to the prospects of a fully-developed world market. It was enough for her to establish that the crises of 1900 and 1907 had broken the mainstays of Bernstein's theory. And obviously her critical consciousness did not tolerate the maintenance of a hypothesis conceived in a burst of creative enthusiasm so long as it could not be thoroughly examined. She was to undertake this examination in 1912 in her *Accumulation of Capital*.

The labour of Sisyphus

With the refutation of Bernstein's 'adaptation' theory, any hopes for a steady weakening of class antagonisms were virtually destroyed. As far as Luxemburg's chief ideas about Bernstein's theory are concerned, we can dispense with the details of her arguments against his fantasies. These have been thoroughly refuted in the meantime by events themselves. The hopes of Bernstein and his followers that, as a result of the continuing class struggle, capitalist exploitation would be progressively overcome, seemed to have a better basis. In all the capitalist countries, and particularly in Germany, the 1890s had ushered in a powerful upswing for the trade-union movement. In big waves of strikes the German workers made up for the time lost in the period of Bismarck's Anti-Socialist Laws, when the opposition movement was almost completely suppressed; and in these struggles the German trade unions became a veritable power. It was a theoretician much despised by the trade-unionist 'realist politicians' (*Realpolitiker*)–Parvus–who had stressed the great importance of the trade unions for the socialist class struggle and who had criticised the underestimation of their value by some party leaders. On this issue, Rosa Luxemburg was doubtless in complete agreement with Parvus, her close political collaborator at that time. But now the problem was to fight against certain illusions connected with the rise of the trade unions. In his book Bernstein had declared that, in the struggle between the rate of wages and the rate of profit, the trade unions would gradually depress the rate of profit until, in the end, no surplus-value would remain and capitalist exploitation would cease. It was now necessary to stake out the limits of the trade-union struggle.

Rosa Luxemburg pointed out that the trade unions were essentially not weapons of attack against capitalist exploitation, but rather the organised defence of the working class. They battled against the tendency to progressive impoverishment (*Verelendungstendenz*) continuously operating in the capitalist economic order, if not always able to win out. They were instruments for giving free rein to the capitalist law of wages–i.e. the sale of labour-power at its prevailing market price–rather than instruments for abrogating it. The workers should not let themselves be deceived by momentary successes:

If we consider the longer periods of social development, it is impossible to shut our eyes to the fact that, on the whole, we are approaching times of growing difficulties for the trade-union movement rather than times of a victorious display of power. Once industrial development has reached its zenith and the "descending phase" (*absteigende Ast*) of capitalism sets in, the trade-union struggle will become doubly difficult. In the first place, the objective market conditions for the sale of labour-power will deteriorate, because the demand for labour-power will increase more slowly and the supply more rapidly than is the case at present. In the second place, in order to recoup its losses on the world market, capital will encroach more and more persistently on that part of the product which should go to the workers. After all, the reduction of wages is one of the most important means of retarding a fall in the rate of profit.[28]

As a matter of fact, the difficulties predicted by Rosa Luxemburg arose long before the descending phase of economic development set in. Even before the First World War the formation of trusts and of militant employers' associations threw back the trade unions in the most important industries (heavy industry, dockyards, etc.) into a state of almost complete powerlessness. And only the voracity of capital for qualified labour-power in that stormy period of economic upswing and the armaments race prevented a rapid decline of wages.

However, Rosa Luxemburg was not content merely to point out the general tendency of development; her theoretical insights impelled her to define more sharply the limits of the trade-union struggle:

> Thanks to objective processes at work in capitalist society, (the trade-union struggle) is transformed into a kind of labour of Sisyphus. However, this labour of Sisyphus is indispensable if the worker is to obtain at all the wage-rate due to him in the given situation of the labour market, if the capitalist law of wages is to operate, and if the effectiveness of the depressive tendency of economic development is to be paralysed, or to be more exact, weakened. But a proposed transformation of the trade unions into an instrument for the gradual reduction of profits in favour of wages presupposes, above all, the following social conditions: first, a halt to the proletarisation of the middle strata of society and to the growth of the working class; second, a halt to the growth of labour productivity, i.e. in both cases . . . *a reversion to pre-capitalist conditions.*[29]

Labour of Sisyphus! The expression evoked outbursts of indignation from trade-union leaders. They did not examine its meaning or pay any attention to Luxemburg's line of argument (which would, of course, have demanded some knowledge of Marxist theory). They interpreted it to mean that all trade-union work was utterly useless. They did not appreciate how highly she was rating trade unions when she assigned them the task of protecting working-class standards-of-living against the tendency to impoverishment, immanent in the capitalist mode of production, against a complete slide into the abyss. For them Rosa Luxemburg became the most-hated and repeatedly reviled 'enemy of the trade unions'.

In 1908, when Karl Kautsky took up the expression Sisyphus-labour in his book *Der Weg zur Macht* (*The Road to Power*), using it in the way Luxemburg had done, the General Commission of the Trade Unions replied with the publication of *Labour of Sisyphus or Positive Successes*, which fell upon Kautsky and other 'anarcho-socialists of the same cut as Rosa Luxemburg' with bitter hatred, demonstrating in their relevant arguments that they had still not grasped Marx or the meaning of that catchword. The limited mind of the specialist balked at recognising the limits of his speciality. Kautsky, by the way, was soon to off-load the designation 'anarcho-socialist' onto Rosa Luxemburg, too, when he began to liquidate his revolutionary views.

4
The conquest
of political power

The limitations of parliamentarism

Rosa Luxemburg analysed the institution of democracy as she did
all social phenomena: as a product of historical processes. She came
to the conclusion that to regard democracy as Bernstein did, namely
as the 'great fundamental law of all historical development', was absolutely and thoroughly wrong, and nothing but a petit-bourgeois,
superficial and mechanical generalisation of the features of one tiny
stage in this development, i.e. the period since about 1870. She also
found that there was no intrinsic relationship between capitalist development and democracy; and that the political form of government was always the result of the whole sum of internal and external
factors, and, subject to this proviso, it could range from an absolute
monarchy to a democratic republic.[30]

And what about parliamentarism? While the reformists waited
for it to come into its own, Rosa Luxemburg saw clear signs of its
decline. Contributing to this decline were both the collision between
the proletarian class forces and the bourgeois, as well as bourgeois
world politics, which 'is plunging the whole economic and social life
of capitalist countries into a whirlpool of incalculable and uncontrollable international disturbances, conflicts, and transformations, in the
midst of which bourgeois parliaments are tossed about impotently
like flotsam in a stormy sea':

> Parliamentarism is far removed from being the absolute programme
> of democratic development, of human progress, or any such noble
> thing; it is rather the particular *historical form of the class rule of
> the bourgeoisie* and—this is only the other side of this class rule—*of
> its struggle with feudalism*. Bourgeois parliamentarism will remain
> alive only so long as the conflict between the bourgeoisie and feudal-
> ism continues. Once the animating fire of this struggle has died
> down, parliamentarism will lose its historical *raison d'être* from the
> standpoint of the bourgeoisie. For a quarter of a century, however,
> the general trend of political development in capitalist countries has
> been towards a *compromise between the bourgeoisie and feudalism*.
> The blurring of the differences between the Whigs and the Tories

in England, and between the Republicans and the clerical-monar-
chist aristocrats in France is the product and the expression of this
compromise. In Germany the same compromise was already present
at the birth of the class emancipation of the bourgeoisie. . . .[31]

The party struggles of the bourgeoisie had given way to
cliquish squabbles, and, as a result, the striking features of parliamentarism, the great personalities and the great orators had dis-
appeared. After all, 'the oratorical battle as a parliamentary tactic is
generally useful only for a militant party seeking support from the
people'. The decline of bourgeois parliamentarism was clear enough
even at that time to anyone who bothered to survey the whole development of historical processes. Although a kind of revival of parliamentarism did take place after the First World War, this was only
a last flicker to be extinguished in most of the countries on the
European continent by fascism.

Should Social Democracy therefore simply reject parliamentarism? Rosa Luxemburg regarded parliamentary elections as an
opportunity for the powerful development of socialist propaganda
and for the assessment of socialist influence among the masses. Parliament itself she regarded as the widely audible and internationally
visible rostrum from which to arouse the people. But she did not
insist merely on agitation: the task of a socialist parliamentarian also
consisted in taking part in the positive legislative work, whenever
possible with practical success—a task which would become increasingly difficult with the strengthening of the party's representation in
parliament. The task could be correctly fulfilled only if Social
Democracy retained an awareness of its role as an oppositional party
and, at the same time, found the golden mean between sectarian
negation and bourgeois parliamentarism—always remembering that
its real strength lay outside parliament, in the proletarian masses.
Above all, however, it had to give up without reservation the illusion
that a working-class party could overpower a capitalist state by a
majority vote in parliament, i.e. solely by parliamentary means.

An experiment in government

A clear, practical test of reformist theories could not be carried out
in Germany so long as the semi-absolutist constitution existed. They
were, however, put to the test in France, at a time when the theoretical dispute in German Social Democracy had reached its highest
peak, and Rosa Luxemburg's views on parliamentarism now had to
stand trial as well.

In June 1899, the socialist Alexandre Millerand entered the
Radical Ministry of Waldeck-Rousseau along with that butcher of

the Commune, General Gallifet. His action was acclaimed as a turning-point in world history. Jaurès extolled the courage of the French Socialists in casting one of their own people 'into the fortress of bourgeois government', and reformists throughout the International indicated their agreement when Jaurès justified the move in theoretical terms: the development of capitalist society towards socialism had reached a transitional stage in which political rule was being exercised jointly by the proletariat and the bourgeoisie, and the participation of socialists in the government was the outward expression of this rule.

Rosa Luxemburg followed this experiment with the closest attention and criticised it in thorough investigations which revealed an astonishing knowledge of both French political history and French current affairs. She judged the general significance of the great political crisis troubling France far more coolly and far more accurately than any of the party leaders directly involved. Even in those rare instances where her characterisation of existing conditions over-shot the mark, it turned out that she was only anticipating future developments. In her analysis as well as in her tactical conclusions, she again demonstrated her knowledge of the anatomy of bourgeois society, its laws of development and the prerequisites of the proletarian class struggle.

Since the middle of the 1880s, France had been shaken by continual crises, beginning with the Boulanger crisis, in which a general had reached out for dictatorial powers, through the great corruption-scandal connected with the building of the Panama Canal, up to the Dreyfus affair. General conditions resembled those in times of fascist intrigues: a blatant nationalism; anti-Semitic outrages; rabble-rousing baitings by the press; street-fighting; a comical occupation of a residential quarter, 'Fort Chabrol', by Anti-Dreyfusards; culminating in an attack on the President of the Republic by the *jeunesse dorée* (idle young rich). It seemed as if the last hour of the Republic was at hand.

Rosa Luxemburg recognised, however, that the confusion and uproar which were splitting France into two camps had nothing to do with the existence of the Republic itself, but with a contest between the clerical-militarist forces of reaction and the bourgeois radicals for control of the Republic. But she did not in the least advise socialists to keep away from the struggle. She condemned the party of Jules Guesde, which put forward the slogan *"Ni l'un, ni l'autre!"* (Neither the one nor the other) and which explained that just as people should not have to choose between cholera and the plague, so they should not have to choose between the corrupt bourgeois forms of the right and those of the left. She welcomed the fact that Jaurès was throwing himself impetuously into the struggle, but complained that he did not know how to keep to his side of the demarcation between the bourgeois and the proletarian camps. From the socialist movement, in every political crisis, she demanded activity and firm adherence to principles, and hard work to advance politically and safeguard the road leading to the final aim.

Her attitude to the Millerand experiment was characteristic of her approach. Immediately after his entry into the government, she wrote an article in the *Leipziger Volkszeitung* ['*Eine taktische Frage*' (A Tactical Question), 6 July 1899] dealing with the whole question of government and power on the basis of general Marxist principles. At every successive turning-point she examined the facts of this experiment in the greatest detail, drawing tactical conclusions whose significance went far beyond that of the Millerand case. Since then, the experience of the coalition policy of German Social Democracy [1919-33], of MacDonald's government policy in Great Britain [1924, 1929-31, 1931-35], and finally of the French Popular Front [1936] have corroborated these conclusions to such an extent that Rosa Luxemburg's criticism appears prophetic at all points. No essential feature of these later events is missing in her analysis.

With the whole reformist movement applauding the putting of Bernstein's ideas into practice, Jaurès had justified the participation of the socialists in the government by stating that their party had to occupy every position that came their way. Rosa Luxemburg agreed, provided the positions were such that the class struggle against the bourgeosie and its state could continue to be waged. Parliament offered such positions, for there the party, even in opposition, could represent the interests of its class. The government, however, allowed no room for any real opposition: all its participants had to operate from one common base–the bourgeois state. Therefore, under certain circumstances, the representative of the most extreme bourgeois radicalism could work together in one government with the most dyed-in-the-wool reactionary. A really principled opponent of the existing order, however, would be bound to fail in his very first attempt to oppose the government, or else he would have to carry out the daily functions necessary for the continued existence of the bourgeois state machine and thereby cease to be a socialist. A social democrat striving as a member of government to obtain social reforms and, at the same time, to support the bourgeois state as a whole, was, in the best case, reducing his socialism to the level of bourgeois-democratic or bourgeois working-class politics:

> In bourgeois society Social Democracy by its very nature is *prescribed* the role of an *opposition party*; it may appear as a *ruling party* only on the ruins of that bourgeois state.[32]

Did this fundamental insight exclude all co-operation with

bourgeois democracy? Not at all, according to Rosa Luxemburg. Thanks to its position between the bourgeoisie and the proletariat, the petit-bourgeoisie (which in essence provides the representatives of bourgeois democracy today) had many aims in common with the working class. But whatever the alliance, the working class had to secure its hegemony:

> In the present period, however, the proletariat is called upon to build the leading, dominating element; the petit-bourgeoisie is the incidental hanger-on, and not the other way round. In other words, where the path of the socialist party coincides for a stretch with that of bourgeois democracy, it has the task, not of confining its own struggle to the terrain it shares with the petit-bourgeoisie, but, on the contrary, of systematically overtaking and far outstripping the efforts of the petit-bourgeoisie.[13]

But it is precisely this task which is impossible to carry out within the government of a bourgeois state. Here, under the pressure of the capitalist powers, bourgeois radicalism dictates the character and the extent of the policy of the socialist ministers and therefore of the socialist party. And in all social and democratic questions, this radicalism has proved to be unreliable, even from the standpoint of its own programme, its exponents always liable to defect to the reactionary ranks, and unwilling to go further than is necessary to appease the popular masses.

After Millerand's initial attempts to have social reforms enacted, the government announced a 'pause' and then proceeded to drop even the appearance of concessions to its socialist allies and to adopt brutal, reactionary measures. Every attempt at resistance by the socialists was smothered by the threat to dissolve the government coalition and to leave the field to the reactionaries. Thus it turned out that the principle of the 'lesser evil' determined the whole socialist policy and forced the party to compromise itself more and more. It became increasingly dependent on the government, which in turn became less dependent on it, and the socialist critique of the existing state of affairs was transformed into a mere display of the 'wide horizons' of socialism—without any influence whatsoever on the practical politics of the government.

Jaurès and his friends exuberantly extolled the social reforms proposed by Millerand as Trade Minister. They regarded them as 'socialist saplings, planted in capitalist soil, which would bear wonderful fruits'. Even the speeches of the Minister became 'the greatest and most fruitful moments ever recorded by the history of socialism and of the Republic'. Rosa Luxemburg summarised the commentaries on this reformist politics in the following acclamation:

> At a stroke the classic land of *laissez faire* (*Manchestertum*) is now standing at the summit of progress; the French working class, the

Cinderella of yesterday, is now standing before us as the proud princess. It is clear that only a socialist Minister could evoke such wonders.

However, an examination of reformist activities in France showed that their essential purpose was to obscure social antagonisms.

> The simultaneous protection of the interests of both workers and employers, the former by means of illusory concessions, the latter by means of material ones, finds its palpable expression in the simultaneous working out of measures designed to make the workers happy on paper and to protect capital with the iron reality of bayonets.[34]

Thus an initiative to shorten working hours actually ended in the lengthening of working hours for children, with a mere residue of hope for future reform. Similarly, the measure aimed at securing the right to strike ended with it clamped in legal shackles. And the reform era culminated in a massacre of striking workers.

We find the same picture in the whole policy of the coalition cabinet. The struggle against those perverters of justice in the Dreyfus case, which was supposed to be the chief task of the cabinet, ended with a disgraceful general amnesty for the victim and the criminals alike. The struggle for the secularisation of the state resulted in offerings to the Catholic Church. Foreign policy was characterised by French participation in the expedition of the European powers against China, by an expedition against Turkey to satisfy certain demands being made by French banks, and finally, by the whipping up of republican, monarchist and imperialist elements into a frenzy of enthusiasm during the visit of Tsar Nicholas II.

Rosa Luxemburg drew the following conclusions from the French ministerial experiences: the much celebrated 'practical politics' had proved to be most unpractical for the working class, because it was bound hand and foot by the participation of the Socialist Party in the government and therefore unable to make its own power felt. The 'unfruitful' opposition, however, had turned out to be the truly realist policy for the working class, because,

> far from rendering practical, tangible and immediate reforms of a progressive character impossible, a principled policy of opposition is the only real way in which minority parties in general and socialist minority parties in particular can achieve practical successes.

Participation in the government had led to the complete cleavage and crippling of the working-class movement, and had driven large numbers of workers to turn sharply away from politics and parliamentarism altogether, towards the illusions of ultra-radical syndicalism.

Jaurès was the staunchest supporter of the coalition policy and its most enthusiastic defender even against Luxemburg's criticism. Ten years after the opening act of this policy, however, he was cursing Millerand and two other socialist ministers (Briand and Viviani) for being 'traitors who let themselves be used to advantage by capitalism'.

Rosa Luxemburg's series of articles on the Millerand experiment form one of the most hard-hitting documents in the whole of socialist literature. Written in a language whose indignation over the wretchedness of the politics analysed never explodes but is restrained, the utmost trenchancy is evident in its antithesis, in the confrontation of appearance with reality, of heroic vows with pitiable capitulations. Her political logic, hammered out on the anvil of hard facts, closed off every loophole, and her final judgment had a universal validity against all attempts to serve the cause of socialism with the methods of capitalist state power. Luxemburg's critique did not prevent the repetition of such experiments. If, at the time, Millerand's policy caused only great difficulties for the working-class movement and no catastrophe as yet, it was only because capitalism was still in its ascendant period, which left the working class time to straighten itself out. But what began in France as sorry farce ended in Germany as tragedy. What farsightedness and force of intuition Rosa Luxemburg must have had, to recognise in 1901 that such policies created the social prerequisites for Caesarist speculators and to declare: 'Jaurès, the tireless defender of the Republic, is preparing the way for Caesarism. It sounds like a bad joke, but, seriously speaking, the day-to-day course of history, is strewn with such jokes.'[35] Thirty-two years later the final fruits of a policy modelled after Millerand's experiment were harvested on German soil—in Hitler's rise to power.

Ultima ratio

In her polemics against Bernstein and Jaurès, Rosa Luxemburg had exposed not only the inadequacy and the utopian character of reformist ideas and policies, but also the threat they posed for the working-class movement. And when the reformists declared that nothing was left for the realisation of socialism and the conquest of political power except violence, Rosa Luxemburg coolly agreed. Every thorough examination of revolutionary tactics, after all, runs into the question of violence, and the problem arose at every turn throughout the whole course of the discussion with the reformists. Rosa Luxemburg dealt with it most comprehensively in a polemic against Emile Vandervelde in connection with the Belgian general strike of 1902.

In the German social-democratic movement the policy of re-
pudiating the use of violence in the political struggle had become
practically a dogma. Wilhelm Liebknecht, whose tongue often enough
ran ahead of his ideas, had once declared that violence only served
reactionary ends—a remark which was repeated with gusto on every
possible occasion. Engels's Introduction to Marx's *Class Struggles
in France* was appealed to as confirming Liebknecht's attitude. Bernstein claimed that what he called the over-estimation of creative
violence in the transformation of society was a Blanquist remnant in
Marxism. In France Jaurès employed all his eloquence to advocate
legal action as the only way to capture political power. Stronger even
than the propaganda of these 'leading lights' were the effects of the
daily practice of organising the working class for elections and parliamentary action, which for decades had been the only activity of
international Social Democracy. And with respect to the last great
proletarian insurrection, Georg von Vollmar, in an oratorical duel
with Rosa Luxemburg, even declared that the Parisian workers
would have done better if they had gone home to bed instead of taking up arms and creating the Commune.

First of all, Rosa Luxemburg exposed the respectably narrow-
minded (*spiessbürgerlich*) and superficial misconception hidden behind the legalist theories. The woman who was ceaselessly decried
as a dreaming visionary by all the 'realist politicians' once again
proved her incorruptible realism and, at the same time, her pedagogical talent. In an attack on Vandervelde she wrote:

> What is actually the whole function of bourgeois legality? If one
> "free citizen" is taken by another against his will and forcibly
> confined in small, close and uncomfortable quarters for a while,
> everyone understands that an act of violence has been committed.
> However, as soon as the process takes place in accordance with the
> book known as the penal code, and the quarters in question refer to
> the "Royal Prussian Prison or Penitentiary", then it is transformed
> into an act of peaceful legality. If one man is compelled by another
> against his will systematically to kill his fellow men, then that is
> obviously an act of violence. However, as soon as this same process
> is called "military service", the good citizen is deluded into believ-
> ing that he can breathe in the full peace of legality. If one person
> is deprived against his will of some part of his property or earn-
> ings, no one doubts that an act of violence has been committed, but
> if the process is called "indirect taxation", then it is merely the
> exercise of legal rights.
>
> In other words, what presents itself to us as bourgeois legality is
> nothing but the violence of the ruling class, a violence raised to an
> obligatory norm from the outset. Once the individual acts of
> violence have been raised in this way to an obligatory norm, then
> the process may be reflected in the mind of the bourgeois jurist

(and no less in the mind of the socialist opportunist) not as it really is, but upside down: the "legal order" appears as an independent creation of abstract "justice", and the coercive violence of the state as a mere consequence, a mere "sanctioning" of the law. In reality, the truth is exactly the opposite: bourgeois legality (and parliamentarism as legality in the process of development) is itself only a particular social form expressing the political violence of the bourgeoisie, a violence which has grown up out of the given economic base.[36]

Thus, far from being dethroned by 'legality', violence is rather its basis and its protector at the same time. And the well-intentioned idea of overcoming the ruling powers by using their own legal forms –i.e. the idea that the legality which makes the violence of the bourgeosie the prevailing social norm can be turned into a deadly weapon against the bourgeoisie itself–is nothing but fantasy.

According to Rosa Luxemburg, behind this mad insistence on legality was the idea of making revolutions at will, the view that revolutions could be made or not according to whether they were considered useful, superfluous, or harmful. However, the idea that violent popular movements were the products of decisions made by leaders or parties could only be conceived in the minds of policemen and certain historians. Revolution was a matter of historical development. German Social Democracy could certainly claim the dubious distinction of having rid itself of the belief in violent revolution as the only method of waging the class struggle and the means, applicable at all times, of ushering in the socialist order. But that did not do away with the problem either of violence in general or of using violent revolution as an instrument of the proletarian struggle. The day-to-day struggle for parliament and in parliament would succeed only if it were backed by the latent violence of the working class:

> Violence is and remains the *ultima ratio* (the last resort) even for the working class, the supreme law of the class struggle, always present, sometimes in a latent, sometimes in an active form. And when we try to revolutionise minds by parliamentary and other activity, it is so that, when finally needed, the revolution may move not only the mind but also the hand.[37]

In this respect as well, Rosa Luxemburg thought through the ideas of the reformists to their final and logical conclusion, and like a Cassandra, she warned of the looming spectre of what came to be called fascism:

> If Social Democracy were really to accept the opportunist standpoint–to renounce once and for all the use of violence and to pledge the working masses to follow the path of bourgeois legality–then its whole parliamentary activity and general political struggle would

sooner or later collapse miserably, leaving the field to the unbounded rule of reactionary violence.[18]

A fighting spirit

It is in these polemics with the reformists that Rosa Luxemburg
gives us the decisive elements of her views on the historical development of capitalist society, on the nature of the proletarian class
struggle and its strategic and tactical requirements. We can only
regret that she never elaborated the world-view which governed her
actions in compact book-form. However great her scholarship was,
she never became a professor and never had the desire to write ab-
stracts for industrious students. She was, above all, a fighter, subordinating herself to the commands of the day and to the given
situation. Her polemics were both a weapon and a means of representing her ideas, and her mind never worked more creatively than
when she had her opponent at the point of her sword. She loved
intellectual skirmishes. Writing to Karl Kautsky from a prison-cell
in Zwickau [1 September 1904] to spur him on in his political
battles, she ended up describing what she herself felt about being
active: 'But you must do it with gusto and joy, not as if it were a
boring intermezzo, because the public always feels the spirit of the
combatants, and the joy of battle lends the arguments a clear reson-
ance and ensures moral superiority.' Indeed, this joy shines out of
all her polemic writings, especially out of her pamphlet *Social
Reform or Revolution*.

When Professor Sombart was still flirting with Marxism, he
once wrote that one could read the *Communist Manifesto* over and
over again, and every time discover new beautiful passages and unexpected profound thoughts. This is exactly the case with *Social
Reform or Revolution*. Each new reading brings out new ideas and
solutions to problems, which even twenty or thirty years after they
were formulated could be regarded as completely new. Prophecies
turn out to have been fulfilled. Time and new experiences have
called into question only a few points in the argument. The fact that
Rosa Luxemburg was compelled to follow the paths of thought taken
by her opponents doubtless prevented her from making the pamphlet
a highly finished piece of work. While some aspects of the question
had to be examined in great detail, others were not developed at all.
The author tackled the problem on two different occasions: first,
in answer to Bernstein's articles in *Neue Zeit* [*Leipziger Volkszeitung*, September 1898], and half a year later [April 1899] in
answer to his *Voraussetzungen des Sozialismus*. Nevertheless, *Social
Reform or Revolution* is an integral whole, as naturally grown as a

tree with two trunks, springing from the roots of a unified and un-compromising conception of the world.

In the party, but also far beyond it, the articles in the *Leipziger Volkszeitung* caused a real sensation. In Leipzig people rushed to get the paper, and everywhere, particularly in party circles, the articles were passionately discussed.

The pamphlet was certainly strongly influenced by the *Communist Manifesto*, in the daring flow of its ideas, its broad perspectives and impressive style. However, as is the case with all great artists who have assimilated the art of their predecessors, influences and stimuli are sublimated in a new creation. This was characteristic also of Rosa Luxemburg's attitude to the Marxist world-view. She had absorbed it into her flesh and blood so that she could become a creative Marxist in her own right, without the need to appeal all the time to the authority of Marx and Engels. She had a strong grasp of the revolutionary nature of this world-view, much more so than did the German Marxists, who were considered at that time to be the true heirs of the spirit of Marx. This is clearly evident if one compares *Social Reform or Revolution* with Kautsky's *Bernstein and the Social Democratic Programme* [Stuttgart 1899]. His book was a pedantic examination of Bernstein's individual claims, a mere confrontation with the present, a defence of long-standing traditions. Rosa Luxemburg's pamphlet showed an intellectual mastery of the historical process and a steady awareness of great upheavals to come, motivated by a tremendous will to revolutionary action.

This contrast was not just pure chance. The Marxist view of history owed its conception not only to the genius of its originators but also to the particular historical conditions prevailing just before the [March] revolution of 1848–a situation which demanded the overcoming of theoretical problems from a new and revolutionary point of view. The Western European epigoni of Marx and Engels had developed their ideas in a period of creeping movement, when history flowed like a sluggish stream and the distant cataracts remained hidden from eyes accustomed to broad plains. Their Marxism lacked a revolutionary throb. Even someone like Mehring, who surpassed everyone else in militancy of spirit and in understanding of history, had certain limits to his powers of perception, as his uncritical defence of Lassalle proved. As a Russo-Polish revolutionary, Rosa Luxemburg also grew up in a 'pre-March' (*vormärzlich*) situation: the revolution was approaching; it was already determining the politics of the day and posing problems which could not be solved along the old traditional lines. She was thus capable of recognising the revolutionary principle in Marxism, and of seeing the Western European situation very differently from the routine way of native observers. It was this historical situation which also explains why, since the end of the 1890s, it was the Russians who advanced more and more to the forefront of the Marxist ranks and who played an increasingly important role in matters of theory.

When Rosa Luxemburg took up the struggle against reformism, she was as old as Marx and Engels when they made their 'agreement' (Selbstverständigung) and worked out their theory of historical materialism–she was almost thirty. It is an age at which an individual has developed his essential characteristics and created his own picture of the world. The mature and forceful consciousness of Luxemburg's writings in this period are expressed in a youthful freshness, which reaches out to us even today; a militant spirit and a bold self-assurance, which unhesitatingly follows arguments to their logical conclusions.

Skirmishes

'The upholding of principles–anyone can do that, even an ignoramus; it doesn't require anything', Vollmar had asserted during the discussion. Herein was expressed the whole arrogance of the practical man for the theoretician who secluded himself from the world and was forever impeding action. However, practical experience was demonstrating even then how much knowledge and wisdom were necessary to steer the ship of the working-class movement, which was very deficient in theoretical insight. Rosa Luxemburg also recognised that a period of political calm favoured the spreading of reformism, and wanted therefore to nip the danger in the bud. In several of her articles she demanded the expulsion of Bernstein from the party and reproached the party leaders with making too great concessions to him, although they were much better situated than anyone else to see clearly the reality of Bernstein's position. In a letter to Bebel on 31 October 1898, she wrote:

> . . . It was clear to me, of course, that Bernstein's arguments are no longer in accordance with our party's programme, but it is very painful to think that we might have to abandon all hope for him. However, I am amazed–if you view the matter *in the same way I do*–that you and Comrade Kautsky did not want to use the favourable atmosphere created by the Party Congress to open an immediate and vigorous debate, but instead induced Bernstein to write another pamphlet, which will only drag out the whole discussion. . . . If Bernstein is really lost to us, then the party will have to get used to the idea–however painful–of treating him henceforth like Schmoller* or any other social reformer.[19]

* Professor Gustav Schmoller, liberal social reformer and one of the so-called *Kathedersozialisten* (academic socialists).–Tr.

However, the party leaders were not prepared to adopt vigorous measures. They were intent on preserving the 'old victorious tactics'. And although the rank-and-file members were nine-tenths behind the radicals, they could not recognise the deep-seatedness of the antagonisms. Anyway, things seemed to be going very well. After the Dresden Party Congress in 1903, even Rosa Luxemburg believed that the reformist fog had dissipated, but she therefore insisted all the more that the party should be 'cleansed of those decaying elements which have appeared as a result of the last five years of its history'. However, the best time for such an operation had probably been let slip. Reformism already had strong cadres among the leading functionaries of the party and occupied high commanding positions in the trade unions. Any operation now would threaten to lead to a split. But this was out of the question, because, despite the deeply antagonistic viewpoints, on the whole it was still possible to carry out a unified policy. Constitutional conditions in Germany prevented reformist experiments such as were possible in democratic countries. Thus the reformists had to be content with provoking the party by useless compromises with the ultra-capitalist National Liberals or with the Catholic Centre Party, by lunching with the monarchs of South German states, and similar humbug. As a result, every year insufferable debates were renewed in the party press and at party congresses, but they led to nothing.

Rosa Luxemburg participated in these verbal encounters only when they gave her an opportunity to work out general principles. For the rest, she worked intensively for the Polish movement, which since 1898 had shown signs of another upswing. In November 1899 the party leadership offered her a place on the editorial board of *Vorwärts*. She rejected it. Her experiences in Dresden with the *Sächsische Arbeiterzeitung* were enough for the time being. Besides, her relations with the chief editor, old Wilhelm Liebknecht, were still strained, and it was clear to her that, if she accepted the offer, she was bound to come soon into conflict with his very impressionist policies. That would have been a much more serious matter than a slanging match with the likes of a Gradnauer, not only because of the objective consequences, but also because she deeply respected the old 'Soldier of the Revolution'. When the old man made her a peace offer in the last year of his life, she accepted delightedly.

Her personal life was subordinated to her writing, to her participation at national and international congresses, and to her speaking tours. In 1900 Jogiches moved to Berlin. Thus began a period of close intellectual and political cooperation for the tasks which their comrades and the situation in Poland now imposed. The establishment of a more theoretical journal, modelled on *Neue Zeit*, was their first concern, and in 1903 *Przeglad Socjaldemokratyczny*

(Social-Democratic Review) began to appear. Luxemburg and Jogiches were the intellectual standard-bearers; the contributors were internationally known and important Marxists. Jogiches wrote under the pseudonym Jan Tyska, the name he was to retain henceforth in his political work. Rosa Luxemburg wrote mostly under her own name, but also under different pseudonyms such as R Kruszynska, R K, Maciej Rozga, M R, Josef Chmura, Spartakus, and X. Right away, in the first two issues (January-February 1903), she published a brilliant historical retrospect on the Polish socialist working-class movement under her own name: 'In Commemoration of the [First] *Proletariat'*. She wanted in this work not only to keep alive the memory of this heroic vanguard, but more especially to pass on to later generations the lessons to be drawn from the failure of this movement, and to strengthen and consolidate her own comrades.

On 30 October 1901, Bruno Schönlank, the editor-in-chief of the *Leipziger Volkszeitung*, died. The Leipzig party organisation now turned over the job of running the paper to Rosa Luxemburg. When the news of her appointment was published, the whole bourgeois press howled in protest. The extreme right called for the police to whisk her over the border. The left-wing bourgeois *Vossische Zeitung* demanded that the executive of the SPD should expel 'that Donna Rosa Luxemburg who believes herself called to be the standard-bearer of the red revolution'. The Christian Nationalist clergyman, Friedrich Naumann, raised a hue-and-cry about 'bloody Rosa' in chorus with the *Frankfurter Zeitung*, and her reformist party-brothers joined in the concert with barely muffled drums. Several months later they had the pleasure of hearing that Rosa Luxemburg was now resigning from the editorship of the *Volks- zeitung*. The Press Commission had refused to give her–a woman! –the authority which had enabled Schönlank to make the Leipzig paper the most distinguished organ of the international socialist press, and which Rosa Luxemburg regarded as absolutely necessary for the creation of a militant paper, prepared to fight with a unity of spirit. It should be noted that, although the good Leipzig socialists were inordinately proud of their red banner, glimmering in the depths of their hearts was the quiet hope of the gallant soldier Schwejk for 'moderate progress within the limits of party discipline'.

Beginning in October 1902, Rosa Luxemburg suspended even her contributions to the paper. Her reasons are not quite clear. It is known that many of her articles were thrown into the wastepaper basket, and that she accused her successor as editor-in-chief, Franz Mehring, of not having explicitly defended her interests. This was apparently the first violent discord between the two. She later gave a light-hearted account of it in a letter to her friend Diefenbach

while telling him how she had made the acquaintance of the poet
Friedrich Hebbel:

> . . . I've known Hebbel longer than I've known you. I borrowed
> his works in fact from Mehring during that time when our friend-
> ship was going through a very passionate stage and the neighbour-
> hood between Steglitz and Friedenau* (where I was still living)
> represented a tropical landscape where Elephas Primigenius grazed
> and the slender giraffe plucked the green fronds from the phoenix-
> palms. At that time . . . I read Agnes Bernauer, Maria Magdalena,
> Judith, Herod and Mariamne. However, I didn't get any further be-
> cause the tropical climate suddenly had to give way to the first great
> glacial period, and my fat Gertrud [Gertrud Zlottko, Rosa's house-
> keeper] had to walk to Steglitz carrying a washing-basket full of his
> presents and borrowed books, in answer to a similar transport which
> had just arrived in Friedenau–something that invariably happened
> every time we got disengaged.⁴⁰

With regard to friendships Rosa Luxemburg's motto was: all
or nothing! And Franz Mehring was a touchy and sensitive man
given to nursing grudges. No wonder they were often clashing and
breaking up. Even the difficult period of struggle during the World
War did not pass without trouble between them. Nevertheless, their
mutual respect for each other's intellectual achievements, their related temperaments, and finally their common aims and enemies
brought them together again and again. Their first discord lasted
almost a year. Not until Mehring was attacked at the Dresden Party
Congress in 1903 by a group of revisionists, who cast ignominious
aspersions on him, and he had been practically ostracised by the
party for a rather long time, did she put aside all ill-feeling and
come to place herself resolutely at his side.

Her relationship with Jean Jaurès was of an entirely different
character, and it refutes the claim that she had no understanding for
anyone who did not share her views, and had nothing for them but
repulsion, hate and malice. It is true that she could be inexorably
hard on anyone in whom she discovered intellectual vacuousness or
low-mindedness hiding behind an inflated arrogance. But from a
worthy opponent she could put up with even excessively sharp words
and say to herself: à la guerre comme à la guerre! Even from Jaurès.
They contrasted sharply with each other, both in their ways of thinking and in their politics. She had certainly attacked him often
enough. But even when the trenchancy of her argumentation remained undiminished, there was always something conciliatory in its
tone, something that was almost unheard-of in her polemics with
others. She esteemed his personality, the soaring sweep of his

---

*   These are both suburbs of Berlin–Tr.

thoughts–even when she felt he was wrong–his deep-welled enthusiasm and his unswerving devotion to the cause of the working class. After one of his speeches she observed (as if to placate her own rebellious and critical conscience): 'What the man says is all wrong, but you can't help it–you've just got to applaud. He carries you away!' At the International Congress in Amsterdam (1904) she had a very vigorous exchange of blows with him over the question of 'ministerialism' or 'class collaboration'. After Jaurès had made his speech, however, there was no translator for him. Rosa sprang into the breach and recast the bolts directed against herself from French into German. In thanking her, Jaurès declared, 'Comrades, you have now seen that in-fighting is not always a hindrance to cooperation'. Rosa Luxemburg was always ready to engage in such 'collaboration' and all the more so with a man of the calibre of Jaurès.

Naturally it was not long before the Public Prosecutor developed a keen interest in this woman who used language endangering the national interests. In 1900 Rosa Luxemburg issued a pamphlet in Polish entitled *In Defence of Nationality*, vigorously inciting resistance to the official attempts to Germanise Prussian Poland. This resulted in proceedings against her on a charge of having insulted the Prussian Minister of Culture. The 'crime' was atoned with a fine of 100 marks. In July 1904 she was sentenced to three months' imprisonment, because she was supposed to have insulted Emperor Wilhelm II by remarking [in a speech during the 1903 *Reichstag* election campaign]: 'Any man who talks about the good and secure living of the German workers has no idea of the real facts'. She had almost finished serving her sentence in Zwickau, when King Albert of Saxony died, and the favour of a general amnesty was granted even to her. She was indignant that she, a republican, should be expected to accept grace from a king, and did not want to leave her 'hospitable cell' at all. But she finally yielded to gentle pressure and undertook the march to the freedom of the outside world. This was three months before the first great storm began to shake Russian absolutism, 'the prison house of nations'.

5
The Russian Revolution
of 1905

Russia awakens

The first Russian Revolution dates from Bloody Sunday, 22 January 1905. Russian Marxists were not taken by surprise: they had foreseen and foretold its coming, and defined its character. As early as the inaugural congress of the Second International in Paris in 1889, Plekhanov had proclaimed that the coming revolution against Tsarism would be a workers' revolution or no revolution at all. That was at a time when it was still a moot point whether capitalism would make headway in Russia. The Russian working class was only just beginning to develop. Only in Poland, which, economically speaking, was practically a foreign country, did a working-class movement exist. In Russia proper, socialist ideas were at first confined to small circles of intellectuals which only rarely included working-class elements.

The decisive turn came in 1896. The coronation of Nicholas II proved to be the accidental starting-point. At the coronation, on 18 May, the finger of history spelt out a twofold writing on the wall for Russian autocracy: the approaching collapse of the blind faith of the masses in absolutism, and the first appearance of the proletariat in the historical arena. On the Khodynka Field near Moscow many hundreds of people, who were among the vast throngs who had come to greet the new Tsar in the hope of receiving presents, were crushed and trampled to death. In St Petersburg, however, 40,000 workers went on strike, because they were unwilling to sacrifice their wages for the three coronation days on the altar of Tsarism. The strike was put down. However, in January 1897 another strike broke out which brought the working class its first great success: a legal maximum working-day of eleven-and-a-half hours. The Tsarist sway was now broken, and social-democratic propaganda began to filter through to the proletarian masses. Lenin began to be active in St Petersburg. Socialism in Russia moved from the realm of pure theory to the realm of action; it grew from small circles into a political movement. In 1898 a small group of people founded the Russian Social-Democratic Party.

Years of underground work followed throughout the country, and its effects were manifested suddenly in violent explosions. In March 1902, a mass strike broke out in Batum, followed immediately afterwards by giant demonstrations in Nishni-Novgorod and Saratov. In December 1902 the total working force of Rostov-on-the-Don went out on general strike; for the first time in Russian history freedom of assembly and of speech were won by the determination of the masses. The years 1903-04 brought social convulsions which shook the whole of southern Russia. General strikes spread from one town to the next: from Baku to Tiflis, Batum, Yelisavietgrad, Odessa, Kiev, Nikolayev, and Yekaterinoslav. These struggles differed from strikes in Western Europe in their spontaneity, their extent, the rapid surmounting of craft barriers, and in the shift from purely economic to political aims. They all bore a revolutionary character—not in their various starting-points, but in the force of their clash with the state power. Most of the strikes ended in bloody street-fighting. They were echoed by numerous local peasant insurrections against the landowners. 1902-04 were the years of revolution in the process of development.

The Russo-Japanese War of 1904-05 led briefly to another flare-up of a wave of chauvinism among the broad masses, and for a while the working-class movement was pushed into the background. But then came the severe defeats on the battle-fields of Manchuria, and the rotten depths of the absolutist regime were exposed. The defeats brought the liberal bourgeoisie out into the open: at banquets and congresses, in long-winded speeches, addresses, and manifestos, feeble demands were made for democratic liberties. It seemed as if the liberal landowners, manufacturers, and lawyers had taken the leadership of the opposition movement into their hands in order to force the granting of the most necessary reforms. But in December 1904, when absolutism managed to let out a few vigorous threats, that whole opposition which was considered respectable in the eyes of 'society' collapsed.

At the same time, however, the working class struck out, beginning with a general strike in Baku. There followed, in mid-January 1905, a strike in the Putilov works in St Petersburg. Having begun in protest against the dismissal of two workers, it had spread rapidly; by 20 January it involved 140,000 workers and had taken on a clear political character. Ironically enough, history willed that this mighty rising should be led by a trade-union organisation (the Assembly of Russian Workingmen) which had been founded by the Moscow Police Chief, Subatov, for the purpose of keeping the workers away from the influence of Social Democracy, and that it was not a well-known revolutionary, but a dubious adventurer, the priest Gapon, who stood at its head. But behind the backs of Subatov and Gapon social-democratic agitators were active; they brought revolutionary ideas into the seething masses, and pushed and thrust their way forward.

In the consciousness of even the working masses the Tsar was still the Father of the people, who could and should help them. It was to him they wanted to go and submit their grievances; it was from his fatherly hand that they hoped to receive the rights they needed to live. On Sunday, 22 January 1905, 200,000 workers carrying portraits of the Tsar and sacred icons set off for the Winter Palace. They took with them a petition describing their troubles and pointing out the oppression and the degradation under which the whole nation groaned. They demanded a general amnesty, civil liberties, the separation of church and state, the eighthour day, a minimum wage, the transfer of land to the people, and the convocation of a constituent assembly on the basis of a universal suffrage. Although they devoutly beseeched him, their plea ended with an abrupt threat; the imploringly clasped hands became clenched fists:

> These, Your Majesty, are our chief wishes. Give the order and swear to fulfil them, and you will make Russia happy and glorious, and your name will be imprinted on our hearts and on the hearts of our descendants for all time. But if you do not grant or heed our supplications, we shall die here, on this very square before your palace. . . . May the sacrifice of our lives be for Russia, who has suffered too much; we shall make it readily.

They made their sacrifice. They marched to the palace, right into a well-prepared trap. 2,000 men, women and children were shot to death, 4,000 wounded. But the blood-bath which was to have banished for all time all thoughts of rebellion from the minds of the Russian working class became the baptism-in-blood of the revolution. The salvos of Vassily-Ostrov awoke the whole Russian proletariat. By the end of January a wave of strikes, encompassing over a million workers, surged throughout Russia. The revolution had begun.

Under the fresh impression of these events Rosa Luxemburg wrote on this, 'The Proletariat's Pilgrimage of Supplication' (*Der Bittgang des Proletariats*), in *Neue Zeit*, February 1905:

> History, like nature, is really much more bizarre and richer in its caprices than the intellect with its powers of classification and systematisation. . . . The humble "petition" of the masses of the people to the Tsar was in reality nothing but a request that His Sacred Majesty would most graciously condescend with his own hands to decapitate himself as supreme monarch of all the Russians. It was a request to the autocrat to put an end to the autocracy. It was the very modern class urge of a deadly serious and mature

proletariat fitted into the fantastic whim of a colourful old wives'
tale. . . . It is enough that the excited masses should hit upon the
idea, formally childish, but actually awful, of going to see the
father of their people face to face and of wanting to make the myth
of a "social kingdom or empire" come true, so that the struggle
could be transformed with iron logic into the death-lock of two
irreconcilable enemies, into the contest of two worlds, into the
battle of two ages of history.

Rosa Luxemburg joyfully greeted the awakening of the
Russian people who, roused by the volleys before the Winter Palace
and by the whips of the Cossacks, had risen in their millions to go
out on the first general strike throughout Russia. Everything she
had achieved up to then–the scientific investigations, the intellectual struggles, the training and organisation of revolutionary cadres,
the dogged wrestling with the state power in order to bring a little
light into the minds of the workers–everything had been guided
by the ever-present thought of revolution. And now it was there.
Its powerful force urged her to go to the front lines, to immerse
herself in the masses who were making history at the great turning-
point of the epoch.

But even if she had not been confined to a sick bed for long
weeks, as she was at the time, she knew that she could not yield to
this urge. She had learned to bring her flaming temperament under
control and not to yield to romantic inclinations. She now belonged
to the general-staff of the party, and conditions did not favour as
yet the transfer of headquarters to Poland itself. The demands
made on her could not be carried out in the trenches, where local
events of the moment obscured the view of the conflict as a whole.
Her tasks were to interpret the meaning of events, to define the
next goals of the movement, to examine the means and methods
used in the struggle, and to teach while learning. They also entailed
a reconsideration of the ideas which had guided Polish and Russian
Social Democracy in their preparations for revolution, and their
testing against revolutionary reality.

The organisation of the party

Russian Social Democracy had longed for, expected, and prophesied this contest of two worlds, this battle of two ages of history.
However, it was not prepared for it organisationally, politically, or
strategically. In fact, when the preliminary skirmishes of the revolution were already taking place, it split into two parts which
could never really be forged into a unity again and which finally
formed two irreconcilably hostile camps.

The proclamation of Russian Social Democracy in 1898 had been in reality no more than the definition of the task of creating a party. Numerous small and completely autonomous circles continued to exist throughout Russia with only very little connection with one another and without any stability or unity. When Lenin left Russia, it was with the aim of remedying this situation. In 1900 the newspaper *Iskra* (Spark) was founded; its editorial board consisted of the 'old ones', Plekhanov, Akselrod, and Vera Zasulich, and the 'young ones', Lenin, Martov, and Potresov. Later Trotsky joined the board after his escape from Siberia.

The main purpose of *Iskra* was to prepare for a new party congress which was supposed to create a really strong and tightly organised party with a Marxist programme. To this end, clarity on theoretical matters was first needed. To begin with, accounts were finally settled with the *Narodniks* (Populists), those opponents of Marxism who denied the necessity of capitalist development in Russia and pursued a utopian socialism based on the peasant commune. Meanwhile, however, a new group arose out of the Marxist circles: from the experiences of the strikes of 1896-97 it drew the conclusion that Social Democracy should confine its activities to organising the working class for the economic struggle and to leading this struggle; politically it should advocate social reforms only within the framework of the existing regime. Only in this way, it was argued, could it remain a purely working-class movement. Moreover, Social Democray should leave the general political struggle and the carrying out of the bourgeois revolution to the bourgeoisie, so that after the victory of the latter, it could make use of the new basis to establish a working-class movement along the usual Western European lines. This tendency received the name 'economism'.

The *Iskra* group, and in particular Lenin, condemned these ideas very sharply, regarding them as a denial of the socialist and revolutionary nature of the class struggle, in which the daily struggle for wages and social reforms was only the means to an end, only the preparation of the working class for still greater tasks. According to the *Iskra* group, Social Democracy had to fill the working class with a consciousness of its mission: to become the champion, over and above its immediate interests, of all oppressed classes and the protagonist of historical progress as a whole. Only a political struggle with revolutionary aims could give the working-class movement a social-democratic character.

In these theoretical discussions Rosa Luxemburg stood on the side of the *Iskra* group, although one of the leaders of the 'economists', Krichevskii, had belonged to her closest circle of friends in Zürich. However, she ran into vigorous opposition from

Lenin with regard to the organisational form which Russian Social Democracy should have. In various articles and in *What Is To Be Done?*, Lenin had dealt with this point, and it seemed as though the *Iskra* group was in complete agreement with him. In the summer of 1903, however, at the second Congress of the Russian Social-Democratic Party, held in Brussels and London, Lenin's ideas provoked violent discussions, which finally resulted in the party's split. A truly Homeric dispute was carried on, with protracted debates over Paragraph 1 of the proposed statutes, a dispute which may seem absurd to the Western European reader of the minutes and of the literature published after the Party Congress. These leave the impression that the debates were nothing but obstinate quarrels over mere words with a terrific amount of hair-splitting.*

In order to understand these debates, it is necessary to keep in mind the state of the social-democratic movement at that time, with its unstable and anarchical network of circles, and the conditions in which an illegal party organisation had to operate under absolutism. At the same time, it is necessary to understand that deep political antagonisms were coming to a head in the discussions on the statutes, antagonisms which were still only felt rather than clearly expressed in any single argument. Lenin sensed grave dangers ahead and wanted to ward them off by organising the party more tightly. He was aware of the tremendous tasks which would face the party in the approaching revolution, and wanted to forge it into a weapon of iron. And, finally, he recognised that he alone out of the whole *Iskra* group would be able to lead the party with the necessary confidence and determination. The very impersonal and objective way in which he reached this conclusion explains his obstinacy on this question.

The wording of the two proposals for Paragraph 1 of the statutes gives hardly an inkling of the antagonism. It is certain that Martov wanted a party with ill-defined boundaries in accordance with the actual state of the movement, and with strong autonomy for the individual groups; a party of agitation which would broadly and loosely embrace everybody who called himself a socialist. Lenin, however, felt it was important to overcome the autonomy and the isolation of the local groups, and thus avoid the dangers inherent in their over-simplified and ossified ideas, not to speak of

---

* Two formulations of Paragraph 1 were under consideration:
Martov's proposal: 'A member of the Russian Social-Democratic Workers' Party is everyone who, in acceptance of its programme, works actively to carry out its tasks under the control and direction of the organs of the party.'
Lenin's proposal: 'A party member is everyone who accepts its programme and supports the party both in material ways as well as through personal collaboration in one of the party organisations.'

their backward political development. He wanted a firmly and tightly organised party which, as the vanguard of the class, would be closely connected with it, but at the same time clearly distinct from it; a hierarchically structured party which would include various organs (party committees, factory cells, educational circles, etc.), but whose core was to be made up of full-time professional revolutionaries. The party was to be organised from the top downwards, and headed by a central committee responsible to the party congress only and possessing almost unlimited political and organisational powers. This omnipotence of the central committee was underlined still further by the statutes commission of the Congress, which gave the central committee full powers to organise the lower party committees at its own discretion, to dissolve them at will, and to decide on the tasks of the members of such committees (the professional revolutionaries). In the end, therefore, even the responsibility of the central committee towards the party congress could be made into a mere fiction.

At the Congress Martov was victorious, and Lenin gave way on this point. But when the radical point of view prevailed in the discussions on the party programme, various reformist groups left the Congress altogether, and the Lenin group thus obtained a majority of the votes determining the members of the central organs. Shortly thereafter a change of alignment occurred in these policy-making bodies: Plekhanov went over to Martov's side, thereby helping him to gain a majority again and soon after this the party split. In accordance with the final voting at the Party Congress, the two groups were called Bolsheviks and Mensheviks (from the Russian words for majority and minority respectively).

After the split Lenin published a book, *One Step Forward, Two Steps Back,* in which he vigorously criticised the proceedings of the Party Congress and dealt in particular with the organisational question. With the utmost trenchancy Lenin argued his centralistic standpoint. It seemed as though he wanted to provoke his opponents, and he made very bold declarations, for example: 'Bureaucracy against democracy – that is, in fact, the organisational principle of the opportunists.' Rosa Luxemburg replied to Lenin's book, simultaneously in *Iskra* and in *Neue Zeit* (July 1904), with an article entitled 'Organisational Questions in Russian Social Democracy'. At the time the work made scarcely any impression on the Western European working-class movement; at most it caused astonishment that the Russians should be fighting about such peculiar ideas. It later became quite significant in the discussions which took place in the international working-class movement after the seizure of power by the Bolsheviks in Russia.

Rosa Luxemburg was in agreement with Lenin that the revolutionary party had to be the vanguard of the working class, that it had to be centralistically organised, and that the will of its majority could be carried out by means of strict discipline in its activities. But she rejected his ultra-centralism. In her opinion, Social Democracy was the first political movement in history to reckon on the independent action of the masses in all its phases. It therefore had to create an organisational form very different from that, say, of the conspiratorial Blanquist organisations. When Lenin characterised revolutionary social democrats as 'Jacobins indissolubly bound to the organisation of the class-conscious proletariat', he forgot, she declared, that the antagonism between Social Democracy and Blanquism was not exhausted in the contrast between the organisation and class-consciousness of the proletariat on the one hand and the conspiracy of a small minority on the other. The difference between Blanquism and Social Democracy was rather that there was no inherent connection between the conspiratorial activity of Blanquism and the daily life of the popular masses. For this reason, Blanquism could, and, in fact, had to shut off its organisation hermetically from the popular masses. At the same time, she continued, the activities of the Blanquists were based on a definitely fixed plan, conceived freely, whereby the members of their organisation necessarily became the tools of a previously determined will—a central committee vested with broad powers and demanding blind obedience from all the individual organs:

> The conditions of social-democratic activity are fundamentally different. This activity grows historically out of the elemental class struggle. It thereby develops in accordance with the dialectical contradiction that the proletarian army recruits its forces only in the course of the struggle itself, and only in the course of the struggle does it also understand the tasks of this struggle. Organisation, enlightenment, and struggle are thus not isolated factors, separated mechanically and chronologically, as they would be in a Blanquist movement; they are only different aspects of the same process. On the one hand—apart from the general principles of the struggle—there can be no ready-made fighting tactics, fixed down to the last detail, which could be drilled into social-democratic members by a central committee. On the other hand, the very process of struggle in creating the organisation causes a continual fluctuation of the social-democratic sphere of influence. From this it follows that the social-democratic organisational form cannot be based on blind obedience and on the mechanical subordination of the party militants to some centralised power. . . . The character of social-democratic centralism must therefore be essentially different from that of Blanquist centralism. This social-democratic centralism can be nothing but the authoritative concentration of the will of the

enlightened and militant vanguard of the working class as against its separate groups and individuals. It is, so to speak, a "self-centralism" of the leading section of the proletariat; it is the rule of the majority within its own party organisation.[41]

Rosa Luxemburg regarded the existence of an all-powerful central committee as a danger to the development of the struggle itself. Experience in Russia and in other countries showed that every new form of struggle had not been 'invented' by leaders, but had arisen from the creative initiative of the masses. Here, too, she wrote, unconscious action preceded conscious action; the logic of the objective historical process preceded the subjective logic of those bearing it. She made the significant observation that in this process the organisational leadership naturally tended to play a strongly conservative role. It worked out the newly adopted methods of struggle to their final consequences, but then became a bulwark against further innovations on a large scale. A particularly clear example of this was to be found in German Social Democracy, whose leadership offered almost insurmountable resistance to any attempt to go beyond the parliamentary routine, worked out to be the last detail, towards new forms of struggle:

> This inertia is explained to a large extent, however, by the fact that it is also very difficult to present the contours and tangible forms of a political situation which does not yet exist, i.e. an imaginary one, in the empty air of abstract speculation. Moreover, it is not so important for Social Democracy to foresee and draft complete formulae for future tactics as it is to preserve in the party a correct historical appreciation of each prevailing form of struggle, to preserve a vivid feeling for the relativity of the given phase of the struggle and for the necessary intensification of revolutionary factors from the standpoint of the final aim of the proletarian class struggle. However, to vest a party leadership with such absolute powers of a *negative* character, as Lenin wants to do, would intensify in a downright artificial and dangerous way the conservatism necessarily inherent in every such body.[42]

There is no doubt that Rosa Luxemburg attached special importance to this argument against Lenin. Even at that time she observed in him—and later in the Bolsheviks—a dangerous rigidity in argumentation, a certain scholasticism in his political ideas, and a tendency to ignore the living movement of the masses, or even to coerce it into accepting preconceived tactical plans. This thoroughly violated her dialectical sense of the political process. She had encountered such rigidity and narrowness among the French Guesdists and regarded these tendencies as a serious hindrance to political action.

Lenin himself was confident enough that he would not succumb to this danger. Later, when he looked back at the discussions of 1903, he openly admitted in one of his works that he had adopted that rigid and exaggerated form of argument in order to hammer home to his followers the decisive political truths. In any case, when big decisions had to be taken, he demonstrated a tactical elasticity which one would not have suspected from his writings. His associates, however, manifested that conservative inertia, as decried by Rosa Luxemburg, at almost every historical turning-point when they were left to make decisions on their own initiative-for example, during the formation of the workers' soviets in 1905 and at the outbreak of the revolution in 1917 [before Lenin's return to Russia].

According to Rosa Luxemburg, the only guarantee against socialist tactics becoming rigid formulae was to keep alive those forces in the party capable of exercising criticism within the framework of Marxist principles and to secure an effective control of the party organs from below. Thus she came to the following conclusion:

> The ultra-centralism advocated by Lenin seems to us, in its whole character, to be sustained not by a positive creative spirit but by a sterile night-watchman spirit. The drift of his thought is mainly directed at the *control* of party activity rather than its *fructification*, at its *constriction* rather than its development, and at the harassment rather than the *unity* (*Zusammenziehung*) of the movement.[43]

Rosa Luxemburg valued the creative role of the masses to an extraordinarily high degree, and believed it could be realised within the party by allowing an unlimited amount of freedom to criticise all the higher organs of the party. She regarded this freedom of criticism as the way to prevent ossification, and as the living spring at which all the inadequacies of the movement could be cured. In her opinion, it was the duty of the party leadership to execute the will of the majority, and to influence the formation of this will by the use of its higher insights, but not to force its own will onto the organisation in a dictatorial manner. She spoke bluntly against any any attempt to have an omnipotent party leadership play the part of a divine providence: 'Mistakes made by a really revolutionary working-class movement are historically immeasurably more fruitful and more valuable than the infallibility of the best "central committee" that ever existed.'[44]

Lenin and Luxemburg

Lenin answered her criticisms of his ideas at the time in an article intended for *Neue Zeit*. Curiously enough, he did not deal with the positive content of her criticism, but only contested its validity. He did not favour absolute centralism, but advocated the elementary rules necessary in any conceivable party organisation. In her analysis Rosa Luxemburg had ignored the Party Congress and the facts of the party struggle. The main part of his retort was devoted to the internal struggles of the Russian social-democratic movement, and these were described in a way that must have rendered them completely unintelligible to anyone unfamiliar with the subject. It is not surprising, therefore, that Kautsky, the editor of *Neue Zeit*, refused to publish the article; it did not appear until two decades later in the periodical *Leninski Sbornik*.[45]

Later Lenin often ridiculed Luxemburg's idea of 'organisation as a process'. However, he himself was destined to experience this fact, namely that changes in the organisational forms were subject to the developmental process of the movement as a whole. When the Russian Revolution of 1905 won the freedom of association, he himself gave the party a form which had little in common with the ultra-centralism he had recommended. Under pressure from the greatly increased party membership, he even agreed to the re-establishment of party unity, and although the majority thereby passed once again into the hands of the opportunists, he nevertheless submitted to their decisions even in very important questions.

This leads directly to the question as to whether the present form of rule in the Soviet Union and the situation in the Communist Parties are the result of Lenin's organisational principle. First of all, it is necessary to make some observations. Lenin himself explained that in his book *One Step Forward* . . . he had deliberately exaggerated his demand for centralism in order to counteract the anarchy prevailing in the Russian party at the time. When the organisational theses were laid down for the parties of the Third (Communist) International in 1920, he insisted that they were much too 'Russian' to be suitable for Western European conditions. And these theses were, in fact, founded on 'democratic centralism' and provided for freedom of criticism and for the control of the party leadership from below. It is true that in Lenin's own ruling Communist Party centralist control was very strenuously exerted, but that was because the Civil War [1918-21] demanded a rather military form of party organisation. Nevertheless, during those years when Lenin stood at the helm of the Soviet state, the great political decisions were not in the least dictated from above, but were hammered out in vigorous intellectual struggles. And Lenin, who once flippantly wrote of 'bureaucracy as the principle of revolutionary Social Democracy', finally came to regard the struggle against the state and party bureaucracy as such an urgent task that, just shortly before his death, he dictated his thoughts on the matter as a kind of testament.

A survey of the whole development since 1903 would lead to the following conclusion: Lenin's old ultra-centralistic ideas obviously had an effect on the practice of the Bolsheviks insofar as they helped to overcome objections and resistance to an exaggerated centralism. However, these views were modified continually and in different directions by the tasks and the conditions of the struggle. Here again reality turned out to be stronger than any preconceived theory. And the grotesque forms of life of the official Communist organisations of the present have their origin not so much in a theory created decades ago as in the decline of the Russian Revolution, whose most important characteristic had been the construction of a party bureaucracy which rules the state with unlimited power and is guided by special interests and particular social ideas.

The symptomatic role of Lenin's organisational views is thus exaggerated and distorted if passages from his writings of 1902 and 1904 are simply linked up with the results of decades of development. On the other hand, one should be wary of thinking that Rosa Luxemburg imagined the party to be a loose collection of like-minded people. It is true that she strongly supported the freedom to express opinions and criticisms within the party as a vital necessity, as the only sure way to combat the dangers of rigidity and degeneration, but she also stressed very much that this freedom had to be limited by the commonly shared Marxist principles within the party. At the same time she valued very highly the unity of the party and of the working-class movement, and welcomed the fact that in the German social-democratic ranks there was room for widely diverging views. 'A great and serious party will not split as a result of newspaper articles or even as a result of isolated cases of political disloyalty (*Seitensprünge*).' However, general agreement on the ultimate aim of the party was not sufficient as the basis of party unity; common political practice was also necessary. She firmly opposed any 'blurring of the distinction between the staunch elite troops of the working class and the unorganised masses of the people'. She took the matter of the party's centralism very seriously: in the International she fought all attempts of the parliamentary fractions to assert their autonomy and to evade the control and policy decisions of the party as a whole, and she herself was very energetic in seeing to it that the will of the central committee in the Polish party was respected.

This first disagreement between her and Lenin—even if all the various background factors are taken into consideration—nevertheless revealed characteristic differences between these two great leader-personalities. Luxemburg underestimated the power of organisation, particularly when the reins of leadership were in the hands of her opponents. She relied all too believingly on the pressure of the revolutionary masses to make any corrections in party policy. Lenin's total political view prior to 1917 shows traces of unmistakably Blanquist influences and an exaggerated voluntarism, though he quickly overcame it when faced with concrete situations. To overstate the point, it can be said that Rosa concerned herself more with the historical process as a whole and derived her political decisions from it, while Lenin's eye was more concentrated on the final aim and sought the means to bring it about. For her the decisive element was the mass; for him it was the party, which he wanted to forge into the spearhead of the whole movement.

The character of the 1905 revolution

Russian Social Democracy had broken apart in 1903, seemingly because of personal rivalries and strongly exaggerated differences on the question of organisation. However, when the revolution became reality, it was evident that underlying the cleavage were deep antagonisms which had been only vaguely felt up to then. It was now necessary for the movement to make up its mind about the character, aim, and strategy of the revolution.

Generally speaking, in and beyond the social-democratic ranks, the conception of the Russian Revolution was that it would be a bourgeois revolution, aiming at the overthrow of absolutism and the realisation of bourgeois-democratic liberties. But underneath this general postulate were hidden very deep-seated differences of opinion. The various bourgeois-democratic groupings, the Social-Revolutionaries, and certain theoreticians of the PPS let themselves be carried along by events, without attempting any deeper analysis of social relations. From the general formula most of the Menshevik leaders drew the conclusion that because the revolution in question was a bourgeois one, its leadership and, later, the governmental power belonged rightly to the bourgeoisie. The working class had to confine itself to supporting the bourgeoisie's strivings for power; beyond that, it had 'to exert revolutionary pressure on the will of the liberal and radical bourgeoisie', and 'to force the upper strata of society to lead the bourgeois revolution to its logical conclusions'. (A S Martynov, *Two Dictatorships*, 1904.) They thus thought that the task of Social Democracy was to urge on the radical bourgeoisie, but that the movement itself should remain within the framework of bourgeois politics and should not fight with its own weapons for the objectives of the proletariat or even snatch the leadership away from the bourgeoisie in the gigantic struggle. Any attempt to overstep these limits would prove to be fatal. It would drive the bourgeoisie into the camp of the reaction and thereby wreck the revolution altogether.

The social-democratic left-wing–the Bolsheviks, Parvus, Trotsky, Rosa Luxemburg, and Kautsky (who was strongly under her influence)–reproached the proponents of this tactic for being utopian and reactionary. They examined the experiences of earlier revolutions and pointed out that the great French Revolution was guided to victory only because under the Jacobin leadership the plebeian element–the petit-bourgeois and proletarian masses of the people–seized power and tore out feudalism by its deepest roots even against the opposition of the bourgeoisie itself. The Revolution of 1848 in Germany failed precisely because the bourgeoisie, fearful of the proletariat, which was just taking its first hesitant political steps, joined forces with absolutism right after the first storm and thereby saved it from destruction. The Russian bourgeoisie would take the same course, and very quickly, too, because in the meantime, since 1848, the strength of the international and even of the Russian proletariat had grown enormously.

This historical experience suggested that the Russian Revolution could be victorious only if the proletariat succeeded in capturing the leadership, hegemony. An analysis of the concrete situation could only confirm this view. The Tsarist empire harboured the most glaring social contradictions. In agriculture a wide variety of production methods existed, from the peasant's tiny plot of land tilled with the mediæval wooden plough to the modern large-scale farm of the 'liberal' landowner. In the towns there was a petit-bourgeoisie which had never experienced the heyday of craft production, because it had been unable to compete against the cheap cottage-industry of the peasants; and finally there was a modern, highly concentrated industry* which, like a hotbed, had been specially fostered by absolutism.

Even from this sketch of the Russian economic structure there emerge significant differences in class attitudes as compared with previous revolutionary situations. The liberalism of the Russian bourgeoisie was bound to be even shorter-lived than that of its

* The large-scale industrial concern was relatively much more strongly developed in Russia than in Germany, which was marching at the head of capitalist countries in Europe. This is shown by the following comparison:

	GERMANY Statistics for 1895		RUSSIA Statistics for 1902	
Firms employing	No of firms	Workers employed	No of firms	Workers employed
51-1,000 workers	18,698	2,595,536	6,334	1,202,800
over 1,000 workers	255	448,731	458	1,155,000

Western counterpart; even more quickly would it have to seek a compromise with the old powers because of its involved relations with the absolutist regime and because of its fear of the working class. The urban petit-bourgeoisie was not at all in a position to play the leading role it had played in all previous revolutions. It lacked political will and vegetated in a dull and sluggish fashion; the most that could be expected was that it would be swept along by the revolution's momentum. In other countries and in former times the work of politically educating the working class had been done by the petit-bourgeoisie, but in Russia this had been carried out by the revolutionary intelligentsia, organised in the various socialist parties. The peasantry, on the other hand, hungered for land and strove to liberate itself from the oppressive burdens of absolutism; it was therefore revolutionary. However, peasant action was necessarily confined to a local arena. The peasantry could not take over the leadership of the whole struggle; on the contrary, it needed a leader itself. And Rosa Luxemburg foresaw that, once its urgent social needs were satisfied, it would fall prey to the reaction.

Thus, the only class left to lead the revolution through to the end was the working class. It is true that in relation to the total population in Russia it was weaker than the working class in the large-scale capitalist countries. But at least it was concentrated in large masses at the politically crucial points and had already proved its strength in struggles of gigantic proportions. In addition, international social relations had their effect on Russia. The fact that the bourgeoisie in the West had given up the struggle for its own freedom and had deserted to the camp of the reaction must have sapped the resolution of the Russian bourgeoisie. At the same time, the attitude of the Russian working class expressed something of the power and the maturity of the international proletariat.

Out of these considerations Rosa Luxemburg, writing in *Neue Zeit* (January 1905), drew the following conclusion:

> The Russian Revolution will, formally speaking, bring about in Russia what the February and March Revolutions [1848] brought about in Western and Central Europe half a century ago. At the same time, however–and just because it is a belated and straggling fragment of the European revolutions–it is a very special type in itself. Russia is stepping onto the revolutionary world-stage as the politically most backward country. . . . Precisely and only for this reason, contrary to all the generally held views, the Russian revolution will have a more pronounced proletarian class-character than any previous revolution. It is true that the immediate objectives of the present uprising in Russia do not go beyond the limits of a bourgeois-democratic constitution, and the final result of the crisis (which may, and most probably will, last for years, alternating between flood and ebb-tide) may, if anything at all, be no more

than a wretched constitution. And yet the revolution which is condemned to give birth to this political changeling will be a pure proletarian one, unlike any before it.

Thus Rosa Luxemburg was far more sceptical in her estimation of the probable outcome of the revolution than the Mensheviks. But this in no way crippled her resolution. She valued the revolutionary process itself higher than its immediate result; for the first time the proletariat would play the leading and decisive role, and its interests and its fighting methods would determine the character of the revolution. She therefore set before the working class the task of acting, not as the auxiliary troops of liberalism, but as the vanguard of the revolutionary movement and as a class which, although it determined its policy while still being dependent on the other classes, nevertheless derived that policy exclusively from its own class tasks and class interests. Thus, in a formally bourgeois revolution the antithesis of bourgeois society and absolutism would be superseded by the antithesis of the proletariat and bourgeois society.

The character of the revolution would also express itself in the strategic aim put forward by the socialist party, namely in the question of the revolutionary government. For the Mensheviks it was clear that after the overthrow of Tsarism this revolutionary government could only be a bourgeois class-government. At their party conference in May 1905 they explained that they had to take a position which, in the struggle against the inconsistent and self-seeking policies of the bourgeois parties, protected them from being absorbed into bourgeois democracy. Therefore Social Democracy should not aim at taking over power in the provisional government or at sharing it with others, but it had to remain the party of the most radical revolutionary opposition. This attitude, the Mensheviks believed, was proof of their singularly firm adherence to Marxist principles, and they appealed to the resolution adopted by the Amsterdam Congress of the International in 1904, which had condemned 'ministerialism', the participation of social democrats in the government of bourgeois states. They warningly quoted Engels's observation that, if socialists came to power in an unripe situation, they might,

> in the interests of the movement itself, support the interests of another class, alien to them, and fob off their own class with claptrap and promises, and with the assurance that the interests of that alien class are really their own interests. Whoever falls into this devious position is irretrievably lost.[46]

The attitude and argumentation of the Mensheviks appeared to be boldly radical and rigorously principled to an extreme degree. This, however, is an excellent example of how a tactical principle, which imparts a definite character to a policy in a definite historical situation, can have the opposite significance and effect in another, basically different situation.

It was Lenin who exposed the Mensheviks's 'Marxist' entrenchment for what it was. How on earth could anyone talk as if the participation of the working class in a democratic revolution and its organs of power could be lumped together with its participation in a government which opposed a socialist revolution! Engels's warning, however, should only serve to protect people from being deluded by the total situation; it would aid in limiting aims and propaganda to the practically attainable. Lenin saw the possibility of this in a 'revolutionary-democratic dictatorship of the proletariat and the peasantry', in a revolutionary government composed of socialists and representatives of a peasant party (which would undoubtedly be formed); such a government would create dictatorially the basis of a bourgeois-democratic state.

Parvus, Trotsky, and Rosa Luxemburg were in complete agreement with Lenin's efforts to counteract the Menshevik programme of total abstention from governmental participation. But they parted company with him over objectives. They regarded his 'democratic dictatorship' as an attempt to force the revolutionary process into the desired channels by violence. With Trotsky assenting, Parvus announced: 'The proletarian-revolutionary government will be a government of the working class. If Social Democracy stands at the head of the revolutionary movement of the Russian proletariat, then this government will be a social-democratic one.'

Rosa Luxemburg defined her basic attitude to these questions in articles appearing in the Polish publication *Przeglad Socjaldemokratyczny* (Social-Democratic Review). In her opinion, Lenin's slogan could not be realised, above all for two reasons. He was certainly right in opposing the Mensheviks for their hidebound scholasticism in regarding the peasantry simply as a reactionary class, contrary to the realities of the Russian experience. However, he overlooked the great social differentiation within the peasantry as a class, and also the fact that it would certainly, and probably very soon, turn away from the revolution. Above all, Lenin was mistaken with regard to the attitude of the working class. No power on earth could restrain the proletariat from using its political authority for its own interests, irrespective of the limits of the bourgeois social order. A government of socialists which tried to confine the activity of the working class within these limits would necessarily have to take up the cudgels against its own class, inevitably preparing the way for the counter-revolution.

Social Democracy therefore had to seek allies among the peasantry and rely on their revolutionary action to bring about the overthrow of absolutism. It had to take governmental power into its own hands, arm the revolutionary masses of the people right away, and organise the armed working class into military units. Quickly and by dictatorial means it had to carry out all the fundamental measures necessary for the political and economic transformation of society. Once this was done, a constituent assembly could be called on the basis of the general suffrage. Moreover, while this parliament was thrashing out the constitution, the revolutionary government had to secure dictatorial power for itself, and the popular masses had to remain armed in order to keep parliament from sliding onto the counter-revolutionary path, and possibly in order to take action against parliament. Here she was thinking of the experiences of the Long Parliament during the English Revolution and of the National Convention during the French Revolution. To be sure, she was generally not inclined to force political aims into the strait-jacket of a rigid formula, since she viewed them as always being the result of a complicated process of development. Nevertheless—probably as a counter-blast to Lenin's 'revolutionary-democratic dictatorship of the proletariat and the peasantry'—she coined the slogan: 'revolutionary dictatorship of the proletariat relying on the peasantry'.

There was no doubt in Rosa Luxemburg's mind that conditions in Russia were not yet ripe enough for the proletariat to retain political power in its hands indefinitely. However, the overthrow of absolutism seemed possible to her only as the result of the class victory of the proletariat, which would inevitably lead to its seizure of power. And absolutism could be overthrown only if the working class and its leading party directed their whole policy towards this aim. Undoubtedly, once in possession of power, the working class would enforce measures breaking through the barriers of the bourgeois social order, thereby overtaxing its strength and coming into conflict with social 'possibilities'. As a result of this policy it would provoke the hostility of the other social forces, and in the end succumb to the counter-revolution. The only way to avoid this fate would be to abandon revolutionary politics altogether. Only by calmly and resolutely submitting to these historical necessities, would Social Democracy lead the revolution to victory, extricate Russian society from the trammels of backwardness, have a progressive influence beyond Russia's borders, and bring lasting gains to the international working-class movement.

Skirmishing in the rear

The events of 1905 confirmed this daring conception step by step. During that whole year the working-class determined the law of action for all other social forces. Immediately after Bloody Sunday, 22 January, mighty waves of political mass strikes surged across the whole of Russia. In the name of society as a whole the working class raised its fist against absolutism. Demands for civil liberties and a constituent assembly spread like wildfire. Taken by surprise, the authorities seemed to be completely helpless in the face of this outburst. Victory seemed quite near. Barricades were already being erected in Warsaw. However, it was only a start. The gigantic wave of political strikes suddenly broke up into innumerable rivulets of small strikes which no longer had great political aims, but fought for purely economic ones: for higher wages, shorter working hours, and improved working conditions. The antithesis of bourgeois society and absolutism was superseded by the antithesis of the proletariat and capitalism.

In March the movement received a new impulse as a result of the defeats of the Russian army in Manchuria. The working class swept larger and larger sections of the population into the revolutionary maelstrom. Workers' strikes blazed up in all parts of the empire, accompanied by students' strikes. Peasants set fire to the property of the rich landowners. In Tiflis troops mutinied for the first time. In April sailors of the Baltic Fleet demonstrated in St Petersburg. Peasant disturbances broke out in the Baltic provinces, as well as strikes and demonstrations in the industrial towns. The following month saw clashes between demonstrators and the military in Warsaw and Kalisz, the annihilation of the Russian fleet by the Japanese in the Straits of Tsushima, the founding of the 'Union of the Russian People' (the notorious Black Hundreds), and pogroms. In June there followed a general strike and barricade-fighting in Warsaw; the mutiny on the battleship *Potemkin*; the mutiny of troops in Libau, Riga and elsewhere; peasant disturbances and terrorist acts. July saw mutiny in Kherson [Ukraine], strikes of the railwaymen, peasant disturbances in the Baltic provinces. In August the Minister of the Interior, Bulygin, issued a manifesto announcing the summoning of a Duma (Council of State) with extremely limited rights, and the granting of a suffrage which excluded the bulk of the workers and peasants. In September Russian Social Democracy decided to boycott the Duma. In October a political general strike broke out: it began in Moscow, spread to embrace millions, and paralysed economic life and the state apparatus for weeks. It ended in the first great victory: on 30 October the Tsar issued a manifesto proclaiming the introduction of certain civil liberties and the calling of a Duma based on indirect suffrage by a graded electorate.

Throughout this period the whole Tsarist empire was one bubbling cauldron in which all social forces—workers, peasants, students, and soldiers—came to the boiling-point. But where was the bourgeoisie, which supposedly had been destined to take the initiative and command the obedience of others in this bourgeois revolution? Torn between fear and hope, it was to be found trotting around with petitions and meeting at various congresses whose proceedings were so insignificant that history has hardly taken note of them. The working class was the leading force, churning and sweeping along everything else, and the general strike was the effective weapon of the revolution. The hegemony of the proletariat was manifest in the formation of the St Petersburg Soviet of Workers' Deputies (26 October), which became the central leadership of the struggle and, at the same time, proved to be the embryo of future public organs of revolutionary power. Up to this point the prophecies of the left-wing socialists had been borne out in an astonishingly dynamic and forceful way. And the Mensheviks? Their leaders were sceptical and let themselves be carried along with the tide. The rank-and-file members co-operated with the Bolsheviks in thousands of committees, and together they propelled and guided the movement forward.

Rosa Luxemburg was living in Berlin at the time, and working with the feverish exertion of all her energies despite ill health. Even if some of the plans she mentioned in her letters could not be carried out, her achievements during these months were remarkable. She studied political events closely in order to learn from the historical process at first hand. In a series of Polish pamphlets and articles she interpreted the significance of contemporary historical events to those who were experiencing and shaping them. From chaotic and contradictory phenomena she created a clear picture, indicating the next stages of development, vigorously controverting illusions and erroneous ideas prevalent in the revolutionary camp, restraining romanticism, calming down impatience, and utilising the still scanty experiences of the initial struggles to solve burning tactical questions with creative intuition and to concentrate the will of the party on the most urgent tasks.

At the same time she devoted her entire strength to her activities in the German and in the international working-class movements in order to work out the significance of the events in Russia for the proletariat as a whole. The Russian Revolution had strengthened the revolutionary consciousness of the German workers and made them ready for action. In January the miners of the Ruhr district, who for 15 years had felt defenceless in the face of the overwhelming power of capital, went on strike. It was a huge struggle fought around purely economic demands, but it had nevertheless a political character, because it aimed beyond Stinnes and Thyssen at the state itself, and after four weeks it succeeded in extracting at least a promise of serious reforms. German workers were affected by an intense thirst for information about the Russian Revolution. People throughout the country wanted to hear Rosa Luxemburg, and the series of innumerable meetings where she spoke as a representative of the Russian Revolution became a tour of triumph. Because of the pressure of the enthusiastic masses she was now allowed to speak even on trade-union platforms, which up to then had been forbidden territory for her. Clara Zetkin helped a great deal in making her friend's conquest possible; with equal energy she had also thrown herself into the forefront of the work of propagating the ideas of the Russian Revolution.

Another result of events in Russia was that the old antagonism between reformists and radicals burst open again, but this time the latter took the offensive. The social-democratic right-wing revealed a symptomatic inability to understand the problems of the Russian Revolution. Its spokesmen were, of course, enthusiastic about it, but although they prided themselves on their Marxism, they were unable to interpret the revolution in terms of the class struggle. They regarded it as an outgrowth of the 'Russian soul'. They justified it only as an exceptional case, as a struggle against a despotic regime, for they felt that such a struggle would be senseless in a constitutional society resting on a secure legal basis. In other words, they were saying that the Russian Revolution was merely an interesting spectacle for European democrats, and they did not have to draw any conclusions from it about their own future. The politics of Russian Social Democracy, a brother party in the International, was a closed book to them. They acknowledged their sympathy for the liberal Cadets (Constitutional Democrats) and the populist-terrorist Social-Revolutionaries. They passed over the violent actions of the proletarian masses almost without notice, but they were all the more enthusiastic about dramatic spectacles, such as the shootings of governors and grand-dukes.

Rosa Luxemburg felt deeply provoked by the antagonism of these views to her own ideas. She scoffed at those who sought to get the feel of the revolution

> with phrases about cracked ice floes; endless steppes; tired, apathetic, and weeping souls; and similar cracked belletrist nonsense out of the minds of bourgeois journalists whose entire knowledge of Russia is derived from the latest performance of Gorky's play *The Lower Depths* or from a couple of Tolstoy's novels, and who gloss over the social problems of both hemispheres with an equable and well-intentioned fatuity.

It caused her deep chagrin that such insipid bilge should swell the columns of *Vorwärts*. And she must have been delighted when her merely incidental criticism triggered off a half-amusing, half-serious battle over the Marxist versus the 'ethical-æsthetic' conception of history, in which her friends Mehring and Kautsky led the attack in defence of the former.

To her it was more important to draw lessons from the Russian experience which could be used for the struggle of the Western European proletariat in the foreseeable future. The great lesson of the Russian Revolution was contained in the political mass strike, and Rosa Luxemburg expected it to bear fruit in the next stage of the German and Western European working-class movement. For years she had been labouring to obtain recognition for this weapon, but without making a particularly deep impression. As late as 1904 the German Party Congress had rejected a motion by Karl Lieb- knecht and Clara Zetkin to examine the feasibility of this form of struggle. But now, because of the Russian example, the working masses were responsive to the idea, and a big discussion on the issue got under way. In vain did the trade-union leaders seek to prevent this 'playing with fire'. The Trade-Union Congress in Cologne (May 1905) almost unanimously condemned the idea of the mass strike. Nevertheless, the SPD Congress in Jena in the autumn of 1905 sanctioned the political strike as a weapon that could be employed under certain conditions even by the German working class.*

The resolution of the Jena Party Congress was a victory for Rosa Luxemburg. But it did not satisfy her. Even though the up- swing in party militancy was manifested strongly, the positive con- tent of the resolution remained far below her expectations, com- pletely oriented as it was to the safeguarding of parliamentarism. Moreover, the circle of comrades who were close to her in spirit turned out to be very small indeed. Even Bebel was not one of them. In her speech at the Jena Congress, Rosa Luxemburg de- clared, among other things:

> Anyone listening here to the previous speeches in the debate on the question of the political mass strike must really feel like clutching his head and asking: "Are we actually living in the year of the glorious Russian Revolution, or are we ten years behind the times?" . . . Previous revolutions, especially the one in 1848, have shown that in revolutionary situations it is not the masses who have to be held in check, but the parliamentarians and lawyers, so that they do not betray the masses and the revolution. . . . In the face of all this small-mindedness we must tell ourselves that for us the final words of the *Communist Manifesto* are not merely a pretty phrase to be used at public meetings, but that we are in deadly earnest when we shout out to the masses: "The workers have nothing to lose but their chains; they have a world to win."[47]

---

* For an account of the dispute over the mass strike see below, Chapter VII second section.

Her words got on Bebel's nerves, so much so that he protested ironically: 'Listening to all that, I could not help glancing a couple of times at the toes of my boots to see if they weren't already wading in blood.' Occasionally the grand old warrior revealed himself to be the skilled turner that he actually was. It is interesting to note, by the way, that the Public Prosecutor used these same words as evidence in charging Rosa Luxemburg with incitement to violence, and a year later she was sentenced to two-months imprisonment by the Weimar court (*Landgericht*) for this offence.

For all that, the Russian Revolution inflamed the passions of even the Party Executive. Under pressure from the Berlin district organisation, which was deeply dissatisfied with the shilly-shallying of *Vorwärts*, it dared, for the first time, to strike out against the right-wing. Six editors of *Vorwärts*, with Kurt Eisner and Gradnauer (Rosa Luxemburg's old enemy) heading the list, were dismissed, and their places taken by radicals, including Rosa Luxemburg. In a letter to Leo Jogiches, who was leading the Polish movement from Cracow at the time, she expressed cautious doubts about the new editorial board:

> The editorial board will consist of mediocre writers, but at least they'll be "*kosher*". This is the first time since the world began that *Vorwärts* has experimented with forming a thoroughly radical cabinet on the premises. Now the Leftists have got to show that they are capable of governing (*regierungsfähig*). . . .

In fact, they proved too 'capable of governing', i.e. too loyal to the official party line, to please Rosa's taste in the long run. But before this became too obvious, Rosa herself was active on a very different battlefield.

6
In the line of fire

Warsaw

> Rosa Luxemburg, that gallant and heroic female, doesn't think it
> right to expose herself to the dangers of the proletarian revolution,
> but she will continue to preach revolution with that screeching
> rhetoric of hers. . . . Rosa Luxemburg will not risk her own neck–
> something we regard as quite understandable and human. But what
> an impudence it is that a Polish woman who takes good care to
> avoid the dangers in her homeland should goad the German workers
> on to revolution! What on earth would this gallant lady do in the
> unlikely event of her speeches and articles really setting off a con-
> flagration in Germany! Would she stick it out here or would she
> decamp to yet another clime on the "international" scene?

That was Pastor Friedrich Naumann writing in his mouth-piece,
Die Hilfe (Help), around this time; the very man who, several years
before, himself far removed from the theatre of operations, had
whipped up the 'bearers of German culture' (*Kulturträger*) to per-
form Hunnish deeds against the Chinese. For months the tune 'Off
to Poland!' made the rounds of the German press; the keynote was
given by the reformists, who titteringly piped out the refrain long
after Rosa became active on the revolutionary front.

As soon as two conditions were fulfilled–a sufficient improvement in her health and a situation which demanded the presence of
the party leadership directly on the battlefield–she left Germany.
She did so against the wishes of her own comrades and behind the
backs of the SPD Executive, who, for political and personal reasons,
would hardly have let her go. Using the passport of a Berlin comrade, Anna Matschke, she smuggled herself over the border into
Russian Poland towards the end of December 1905.

It was an adventurous journey. In Russia the decisive struggle
between revolution and absolutism was raging. After it had become
clear that behind the October Manifesto of the Tsar there had been
nothing but a desire to gain time for a new attack on the revolutionary masses, the working class had resorted to a general strike for the
last time. In Moscow an uprising had broken out. No trains were

running. The Tsarist regime was mobilising all the troops which seemed still reliable, and concentrating them against the big towns. At the German-Polish frontier railway traffic ceased. An attempt to get to Warsaw on the direct line via Toruń and Aleksandrów Kujawski failed. Rosa had to make a wide detour along the border as far as Ilowa. Here trains were also at a standstill. And there was no possibility of continuing the journey with horses – which would have been a dangerous undertaking in any case. Then she found out that a troop train was supposed to leave for Warsaw, and decided to travel with it. She was the only civilian squeezed between soldiers and weapons which were supposed to bring the rebellious city of Warsaw to reason. Despite the bitter December cold, the train was unheated. It was also unlit, to avoid being discovered by the population insofar as this was possible. It crawled along, for fear of derailment; there was the possibility of the track being destroyed by striking workers. When the train went by the stations, soldiers could be seen standing at the ready. And in these conditions of continuous nervous tension Rosa had to contend with the possibility of being discovered at any moment throughout the two-day journey. Thus it happened that the counter-revolution brought the leader of the revolution with military protection to her goal.

Warsaw was under martial law. The inner city was deathly quiet. Everywhere soldiers were on patrol. The workers were still out on general strike, but it was to end without success. The uprising in Moscow was crushed. Still Rosa Luxemburg was full of confidence. She wrote to Kautsky on 2 January:

> The mood everywhere is one of vacillation and a wait-and-see attitude. The cause of all this, however, is the simple circumstance that the *mere general strike as such* (*blosse Generalstreik*) has played out its role. Now only direct and general street-fighting can decide matters, but the right moment for this must still be prepared.

As yet no one on either side of the barricades recognised that by this time the high-point of the revolution had already passed. All public meetings were forbidden. Nevertheless, the workers met in the factories without interference and heard the agitators of the various parties, for the factories were their strongholds. Workers' organisations were forbidden. Yet the trade unions were growing by leaps and bounds. The revolutionary newspapers were banned, but the paper of the Polish social-democratic movement, *Czerwony Sztandar* (Red Flag), appeared daily. It was typeset in secret by fly-by-night crews of compositors, and frequently the printing premises were changed. Often print-works were raided, and the printing of the paper was carried out by force, even at gunpoint. Sometimes, to keep up appearances, even those printers who were willing to do the work demanded that they, too, should be raided and 'coerced'. And every day, despite the police and the military, the newspaper boys of the proletariat went through the streets crying out '*Czerwony Sztandar!*'.

However, the difficulties of the revolutionaries grew with each passing day. The failure of the strike and the defeat of the Moscow uprising brought new cheer to the reaction. The state apparatus consolidated itself again. The police, who in face of the mood of popular indignation had become hesitant, now noticed faint signs of the wavering resolve of the workers, and made more energetic efforts to get a grip on the situation. They were whipped up by the bourgeois press, which now took an odious stand against the revolutionaries, even in Poland. The social-democratic organisations were harassed, and police raids and arrests took place almost daily. Those apprehended were threatened with execution by firing-squad. The leading comrades were weighed down with a crushing burden of work: besides agitating in factories and barracks, and publishing half a dozen papers to meet the various needs of the movement, they had to surmount new difficulties and introduce new organisational measures every hour. In this confusion Rosa Luxemburg regarded it as her chief task to assist the movement in achieving an overall view and an understanding of the situation as a whole as well as clarity concerning the immediate objectives. For this purpose she wrote a pamphlet called 'From the Days of Revolution. What Next?' [*Z doby rewolucyjnej. Co dalej?*], the third in a series of three essays in Polish under the same title. The two earlier ones had been written in April and May 1905 in Berlin.

The problem of armed uprising

The revolutionary movement had got off to an even more vigorous start in Poland than in the rest of Russia. The level of industrialisation here was higher, and the national antagonism to Tsarist rule made the urban petit-bourgeoisie more active. As early as March 1904 large demonstrations occurred, spreading increasingly month by month. Police and military proceeded against the movement with that special brutality characteristic of foreign rule. In the autumn of 1904 the PPS (Polish Socialist Party) decided to offer armed resistance to the police. On 13 November fierce fighting took place in Warsaw. At the beginning of January 1905 fighting broke out in Lódź, Radom, Siedlce; and after Bloody Sunday there were strikes—often accompanied by violent clashes—in Lódź, Vilna, Kovno, Bialystock, Dombrowa, Záwierce, Czestochowa.

The PPS prided itself on having the initiative and leadership in this movement, and it probably did. It gathered within its ranks strong sections of the working class, and was better organised than the SDKPiL (Social-Democratic Party of the Kingdom of Poland and Lithuania). Events seemed to justify its strategy of revolutionary struggle for Polish independence, and it was already rejoicing over its victory: 'The PPS will cope with its internal and external enemies. It will also cope with those disruptive cliques patronised by people who are uncalled for and imported into Poland from abroad, people who can't even speak Polish.'[48] This comment was aimed directly at Tzsyka (Jogiches), who since 1904 had been guiding the illegal work of the SDKPiL from Cracow and who had certainly repeatedly warned his organisation against collaborating with the adventurists of the PPS.

Thus, the PPS leaders were not wanting in self-assertiveness and strong hate. However, they were political romantics who always viewed reality through rose-tinted spectacles, i.e. as they wished to see it. For decades they had regarded the Polish people as the revolutionary nation *par excellence*, and had arrogantly scoffed at those who expected revolutionary deeds from the barbaric and servile Russians, Ukrainians, Georgians, etc. For this reason they had considered the overthrow of Tsarism to be completely impossible, and had sought Poland's salvation in its forcible severance from Russia. They did not rely on the class forces in the Tsarist empire, but imagined that the liberation would be a military action along the lines of the 1863 revolt, and always based their speculations solely on a favourable international situation. This also explains why their leader, Pilsudski, journeyed to Japan immediately after the outbreak of the Russo-Japanese War in order to beg the Mikado for arms and financial aid.

When, contrary to their expectations, the whole of Russia rose against absolutism, the PPS leaders were swept along into the general movement for a short time. But the entire character of this revolution was foreign to them. Consequently their revolutionary romanticism boiled over immediately after the first big events. In the spring of 1905 their party paper, *Robotnik* (Worker), asserted: 'We already have the revolutionary forces. Now we must have the revolutionary methods. Let us form fighting detachments, and obtain arms and other weapons, and we shall soon have political freedom.' The most important tasks, as they saw them, were to organise their followers and, if possible, the entire Polish people militarily; to purchase arms from abroad; and to manufacture bombs.

Rosa Luxemburg regarded this view as a serious danger to the revolution. Her first pamphlet entitled 'What Next?' was devoted to this theme. Such a conception was a typical outgrowth of parties whose attachment to the working-class movement was purely verbal.

After all, the bourgeoisie, too, looked upon social struggles as being merely a question of brute physical force. If one asked the average factory-owner or member of the *szlachta* (gentry) why he considered the restoration of Poland to be impossible, he would answer: Where on earth will we get the strength to deal with the strong armies of the conqueror? The PPS, however, trusted its ability to create this military strength. It simply transferred the views of the conspiratorial terrorist circles to the working class, and thought that by some plan or other it could arm the workers and strike out. Absolutism would certainly be overthrown only by a general uprising, but the masses themselves would have to procure the necessary arms by disarming the military, by storming arsenals, and so on. Such actions, however, could only develop as a result of a prolonged revolutionary mass movement:

> In popular revolutions it is not the party committee under the all-powerful and brilliant leader or the little circle calling itself a fighting organisation which counts, but only the broad masses shedding their blood. The "socialists" may imagine that the masses of the working people must be trained under their orders for the armed struggles, but, in reality, in every revolution it is the masses themselves who find the means of struggle best suited to the given conditions.[49]

Social Democracy had to confine itself to doing what was possible. In the best case it should direct all its exertions towards seeing to it that individual workers in the party and groups of workers were armed to resist the brutalities of the state power. But to lead the workers to believe that the party would provide them with sufficient arms to attack the military and to do battle with the standing army would be to deceive the working masses.

Should socialists then wait with folded hands for the outbreak of street-fighting and leave to fate their concern for the lives of thousands of workers? Of course not. But to prepare for these struggles Rosa Luxemburg had only one method (which must have astonished all those who maligned her at the time as a Blanquist, a Bakuninist, or as 'bloody Rosa')–agitation!

Agitation above all in the countryside. To win over the agricultural labourers and the peasants, not for a directly military struggle, but to capture their minds for socialism and awaken in their breasts the fire of revolt and the will to be liberated:

> We must carry the banner of class struggle to the countryside, without masking our political demands with the ambiguous and cowardly phrases of patriotism. We must point out to them all aspects of their proletarian or semi-proletarian existence, and explain to them what their interests are, above all, those interests they have in common with the working masses of the whole of Russia: the overthrow of absolutism![50]

In this way the revolutionary movement could be generalised; absolutism would be weakened by being forced to disperse its forces over the whole empire.

The present task was not the formation of fighting detachments for a frontal attack, but agitation among the soldiers. It was precisely here that the failure of social-patriotic slogans manifested itself. One could obviously not approach Russian soldiers stationed in Poland with a cause which was not expressly their own. Socialists had to appeal to their class interests as workers and peasants. Socialist agitation would draw a section of the military into the revolutionary front and make others waver, thus eroding the strength and discipline of the army. 'We must arm the proletariat, both in peasant smock-frock and in military uniform, with the weapons we can give: enlightenment concerning its economic and political class interests.' Enthusiasm for mere acts of violence was misplaced:

> There are two ways of accelerating the revolution and disorganising the government. The government is being thrown into disarray by the war with Japan, by the Tungus in Manchuria, by famine and bad harvests, and by the loss of credit on European stock-exchanges. These factors are independent of anything the popular masses may do. Bomb-throwing by individuals falls into the same category. Another method altogether is the involvement of the popular masses, and this is not dependent on chance: general strikes; partial strikes; sabotage in industry, commerce and transport; military uprisings; the stopping of trains by strikers, etc. Throwing a bomb is about as dangerous to the government as killing a gnat. . . . Only people incapable of thinking, believe that terrorist acts of bombing can make anything more than a momentary impression. Just by themselves, mass actions as a disorganising tactic are a danger to absolutism. Not only do they disorganise the ruling system, but they also organise at the same time the political forces which will overthrow absolutism and create a new order. This is the only course for Social Democracy. Agitation will win over the countryside. It will undermine discipline in the army; call the broadest masses into open struggle; and generate the forces to build barricades, procure weapons, win victories here and others there, and finally collect and pull everyone into the struggle.[51]

For Rosa Luxemburg the tasks of a revolutionary party were not to be found either in the heroic deeds of individuals or the daring coups of small minorities. The decisive factor was agitation, the winning of people's minds for socialism in such a way that their will to achieve socialism would, so to speak, move from head to fists, and vent itself in mass actions. It was the same attitude shown by Marx in Paris at the beginning of the 1848 Revolution when he opposed [Georg] Herwegh's adventurous intention of raising volunteer troops to bring the revolution into Germany by force of arms. Rosa

Luxemburg's chief concern was that the revolution should reach organic maturity; this could be achieved by utilising and furthering the dynamic of events themselves—which was the role of leadership. She knew very well that the party would also have definite technical tasks to fulfil in preparation for an uprising. In January 1906, at a time when she no longer held that the mere general strike as such was sufficient to carry the movement to victory, and believed that the period of mass uprisings was dawning, she wrote, in the third pamphlet of the 'What Next?' series:

> The phase of open struggle which has now begun makes it incumbent on Social Democracy to arm the most advanced fighters as well as possible, to work out the plans and conditions for street-fighting, and, above all, to learn the lessons of the Moscow struggle. This technical preparation for the armed struggle is tremendously important and necessary, but it is not the chief guarantee of victory. In the last resort, the decisive factor will not be the fighting detachments of an organised minority (although they do have their special tasks in the revolutionary struggle), but the broad masses of the proletariat. Only their readiness and their heroism can guarantee final victory in the street-fighting. However, these masses cannot be organised in fighting detachments; they can be prepared and organised only on the basis of the continuous and daily class struggle, both economic and political. Social-democratic trade unions and social-democratic associations, the creation of units within the military—these are our chief tasks for the coming victory. The organisation and enlightenment of the working masses in accordance with their general class interests and their particular present-day tasks will enable the fruits of the class struggle to endure. This work will also give the revolution such an impetus that a return to reaction will be impossible. The militant mood of the masses and their readiness to be victorious at any cost will bring this about.[52]

Rosa Luxemburg did not imagine the uprising to be a frontal attack on the armed forces of the state. In her opinion, the prerequisite for the uprising was a deep demoralisation among the troops; agitation would pave the way for it, and the fighting itself would complete the process. The victory of the uprising depended on the defection of strong sections of the troops to the revolutionary masses.

The content of the two pamphlets cited above stands in glaring contradiction to the picture of Rosa Luxemburg's ideas drawn by certain malicious 'Bolsheviks'.* A textual comparison of Lenin's and Luxemburg's writings on this point might lead to the conclusion that they agreed in every respect. That would be wrong, however:

---

* Cf., e.g. Jemeljan Jaroslawski, *Rosa Luxemburg on the Question of Insurrection*. The author mentions only random passages in Luxemburg's text and draws hasty conclusions. He is obviously unfamiliar with her two basic writings on the point.

they approached the question from a totally different perspective—
as the following statement by Lenin demonstrates:

> There is no doubt that we still have much, very much, to do for the
> enlightenment and organisation of the working class. But the whole
> thing now is a question of knowing where the centre of gravity of
> this enlightenment and organisation must be. Should it lie in the
> trade unions and legal organisations or in the armed uprising, and
> the creation of a revolutionary army and a revolutionary govern-
> ment?[58]

The same can be shown in a passage from Lenin's *What Is To
Be Done?*, where he says that the party must create a network of
militarily organised agents whose work at the moment of the uprising would offer the greatest probability of success:

> The ability to estimate the general political situation correctly, and,
> in consequence, also the ability to choose the opportune moment for
> the uprising, would be developed precisely in such work. . . . Pre-
> cisely such work would finally spur on all the revolutionary organ-
> isations in all parts of Russia to maintain permanent and at the
> same time strictly conspiratorial links with one another. . . . With-
> out this it is impossible to discuss plans for the uprising collectively
> and to take the necessary collective measures on the eve of the up-
> rising, both of which must be kept in the strictest secrecy.

Like Rosa Luxemburg, however, Lenin also learned from the
experiences of the Moscow uprising. Thus both developed their
ideas in a similar direction. While Rosa at first put her whole stress
on the spontaneous activity of the masses and—so it seems—recognised the great importance of conscious organisation and leadership
only as a result of the events of 1905, Lenin first started from a
conspiratorial conception and then recognised its limitations. Before
the 1905 'rehearsal' it seemed to him that the task facing the leadership of the struggle was to create an organisation which would be
able to choose the right moment for the uprising, and which would
have to operate 'without expecting help from any quarter, but
rather by managing everything itself'. Now he saw in fact that the
workers were moving from the strike weapon to armed uprising over
the heads of the organisation, 'the biggest achievement by far of the
Russian Revolution'. The views of both theorists thus came so close
that there hardly seemed to be any difference between them. However, they did develop from different starting-points, and this fact is
significant for an understanding of certain, very essential, differences
in their political thought.

History has pronounced judgment on both these conceptions
of armed uprising. In all revolutions, fighting units attached to the
revolutionary parties and organised on conspiratorial lines have
never been able, even at best, to act as more than a skeletal frame

for the fighting masses. In the worst case, whenever the situation has failed to come to a head as they hoped, they have inevitably become a danger to the party by threatening to set off putschist actions or to take over party rule, and have had to be dissolved by the party. On the other hand, the uprisings of 1905-06 came nearer to the picture that Rosa Luxemburg had in mind. The December uprising in Moscow was begun spontaneously by the masses. The leadership of the uprising (the Soviet of Soldiers' Deputies) played essentially the role of a military adviser. The February uprising of 1917 was also a completely spontaneous action of the St Petersburg workers and soldiers. In contrast, the uprising of 7 November 1917 was systematically prepared and laid down according to a definite plan. It was carried out almost exclusively by regular army troops; this was possible because a significant part of the ordinary soldiers–in Petrograd the preponderant part by far–already stood on the side of the revolution and pressed for action, and the rest of the soldiers were wavering in their support of the old regime. We can see a similar development also in the great French Revolution: a spontaneous action on 14 July 1789 which shook absolutism to its foundations, and a systematically planned action on 10 August 1792 which brought the decisive victory.

It is obvious that in a rising revolutionary movement the significance of the organisation grows together with the initiative of the leadership, and that victory depends very substantially on these factors at the climax of the movement. Rosa Luxemburg's treatment of this problem shows a characteristic feature which often appears in her writings. She really examined the question of the uprising in detail only when and insofar as it achieved practical significance during the Russian Revolution. Later, when she dealt with the experiences of the Revolution for the parties of Western Europe, she went deeply into the question of the mass strike, which was a burning issue there; she mentioned the question of the uprising only incidentally. There is no doubt at all that she thought out the consequences of each of her tactical decisions to their logical conclusion. Nevertheless, she was aware that each new experience would bring new insights, and each new situation new possibilities and exigencies. She therefore mostly confined herself in propaganda to clarifying the next tactical step. In this way she preserved for herself and the movement a certain flexibility in political action.

Polish Social Democracy and the Polish Socialist Party

In the second of her 'What Next?' pamphlets (published in May 1905) Rosa Luxemburg dealt with the remarkable phenomenon of the disintegration of the first great political mass strike of January 1905 into innumerable isolated strikes of an economic nature which then dominated the scene of struggle for months. She raised a question which was occupying the minds of all conscious revolutionaries at the time:

> Does this transition to economic strikes not mean a temporary decline in revolutionary energy, a retreat; are these current economic strikes not just an aimless skirmish with capitalism? Therefore, in the future, ought we not to counteract such a splintering of the general strike by quickly breaking off the strike while it still has the power of a political demonstration?[54]

Rosa Luxemburg saw the solution of the problem as lying in an understanding of the double character of the revolution. It was a bourgeois revolution as far as political liberties, the republic, and the parliamentary form of government were concerned. At the same time, however, it had a proletarian character because the working class was the leader and the strongest supporter of revolutionary action, because its fighting methods dominated the conflict, and because it had become the most important social factor. This new-found force had, of necessity, to express itself in a direct struggle against capital for the improvement of working-class conditions, irrespective of the effects this action might have on the political attitude of the bourgeoisie. According to Rosa Luxemburg, Social Democracy should therefore not oppose these economic strikes under any circumstances, but should try to steer them into the main current of the revolution. She also regarded the outbreak of these strikes as proof that it would be impossible to keep the working class within the bounds of the bourgeois economic order once power fell into its hands during the course of the revolution.

At the same time she warned against systematically judging all economic strikes by the same standard. Strike fever suddenly seizing hold of great masses of workers was something quite different from the usual strike in a single factory. Far more significant than the immediate winning of improvements in working-class economic conditions was the phenomenon that during these strikes entirely new strata had been swept into the struggle for the first time: industrial workers in the provincial towns, the army of clerical workers and members of certain intellectual professions, and the great mass of the landless proletariat together with the proletarianised peasantry. Thus for Rosa Luxemburg these economic strikes indicated a tremendous expansion of the sphere of struggle which would help eventually to secure the revolution. The task of Social Democracy was therefore to group the demands of these strikes around the central slogan of the eight-hour day, in order to create a united mass movement which would then, in its turn, develop organically into a political struggle.

This statement was again directed at the PPS, which only sulkingly participated in the economic strikes in order not to lose every vestige of its influence on the masses, while at the same time bemoaning the degeneration of the revolution into a mere movement for wages. It tried to act as if it were much more revolutionary than the Social-Democratic Party, which it claimed was leading the working class astray. In reality, the two basic conceptions which had been wrestling with each other in the Polish socialist movement since 1893 were here put to the test of history: the view of the PPS, which aimed at achieving the political restoration of an independent Poland; and the view of Rosa Luxemburg, which declared that the overthrow of absolutism would come through a revolution in which the Polish proletariat would ally itself with the Russian proletariat, together establishing their hegemony over all the revolutionary forces. It was to become evident that the former conception was the wishful fantasy of petit-bourgeois nationalist intellectuals, while the latter was the expression of the real historical process as seen from the working-class standpoint.

The PPS should have realised very soon that the real revolution did not consist in bomb-throwing and putschist undertakings by small fighting detachments, but in the mass actions of millions of people. But it persisted in resisting these insights and, as a consequence, rapidly lost the leadership of the struggle. For a while it let itself be taken in tow by the SDKPiL. The proletarian supporters of the PPS simply followed the social-democratic slogans, and compelled their leaders to do the same. This resulted in a deep cleavage in the leadership of the PPS itself. The pure nationalists, the 'social-patriots', saw with horror that their hopes of an independent Poland were ebbing away as fast as that the Russian Revolution was advancing. They thus ended up turning sharply against the revolution itself.

As early as June 1905, the leadership of the PPS openly opposed the general strike which had broken out in Warsaw and Lodz and had led to barricade-fighting. They raised a hue and cry against the SDKPiL for driving the masses into the strike for purposes of senseless self-aggrandisement. This was an admission by the PPS leaders of their loss of influence on the working class to the SDKPiL, which meant a loss of influence even on the proletarian members of their own party. However, worse was yet to come. After the great general strike throughout the Russian empire in December 1905, Daszyński, the leader and parliamentary deputy of the Galician Socialist Party and the recognised head of the PPS in all three partition areas, published an 'Open Letter' [3-5 January 1906] in the

Cracow *Naprzód* (Forward). There he thundered against any general strike on Polish territory. At a time when the Tsarist conception of the state was undergoing its most severe crisis, the Poles should pursue their own aims and use their own methods of struggle. They had to live their own lives and free themselves from movements originating elsewhere, and consequently having other aims which threatened to corrupt or even destroy Polish life. The aim of the Poles was to win Polish independence. The possibility of a victorious struggle was emerging more and more clearly. The Polish people had to prepare for this struggle and not waste its strength prematurely in pursuit of foreign objectives – the victory of an all-Russian revolution. In Tsarist Russia proper a general strike might be a suitable and even a lastingly victorious weapon; in Poland it might be fatal. What was the sense of a strike on the Warsaw-Vienna railway line, which was not state property, but belonged to Polish capitalists?

For the sake of the phantom of national liberation, Daszyński denied the existence of working-class interests. In defiance of the obvious facts, he asserted that 'not classes, but peoples were now fighting in Russia'. He dreamed of the union of the whole Polish people aiming for national independence; and this dream was even more fantastic, considering that the Polish *haute bourgeoisie* did not waver for one moment in their loyalty to Russian absolutism, and even the bourgeois nationalist party of the National Democrats had given up the idea of a national uprising and Polish independence. It was really quite clear that a national revolution was conceivable only within the framework of a social revolution. The PPS leaders were the only ones who clung to the aim of national independence and placed it above all else. Daszyński, Piłsudski, and their comrades now clutched at the last possibility of achieving their aim: absolute separation from the Russian Revolution, but a national uprising at the moment of Russian revolutionary victory. Thus the PPS leaders, who just a year before had boasted of being the true leaders of the Polish proletariat, were now compelled by logical necessity to dissociate themselves from the proletariat and abandon socialism. At the moment of its great critical test their nationalistic conception had cast them into utter confusion and political impotence.

Daszyński's 'Open Letter', which was extensively analysed by Rosa Luxemburg with great trenchancy (*Czerwony Sztandar*, 16 and 27 January 1906), brought the crisis in the PPS out into the open. A split took place at its Party Congress in February 1906. The overwhelming majority of the party stood behind its left-wing (the 'PPS-Left'), which dropped the slogan of Polish independence and adopted in substance the programme of the Social-Democratic Party. Under Piłsudski's leadership, the armed and disciplined 'Fighting

Organisations' (*Bojowka*) separated from the party and called themselves the 'PPS-Revolutionary Fraction'. Rosa Luxemburg's strategy had captured the whole Polish working-class movement—a complete victory, after twelve years of intellectual struggle. It was a victory which bore out her deep and incorruptible insight into the historical process and a strength of character enabling her to stick to her guns once she became convinced of the soundness of the policies she advocated.

The 'Revolutionary Fraction' sank into pure adventurism in the reactionary period that followed. The *Bojowka* shifted their activities to 'expropriations', hold-ups of railway ticket-offices, post offices, licensed liquor shops, etc., finally becoming brutalised and sinking into banditry. In an essay (1909) expressing anger, indignation, and, at the same time, deep human understanding, Rosa Luxemburg depicted the great degeneration of this movement which was evident at the courts-martial of its members in 1907-08:

> Common bandits appear side by side with revolutionary workers before the courts-martial. These bandits cling to the class movement of the proletariat, they figure statistically as victims of the counter-revolution, they sit together with revolutionary workers in the prison cells and die on the gallows with the Song of the Red Flag on their lips. A large number of these bandits were once revolutionary workers and members of various socialist parties. Finally, what is even worse: the revelation that banditry, provocation, spying and revolutionary activity are sometimes intertwined in one and the same case, and that working-class circles are involved. How could this association arise between the drama of the proletarian revolution and, working at cross purposes to it, the partisan struggle of the *Lumpenproletariat* against private property?[55]

Rosa Luxemburg found the answer to this question in the terrible privations of untold masses of people during counter-revolutionary period, and in the political spinelessness of the 'Revolutionary Fraction', which sank into the depths of political terrorism.

After the utter bankruptcy of this sort of revolutionary action became obvious, its inspirer and leader, Josef Pilsudski, decided to try to achieve Polish independence by other means. In 1909, when war between Austria-Hungary and Russia seemed imminent as a result of the Austro-Hungarian annexation of Bosnia, Pilsudski came to terms with the Austro-Hungarian government, whereby he founded Polish rifle-brigades (*Strzelcy*) to provide cadres for a future Polish Legion, and placed them and himself under the General Staff of the Hapsburg Army. This marked the final break between social-patriotism and the working-class movement, and the alignment of Pilsudski and his followers with the imperialist conqueror's front.

This complete slide of Polish nationalist socialism into the camp of the reactionary powers had been predicted by Rosa Luxemburg as early as the beginning of her campaign against the PPS leadership. Her theory could not have been more emphatically justified. The direct consequence of this development was the affiliation of Polish Social Democracy to the Russian party in the spring of 1906. From that time onward the proclamation of the right of self-determination of peoples by Russian Social Democracy represented no danger for revolutionary strategy in Poland; together the principle of self-determination and the policy of the Polish working class formed a dialectical unity.

In prison

In the course of 1905, not only did Polish Social Democracy become the undisputed leader of the Polish working class, but also Poland herself marched at the van of the revolution, outstripped in activity only temporarily by St Petersburg and Moscow. The chief reason for this, of course, was the heavier industrialisation of Poland. In addition, however, the revolution was furthered by the political firmness of the SDKPiL which was secured by the intellectual superiority of Rosa Luxemburg. Leo Jogiches, who had come to Warsaw under the name of Otto Engelmann, developed his great organisational abilities and held the party together in a strictly disciplined fashion. An outstanding group of revolutionaries supported them: Feliks Dzierzyński, who with the Russian Petrienko led the military organisation of the party; Warski, Karski, Radek, Aussem, Hanecki, Malecki, Domski, Irene Semkowska, Unszlicht, Leder, Brodowski-people who rendered outstanding services to the Russian Revolution after 1917. In 1901 the party numbered hardly 1,000 members; by 1905 it had grown to 25,000 and by 1907 it reached about 40,000. It published newspapers in Polish, German, and Yiddish, distributed leaflets in Russian to the occupation army, organised trade unions, and directed strikes and barricade struggles.

Naturally the work entailed sacrifices. Especially after the December strike persecutions by the police intensified, and arrests became more frequent. On 4 March 1906 Rosa Luxemburg and Leo Jogiches were arrested in the house of Countess Walewska. The Warsaw police had been put on the track by informers' reports from Germany, and, after their arrests, incendiary articles in the German reactionary press, particularly in the conservative *Post*, furnished material for the prosecution's indictment. At first Rosa and Leo were held in protective custody under their assumed names, Matschke and Engelmann. However, the police already had an inkling of the catch they had made. A week later, after they found a photo of Rosa in the possession of her sister, she had to lift the 'veil' concealing her identity. Not until June were the police given indications of Leo's real identity, again thanks to the direct denunciation of the *Post*, and only in August did they succeed in definitely uncovering his alias.

Rosa was first confined in the police prison in the Warsaw Town Hall. Conditions were terrible: they were such as could be imagined at the onset of reactionary periods, when the police are out man-hunting and emptying their hauls into the prisons every hour. In a letter to Kautsky, Rosa depicted this 'idyll':

> They found me in a rather embarrassing situation. But let's forget about that. Here I am sitting in the Town Hall, where "politicals", common criminals, and lunatics are all cooped up together. My cell, which is a jewel in this setting (an ordinary single cell intended for one person in normal times), now contains 14 guests, fortunately all political. On either side of us are two big double cells, each with about 30 prisoners, all on top of one another. . . . Now we all sleep like kings on plank beds right across one another, side by side, packed like herrings, but we are doing all right–as long as extra music doesn't come our way, as it did yesterday, e.g. when we got a new colleague, a Jewess, stark raving mad, who gave us not a moment's rest for 24 hours with her screams and her running about in all the cells, and causing a number of politicals to break out in hysterical sobs. Today we are finally rid of her and have to cope with only three quiet *"myschuggene"* (loonies). Going for walks in the courtyard is quite unknown here, but during the day the cell doors are left open, and we are allowed to walk the whole day in the corridor, to mix with the prostitutes and listen to their lovely ditties and expressions, and to enjoy the odours wafting from the equally wide-open lavatories.

Rosa's health had already been considerably strained by the overwork of the previous months, and living in these crammed, hardly ventilated cells soon made her seriously ill. In addition, she was weakened by hunger strikes, the only weapon the prisoners had in their struggle for more bearable conditions. Last but not least, there were the psychological torments as well. On 11 April Rosa was transferred to the notorious Pavillion X of the Warsaw Citadel, where outwardly conditions were somewhat better. However, the severe extent to which Rosa suffered under them is evident in a letter that she wrote to Sonja Liebknecht, Karl's wife, in February 1917:

> . . . It's been a long time since anything has shaken me so much as Martha's short report of your visit to Karl, how you found him behind bars and how it affected you. Why didn't you tell me about it? You know I'm entitled to know about everything that gives you

pain, and I won't be done out of my rights of possession. The episode vividly reminded me, by the way, of my first reunion with my brothers and sister ten years ago in the Warsaw Citadel. There the prisoner is exhibited in a veritable double wire-cage, i.e. a smaller cage stands freely within a larger one so that the prisoner and his visitor have to converse through the glinting double wire network. It was just after a six-day hunger strike, and I was so weak that the Commandant of the fortress (a cavalry captain) had practically to carry me into the visitors' room; I clung with both hands to the wire netting of the cage, and this must certainly have intensified the impression of a wild animal in a zoo. The cage was standing in a rather dark corner of the room, and my brother pressed his face right against the wire netting. "Where are you?" he kept asking, wiping away the tears behind his spectacles which prevented him from seeing.—How willingly and gladly I would now sit in the Luckau Cage to relieve Karl!

But there were still worse experiences. There were days when gallows were erected in the courtyard of the fortress, and an agonising silence fell upon the whole prison until the steps of the condemned prisoners and of the execution commando could be heard and the funeral march echoed through all the cells. And, with ominously grave words and special ceremonies, revolutionaries were often summoned from their cells, never to return. Without the benefit of legal procedure or a verdict, their lives were blotted out through 'administrative channels'. Once this fate seemed about to befall Rosa. Leo Jogiches, reserved and unsentimental, recounted the incident after her death. Her eyes were bound, and she was led away. But it proved to be only an interrogation; the unusual procedure was due either to an error or to a deliberate act of mental cruelty. Asked later what she felt at the time, Rosa replied: 'I was ashamed because I felt myself blanching!'

It would be far from the mark to believe that Rosa was downcast by all these wrongs and horrors. She knew that her situation was, to use her own words, 'rather serious', i.e. damned serious; she was sick, and her hair began to turn grey. However, her letters from this prison-sepulchre breathe a natural cheerfulness, and are full of amusing anecdotes and self-irony. She loved to live with danger. Even though her body was weak and her health was threatening to break down, her intellectual and psychological strengths rose to the danger and transcended all the sufferings and menacings of fate. And she was able to defy her oppressors and was delighted whenever she succeeded in outwitting them. She saw visitors through the wire netting of the cage she later described. The supervising gendarmes were not allowed to speak to the prisoners, and when they dared to undertake errands for the prisoners, they were ruthlessly transferred to a punishment battalion. The prison itself was within the walls of the fortress; the authorities took great pains and used brutal means to cut it off from the outer world. And yet Rosa remained in continual lively contact with the struggle outside. Not only did she know what was happening in the Polish party so that she could intervene with advice and instructions, but she also received reliable news from the 'North Pole' (the code for St Petersburg) about the internal developments in the social-democratic movement there, news which unfortunately reported nothing but great confusion and the lack of decisiveness and vigour. 'There, that's where I'd like to go as soon as possible! . . . Damn it all! (*Kreuzhageldonnerwetter*) I think I'd shake them all awake until they were completely black and blue!'

News came not only from outside, and Rosa's messages, smuggled to fellow-prisoners and to the outer world, were not the only products of her pen being circulated. After four weeks imprisonment, she was able to report that she had finished her third pamphlet; the first two had already been smuggled out and printed. Moreover, she wrote articles for *Czerwony Sztandar*. Kautsky promised her that everyone would split their sides with laughter if she should some day get the chance to recount her 'travel experiences'. 'I'm especially tickled pink about all the "improper things" (*Unanständigkeiten*) which I daily spirit out of here and get back one or two days later "black on white".' The achievement is all the greater in view of the fact that, in all the tumult of discussions, the bickering of the 'common' criminals, and the fits of rage of the '*myschuggene*' prisoners, Rosa could only work undisturbed from 9 p.m. to 2 a.m. Since the pandemonium of the others began as early as 4 a.m., the work was done at the cost of her sleep.

Imprisonment oppressed Rosa. Her relatives were, of course, moving heaven and earth to secure her release. They had turned to the SPD Executive and were hoping, in view of her German nationality, for an intervention from the German government in her behalf. Rosa complained about this intercession: 'Unfortunately anyone sitting in prison is immediately made a ward not only of the authorities, but even of his own friends.' In any case, she wanted Bülow, Chancellor of the Reich, to be kept out of the affair, because then she would not be able to speak her mind about him and his government as freely as she would like. Her German nationality was a matter of much brain-racking for the Public Prosecutor in Warsaw, for respect for internationally valid pieces of paper had not yet died out in those days. Finally, on the basis of expert legal opinion, a decision was reached: Rosa's marriage with Lübeck was valid in Germany, but since it had not been performed by a rabbi, it was not valid in Russia, so that although she was a German in Germany, she was still a Russian in Russia.

In June a medical commission reported: 'Luxemburg is suffering from anæmia, hysterical and neurasthenic symptoms, catarrh of the stomach and the intestines, and dilation of the liver. She needs hydropathic and spa treatment under appropriate hygienic and dietetic conditions.' On 28 June she was released from prison on the basis of this diagnosis, but ordered to remain in Warsaw. Bail of 3,000 rubles had to be provided.* Further intercessions were made. A second medical report pointed out the absolute necessity of treatment at a foreign spa, and on 31 July she was permitted to leave Warsaw.

There were, however, reasons for her unexpected release other than those recorded in the official documents of the case. The police apparatus had already become heavily demoralised during the Revolution. High officials had been bribed, and, in addition, the Fighting Organisation of the Social-Democratic Party had let the Okhrana know that any harm befalling Rosa would be avenged.

Rosa went first to St Petersburg, where she met Akselrod, with whom she became involved in violent arguments about revolutionary tactics. After that she stayed about a month in Kuokkala in Finland. From there she visited Parvus and Leo Deutsch in the notorious Peter-Paul Fortress, where they were getting ready to be transported to exile in Siberia. It was in Kuokkala that Rosa wrote her pamphlet *The Mass Strike, the Party, and the Trade Unions*, which summed up the lessons of the Russian Revolution for the German working class. But she was itching to plunge into the intellectual fray in Germany. There was one hindrance: an indictment based on her speech at the Jena Congress of the SPD in 1905 was pending. She knew that an arrangement had been made between the Russian and the German police that she should be deported to a point on the German border even before the beginning of the next parliamentary session. This hinted at her immediate arrest. Needless to say, she had little desire to return to state custody so quickly. In September she left for Germany and travelled almost non-stop to the Party Congress in Mannheim. Some time later she managed to take an urgently needed recuperation-holiday in Maderno on the Lago di Garda: 'Sun, peace, and liberty–the finest things in life–except for sun, storm, and liberty.'

In the meantime Leo Jogiches remained in Pavillion X of the Warsaw Citadel. Up until August he had been able to sustain his alias. Permission was given for his release on bail, but for some reason it was retracted again. On 14 November 1906 came the in-

* The bail was probably paid by the SPD Executive. At any rate Rosa was later accused in inner party circles (but occasionally also publicly) of displaying abysmal ingratitude because she dared to attack the Party Executive on tactical matters.

dictment against him and Rosa in the name of the notorious commander of the Warsaw military district, Skalon, a real bloodhound:

> According to an investigation conducted by the Gendarmerie,
> charges are being brought against the *Kleinbürger* [citizen of the
> lower-middle class] Leo Jogiches (alias Otto Engelmann) and the
> merchant's daughter Rosalie Luxemburg (alias Anna Matschke)
> that in 1906 they joined the Fighting Organisation of the Social-
> Democratic Party of the Kingdom of Poland and Lithuania, an
> organisation which aims to overthrow by armed uprising the monar-
> chical form of government in Russia as laid down in the basic laws,
> and in this way to obtain the autonomy of Poland–a crime as pro-
> vided for in §102 of the Penal Code. For the aforesaid criminal act
> the *Kleinbürger* Leo Jogiches (alias Otto Engelmann) and the mer-
> chant's daughter Rosalie Luxemburg (alias Anna Matschke) . . . are
> being handed over by me to the Warsaw Military Court.

On 10 January 1907 Jogiches's trial began. Rosa Luxemburg
had refused to appear before the court at all. At the very beginning
of the proceedings an incident occurred which determined Leo's
conduct throughout the trial. The President of the court, a General,
addressed him with '*du*' (thou), as it befitted a man of his social
rank to address a '*Kleinbürger*' in accordance with the old caste
system. Leo and his lawyers protested. The court decided, since
Jogiches was regarded as a Russian subject, to reject the demand of
the lawyers and to take away their right of defence if they again
brought up questions of discipline. Thereupon Leo declined to give
evidence and remained silent throughout the three-day trial. He was
convicted of military desertion (committed in 1891 by going abroad)
and high treason, and sentenced to eight years hard labour. Rosa
Luxemburg would have received similar treatment, and for her it
would have meant a death sentence. On 5 April 1907, just before
he was to be sent to Siberia, Jogiches escaped from prison. The
escape was a masterpiece of ingenuity. It was above all his clever
way of handling people, together with Hanecki's aid, which enabled
him to win over a gendarme for his undertaking. Several weeks later
he was among the participants at the London Congress of the
Russian Social-Democratic Party, and immediately afterwards, back
in Berlin, he again took up his place in the leadership of the SDKPiL.

Criticism of the revolution

When Rosa Luxemburg drew up the balance of the first year of revolution, she was full of confidence. She expected a further increase
in proletarian activity, the deepening disintegration of the Tsarist
state and military apparatus, and uprisings in town and country

CRITICISM OF THE REVOLUTION | 119

finally culminating in a general mass uprising, strong enough to deal the death-blow to absolutism. Indeed the events of 1906 seemed to confirm this perspective. Demonstrations, strikes, peasant disturbances, insurrections, and mutinies broke out again and again, proving that the flame of revolution had not been extinguished. At the same time, however, the official terror of the absolutist power intensified: pogroms, punitive expeditions (particularly in the Baltic provinces), mass shootings, summary courts-martial, executions and an ever-increasing flow of exiles to Siberia. The workers gradually lost the positions they had conquered from the capitalists in the revolutionary upheaval; in the end the strikes gave way to big lockouts.

It became clear that December 1905, with its general strike and the Moscow uprising, had been the highest-point of the revolutionary wave. Even if the revolutionary masses were still capable of strong blows, it was nevertheless evident that they were progressively losing the initiative; the centre of events was shifting from mass action to parliamentary skirmishing. Despite the reactionary electoral law, the liberal party of the Cadets (Constitutional Democrats) won a big victory in the elections (March 1906), and its attempt to uproot absolutism by parliamentary means caused new hopes to spring up among the right-wing socialists of Russia. Rosa Luxemburg had prophesied that the Duma would become the fig-leaf of absolutism, and that it would be a Cossack Duma. And it was true: such parliamentary action only reflected the agony of the revolution. Absolutism was preoccupied with balancing the class forces in its favour: it dissolved the first Duma in June 1906, ruled without a parliament until March 1907, broke up the second Duma in June 1907, and then had a third Duma elected on the basis of an even more unjust suffrage, so that it was dominated by hardened reactionaries. The counter-revolution was spreading its shroud over the whole of Russia.

Later, in the *Juniusbroschüre*, Rosa Luxemburg analysed the decline of the revolution:

> Two causes explain why, despite its unexampled display of revolutionary energy, clarity of purpose, and tenacity, the Russian revolt of 1905-06 suffered defeat. The one lies in the inherent character of the revolution itself: in the enormous historical programme and the mass of economic and political problems it laid bare, some of which, like the agrarian question, are completely insoluble within the framework of our present social order; and in the difficulty of creating a modern state for the class rule of the bourgeoisie against the counter-revolutionary resistance of the whole bourgeoisie of the empire. From this angle, the revolution failed because it was a proletarian revolution with bourgeois tasks, or, if you prefer, a bourgeois revolution with proletarian-socialist fighting methods, a col-

lision of two epochs amid thunder and lightning, a fruit of the delayed development of class relations in Russia as well as of their overripeness in Western Europe. Similarly, from this angle, the defeat of 1906 does not represent the bankruptcy of the revolution, but merely the natural close of its first chapter, which will inevitably be followed by other chapters. The second cause was of an external nature; it lay in Western Europe: European reaction once again hurried to the aid of its hard-pressed protegé.[56]

The defeat of the revolution caused great confusion in the Russian socialist movement, and to a lesser degree in the SDKPiL, which continued to be firmly organised and ideologically coherent. It was only natural that in the new period of illegality the organisations should shrink and that the working masses should fall back into political apathy. Highly disturbing, however, was the fact that large numbers of intellectuals were now dropping out of politics altogether. In addition, all sorts of aberrations began to appear in Social Democracy. Among the Bolsheviks some groups took refuge in philosophical speculations (Machism), and even in mysticism ('Godseeking'). Theories were also mooted which–had they been put into practice–would have led to sheer adventurism (e.g. Otsovism, a policy demanding the recall of the party Duma fraction and a boycott of the Duma on principle). The Mensheviks, who had not found any opportunity to make a reality of their tactical ideas during the great period of the revolution, now succumbed to defeatism. They declared that the revolution was absolutely finished, and accordingly believed that socialists should now make themselves at home in the new situation. A strong group even came right out and demanded the liquidation of the illegal party organisations–which was practically synonymous with the dissolution of the party altogether.

Heated discussions on fundamental revolutionary problems now began anew; these took up the old theories which had meanwhile been enriched by the experiences of 1905-06. Rosa Luxemburg took a greater part in them than the needs of the Polish movement really demanded.

Among the Mensheviks it was Cherevanin[57] who, in two works, did most to examine the revolution. He concluded that the working class, and with it Social Democracy, had not sufficiently respected the bourgeois character of the revolution; their stormy actions and their direct attacks on capital had driven the bourgeoisie into the arms of the reaction, and thus caused the collapse of the revolution. However, he had to admit that, in view of the given class relations, the working class could not be compelled either to play the role of henchman to the bourgeoisie or to sacrifice its own class interests. Logically, therefore, a 'correct' Menshevik tactic

CRITICISM OF THE REVOLUTION | 121

would have failed too. He came to the peculiar conclusion that in the given circumstances no correct working-class policy was feasible at all, and thereby revealed the helplessness and uselessness of the Menshevik view.

Even in this period, Lenin was consistent in his standpoint, advocating a democratic dictatorship of the proletariat and the peasantry. Trotsky continued to develop his theory of permanent revolution, particularly in articles published in 1908 in the journal of Polish Social Democracy. He came to the conclusion that, although the revolution was directly faced with bourgeois objectives, it should not be satisfied with them. In fact, the revolution could solve its immediate bourgeois tasks only if the proletariat seized power. But once that happened, the proletariat could not confine itself to carrying out the bourgeois revolution. To secure its aims, the proletarian vanguard would have to interfere not only with feudal property, but with bourgeois property as well. It would then come into conflict not only with the bourgeoisie, but also with large sections of the peasantry. Thus, the contradictions confronting a workers' government in a backward country could be solved only internationally, in the arena of the proletarian world revolution. Compelled by historical necessity to burst the bourgeois-democratic framework of the Russian Revolution, the victorious proletariat would then have to break through its nation-state framework–i.e. consciously strive to make the Russian Revolution the prelude to world revolution.

Rosa Luxemburg defined her attitude to these questions and standpoints in several extensive works analysing the course of the revolution and the counter-revolution. She attacked the views of the Mensheviks, particularly in two great speeches at the London Congress of the Russian Social-Democratic Party in May 1907, both masterpieces of polemic oratory. Her opinions were most graphically summed up in a speech delivered by Leo Jogiches in December 1908 at the Congress of the SDKPiL. After summarily rejecting the Menshevik ideas, he dealt with Lenin's views. The following represents the gist of his words.

According to the Bolsheviks, the interests of the proletarian and the peasant classes in the revolution were identical. If this standpoint were to be logically maintained, then, for a time at least, all efforts should be directed at forming a proletarian-bourgeois party. But then at a certain stage of the revolution the 'dictatorship of the proletariat and the peasantry' might turn into a weapon against the proletariat and the revolution. The Bolsheviks were ahead of the Mensheviks, thanks to their greater sense of historical development; they demonstrated that they were no doctrinaires by taking into account the great potential strength of the peasantry. The error of the Bolsheviks was that they saw only the revolutionary aspect of the peasantry. In this respect they represented the antithesis of the Mensheviks, who, in order to justify their own conception of a revolution led by the bourgeoisie, only saw the reactionary aspect of the peasantry.

However, history could make nothing of dead schemas. In reality, they (Jogiches and his friends), the Bolsheviks, and a section of the Mensheviks were fighting for the dictatorship of the proletariat–the Mensheviks despite their erroneous views. It would be difficult to formulate the position more abstractly and less dialectically than the Bolsheviks did. At the bottom of their conception was something like a military advance according to a preconceived plan. In reality, however, the vital content of the historical process itself would be determined by its own course and by its own results–i.e. by objective aims, in spite of and independently of the subjective aims of its participants. The very character of classes and parties changed under the influence of momentary events and new situations. He (Jogiches) did not fear that the views of the Bolsheviks would lead to dangerous concessions to the peasantry. He had faith in the healthy proletarian spirit which underlay all their ideas.

He and his friends were in favour of the dictatorship of the proletariat based on the peasantry. Without a doubt, the attitudes of Parvus and Trotsky were closely related to the views prevailing in his party. But the party did not accept the idea of permanent revolution, which based its tactics not on the Russian Revolution, but on the effects of that revolution abroad. It was not possible to base tactics on combinations which could not be properly estimated. Such horoscopes were determined in a too subjective manner.

Thus both Leo Jogiches and Rosa Luxemburg were more reserved in their judgment than Trotsky, Rosa, however, very readily recognised that the proletarian dictatorship she had in mind could be secured only by the victory of the working class in the advanced capitalist countries; failing this, it would have to give way to the counter-revolution.

Rosa Luxemburg's attitude towards the peasantry is important, particularly because certain anti-Luxemburgists have again and again made the assertion that she underestimated or even ignored the significance of the peasantry in the revolution. This is downright wrong. In numerous writings Rosa Luxemburg pointed most emphatically to the agrarian question as the crux of the revolution because of the significance of the peasant movement in any seizure of power by the working class. At the Congress of the Russian party in 1907 she attacked especially the views of Plekhanov and the Mensheviks on the peasant question as sterile and schematic. Even though she often compared the Bolsheviks with the French

Guesdists, finding their theories too narrow and rigid in many respects, she largely agreed with their practical policy throughout those years, and even with their broader revolutionary perspectives. She always stressed that such a mighty upheaval as was bound to happen in Russia, could not attain its end in one quick surge: she reckoned with a lengthy revolutionary period in which defeats and ebb tides would be inevitable. But she knew and underscored the fact that the reaction setting in after 1905-06 would neither reestablish the old power of absolutism with its old class relationships nor solve the great political questions so well that it could just develop in peace and quiet. For her the revolution was not dead. It would rise again more powerful than ever. In 1912 she was one of the first to observe the new upswing in the revolutionary tide. It was to be smothered again by the World War, only to reappear in 1917 with an even stronger momentum propelling it towards its goal.

7
A new weapon

Disappointment

> ... I am dying to get to work and start writing; among other
> things, I am ecstatic about the prospect of plunging into the dis-
> cussion on the general strike. Only a few more days of patience till
> I get a secure roof over my head and better working conditions, for
> here there seems to be no end to the running around to the
> gendarmerie, the Public Prosecutor, and similar such pleasant in-
> stitutions.
> The latest "squabble" (*Krächle*) in the party made me laugh and–
> excuse me–laugh like the devil himself to boot! Oh! to hear about
> the world-shaking events between Lindenstrasse and Engelufer*
> which have unleashed such a storm! To imagine how this same
> "storm" would look *here!* What grand times we are living in! I
> call them grand because they raise masses of problems, *enormous*
> problems; they provoke though, and stimulate "criticism, irony,
> and deeper significance"; they stir up passions; and above all–
> these are fruitful and pregnant times which give birth every hour,
> emerge even "more pregnant" after every delivery, and give birth
> not to dead mice or even dead (*krepierte*) gnats, as in Berlin, but
> to gigantic things, like gigantic crimes (*vide* the government),
> gigantic disgraces (*vide* the Duma), gigantic stupidities (*vide*
> Plekhanov & Co.), etc. I am all agog at the idea that I shall soon
> be able to sketch a nice picture of all these gigantic happenings–
> especially, of course, in the NZ [*Neue Zeit*]. So reserve for me an
> appropriately gigantic room.[58]

Highly enthusiastic about the great experience behind her and the
work ahead, Rosa Luxemburg hastened to return to Germany after
her release from prison in Warsaw. Her high spirits did not flag as
far as the Russian Revolution was concerned. But the nearer she
came to her second homeland, the homeland of German Social
Democracy, the more dispirited she felt. In Finland, she received
her first German greeting in the form of a copy of *Vorwärts*. The
triviality of the articles, the narrow-mindedness of the points of

* The headquarters of the SPD were in the Lindenstrasse, the headquarters
of the trade unions on the Engelufer–Tr.

view, and the dullness of the ideas expressed by these 'kosher' left-wing pens made her sigh: 'I felt wretched at Plevna!' as the Tsar did at the prospect of confronting the Turks in 1877. Then, barely having arrived in Germany, she attended the Party Congress in Mannheim, where she breathed in the stuffy intensity of the atmos-phere which surrounded the leaders of the German working-class movement, and she felt like a fish out of water.

Indeed, the fresh breeze from the East which had aired the party headquarters for a while had dropped. Inclined to defeatism from the outset, the party leadership, like a sensitive barometer, had immediately registered the regressive development of the Russian Revolution after the December struggles. Increased working-class activities on behalf of the general suffrage in the 'red kingdom' of Saxony* and in Hamburg had been suppressed. After some sabre-rattling by the government, the Party Executive had immediately rendered quite innocuous a great demonstration called in support of the Russian Revolution on the anniversary of Bloody Sunday by depriving it of any revolutionary meaning. In February 1906, after having discussed the implications of the mass-strike resolution passed by the Jena Party Congress, the Party Executive and the General Commission of the trade unions made a secret agreement to the effect that the resolution should remain a dead letter. In fact, the trade-union leadership had practically taken over the party, and the Party Congress in Mannheim merely confirmed the general watch-word: backwards!

Rosa Luxemburg took these developments very seriously. Even in Jena she had felt that the old party leaders held views com-pletely different from her own. The Mannheim Congress made it clear to her that these were not temporary aberrations, and that in future she would have to regard Bebel and the great majority of the leading party cadres as enemies. Replying at the beginning of 1907 to Clara Zetkin, who had expressed anxiety over future party policy, she declared:

> Since my return from Russia, I feel rather isolated. . . . I feel the irresolution and the pettiness of our whole party more glaringly and more painfully than ever before. However, I can't get so ex-cited about these things as you do, because I have already seen with terrible clarity that these things and these people cannot be changed until the situation becomes completely different, and even then–I have coolly reflected on the matter before coming to this conclusion –we shall just have to reckon with the inevitable resistance of such

* At the Reichstag elections in 1903 the SPD captured all the constituencies in Saxony with one exception, but in Saxony itself–i.e. for the Saxon Diet elec-tions–the three-class franchise, in force since 1896, effectively excluded SPD candidates from the Diet.

people if we want to lead the masses on. The situation is simply this: August [Bebel], and still more so the others, have completely spent themselves on behalf of parliamentarism and in parliamentary struggles. Whenever anything happens which transcends the limits of parliamentarism, they are completely hopeless–no, even worse than that, they try their best to force everything back into the parliamentary mould, and they will furiously attack as an "enemy of the people" anyone who wants to go beyond these limits. The masses, and still more the great mass of comrades, are inwardly tired of parliamentarism, I feel. They would joyously welcome a fresh breeze in party tactics; however, the old experts (*Autoritäten*), and even more the upper stratum of opportunist editors, deputies, and trade-union leaders, are a dead weight. Our task is now simply to counteract the stagnation caused by these experts by being as blunt as possible in our protest, knowing that we are likely, depending on circumstances, to have not only the opportunists but also the Executive and August fighting against us. As long as it was a question of defending themselves against Bernstein & Co., August & Co. put up with our presence and assistance–since they, after all, launching an offensive against opportunism, then the old ones, together with Ede [Bernstein], Vollmar, and David, stand against us. That's how I see matters, but now to the main point: keep well and don't get too excited about it! Our tasks will take years! [59]

In the struggle for which she was arming herself Rosa Luxemburg reckoned with the support of the working masses and with the objective development of the situation at home and abroad. Some reflection of the prevailing mood of the social-democratic masses had found expression at the Jena Congress. Moreover, at the many public meetings she addressed on the Russian Revolution and its lessons for Western Europe, she could see, from the serious interest and enthusiasm of the audiences, that the revolutionary spirit had not been extinguished among the rank-and-file of the party as it had in its higher strata. In Austria the Russian Revolution had triggered off a vigorous mass movement; and just then, towards the end of 1906, the Austrian proletariat was reaping its first great success, general suffrage.

Rosa Luxemburg was indeed more cautious than Trotsky in estimating the effects of the Russian Revolution on the large capitalist countries. But she was unshakeable in her conviction that the rising of the Russian proletariat had ushered in a new historical epoch altogether. The catastrophes foretold in her examination of the social motive-forces in the capitalist world in *Social Reform or Revolution* were on their way to becoming powerfully ripe. The dispute between France and Germany over Morocco had raised, for the first time, the spectre of European war. International imperialist politics was revealing its true character. The period of wars and revolutions had dawned. To assist the working class in its intellectual and moral preparation for these coming struggles–this Rosa Luxemburg regarded as her most important task.

The political mass strike

The problem, above all, was to learn the lessons of the experiences of the Russian Revolution as far as they could be of value, in the present chapter of history, for the proletariat of Western Europe, in particular that of Germany. The Russian Revolution differed from all previous revolutions because of the appearance of the great masses with that characteristic proletarian weapon, the strike, indeed the strike involving millions, no longer just for wages and bread, but for great political aims. Rosa Luxemburg had long been active in favour of the political mass strike, but now she realised its full significance as the specific weapon of the proletariat in times of revolutionary ferment.

The idea of the general strike is very old. As early as 1839, the English Chartists had regarded it–under the catchphrase 'The Holy Month'–as the weapon with which they could squeeze a general suffrage out of the bourgeoisie and thus open up the way to socialism. At its Brussels Congress in 1868 the First International proclaimed the 'strike of peoples against war'. The Geneva Congress of the International Alliance of Bakuninists in September 1873 pronounced that the general strike was the weapon for starving out and overthrowing the bourgeoisie; if all work ceased for ten days, this would suffice to bring about the collapse of the existing social order. The French syndicalists also extolled the general strike as the chief weapon of the proletariat; neither the barricade struggle of the bourgeois revolution, nor the parliamentarism of politicians, but the peaceable action of folding arms would carry the working class to victory. These were all in all high-minded illusions, characterised by an erroneous estimation of the real relationship between the actual strength of the revolutionary forces and their aims, an estimation based on the hope that mere propaganda could bring about a general strike and keep it up until the bourgeoisie finally capitulated.

In the meantime, actual strikes of large masses of people had come about, but in a rather different way. In 1891, 125,000 workers laid down their tools in Belgium, not in order to overthrow bourgeois society with a purely economic weapon, but in order to gain greater political freedom within the framework of that social order by means of the general suffrage.

Although this first attempt failed, a second thrust in 1893, involving 250,000 strikers, achieved an improvement in the suffrage which opened the doors of parliament to representatives of the Belgian working class. However, equality of suffrage had yet to be obtained. To this end the Belgian Labour Party, in alliance with the Liberals, launched another general strike in 1902. 350,000 workers took part, but in parliament the Liberals left their partners in the lurch, and the strike collapsed. In the same year Swedish workers carried out a great demonstration-strike in favour of a general suffrage. In France, 160,000 miners went on strike and drew many other workers into the struggle. In 1903 Dutch railwaymen began a political strike which led to the proclamation of a general strike. In September 1904, a wave of tremendously violent strikes reaching giant proportions swept over Italy; the intensity was such that street-fighting occurred in a number of towns. Thus there had been all sorts of experiences with the mass political strike before its full significance was revealed in the Russian Revolution.

In the two most important capitalist countries of Europe, however, the idea of a general strike was regarded very coolly indeed. In England, the idea seemed to have been buried with the Chartist movement. In Germany, after the great Belgian experiment of 1893, both Bernstein and Kautsky had contemplated the idea of a general strike as a weapon to defend working-class political rights. In 1896, when putschist notions were gaining ground among German reactionaries, Parvus advanced the idea of the political strike as a means of moving the workers from a defensive to an offensive position. But these remained purely academic utterances. The overwhelming majority of social-democratic leaders still mouthed the axiom: general strike is general nonsense! And the few times they considered it at all necessary to put forward their arguments, they fell back on the words of Friedrich Engels, who had firmly rejected the idea of a general strike as propagated by the anarchists. In 1873, in his pamphlet *The Bakuninists at Work*[60], Engels had attacked the idea that the general strike, by starving out the possessing classes, would force them to strike back at the workers, who would thereby be entitled to make an armed uprising. He pointed out that even the Bakuninists themselves thought that, in order to carry out this experiment properly, the complete organisation of the working class and well-filled coffers were necessary. Here the flaw of the scheme was evident, because no government would brook such preparations, and,

> on the other hand, political events and the excesses of the ruling classes would bring about the liberation of the workers long before the proletariat would ever be in a position to create this ideal organisation and these colossal reserve funds. If it ever had them, it

would not need the detour of the general strike to achieve its aims.[61]*

When the Belgian general strike of 1902 ended in defeat, most of the German social democrats who concerned themselves at all with tactical questions considered this to be a confirmation of Engels's verdict. Even the radical ones declared the experiment to be the last gasp of Bakuninist tactics: such power experiments were absurd; they led to armed conflicts and to the abandonment of legal channels; and further–so they distorted Engels's ideas–the working class would have power long before it had sufficient strength to conduct a victorious general strike.

Rosa Luxemburg had a completely different view. At the beginning of the Belgian struggle she was already sharply critical of the conditions under which it had been launched, and, after analysing the situation in depth, she drew conclusions that no one else dared to enunciate. Not that it had been wrong to resort to a general strike in the first place, but it had been wrong to let the Liberals prescribe the way in which it should be carried out. The striking workers had thereby been given mere walk-on parts in a performance on the parliamentary stage. The renunciation, for the sake of legality, of all strike meetings and demonstrations, and the restriction of militant workers to their own homes had robbed them of that important feeling of their own massed strength and had made them falter. The essence of a general strike was that it was a harbinger, the first stage of a street revolution. But it was just this character which the Belgian strike leaders had very zealously done away with.

A general strike forged *in advance* within the fetters of legality is like a war demonstration with cannons whose charge has been dumped into a river within the very sight of the enemy. The advice given in all seriousness by *Le Peuple* that the strikers should threaten their enemies "with fists in pockets" would not frighten even a child, not to mention a class fighting to the death to maintain its political rule. Thus it happened that the mere work stoppages of the Belgian proletariat in 1891 and 1893 were sufficient to break the resistance of the Clericals, but only because the latter had reason to fear a sudden transformation of the calm into a storm, of the strikes into a revolution. This time, too, it might have been quite unnecessary to use actual violence to attain the desired

---

* For a long time this was held to be Engels's final verdict on the general strike. That this was not the case has since been evidenced by the publication of letters written by him to Victor Adler and Karl Kautsky in 1893. At that time there was strong support in the Austrian party for a general strike to secure the general franchise. Although under existing Austrian conditions Engels was decidedly opposed to such a trial of strength, he did not reject the general-strike weapon on principle.

end—if only the leaders had not unloaded their weapons *in advance,* if only they had not turned the war march into a Sunday afternoon parade, and if only they had not turned the thunder of the general strike into the fizzling of a damp squib.[62]

Rosa Luxemburg's attitude towards the problem of the political strike here—the first time she confronted this problem—again demonstrates her refusal simply to accept the conventional view just because it was based on the master's word. She scrupulously examined Engels's conception, and found that it 'was cut out to fit only the anarchist theory of the general strike, i.e. the theory of the general strike as a means of introducing the social revolution, in contrast to achieving the same end through the daily political struggle of the working class'. She regarded the two things as belonging together, as complementary in certain situations. Her second point was that the general strike was a weapon with a strongly revolutionary character. It assumed a heightened militancy among the working masses; it could not be treated according to the rules of everyday small-scale struggles, but it involved revolutionary consequences which, if overlooked, might result in a demoralising defeat.

The general upswing in revolutionary ardour which ensued as a psychological effect of the Russian Revolution, and the direct example of the giant mass strikes in Russia, destroyed the intellectual barriers which had prevented most German social democrats from feeling any sympathy for the idea of the political strike. The consequence was a very interesting constellation of differing opinions.

With few exceptions, the trade-union leaders persisted in rejecting the political strike on principle. Up to that time they had never viewed the general-strike idea as anything but a deformed product of the romantic temperament of the Latin race, to be passed over with a shrug of the shoulders. But as the German working class seemed to be no longer immune to such destructive ideas, they opened up a noisy offensive against the 'Mass Strike Apostles' and 'Romantic Revolutionaries'. This reached its climax at the Cologne Trade-Union Congress (1905) with the motto: 'The trade unions need peace and quiet above all!' the delegates condemned even the mere discussion of the question as a dangerous and senseless playing with fire. The motives were clear: the trade-union leaders were fearful of losing their tactical independence of the party, they feared that their well-filled coffers would be plundered, and they even feared the destruction of their organisations by the government as a result of such a confrontation. In addition, they were completely opposed to 'experiments' which could disturb their very ingenious system of daily skirmishing with employers. A comparatively small group of reformist party leaders stood by them because they smelt the revolution behind the mass strike and wanted at all costs to prevent the smashing of the legal barriers. One of their spokesmen, the lawyer Wolfgang Heine, painstakingly consulted the penal code and then declared the political strike to be illegal, because it violated both the paragraphs concerning breach of contract as well as those concerning high treason, and was thus both a venial and a mortal sin against the bourgeois social order.

A large number of other reformist politicians, in contrast, wholeheartedly supported the idea of the political mass strike: they regarded it as a weapon to defend the continually threatened general suffrage exercised in Reichstag elections, and perhaps to win a similar suffrage for German provincial diets. Some of them even hoped its use would result in a truly parliamentary regime and thus fulfil their boldest dreams: the step-by-step conquest of political power through a coalition policy. Among these were Eduard Bernstein, Friedrich Stampfer, and Kurt Eisner. They were enthusiastic about the idea of the political strike especially because they regarded it as a weapon which could take the place of barricade-fighting, and it seemed a peaceable weapon into the bargain.

Closely allied to them were most of the deputies, editors, and officials who clustered around the Party Executive and who later termed themselves the 'Marxist Centre'. They spurned the idea of working together with the bourgeois parties in a coalition government, but hoped, on the basis of a really democratic suffrage, to obtain a parliamentary majority with which they would carry out the socialist transformation of society. For them, too, the mass strike was a substitute for armed uprising. As early as October 1903, Rudolf Hilferding had expressed the views of this group in *Neue Zeit*, as paraphrased below.

Now that barricade-fighting had become impossible, the withholding of labour-power was the only means of coercion available to the proletariat to oppose the coercive violence of the state. The workers had to be ever-prepared to launch a general strike to defend the general suffrage, or one day their enemies might suddenly render all parliamentary activity impossible. The general strike had to become the regulative factor behind social-democratic tactics, regulative insofar as every proletarian had to be willing to defend the achievements of his class by using its power over the vital productive processes of society; regulative, furthermore, insofar as the general strike should not replace parliamentarism, but should rather protect the political activities of the proletariat from attack; and regulative, finally, insofar as the idea of the general strike should remain merely an idea, if possible.

Thus, here, the general strike remained a purely defensive instrument to serve a policy of outwardly clenching one's fist while anxiously hoping that no occasion would ever arise when the instrument would have to be used. All these advocates of the mass-strike idea imagined it to be an action which would be decided upon in orderly fashion by the organising leadership and carried out according to definitely established rules by an army of workers marching in step, strictly disciplined, and subordinated to the will of their leaders.

Karl Kautsky's conception seemed to be fundamentally different from all these ideas: it would never be possible, in a rigidly organised state like Prussianised Germany, to force the granting of political concessions or even to ward off reactionary blows by means of a general strike. If workers resorted to this weapon, then they had to be prepared to go the whole hog and reach out for state power. The general strike was a revolutionary weapon, only applicable in a revolutionary situation. When he first developed these ideas (*Neue Zeit*, February 1904), he also regarded the general strike as the revolutionary weapon which would take the place of armed uprising. Because of the experiences of the Russian Revolution, however, he became convinced that armed uprising as a political weapon should not be consigned to the rubbish heap, and that a general strike might very well culminate in an armed uprising. These views seemed to correspond completely with those of Rosa Luxemburg. Indeed, he was strongly influenced by her. Later, however, a profound difference became apparent. Kautsky was always willing to draw revolutionary conclusions if they concerned other countries, the past, or the distant future. His thesis of the general strike as a revolutionary weapon actually meant adopting a wait-and-see attitude until, some day, historical destiny brought forth the revolution.

The Mass Strike, the Party, and the Trade Unions

At the Jena Party Congress of 1905, Rosa Luxemburg, as we already know, was deeply disappointed by the limited perspectives, stereotyped ideas, and sluggish spirit characterising the debates. She disagreed with Bebel's resolution on two counts: that it limited the application of the mass strike to the defence of the general suffrage, and that it tied the party to using this weapon in case of an attack on the suffrage. Nevertheless, with the other left-wing members, she voted for the resolution. In a letter to Henriette Roland-Holst [2 October 1905], she explained her attitude:

> I entirely agree with you that Bebel's resolution gives a very one-sided and flat interpretation of the mass-strike question. When we learnt about it in Jena, some of us decided to put up a fight against it during the discussion so that we could champion the mass strike, not as a mechanical recipe for a defensive political position, but as

an elementary form of revolutionary action. However, Bebel's speech alone was enough to give the matter a new twist, and still more the attitude of the opportunists (Heine, etc.). As on several previous occasions, we "extreme leftists" (*äusserste Linke*) found ourselves being forced to fight, not against Bebel (in spite of important differences with him), but together with him against the opportunists. To have come out directly against Bebel's resolution in the middle of that discussion in Jena would have been a tactical error on our part. It was rather a case of showing our solidarity with Bebel and then of giving his resolution a revolutionary colouring through the discussion. And this we surely succeeded in doing, even if the newspaper report only gives a hazy idea of it. In fact, in the discussion the mass strike was treated, even by Bebel (though he may not have realised it), as a form of revolutionary mass struggle, and the spectre of revolution clearly dominated the whole debate as well as the Congress. . . . We can be abundantly satisfied with this tactical result.[63]

She hoped that further discussion in the press would develop the inherent logic of the mass-strike slogan. But this expectation was dashed when the Russian Revolution ceased to exercise its inflammatory influence. In the endlessly spun out press debates which ensued, the idea was more and more watered down. The understanding reached between the Party Executive and the General Commission of the trade unions made the Jena resolution into a knife without haft and blade. Immediately after her departure from Warsaw, Rosa Luxemburg decided while in Finland to develop her own conception of the matter by confronting the mechanistic formulae haunting everyone's mind with the living experiences of the Russian struggles. Her pamphlet *The Mass Strike, the Party, and the Trade Unions* appeared just in time for the Mannheim Party Congress in the autumn of 1906.

This pamphlet reveals how Rosa Luxemburg formed her opinions on the forms and methods of action, and the many-sided tactics of the working-class struggle, and how she succeeded in solving problems at a time when even the elementary conditions for their solution barely existed—for instance, the question of the relation between the daily struggle in defence of working-class interests and the greater struggle for the realisation of socialism. It was precisely in the debate on the mass strike that it became evident that most of the party theoreticians had constructed schemas in their heads by which all anticipated difficulties could be most readily overcome and success guaranteed, provided that the rules laid down were followed. Rosa Luxemburg did not calculate or construct any patent solution for future difficulties. She drew her ideas out of living experience and a detailed analysis of the historically formative process of class conflicts, never losing sight of the process as a whole. At the same time she was able to look beyond the immediate events of the day with an almost visionary power, to exclude accidental circumstances due solely to the given situation, and to sum up the factors generally valid for a particular phase of development in such a fashion that her picture of reality pulsed with life.

The work was born out of her great experience on the revolutionary front. The hammer-blows of the Russian Revolution reverberate through it. The mass struggles become alive, the struggles that raged throughout Russia in the previous decade with their bizarre turns and twists, the advance sallies and the occasional sinking of the movement into apparent lethargy, the peculiar lack of proportion between insignificant events and the grandiose scale of the struggles, the knotty entanglement of economic and political motives in the strikes, the successes and the defeats. The work is a mighty fresco of the wrestling of great social forces, painted with a rare power of delineation, in an intensity of colour and of feeling for the dynamic of history.

Her analysis of events led Rosa Luxemburg, first of all, to certain general conclusions which are fundamental to her special conception of the mass strike:

> Instead of the rigid and hollow schema of an arid political "action" carried out at the behest of the highest party authorities according to a cautious plan, we see a bit of life pulsing with flesh and blood which cannot be cut out of the great framework of the revolution, because it is connected to all the odds-and-ends of the revolution by a thousand veins.
>
> The mass strike, as shown to us in the Russian Revolution, is such a changeable phenomenon that it reflects all phases of the political struggle, all stages and factors of the revolution. Its applicability, its efficacy, the factors surrounding its origins alter continually. It suddenly opens up new and broad perspectives at times when the revolution seems to have got into a bottleneck, but it is also liable to fail just when one believes its success can be reckoned on with absolute certainty. At times it surges over the whole empire like a giant wave, at times it breaks up into a giant network of rivulets, at times it bubbles out of the ground like a fresh spring, at times it seeps back into the earth. Political and economic strikes, mass strikes and partial strikes, demonstration-strikes and militant strikes, general strikes in individual branches of industry and general strikes in individual towns, peaceable wage struggles and street battles, barricades—all these run together, inextricably tangled, side by side, crossing one another, overflowing into one another—a perpetually moving and changing sea of phenomena. And the law of motion is clear: it does not lie in the mass strike itself or in its technical peculiarities, but in the relation of social and political forces in the revolution itself. The mass strike is merely the form of the revolutionary struggle at a given moment, and every shift in

the relation of the contending forces, in party development and class divisions, and in the position of the counter-revolution–all this immediately affects the strike action in a thousand invisible and scarcely controllable ways. However, the strike action itself hardly pauses for a moment. It changes only its forms, its extent, its effect. It is the living heart-beat of the revolution and at the same time its most powerful driving force. In other words, the mass strike, as shown to us in the Russian Revolution, is not a cleverly concocted method for the purpose of heightening the effect of the proletarian struggle, but *the way in which the proletarian masses move, the form taken on (Erscheinungsform) by the proletarian struggle in the actual revolution.*[64]

Didn't Rosa Luxemburg generalise too much here from the experience of the Russian Revolution? Didn't she inexcusably identify mass strike and revolution? Didn't she arbitrarily confuse two essentially different things, the economic and the political strike? Naturally, she knew that demonstration-strikes and isolated mass strikes carried on for a definite political purpose are of great importance. But a demonstration-strike whose duration is limited from the outset is no more the broadly developed class struggle than a naval demonstration is naval warfare. As a naval demonstration may be used to support diplomatic action, so the demonstration strike may be used to support the parliamentary and purely economic means of applying pressure available to the working class at certain moments of great social tension. Isolated mass strikes, however, are not initiated and carried out according to a plan, but erupt spontaneously–e.g. both of the Belgian strikes in 1891 and 1893, and the great Italian wave in 1904. In the course of these strikes typically revolutionary characteristics came to the fore arising out of a situation which was revolutionary, even though it could not develop its potentialities to the full. For Rosa Luxemburg these were preliminary phases of the real revolutionary strike, and, as such, of great importance. In any case, the mass strike was not the artificial product of a deliberate tactic, but a natural historical phenomenon. Therefore, she regarded the concept of 'the purely political mass strike, with which people prefer to operate, as a lifeless, theoretical schema'. She also rejected the idea of using the mass strike as a lever to liberate the movement in any impasse. If the prerequisites for elementary actions were missing, any attempt to unleash them artificially would have fateful consequences, for 'in reality, it is not the mass strike which produces the revolution, but the revolution which produces the mass strike'. It was this conception, too, which lay behind her answer to the question concerning the origin, the initiative, and the organisation of the mass strike:

If the mass strike is not an isolated act, but the expression of a whole period of the class struggle, and if this period is identical with the revolutionary phase of that struggle, then it is clear that the mass strike cannot be called at will, even if the decision to do so may have come from the highest levels of the strongest social-democratic party. So long as Social Democracy does not have the power to stage and call off revolutions at its own discretion, not even the greatest enthusiasm and impatience on the part of the social-democratic troops would suffice to inaugurate a real period of mass strikes as a mighty movement of the people. . . . A mass strike born out of sheer discipline and enthusiasm would, at best, play the role of a mere episode, a symptom of the fighting mood of the working class, and then the situation would revert to that of quiet everyday life. Of course, even during the revolution, mass strikes don't exactly fall from heaven. They must be brought about in some way or other by the workers. The decisiveness and resolution of the working class also play a part; indeed, the initiative and the subsequent leadership will fall upon the organised and most enlightened social-democratic core of the proletariat. However, initiative and leadership alone are not enough, for then they are mostly confined to being applied to isolated acts, isolated strikes, when the revolutionary period has already begun, and usually within the limits of a single town. . . . The element of spontaneity has played . . . a great role in all Russian mass strikes without exception, either as a driving force or as a restraining element. The reason for this is not that Social Democracy in Russia is still young and weak, but that in each particular act of the struggle so many incalculable factors are at work–economic, political, and social; general and local; material and psychic–that no such act can be defined and dealt with like an arithmetic problem. . . . In short, in the Russian mass strikes the spontaneous element has played such a predominant role not because the Russian proletariat is "unschooled", but because revolutions can't be school-mastered.[65]

However, if the mass strike is not an artificial product and cannot be decided upon at random, but has to be carried out as a historical necessity with all the impetuousness of mass spontaneity behind it, then it is quite useless to worry much beforehand about the provisioning and aiding of the strikers and the victims. History does not ask whether these prerequisites have been fulfilled or not:

> The moment a really serious mass-strike period begins, all such "costing estimates" become something like an attempt to empty out the ocean with a teacup. It is truly an ocean of terrible privations and sufferings, the price paid for every revolution by the proletarian masses. And the solution given by the revolutionary period for this seemingly insurmountable difficulty [of providing material support for the strikers] is to unleash such a tremendous amount of idealism among the masses, that they appear to be insensible to the most acute sufferings.[66]

Was it possible, then, that the debate on the mass strike with the resulting factionalism and violent clashes was of any more than academic significance, if the outbreak of the mass strike was so highly independent of the will of any organisations, if its course was determined by so many uncontrollable factors, and if the strike itself was the product of unconscious historical processes? According to Rosa Luxemburg, it was certainly absurd to decide beforehand to answer an attack on the general suffrage with a general strike, because it was quite impossible to foresee how the masses would react in such a case. She must have regarded the attempt to confine the mass strike to the role of a purely defensive weapon as a shrinking back from the real tasks facing the party. In her view, although the spontaneous decision of the masses was dependent on innumerable factors which could not be known beforehand, the party nevertheless could and should take responsibility for one essential factor: definite clarity on the character of the proletarian struggle in general and of the mass strike in particular, and the strengthening of the will to fight. The party had to ensure beforehand that it and the masses were aware of the probable, calculable consequences of such historical events, and to regulate in the long run its own activities accordingly:

> Social Democracy is the most enlightened and most class-conscious vanguard of the proletariat. It cannot and must not fold its arms and wait in a fatalistic manner for the onset of a "revolutionary situation", or wait for a spontaneous movement of the people to fall from heaven. On the contrary, it must now, as always, *hurry on ahead* of the development of things and seek to accelerate it. This it cannot do, however, by suddenly and haphazardly issuing the "signal" for a mass strike (it doesn't matter whether the time is right or not), but, above all, by making clear to the broadest proletarian strata the inevitable *onset* of this revolutionary period, the inherent *social factors (soziale Momente)* leading up to it, and the political consequences of it.[67]

In another passage:

> To give the struggle a watchword, a direction; to arrange the *tactics* of the political struggle in such a way that at every moment of the struggle the totality of the available, unleashed and active power of the proletariat can be applied and expressed in the militant attitude of the party, and that social-democratic tactics, in line with their resoluteness and incisiveness, never sink *below* the level of the actual relation of forces, but rather forge ahead of them—this is the most important task of the "leadership" in the period of mass strikes. And this leadership will automatically develop into the technical leadership of the struggle. Consistent, determined, and progressive social-democratic tactics evoke in the masses a feeling of security, self-confidence, and militancy; vacillating and weak

tactics, based on a low estimation of proletarian strength, cripples and confuses the masses. In the former situation mass strikes break out "spontaneously" (*von selbst*) and always "at the right time"; in the latter, even direct calls for a mass strike issued by the leadership sometimes prove a failure.[68]

Leaders without vocation

If it might have appeared before that Rosa Luxemburg assigned a very subordinate role to the leadership of the working class in a mass strike, after this discussion there was no doubt that she regarded its role as of great significance. In her view, the leadership should not go into action to prepare for the immediate technical needs of the struggle, but throughout the period which had just begun the character and the direction of the party policy in general would be decisive for the outbreak and the impact of the great struggles ahead. The leaders of German Social Democracy were worn out in the routine of everyday economic struggles and parliamentary skirmishing; could they prove equal to this task? Rosa Luxemburg had no illusions on this score. Particularly prominent among her adversaries in this discussion was that type of labour officialdom which she found most repugnant: people who combined intellectual complacency, narrow horizons, and a lack of élan with showy arrogance. These bureaucrats, who regarded themselves as the only competent experts and yet, by any historical standards, were beneath contempt, appeared in force at the Cologne Trade-Union Congress in 1905. At that time Rosa Luxemburg lashed out at their 'self-satisfied, beaming and self-assured narrow-mindedness which was a joy unto itself, intoxicated with itself, and considered itself far above all the experiences of the international working-class movement'[69]. In the year since then, this type of official had undoubtedly gained increasing influence on the fate of the German working-class movement, and had subjected the Party Executive to its control. When Rosa Luxemburg wrote her pamphlet on the mass strike, she felt the urge to send these obstinate opponents of an up-to-date revolutionary policy back where they belonged. She analysed the trade-union leader as a type, and even though she sharply reined in her animosity, it none the less burst out vehemently here and there.

In this discussion on the mass strike, however, she was above all concerned with clarifying precisely those questions which most interested the trade unions. Apart from their fear of revolution, the trade-union leaders had raised two objections: was a mass strike at all feasible so long as the great majority of the working class remained unorganised and therefore unable to guarantee that decisions would be carried out in a disciplined fashion? And wouldn't the trade-union organisations collapse under such a tremendous task? Rosa Luxemburg considered these questions to be yet another product of that schematic conception of the general strike as an action which was arbitrarily decided upon and directed according to cleverly worked out rules. If the almost perfect organisation of the working class were a prerequisite to any political strike, then it would be ridiculous even to contemplate such a strike at all; further, it would then follow that all such strikes in the past must have taken place without their basic prerequisites having been fulfilled.

At that time the German trade unions numbered about 1,500,000 members, about one-tenth of the whole working class. The great mass of unqualified and unskilled labourers were still hardly covered. Moreover, trade-union officials regarded the organisation of important categories of the working class—for instance, wage-labourers and salaried workers employed by the state, farm labourers, etc.—as being completely beyond the bounds of possibility. Rosa Luxemburg, however, believed that precisely these strata would provide the great militant body to spark off a mass strike. All the great experiments with this weapon had proved to be a powerful lever of mass organisation; in particular, the Russian Revolution had shown that the revolutionary ferment of a mass strike awakened just those millions of backward and previously inert strata to class consciousness and trade-union organisation. She had no doubt whatever that the revolutionary situation in Russia would have the same exciting effect in the large-scale capitalist countries of Western Europe. While the guardians of the German trade unions feared that their organisations would be smashed to bits like fragile and priceless porcelain in the revolutionary whirlwind, she was convinced that they would rise out of this whirlwind fresh, rejuvenated, and vigorous, stronger than ever before. In addition, a revolutionary period in Germany would alter even the character of the trade-union struggle, and would increase its potential to such an extent that the guerrilla skirmishing hitherto waged by the unions would appear child's play by comparison.

In her pamphlet, she attributed the narrow-minded and schematic ideas of the parliamentarians and the trade-unions leaders to their specialisation in particular, and to their often very difficult, everyday tasks, which blocked their view of the wider horizons of the struggle. Her efforts to provide them with some understanding of the dialectical conception of history and its broad perspectives ran into the same barrier; the trade-union leaders, in particular, regarded everything in her explanations which went beyond their own experiences as nothing but the outpourings of a revolutionary romanticism or of a wild hatred of the trade unions. Without bothering seriously to concern themselves with the problems raised, they fell on Rosa Luxemburg and her pamphlet with a tremendous hue and cry.

The pamphlet was first printed in a limited edition for the delegates to the Mannheim Party Congress. The author then yielded to pressure by the Party Executive and expunged certain particularly sharp phrases. The reformist and trade-union press now made exultant noises about Rosa's 'capitulation'. The matter is worth mentioning, because it gave Franz Mehring the opportunity to say publicly in *Neue Zeit* (July 1907) what Rosa Luxemburg as a theorist meant to the international working-class movement:

> Comrade Rosa Luxemburg displayed that very same "dignified objectivity" (*vornehme Sachlichkeit*) (which the reformists prided themselves on) by refraining from sharp words–despite all the bitter and unobjective attacks directed at her by a certain section of the trade-union press–when the chances of reaching an objective agreement seemed to increase. And for this she is now being scoffed at once again, not, as one might imagine, by the bourgeois press, which has a predilection for provoking her with its dull-witted drivelling, but by a segment of the social-democratic press. That is really not nice, and even less so because this tasteless knocking of the most brilliant intellect of all the scientific heirs of Marx and Engels can, in the last resort, only be rooted in the fact that it is a woman whose shoulders bear this intellect.

A theory of spontaneity

Particularly in her pamphlet on the mass strike, but also on many later occasions, Rosa Luxemburg stressed that revolutionary movements could not be 'fabricated' (*gemacht*); they did not come about as a result of a decision made by party officials, but broke out spontaneously and under certain historical conditions. Although this view has now been confirmed again and again by actual historical experience, it has not prevented a serious charge being made against Rosa in this respect. Her view has been distorted into a caricature of itself, and it has been claimed that Rosa Luxemburg created a theory of spontaneity, and fell victim to a mysticism, or even a mythology of spontaneity. Grigori Zinoviev* was the first to make this claim, obviously in order to enhance the authority of the Russian Communist Party in the Communist International. Others developed and repeated it so often that it has become a political-

---

* Comrade-in-arms of Lenin, and President of the Third (Communist) International. Executed in 1936 as an opponent of Stalin after a show-trial in Moscow.

historical axiom. In order to clarify the attitude of this great woman revolutionary towards revolutionary activity, it is necessary to examine these disagreeable attacks more closely.

The charge reads: the negation or at least the blameworthy depreciation of the role of the party's leading role in the class struggle; an uncritical worship of the masses; an overestimation of the impersonal and objective factors of development; a denial or underestimation of the importance of conscious and organised action; and, finally, an over-emphasis on the automatism and fatalism of the historical process. The conclusion then drawn from all this is that Rosa Luxemburg regarded the party as having no *raison d'être* at all.

Now such reproaches directed at a fighter like Rosa Luxemburg are really grotesque. She was filled with such a headstrong urge to act, and to incite others–both individuals and masses–to act, that the motto of her life was: 'In the beginning was the deed!' She could even feel sorrow about not being more vigorously active, like Ulrich von Hutten [the Protestant humanist, 1488-1523].

Mich reut, dass ich in meine Fehden trat

Mit schärf'ren Streichen nicht und kühn'rer Tat!

I regret that I didn't enter the lists

With sharper blows and bolder deeds!

And this is the woman who is supposed to have espoused the philosophy that history took its course, indifferent to the whole of humanity, and left men to resign themselves to fate! In one of those impressionistic letters revealing something of her inner being (her letter to Karl Kautsky, dated 13 July 1900), she remembered the depressing feeling that gripped her every time she looked at the Falls of the Rhine, and in a lightly malicious undertone directed against Kautsky himself she wrote:

Every time I . . . see that frightful spectacle, the splashing spray, the bleached whiteness of the watery cavern, and hear that deafening roar, it wrings my heart, and something in me says: there stands the enemy. Are you astonished? Of course, it is that enemy –human vanity–which fancies itself to be something else and then suddenly collapses into nothing. A similar effect, incidentally, is achieved by a world-picture which reduces all events, as Ben Akiba did, to: "it was always so", "it will get better by itself", etc., and which consequently represents man with his will, his ability, and his knowledge as superfluous. . . . For this reason I hate such a philosophy, *mon cher Charlemagne*, and shall stick to the idea that it would be better for people to have to plunge into the Falls of the Rhine and go under like a nut-shell than to nod wisely and let the waters go on rushing by, as they did in the time of our ancestors and will go on doing after our time.

So it is better to plunge into the Falls of the Rhine than to give up trying to control the course of history! Of course, even her critics could not overlook this headstrong will to act, and they occasionally had to admit: all right, but Rosa Luxemburg's political activity was in glaring contradiction to her theories. That is certainly an odd objection to make about a woman whose sharp mind guided and governed all her actions. She did commit one 'mistake', however. While writing, she did not think of those super-wise critics who would be correcting her ideas after her death, using dozens of quotations chiselled out of context to prove her 'theory of spontaneity'. She wrote for her own time and for a German working-class movement whose organisation had developed from a means to an end. Once, at a Party Congress, she commented that people could not know beforehand when a mass strike would break out. Robert Leinert [a well-known trade-unionist] called out that, of course, the Party Executive and the General Commission would know! But he was no more expressing a will to act than the others who spoke in a similar vein. They very much feared that the organisation would be jeopardised by any great struggle. Concealed behind their explanation—half excuse and half conviction—that the working class had to be completely organised before launching any political strike was the desire to avoid and prevent any such struggle. Rosa Luxemburg was aware of this, and she therefore put particular emphasis on the factor of spontaneity in all struggles of a revolutionary character, in order to prepare both the masses and their leaders for the events ahead. She should have been immune to misinterpretation because she was clear enough about what she meant by spontaneity. On one occasion, in order to fend off the idea of a general strike prepared by the party leadership, methodically carried out like any ordinary strike for higher wages, and deprived of all its stormy revolutionary character, she pointed to the example of the Belgian strikes of 1891 and 1893:

> The difference is that the mass strikes of the 1890s were spontaneous movements born of a revolutionary situation, of an intensification of the struggle, and of the extremely excited energy of the working masses. They were not spontaneous in the sense of being chaotic, aimless, unruly, or leaderless. On the contrary, in both these strikes the leadership was in complete agreement with the masses: it marched at their head and was in full command of the movement precisely because it felt close to the pulse-beat of the masses, adapted itself to them, and was nothing but their mouthpiece, the conscious expression of their feelings and strivings.[70]

Thus the spontaneity of such movements as Rosa Luxemburg defines it does not exclude conscious leadership but, on the contrary, demands it. And more than that! In her opinion, that spontaneity imputed to her and branded as fatalism by her critics does not simply fall from heaven. This we have already shown and could pile up quotations in support. In 1910, when the German workers began a movement to press for a reform of the Prussian franchise, she demanded that the Party Executive draw up a plan for the carrying out of further action, and she herself made suggestions. She condemned the policy of 'waiting for elementary events', and demanded that the action be continued as a powerful political offensive. During the World War she pointed out in her *Juniusbroschüre* how important parliament, as the one free tribune, could be for triggering off mass actions if people like Liebknecht mastered its use in a systematic and determined way. And her hope in the masses did not obscure for her the importance of the role and task of the party. In 1913, when she was attacking the 'attrition strategy' advocated by Kautsky, she wrote:

> Leaders who hang back will certainly be pushed aside by the storming masses. However, just to sit back and wait calmly for this gratifying result as a sure indication that "the time is ripe" may be all right for a lonely philosopher, but for the political leadership of a revolutionary party it would be a sign of poverty, of moral bankruptcy. The task of Social Democracy and its leaders is not to be dragged along by events, but to be consciously ahead of them, to have an overall view of the trend of events, to shorten the period of development by conscious action, and to accelerate its progress.[71]

Rosa Luxemburg certainly underestimated the retarding influence which an organisation can exercise on the masses if its leaders are opposed to the struggle, and perhaps she overestimated the elementary activity of the masses, expecting it earlier than it actually occurred. She did those things which mattered to her in order to spur on the German social-democratic leadership. And the overestimation of the masses is the unavoidable 'mistake' of every real revolutionary; it springs from a passionate desire to surge ahead and from the deep recognition that great historical upheavals have to be achieved by the masses. But her faith in the masses was not at all mystical. She knew their weaknesses and had ample opportunity to observe their vices in periods of counter-revolutionary activity. Her feelings about the masses are made clear in a letter she wrote to Mathilde Wurm from prison on 16 February 1917, after having been tormented for over two years by the idea that the masses had failed to rise to the historic occasion:

> Your whole argument against my motto: "Here I stand—I can do no other" amounts to saying: that's all very fine and good, but people are too cowardly or too weak for such heroism; *ergo* we must adapt our tactics to their weaknesses according to the principle: *chi va piano, va sano* (slowly but surely). What a narrow view of

history, my dear lambkin! There is nothing more changeable than human psychology. Especially since the psyche of the masses always harbours—like Thalatta, the eternal sea—all sorts of latent possibilities: deathly calm and raging storm, the basest cowardliness and the wildest heroism. The masses are always what they *must* be, what the given historical conditions make of them, and they are always on the brink of becoming something totally different from what they seem to be. It's a fine ship's captain, indeed, who would steer a course according to the momentary appearance of the water's surface and wouldn't know how to deduce from the signs in the sky and on the sea whether or not a storm was brewing! My dear little girl, "disappointment in the masses" is always the most disgraceful attitude a political leader could have. A truly great leader adjusts his tactic not in accordance with the momentary mood of the masses, but in accordance with the iron laws of historical development. He sticks to his tactic despite all disappointments and, for the rest, allows history to bring its work to maturity.

There is not an iota of truth in the allegation that Rosa Luxemburg espoused a mythology of spontaneity. This theory itself is a myth, fabricated for particular political purposes and used by narrow-minded petty officials who are yes-men to those above them, and at the same time believe that they can command and bully a party with impunity.

Well-meaning people have often been misled in this matter by an inability to recognise the dialectical character of historical necessity. Certainly Rosa Luxemburg did believe in the existence of 'iron laws of historical development', but for her the executors of these laws were human beings, the masses in all their millions, their organisations and their leaders, with all their strengths and weaknesses, their actions and their failures. Depending on the activity of these masses and their organisations (the state, the party, etc.), these laws fulfil themselves more or less rapidly, directly or indirectly. And even if the course of history should hit rock bottom, before scaling the heights it will always create anew the conditions which will ensure its development according to these laws. For Rosa Luxemburg the next great turning-point in history would be the overthrow of capitalism, a historical necessity which the working class had to seize upon as their conscious aim and bring about. She had all the impetuous temperament of a Harry Hotspur, but she subjected it to the discipline of her knowledge so that she could effectively summon up the patience to let things and human beings ripen for the decisive deeds ahead.

It was not long before she recognised that the international upswing given to working-class movements by the Russian Revolution of 1905 had exhausted itself. An even though the debate on the mass strike continued, she took hardly any part in it. Purely academic discussions on tactical questions were not to her taste. Only when the masses again came into movement did she again intervene in the debate–in order to rouse people to action.

8
Concerning
the end of capitalism

The party school

In 1906 the SPD set up a party school in Berlin. Every winter up to the outbreak of the World War about thirty comrades and trade-union members, chosen by their district organisations, took courses in the social sciences and in the practical work of agitation. The school was an expression of the organisational strength of the working-class movement and an outgrowth of the need to ensure a supply of qualified editors, agitators, and other officials for the movement. Among the teachers were Franz Mehring, Rudolf Hilferding, Hermann Duncker, Arthur Stadthagen, Emmanuel Wurm, Gustav Eckstein, and Hugo Heinemann, most of them supporters of the radical wing of the party.

Although it appears that Rosa Luxemburg was included on the teaching staff from the outset, she did not, however, participate in the first set of courses, perhaps because she refused to do so for reasons of her own, or because the trade unions objected to her. But the Prussian police forced a change in the teaching staff: they threatened Hilferding, who was an Austrian, with expulsion if he continued his teaching activities, and he therefore withdrew. At Kautsky's suggestion, Rosa Luxemburg was engaged from 1907 onwards to fill the gap, and was assigned the course on economics, an introduction to the economic teachings of Karl Marx.

She proved an outstanding teacher. And not only because she had an absolute mastery of her material: she possessed very considerable natural teaching talent as well. She already owed some of her success as a writer and a speaker to this talent, but now she had a chance to develop it fully. Hers was not an easy task. Marx's *Capital*, which formed the basis of the course, is no popular text-book; a correct understanding of its teachings presupposes a thorough grounding in the economic and social sciences. The pupils, however, were thrown together from a colourful variety of backgrounds: next to raw youngsters who had only a smattering of socialism, but had distinguished themselves in one way or another in their work for the party, there were old and experienced party workers. They represented a very wide variety of occupations: mechanics, carpenters, decorators, miners, party secretaries, trade-unionists, housewives, intellectuals. Most of them had derived their knowledge of socialism only from agitational pamphlets, and were not used to systematic thought. From the first lesson Rosa Luxemburg was able to establish close contact with her pupils. She never lectured at them and promised no ready-made answers, compelling them to work out their own ideas and conclusions.

She began the course by dealing with the various economic systems, their characteristic features, their transformations and the causes thereof. In this connection the most important economic theories before and after Marx were examined. Finally, after long weeks spent in working out a total picture of the actual development of the relationships of production and exchange, and of their reflection in the bourgeois social sciences, the class worked its way through Marxist teachings, using *Capital* as the basic text. Throughout the course Rosa Luxemburg limited the material which she delivered in her lectures to the most necessary facts and concepts. She knew how to get her pupils to use their own minds and imaginations, and, by raising ever new objections and questions, she subjected their knowledge and ideas to a thorough testing until they were able to form a picture of life as it really was. Thus, above all, the actual development of their thinking processes was up to the pupils themselves. And she did not concern herself only with gifted students: she always held everyone under her spell. And if a daydreamer ever managed to evade it, she woke him up without fail by asking a well-aimed question, and helped him get over his embarrassment by making a spirited remark, thereby re-establishing her rapport with the class. In this manner she created an atmosphere charged with tension, in which all the pupils could develop their intellectual capacities, and a spirit of enthusiastic creativity and mutual emulation. All the while that she was apparently going along with the ideas of her pupils and compelling them to come to grips with these ideas down to their last particulars, she was in fact imperceptibly guiding their efforts to the desired aim. After such intellectual gymnastics, the pupils themselves were astonished by their new insights and their clear and accurate grasp of ideas which had not been handed to them from outside like alien dogmas, but which were their self-acquired intellectual property.

Rosa Luxemburg's great skill in handling people stood her in good stead in these classes. Naturally as an intellectual personality, she greatly excelled her pupils in knowledge and in the power of her thought, but when she worked together with them, these qualities receded so far into the background that no one felt oppressed by them–that is, until the hour was over and the spell broken. Only then, in mulling over the lesson, did her pupils feel overwhelmed by the impact of her superiority. She instilled in them a contempt for scientific dilettantism and cowardly thought, and compelled them to show respect and enthusiasm for scientific achievement. Their work with her brought Rosa Luxemburg's pupils not only an intellectual gain but a moral awakening. Some of them had certainly come to the party school filled with prejudices and with the determination not to let her turn them into heretics like herself. Needless to say, she won all of them over, and even those who later became her opponents in the working-class movement never failed to show their gratitude to her or their respect for her. In this way she conquered people and inspired them with the wealth of Marxist ideas and the will to fight for the realisation of these ideas.

Introduction to Economics

Out of her teaching activities at the party school came two important works: the *Introduction to Economics* and *The Accumulation of Capital*. Unfortunately we have the first of these only in fragmentary form. From a letter written by Rosa Luxemburg on 28 July 1916, from the women's military prison (*Barnimstrasse*) in Berlin to the party publisher, I H W Dietz, we know the general plan of the whole work, which was to have included the following chapters:

1   What is Economics?
2   Social Labour (*Die gesellschaftliche Arbeit*).
3   Economic-Historical Perspectives: Primitive Communist Society.
4   Economic-Historical Perspectives: Feudal Economic System.
5   Economic-Historical Perspectives: The Mediæval Town and the Craft Guild.
6   Commodity Production.
7   Wage-Labour.
8   The Profit of Capital.
9   The Crisis.
10 The Tendencies of Capitalist Development.

In the summer of 1916 the first two chapters were ready for printing, and all the other chapters already in draft. However, only chapters 1, 3, 6, 7, and 10 could be found among her literary remains. These were published in 1925 by Paul Levi, unfortunately with many errors, arbitrary alterations, and the omission of important notes. If we had the whole book today, we would have all the material she dealt with in her courses at the party school. From the torso which remains we can see that the work is the product of long fermentation and repeated distillation, a process which Rosa Luxemburg, through her day-to-day contact with her pupils, came to recognise all the difficulties which others might encounter in trying to understand the material, and succeeded in overcoming them. The result is a crystal-clear presentation of economic development and its problems. The language is that of the people, but it is not that popularising style which avoids difficulties by flattening and simplifying the problems, but a straightforward simplicity as is found only in the writings of someone who has a lively view and a complete intellectual mastery of things. It is this down-to-earth language which leads the reader easily from one stage of knowledge to the next, and fascinates even those who are familiar with the subject, revealing to them new and unexpected perspectives, and offering new solutions.

From the torso and the themes of the missing chapters it is clear that the book was to have been a condensed presentation of all the economic teachings of Karl Marx. But Rosa Luxemburg did not follow the earlier popularisers of Marx; she did not even cling to his methods of presentation, which were derived from the elementary economic categories. She sketched the great stages of the economic and social history of mankind, and intertwined all this with a criticism of the social theories which have been the intellectual reflection of this history. And she proceeded to do all this trenchantly. At the party school she had sought to find the solution of problems by thoroughly thrashing out, together with her pupils, their wrong or partially correct answers until the truth became visible; in the book she adopted much the same method, but here it was the errors, stupidities, and small-minded sophistries of the great luminaries of economic thought which provided her with working material. They offered her yet another welcome occasion to give the old fogies a really hard drubbing. With the same pleasure which Lassalle once had in attacking Julian Schmidt, she flayed the old revered authorities and unmasked their seemingly profound revelations as hollow rhetoric. Behind the scientific inadequacies of her opponents she sensed the moral weakness of the class enemy, and took a joy in trouncing them.

However, the sharp blows she dealt the orthodox economists are not mere arabesques designed to make her presentation more vivid, or even polemical excesses. On the contrary, they are closely connected with the subject-matter. In the first place, they are supposed to show precisely how the orthodox authorities on the social sciences are influenced and hindered in their judgments by the historical interests of their class; but, in addition, they are supposed to prove that economics has always been a weapon in the class struggle. Rosa Luxemburg demonstrates how necessary economics as a science became when the anarchistic mode of production in capitalist society obscured actual economic relations or, thanks to competition and the monetary system, showed them as in a distorting mirror. She proves further that this science originated as a weapon of the bourgeoisie against feudalism, and that as such it made bold achievements; but that with the rise of the labour movement it developed into a purblind defender of the existing order, and its exponents gradually liquidated its most decisive intellectual gains until they themselves—as far as they still strove to arrive at theoretical conclusions at all—sought refuge in a kind of economic mysticism or even pseudo-scientific tomfoolery (of which Sombart is a prototype). And, finally, while she shows that Marx's *Critique of Political Economy* represents a weapon in the hands of the proletariat in the class struggle, she also points out that a 'planned economic order, consciously organised and directed by the whole labouring population' will no longer need economics as a science.

The reader learns about the origin, development, function, and final dissolution of all economic and social orders, beginning with primitive communism and going on to modern capitalism, whose internal mechanics are laid bare and whose downfall, as a result of its own inherent contradictions, is seen as inevitable. Thus, together with a history and an analysis of theoretical economic problems, she also gives a historical survey of bourgeois and socialist theories about society illuminated from the historical-materialist standpoint.[72]

The Accumulation of Capital

Rosa Luxemburg worked on her *Introduction to Economics* for several years. Her teaching activity at the party school, her work of agitation on behalf of German Social Democracy, the tactical debates with her opponents in the party, and a tremendous amount of work for the Polish and Russian movements postponed the conclusion of the book again and again. At the beginning of 1912, when she attempted to conclude the work, at least in outline form, she stumbled on an unexpected difficulty:

> I could not succeed in depicting the total process of capitalist production in all its practical relations as well as its objective historical limitations with sufficient clarity. On closer examination I came to the view that this was not merely a question of depiction, but also that a problem was posed which is connected with the theoretical contents of Vol II of Marx's *Capital* and which, at the same time,

impinges on the practice of present-day imperialist politics and its economic roots.

And, as she explained in the Foreword, this was how she came to write *The Accumulation of Capital*.[73]

To be understood properly, the theoretical problem which she stumbled on demands a very exact knowledge of Marxist theory and cannot be explained in brief terms. All that can be attempted here is to give a general idea of it. In this respect, the times which we are now living in will facilitate our understanding. In 1929 the world economy was shaken by a deep crisis unparalleled in the history of capitalism. It broke out just after the destruction caused by the World War had been made good, the broken threads of the world market had been tied together, and a short, but powerful period of prosperity had awakened new optimism. However, even this boom period from 1924-28 had disturbing features which marked it off from pre-war boom periods. Above all, in the most important capitalist countries (USA, Great Britain, Germany, etc.), unemployment was many times greater at the height of the boom than it had been at the lowest point of any pre-war crisis period, and the productive capacity of the industrial plants was no longer being fully utilised. The crisis which began in 1929 lasted as many years as a crisis formerly lasted months. It led to unemployment figures ten to twenty times greater than pre-war figures, and closed down whole areas of production. Overproduction reached such monstrous proportions that starvation in the midst of plenty became a cliché, and the devaluation of products and capital, enormous though it was, no longer proved sufficient (as it had in previous crises) to clear the way for a new economic upswing, so that the authorities had to resort to the desperate measure of destroying vast quantities of commodities. After the crisis had ravaged the world economy for years, production did begin to increase for a short time, but this did not affect the whole world economy. Moreover, the most important cause of this recovery was the fantastic rearmament programme of the fascist states. Meanwhile countries were pursuing policies which were increasingly isolationist and protectionist in character, and were launching increasingly oppressive wars of conquest. A new world war was threatening to become a fatal inevitability.

The question arises: how does such a catastrophic development occur? Is it accidental? Is it the fault of capitalists or governments, individual or collective, who could have avoided it? Or is an inherent law in the mechanics of capitalism at work here?

Along with many other Marxists, Rosa Luxemburg was convinced that wars develop from the essential character of the capitalist social order. Beyond that, she concluded that the same causes which bring about modern warfare also destroy the conditions essential to the continued existence of the capitalist economic system. And she predicted that the final collapse of capitalism would come about in just such economic and political crises as we have been witnessing. But she did not succeed in uncovering such an inherent historical law in her *Introduction to Economics* on the basis of Marx's *Capital*. Was her conviction erroneous, or were Marx's teachings inadequate? That was the question, and it was of tremendous importance, for Rosa's total view of things hang on the answer. All her political activity was based on scientific knowledge: deeply rooted in her was the idea that socialism could become a reality only if it was possible to prove scientifically that capitalism would be destroyed by its own immanent contradictions.

The difficulty arose with the problem of whether the capitalist economic system (which surpassed all other economic systems in its tremendous dynamic of growth and expansion) could develop without hindrance. Economic science does not dispute the fact that this possibility of continuous development is an essential condition for capitalism. In earlier economic systems production took place for direct use, and the things produced were consumed by master and slave. Bad harvests, wars, and epidemics could sometimes cause catastrophes. However, crises arising out of the immanent laws of the economic order – crises of overproduction, widespread starvation in the midst of plenty, mass destruction of useful commodities in an effort to re-establish 'normal' production conditions by force – were quite unknown. The capitalist economic system must satisfy social needs in some way or other, but that is not the driving force of capitalist production. The motivation is profit. Profit arises out of surplus labour, i.e. out of that quantity of labour-power expended by the worker over and above the quantity necessary to satisfy his own essential needs. However, profit is embodied in the commodities produced, and it can be 'realised' only when the capitalist finds enough purchasers for them. The capitalist who has the best chance of selling his commodities, and thus of realising his profit, is the one who can produce most cheaply. The resulting competition compels the individual capitalist to improve and perfect his means of production; if he falls back in the race, he is lost. Every new technical advance brings about an increase in the productive forces and the masses of commodities produced, but at the same time the number of workers employed declines, relatively at least, and consequently the number of paying customers as well. The more powerful the productive forces become, the more 'hands' are rendered superfluous. The unavoidable result is a steadily growing army of unemployed workers, whose existence in turn tends to depress wages, thereby limiting market capacity still further. Thanks to the whip of competition, the capitalist economic system is compelled to produce more and more. The result is inevitably the occurrence of periodic crises during which those productive methods which have proved no longer able to meet competitive demands are weeded out and great capital values destroyed. Once this has happened, the process begins all over again, but this time with an even more striking disproportion between the productive forces and the amount of labour-power required to supply them, so that the risks are greater.

This was the way Marx depicted the course of capitalist economic development. Moreover, despite fluctuations, the reserve army of unemployed was to become greater and greater, wages were to be forced down in the end to a bare subsistence level, and crises were to follow one another with increasing rapidity and increasing devastation. However, these theoretical conclusions seemed to contradict reality. From the 1860s onwards, wages of European workers rose steadily, and the reserve army of unemployed became smaller. The crises, the apoplectic fits which were to signal the approaching end of capitalism, became weaker and weaker, and capitalist prosperity seemed to be more and more on the increase. In an effort to find a way out of this contradiction, many of Marx's followers began to give to some of his words a meaning which they obviously did not have. This was particularly the case with his statements concerning the progressive impoverishment of the working class, the intensification of social contradictions, and the approaching collapse of the capitalist economy. In the face of these new interpretations, Rosa held fast to Marx's theories. Countering Bernstein, she declared that the crises Marx had in mind would set in at a later stage of capitalist development, and that its present unchecked rise was only a passing phase–even if it had already lasted over half a century. She was convinced that capitalist development would sooner or later come up against insuperable barriers and dash itself to pieces against them.

And then, in Vol II of Marx's *Capital*, she found a passage which, if its reasoning was sound, would overturn her whole conception. It related to the possibility of a progressive accumulation of capital, a limitless expansion of production. At first glance the process of accumulating capital appears to be a very simple matter. The capitalist uses that part of his realisable surplus-value which he does not consume himself to purchase machinery, raw materials, and additional labour-power; thus new capital is invested in the economic system. However, if the capitalist economic system is regarded as a whole, the seemingly simple process of accumulation becomes a complicated one, far beyond the control of the individual capitalist. In any particular phase of production, a great variety of commodities must be turned out to meet the consumer requirements of the population, to renew worn-out means of production, and to make new investments. At the same time these various kinds of commodities must stand in a certain relation to one another with respect to their value, and they must find paying customers. Thus, the producers of machinery, raw materials, etc. must turn out commodities according to their own requirements and those of the producers of consumer goods in each new period of production. In the meantime the producers of consumer goods must have succeeded in selling their own commodities if they are to pay for the means of production and for the labour-power they want to use in the new phase of production. In the planless, anarchical capitalist order of society these relations and many other equally necessary ones are determined by the influx of new capital into certain industries, or by falling prices, capital depreciation, bankruptcy, crises, and other such factors.

Now Marx illustrated these often conflicting relations of value in which the expansion of capitalist production and the accumulation of capital take place by means of a very ingeniously constructed model. He proceeded, as he invariably did in all of his economic investigations, from the assumed existence of a society producing in an exclusively capitalist fashion, having no vestiges of pre-capitalist economic factors to complicate its workings, and consisting exclusively of capitalists (and their hangers-on living on surplus-value) and workers. According to his model, each commodity finds its purchaser, and the process of accumulation proceeds in this purely capitalist medium without any restraints or limits, as if in obedience to an economic law of perpetual motion. However, the model made Marx's prophecy of steadily intensifying crises in capitalist society incomprehensible. The view, first argued by Bernstein, that the trusts could overcome the crises by regulating production seemed justified. Since 1815 the great economists have violently debated whether a limitless development of capitalism is possible, whether, above all, it will always be possible to find paying customers for the steadily and enormously increasing volume of commodities. In the last clash on this question of capitalist development, just before Rosa Luxemburg came on the scene, the optimists seemed to have won a full victory—on the basis of Marx's model. The point at issue in this last dispute was whether capitalism in Russia was an unavoidable and viable stage of development or not.

Marx's model also turned out to be a stumbling block for Rosa Luxemburg when she wished to prove the inevitability of capitalist collapse. Up to then, all the theorists had accepted the model without really examining it. However, Rosa discovered the following: first of all, that Marx had not concluded his investigation of the problem of accumulation, but had broken off in the middle, and, secondly, that in his model he had failed to take an essential condition into account. He assumed that the value of labour-power—i.e. the sum of wages—would increase in the same proportion as the value of the means of production. However, the process of expanding production, of course, does not proceed in such a way that every new phase of production requires new equipment, machinery, etc., of the same type as the old which it replaces; it may be that it requires improved machinery, more advanced techniques, and more thorough rationalisation. The result is, as we have seen, that the value of the means of production increases progressively at a more rapid rate than the value of the labour-power employed. In his model Marx had failed to take into consideration this steady shifting of the relations of value. Once this factor is included, then the producers of consumer goods are faced with a difficult dilemma: either they must progressively abandon the accumulation of their realised surplus-value, and consume it themselves except for a steadily shrinking part—a procedure which would invert the whole sense of the capitalist mode of production since it would halt the expansion of production and thus cause the economy to stagnate—or they must accept the fact that a growing proportion of the consumer goods they produce will not be able to find paying buyers. Steadily growing quantities of unsaleable consumer goods together with a steadily growing reserve army of unemployed—such a combination, increasingly intensified, would prove to be the cause of capitalist economic crises.

Up to the First World War the capitalists found a way out of the dilemma created by the contradiction between growing productive forces and relatively shrinking purchasing power by marketing increasingly enormous quantities of commodities among those social strata which did not use capitalist modes of production (peasants, urban craftsmen), or in areas where the mode of production was backward (colonies). But the more vigorously capitalism made inroads into this 'non-capitalist space', the more it kindled the process of accumulation. All this explains the existence of certain social phenomena which could not be reconciled with Marx's theories, especially the temporary abatement of crises and the shrinking of the industrial reserve army.

Rosa Luxemburg discovered the solution of the problem of accumulation in this capitalist penetration into non-capitalist areas. She proved that capitalism could not exist at all unless this possibility of expansion were available. At the same time and despite the model described above, she could still fall back on Marx. It is true that in *Capital*, which examined all questions concerning the mechanics of capitalism, he had postulated the existence of a purely capitalist society in order to work out the laws of capitalist production under the purest possible conditions, just as the law of falling bodies can only be demonstrated in a vacuum. However, he also stressed the fact that a capitalist thrust into non-capitalist areas was one of the most effective means of overcoming economic crises, and that capitalism would inevitably perish when there was no longer any possibility of extending the capitalist market.

Rosa Luxemburg linked this idea to the problem of capitalist accumulation, and this is the great achievement of her chief work. It is true that in her argument she made a number of errors which were uncovered after her death by Bukharin.[74] He did not disprove her main thesis, however, although he thought he did. Fritz Sternberg then rectified her theory of accumulation in one or two points and successfully applied it to other economic questions.[75] It is his ideas which we have followed in our general sketch of the problem.

Imperialism and the theory of capital accumulation

Rosa Luxemburg did not content herself with investigating the theoretical problem of accumulation. Undoubtedly she was helped to a solution of the problem by her studies of primitive communist societies, their decline, and–the point at issue here–their barbaric destruction by the invasion of European 'civilisation'. In her *Introduction to Economics* she had already described this process, taking as her examples the Inca empire, India, and the old Russian *obshchina* (village commune). She now took up the theme again from the viewpoint of the capitalist incursion into non-capitalist economies. She divided this process into three phases: the struggle of capital against the natural economy (primitive self-sufficient society), which begins with the origin of capital under feudalism and soon pushes out beyond the limits of the immediate geographical area; the struggle against the simple commodity-producing economy; and, finally, the competitive struggle of capital on the world-stage for the remaining conditions of accumulation (i.e. for the remaining markets).

With burning hatred she sketches the struggle against the natural economy, and those who wage this struggle–those self-ordained 'bearers of culture' who, rapacious, thirsty for power, and convinced of the values of their civilisation and culture, trample on other peoples, wipe out old cultures and destroy their products on which the lives of millions of people depend, spread famine and mass death, and sweep away whole peoples from the face of the earth. All these things they do without misgivings, flagrantly, hypocritically, and brutally, in order to prepare the ground on which the capitalist seed can thrive.

She describes this cruel and bloody process, taking India and

Algeria as examples. She shows the conquest of markets by 'peaceful trade', taking the example of China from the Opium War to the international campaign against the Boxers. Using the history of the USA, Canada, and South Africa, she exposes how the native red men and black men were deprived of land, freedom, and life; how the natural (primitive) economy was squeezed out by the simple commodity-producing economy; and, finally, how capital moved in and drove the native farmers from one area to the next. There was hardly a crime listed in the penal code, including slave-raiding, head-hunting, and massacre, which was not committed in these economic upheavals for the sake of realising surplus-value. 'The ruin of the independent handicrafts by capitalist competition is a chapter in itself, less noisy perhaps, but no less agonising.' And she draws the following general conclusion:

> The general result of the struggle between capitalism and the simple commodity-producing economy is this: capital takes the place of the simple commodity-producing economy after having replaced the natural economy with the commodity-producing economy. Thus, if it is so that capitalism lives from non-capitalist structures, then it is more accurate to say that it lives from their ruin; and if it is so that it unconditionally needs these non-capitalist areas for capital accumulation then it actually needs them as culture media which it can feed on and suck up in order to carry out this accumulation. Viewed historically, capital accumulation is a metabolic process going on between capitalist and pre-capitalist modes of production. . . . Accordingly, capital accumulation can no more exist without these non-capitalist structures than the latter can continue to exist alongside it. . . .
>
> Thus the assumption Marx made in his model of accumulation is in accordance only with the objective historical tendency of the process of accumulation and its theoretical result. . . . But here we reach a dead-end. Once the final result is reached—which, however, remains merely a theoretical construction—accumulation becomes impossible: the realisation and capitalisation of surplus-value turns into an impossible task. As soon as the Marxist model of extended reproduction corresponds to reality, the outcome—the historical limits of the accumulation process, the end of the capitalist mode of production—is in sight.[76]

As the capitalist incursion proceeds further and further into non-capitalist areas, it is pushed to resort to ever more efficient methods. Such a thrust not only aids in finding a market for commodities which would be unsaleable within the ordinary framework of capitalist production, thereby fully realising surplus-value, but at the same time it stimulates the accumulation process, thereby increasing the productive forces and reproducing on an ever larger scale the fundamental contradictions all over again. Capitalism can

therefore not wait until new markets have been won for its commodities through the traditional methods of deception, fire and
sword. It begins to export capital alongside of its commodities, and
to transplant the most modern capitalist production to countries
which are still deep in the stage of natural economy. In this way,
however, it also creates new competitors for itself, despite its obstinate efforts to prevent by political means the rise of any industry
in the colonial countries. The space available for expansion becomes
more and more limited. Previously the capitalist robbers hunted side
by side, but now they begin to squabble among themselves for the
remaining non-capitalist space which has not yet been confiscated
and for its redivision. This is the age of imperialism.

> Imperialism is just as much a historical method of prolonging the
> life of capitalism as it is the surest and quickest means of objective-
> ly limiting it. This does not mean, of course, that this final point
> will be reached inevitably and methodically. However, the tend-
> ency towards this final point of capitalist development is already
> taking forms which indicate that the final phase of capitalism will
> be a period of catastrophes.[77]

And she summed up her ideas once again in the concluding paragraph:

> Capitalism is the first economic system with the power of propa-
> ganda, a system which has the tendency to spread out all over the
> globe and to crowd out all other economic systems. However, it is
> also the first such system which could not exist alone, without other
> economic systems to provide an environment and fertile soil for it.
> Thus, at the same time that it is developing into a universal system,
> it is being smashed because of its inherent inability to be a univer-
> sal system of production. It is a living historical contradiction in
> itself; its process of accumulation is an expression of the continuous
> solution and, at the same time, aggravation of the contradiction. At
> a certain peak of development this contradiction cannot be solved
> except by applying the principles of socialism–that economic system
> which is universal and harmonious by its very nature, because it
> does not aim at accumulation, but at satisfying the vital needs of
> toiling humanity itself through developing all the productive forces
> of the globe.[78]

The epigoni attack

The Accumulation of Capital was a great achievement: Rosa
Luxemburg had solved a problem with which economists had
wrestled for a full century, ever since the first great economic crisis
in 1815; a problem which had withstood even the intellectual
powers of Marx. The view of history which inspired her and gave

her confidence in her own theoretical and political judgment had been confirmed: socialism had to come not merely because it was the ideal of ever larger masses of people, but because capitalism itself was heading towards its final destruction. At the same time imperialism had been recognised as a historically necessary phenomenon, and with this the way had been barred, at least theoretically, to the illusions and subterfuges in which even prominent Marxists were then indulging, and had been cleared for an understanding of the tremendous convulsions which lay ahead. Her achievement was all the more remarkable because she had not been deterred either by the great prosperity of the capitalist economy in those years, prosperity due precisely to the tremendous capitalist incursion into non-capitalist areas, or by the seeming imminence of a peaceful solution of the most important imperialist controversies among the great powers. Five years later, on 12 May 1917, in a letter written to her friend Hans Diefenbach from prison in Wronke, she described the creative enthusiasm with which she had conceived and composed her masterpiece:

> The period while I was writing *Accumulation* belongs to the happiest in my life. I lived really as if in a state of intoxication, day and night seeing nothing but this one problem that was unfolding itself so beautifully in front of me, and I don't know which afforded me greater pleasure: the thinking process, whereby I pondered a complicated question while walking slowly up and down the room . . . or the shaping of results into literary form on paper. Do you know that I wrote the entire 30 galleys in one go within four months—something unheard-of!—and that I sent off the rough draft to the printer without even once reading it over?

Despite the brilliant literary form of the book, its purely theoretical chapters make very great demands on the reader, and assume a mastery of economics in general and of Marxist economics in particular. Rosa Luxemburg knew that she had written only for a very small elite and that the work 'from this standpoint was a luxury and might just as well have been printed on the finest hand-made paper'. However, she could hardly have expected the response which the book evoked in her own circles. The only authorities on Marxist theory who recognised its value were Franz Mehring and Julian Marchlewski, and they did so with great enthusiasm. But a whole horde of people, competent and incompetent alike, heaped harsh words on *The Accumulation of Capital*, criticism which sometimes degenerated into just a crude tearing-apart of the book.

The science of economics itself, in any case, was to a great extent ignored by the critics. Most of them declared quite frankly that the problem which had caused Rosa Luxemburg so much trouble did not exist at all. Of course, they pointed to Marx's model as mathematically impeccable evidence that the process of accumulation could proceed on its merry way under purely capitalist conditions. They did not take any notice of her proof that Marx's model was inadequate given the economic assumptions of his whole analysis of capitalism. It was not long, however, before the critics got entangled in the most vehement contradictions among themselves in crucial points, thereby demonstrating at least that the problem was not as fully solved as they claimed.

Moreover, those critics who made any serious attempt on their own to present the dynamic of the accumulation process fell victim to the grossest errors. Otto Bauer, who made the most serious effort to come to grips with the problem, declared that the natural increase in the population was the basis for the smooth continuation of the accumulation process—an idea Marx himself had already rejected with scorn. But when Bauer went on to extend the Marxist model in order to adapt it to the real and essential conditions of the capitalist system of economic competition, he discovered that it was indeed impossible for capitalists to realise the whole of their surplus-value within the framework of a purely capitalist society. He thus confirmed Luxemburg's theory. But only up to a point, for he tried to solve the problem by simply transferring the unrealisable commodity surplus in the consumer-goods sector to the production-goods sector. To this Rosa Luxemburg replied laconically: 'One can't purchase copper-mine shares with a lot of unsaleable tallow candles or found a new engineering-works with a stock of unmarketable galoshes.' At the critical point Bauer had overlooked the fact that the accumulation process did not only involve values but also tangible objects belonging to definite categories, both of which had to be properly arranged.

In 1915, when Rosa Luxemburg was condemned to involuntary leisure in the women's prison in *Barnimstrasse* in Berlin, she spent her time in a thorough analysis of the arguments of her critics in a work of great acumen and considerable humour, though with occasional acrimony as well. It was entitled *Die Akkumulation des Kapitals oder was die Epigonen aus der Marxschen Theorie gemacht haben. Eine Antikritik* (The Accumulation of Capital or What the Epigoni Have Done with Marxist Theory. An Anti-critique), and of the altar erected by her critics for the sacrifice of her theories, not one stone remained on top of another. At the same time she used this *Anti-critique* to present her own view of the whole problem again, but in a more popular form, so as to appeal to a wider circle of readers. The work is a masterpiece of scientific investigation and presentation of a problem, and her own verdict on it is just: 'The form has been made very simple, without any accessories, without any coquetry or dazzle; it is plain; everything is reduced to broad outline; "naked", I would like to say, like a block of marble.'

After Rosa's death Bukharin published a criticism of her theory of accumulation. As we have already mentioned, he succeeded in fact in uncovering several weaknesses in her presentation. In various places in her book she made the obviously wrong claim that capital accumulation was the amassing of money capital; this was what mattered to the capitalists. In reality, the building up of money capital is only a link in the accumulation process. The conclusion of every accumulation period is marked by the investment of capital in the productive process itself in the form of new means of production and of wages for additional labour-power. Perhaps this mistake–it is difficult to understand how Rosa made it–led her to overrate the mediating role of money in the process of realising surplus-value and, further, to believe in the complete impossibility of directly exchanging the values to be accumulated between the producers of production-goods and those of consumer-goods. Bukharin was right in criticising this. However, he rejected Rosa Luxemburg's whole theory too hastily. A more careful re-examination of the assumptions underlying the accumulation process shows that a part of the surplus-value to be accumulated in the consumer-goods sector cannot be realised within the framework of a purely capitalist society. And this part grows as the methods of production improve, as the utilisation of means of production increases at a rate consistently higher than the rate at which new labour-power is expended–an essential feature of capitalist accumulation.

Bukharin believed that he had refuted Luxemburg's whole theory. However, his own solution turned out to be an indirect confirmation of her crucial thesis. In his attempt to present the process of capital accumulation in a purely capitalist society, he assumed the existence of 'state capitalism' producing according to plan, and concluded:

> In the event of a "miscalculation" with regard to consumer goods for workers, this surplus could be distributed to the workers as "overfeed", or it could be destroyed altogether. In the case of a miscalculation in the production of luxury articles, too, the "way out" is clear. Thus no crisis of overproduction could possibly arise here.

Bukharin's solution is astonishing. We are presented here with a 'capitalism' which is not economic anarchy, but a planned economy in which there is no competition, but rather a general world trust, and in which capitalists do not have to bother about the realisation of their surplus-value, because they can simply use unsaleable products as overfeed. 'Generally speaking, the process of production proceeds smoothly.' In fact, one has only to eliminate hypothetically all the ordinary conditions of the problem–the anarchy of production, competition, the necessity of selling the produced commodities to realise surplus-value–and the problem no longer exists. 'In Rosa Luxemburg's view crises would be inevitable even in our hypothetical state-capitalist society. However, we have shown, on the contrary, that crises could not exist there.'[79] That was not Rosa Luxemburg's view at all–in fact, given Bukharin's premises, she would probably have completely agreed with him. Only she would never have called 'purely capitalist' a society in which capitalists lived in peace with one another, took command and lived off the fat of the land, while an army of state slaves and (because under such circumstances, the reserve army of unemployed labour must necessarily increase enormously) a broad stratum of have-nots constituted the voracious receptacle for all surplus production. Such a society may correspond to the ideal of fascist dictators, but is not 'pure capitalism' in the Marxist sense. Thus Bukharin's criticism of Rosa Luxemburg's accumulation theory turns out to be the strongest argument in favour of her contention that non-capitalist areas are, after all, necessary for capitalist accumulation.

Various critics, and in particular Bukharin, believed that they were playing an effective trump against Rosa Luxemburg when they pointed to the tremendous possibilities of capitalist expansion into non-capitalist areas. But the originator of the accumulation theory had already removed the sting from this argument by emphasising repeatedly that the death-throes of capitalism would inevitably set in long before its inherent tendency to extend its markets had run into its objective limits. That was not at all a subterfuge on her part to save an untenable theory. Dealing with the general contradictions of capitalism in her pamphlet *Social Reform or Revolution*–fifteen years before she brought these contradictions to a common denominator in *The Accumulation of Capital*–she had written:

> It is true that even the prevailing social-democratic tactic does not consist in waiting for the development of capitalist contradictions to reach their utmost intensity, and in then waiting still further for sudden change to occur. On the contrary, we base our line simply on the tendency of this development, once it has been ascertained, and we then push the consequences of this development to their limits in our political struggle; that is the very essence of any revolutionary tactic.[80]

Expansionist possibilities are not a geographical conception: it is not the number of square miles which is decisive. Nor are they a demographical conception: it is not the statistical comparison of capitalist and non-capitalist populations which indicates the ripeness of the historical process. A socio-economic problem is involved, and a whole complex of contradictory interests, forces, and phenomena has to be taken into account: the driving impetus of the productive forces, the political strength of the capitalist powers, friction among the various modes of production, the acceleration and retardation of expansion by competition among the imperialist powers, the struggle between the heavy and the textile industries in the industrialisation of the colonies (India), maintenance of the ruling interests of the motherlands over the colonies, colonial revolutions, imperialist wars, revolutions in the capitalist countries and all their consequences, convulsions in the capital market, political uncertainty in large areas (China), and many other factors. Today, now that the productive forces have developed enormously, the factors retarding expansion have become so effective that they have already brought about deep economic, social, and political dislocation, and they clearly indicate the decline of capitalism. Theoretically it is quite possible to imagine a new capitalist thrust which could provide more room for the productive forces and introduce a new period of general prosperity. But this is only theoretically speaking.

When Rosa Luxemburg drew her conclusions for the struggle of the working class, she once again demonstrated how little she succumbed to a blind fatalism in uncovering the historical laws of capitalist development:

> Here, as at other times in history, theory does its full service by showing us the *tendency* of development and the logical end towards which it is steering. However, the present period of historical development can no more reach this end than any earlier period could ever unfold to its final consequences. The more social consciousness, this time embodied in the socialist proletariat, intervenes as an active factor in the blind play of forces, the less is the *need* for this end to be reached. And, in the present case too, a correct understanding of Marxist theory offers social consciousness the most fruitful impulses and a most powerful incentive.[81]

9
The struggle against imperialism

The political problem

The Accumulation of Capital did more than solve an abstract theoretical problem: it also proved that imperialism, with all its typical accompaniments – the rivalry of capitalist states for colonies and spheres of influence, for investment possibilities for European capital and for raw-material resources; capital export; high protective tariffs; the predominant role of bank and trust capital; the armaments race, etc. – was not an accidental by-product of certain political measures, nor did it serve merely the interests of narrow capitalist cliques (the armaments industries); rather it was a historically necessary phase of capitalist development – in fact, the final stage of that development, For Rosa Luxemburg these conclusions were of great importance for the policy of the working class:

> As always in such cases, only the exact theoretical understanding of the problem down to its very roots can impart to our practice in the struggle against imperialism that clarity of purpose and that striking power which are indispensable for the policy of the proletariat.[82]

Heated debates on this basic question took place in the SPD, resulting in a very curious state of affairs. The 'reformists' hardly involved themselves in the dispute on the book. Some of them, in fact those who very frankly acknowledged their support for German imperialism (Schippel, Leuthner, Quessel, Maurenbrecher, Winnig, and others), gladly accepted the thesis that imperialism was inevitable and historically necessary. They argued that a real Marxist could certainly not turn against historical progress, but had to further it, particularly since the free development of the productive forces was a preliminary condition for socialism. These well-meaning men were confusing the position of the bourgeoisie with that of the proletariat in the historical process. They overlooked the fact that although capitalist exploitation was historically necessary and historically progressive compared with earlier and more primitive forms of exploitation, nevertheless, socialists were still fundamentally opposed to capitalism.

However, most of the party leaders took a very different stand. The larger the dangers of imperialism loomed up, the more they sought to escape them by sticking their heads in the sand. Kautsky developed a theory of his own to suit the case. He admitted that the expansion of capitalism was proceeding unchecked, and he approved of it. However, according to him, this expansion was not imperialism. The latter was a particular method of expansion, a violent one, used only by small capitalist groups (bank capital and the military), but it was not in the interests of the capitalist class as a whole, and certainly not in the interests of heavy industry. Political power was becoming a less and less suitable instrument for furthering economic expansion. Expenditure on the armaments race merely reduced the funds available for capital investment in Turkey, China, Persia, etc. Therefore the majority of the capitalist class would more and more strongly oppose a policy of imperialist violence, and it could be expected that the capitalist powers would turn more and more away from imperialism and return to a laissez-faire and open-door policy.

It was already evident even when Kautsky was just beginning to develop this theory that experience contradicted all these claims and expectations. What is downright grotesque is the fact that he clung to it and even sharpened it during the World War. It was a perfectly clear-cut case of intellectual flight from ugly reality. And Rosa Luxemburg was thinking especially of Kautsky, the 'super-expert' behind the scenes, when, in her search for a political tendency uniting the critics of *The Accumulation of Capital*, she wrote in her *Anti-critique:*

> The belief in the possibility of accumulation in an "isolated capitalist society", the belief that "capitalism is conceivable even without expansion", is the theoretical formula for a certain definite tactical tendency. This conception tends to regard the phase of imperialism not as a historical necessity, not as the decisive contest between capitalism and socialism, but as the malicious invention of a certain number of interested parties. It is bent on persuading the bourgeoisie that imperialism and militarism are detrimental even from the standpoint of bourgeois interests, and on thus isolating the alleged handful of benefiting parties, so that it can form a block between the proletariat and the broad strata of the bourgeoisie with a view to "damping down" imperialism, starving it out by "partial disarmament", and "removing its sting". Just as liberalism in its period of decay appealed from the less enlightened monarchs to the better enlightened ones, so the "Marxist Centre" wants to appeal from the closed-minded bourgeoisie to the open-minded bourgeoisie in order to dissuade it from the disaster-course of imperialism to a policy of international disarmament treaties, from the scramble for the world-dictatorship of the sword to a peaceable federation of democratic national states. The general conflict to

settle the world-historical antagonism between proletariat and capital is transformed into the utopia of a historical compromise between proletariat and bourgeoisie for the "mitigation of imperialist antagonism between the capitalist states".[83]

Against the danger of war

The tactics of German Social Democracy were in accordance with its basic assessment of imperialism. Despite its sometimes very violent anti-imperialist declamations in the Reichstag, it nevertheless supported German foreign policy on all decisive questions. It criticised only the 'excesses' of this policy, for instance the provocative acts of Wilhelm II and his Foreign Minister, Kiderlen-Wächter. German Social Democracy supported a policy of 'peaceful penetration' into colonial areas because it disliked the bloody consequences of imperialism.

The imperialists in the social-democratic camp continued to pursue their course. Some of them spoke quite openly of the inevitable military contest with Great Britain, though in 1913 Quessel proposed an alliance with Britain to come to terms on the peaceful division of the world, in particular of Africa. They resolutely supported colonialism, and Eduard David even regarded it as an 'integral part of the universal cultural aims of the socialist movement'. They dealt with all imperialist questions from the standpoint of a ruling people whose only duty was to follow a policy of 'welfare despotism'.

The party's 'Marxist Centre' did not take the offensive in foreign-policy matters, but it was full of hope. As late as 1911 Bernstein regarded any fears of war as groundless: the need for peace was universal, and the peaceable assurances of leading statesmen could be viewed as genuine. The armaments race was an anomaly with neither national nor economic justification. The best way to avoid war was by general disarmament, international courts of arbitration, alliances, and the formation of a United States of Europe. In short, the 'Marxist Centre' appealed to the goodwill of the imperialist bourgeoisie rather than to the socialist will of the proletariat.

Rosa Luxemburg came out resolutely against this whole policy, and was supported by the other left-wing party members, though the effectiveness of their goodwill was often diminished by their lack of real insight into things. She declared the general principle that Social Democracy should never take sides in the foreign-policy quarrels of the great powers, because their aim was always the plunder and subjugation of peoples, no matter what diplomatic mask they might put on. The working class should always pursue its own foreign policy guided by its own international and revolutionary interests. The first task in any international conflict was to lay bare the capitalist interests hidden behind it and to show its consequences. She herself did this with extraordinary keenness of vision, always taking in the whole field of world politics and keeping an eye on the complicated problems involved. She mercilessly pulled to pieces both the peace pretensions of bourgeois diplomacy and the peace illusions of Social Democracy. In 1911, when Edward Grey's proposal for a general limitation of armaments was meeting with approval from socialist quarters, she argued in an article on 'Peace Utopias' (*Frieden-utopien*), *Liepziger Volkszeitung*, 6 May 1911, that:

> militarism is very closely connected with colonialism, tariff policies, and world politics as a whole. Thus if all the present-day states seriously and sincerely want to call a halt to the armaments race, they must begin to dismantle their trade policies, and to give up their colonial raiding expeditions as well as their policy of main-taining spheres of influence all over the world—in short, in both foreign and domestic politics they must begin to do the exact op-posite of what is now the very essence of capitalist class-state poli-tics.

Rosa Luxemburg did not often write on foreign-policy ques-tions; she did so only when confusion in the Marxist camp made it imperative to clarify a particular problem and steer party tactics onto the right track. She laid down the guide-lines for judging imperial-ism and outlined the social-democratic position with respect to the various economic and social phenomena in the struggle of the capital-ist powers for the world-market, thus making a very fruitful con-tribution on foreign-policy matters to the German social-democratic press. Several main ideas concerning party tactics emerged: im-perialist politics could not be overcome within the framework of capitalism because it arose from the vital interests of the capitalist social order. Any struggle against imperialism therefore had to be directed against this social order itself. Imperialism or socialism—that was the question! Any attempt to arrive at partial solutions of current foreign-policy conflicts would inevitably lead to supporting one imperialist state against another, and as a rule this meant frater-nising with the bourgeoisie at home in its opposition to other nations and abandoning international working-class interests. Without fail such a policy would lead deeper and deeper into the mire of national-ism and finally end in entanglement in an imperialist war. All ways of trying to save the peace on the basis of bourgeois society—in par-ticular, the propaganda in favour of peaceful expansion, disarma-ment, international courts of arbitration, alliances, 'civilising' colonial policies, etc.—were either an illusion or, indeed, a vindication

through camouflage of imperialism's policy of violence; in any case
they clouded the vision and weakened the strength of the working
class.

The struggle against imperialism (apart from the constant
Marxist exposure of the real background of all diplomatic conflicts)
had to be waged by strengthening international working-class solidarity, by displaying the consolidated might of the international
working class in all world-political crises, and by struggling against
the domestic political repercussions of imperialism–militarism, oppressive taxation, the rising cost of living, and the curtailment of
social policies and democracy–for the winning of democratic rights.
Rosa Luxemburg, and with her the left wing of the SPD, considered
that social development was ripe enough so that in any great future
convulsion socialism–i.e. in political terms, the conquest of power
by the working class–would be on the immediate agenda. The time
had now come for the party to go beyond its previous policy of
mere agitation and organisation to great mass actions. More than
ever before the party had to be determined to take the offensive.

After the Russian Revolution of 1905 the European powers
had grouped themselves into two camps: the Triple Alliance
(Germany, Austria, and Italy) and the Triple Entente (Great Britain,
France and Russia). The Morocco conflict of 1906 had driven home
for the first time the danger of war in Europe. Fear of war increasingly took hold of the masses. How to head off such a war and how
to act in it became burning questions for the International. At its
Stuttgart Congress in 1907 these were dealt with fundamentally for
the first time by considering the nature of imperialist warfare. As the
representative of the All-Russia Social-Democratic Party, Rosa
Luxemburg was a member of the commission charged with working
out a resolution on the party's attitude towards war. She firmly
opposed the proposals (supported by the French and the British
delegates) which called for the proclamation of a general strike and
a general refusal to do military service if war broke out, because she
was against making promises that could not be kept when the crunch
came. She aimed at securing a clear statement against war by the
International and committing the parties to a determined revolutionary policy appropriate to the power of the working class.
Together with Lenin and Martov, she drew up a resolution which,
in consultation with Bebel, was fashioned and re-fashioned until it
was in a form that could not give the German Public Prosecutor any
cause for an indictment, or perhaps even the suppression of the SPD.
The decisive passages of this resolution were:

> In the event of war threatening to break out, it is the duty of the
> workers and their parliamentary representatives in the countries

involved to do everything possible to prevent the outbreak of war by taking suitable measures, which can, of course, be changed or intensified in accordance with the exacerbation of the class struggle and the general political situation.

Should war break out nevertheless, it is their duty to advocate its speedy end and to utilise the economic and political crisis brought about by the war to rouse the various social strata and to hasten the overthrow of capitalist class rule.

In guarded words, down-to-earth and without romanticism, but with the necessary clarity concerning policy aims and character, the resolution indicated a line of action, and it was accepted by the Congress with great enthusiasm and without opposition. Did Rosa Luxemburg seriously believe that it would be adhered to? She knew that there were quite a few nationalists in the International who would consider it nothing but an empty formula. Yet she hoped that the radical socialist leaders, especially those in the SPD Executive would overcome their weaknesses, so that at the critical moment they would rise to the occasion.

The struggle for equal suffrage

It was not long before certain events seemed to justify this expectation; for the first time in its history, German Social Democracy mobilised the working masses for a political offensive. The point of attack was well chosen. The most modern capitalist country in Europe was ruled by a semi-absolutist government propped up by the rotten Prussian Junker class, and the anachronism was becoming more and more glaring. This class monopolised the upper levels of the ruling apparatus and administrative machinery, and buttressed its position above all through the Prussian Diet, in which it had an entrenched majority, thanks to an electoral system which divided the population into three classes according to tax payments, thus in effect putting political power into the hands of a tiny number of wealthy voters. In 1908 Social Democracy succeeded for the first time in winning six seats by polling 600,000 votes, the Conservatives with 418,000 votes obtained 212 seats.

The same year saw the first extra-parliamentary assault by the working class on the bastion of Junkerdom. For the first time Prussian workers demonstrated on the streets in defiance of police bans and managed to prod Wilhelm II into at least making a Royal Speech announcing electoral reform. However, two years passed before any attempt was made to honour this promise, and the Chancellor, Bethmann-Hollweg, then produced a so-called reform which was rather a provocation of the working class. Academics, retired officers, higher civil servants, etc. – a small stratum of 'bearers of culture' – were to move up to the next electoral class. This 'reform' proved to be the signal for vigorous working-class action, which also received the sympathy of sections of the lower-middle classes. Every Sunday in February and March 1910 the streets of the large towns were the scenes of quite large demonstrations. In the provinces frequent bloody clashes with the police occurred, but the bloodshed only inflamed the masses to greater militancy. In Berlin the Police President, Traugott von Jagow (afterwards one of the leaders of the Kapp Putsch against the Weimar Republic in 1920), issued threatening proclamations in Napoleonic style. Troops were called in and drilled in cavalry charges on the streets of Berlin. However, the social-democratic organisers did their work so efficiently that Herr von Jagow suffered one moral defeat after the other. Hundreds of thousands of people were always assembling where they were least expected. The power of the SPD over the working class seemed almost unlimited. Although such direct actions did not gain their immediate objective of equal suffrage for Prussia, at least Bethmann-Hollweg's proposal had to be abandoned and the right to demonstrate on the streets was secured.

It was the first tangible political victory of the German working class, and it was won by the masses, who were really in an aggressive mood. And this was obviously no short-lived wave of feeling: at the same time, the miners were getting ready for a big wage struggle, and 200,000 building workers were holding out for three long months against a lockout, a struggle which led to victory by dint of their determination, endurance, and clever tactics. Rosa Luxemburg viewed the struggle for electoral reform as the basis for an even greater trial of strength. A political strike seemed to her to be the most advisable weapon to intensify the action in favour of equal suffrage and thus prevent it from getting bogged down in inertia. 'In a situation like the present one, long delays, long pauses between the individual actions of the struggle, and hesitation in the choice of the weapons and strategy of further struggle are almost tantamount to a lost battle.'[84] This view was obviously widespread in the party. Numerous organisations (Breslau, Halle, Königsberg, the Rhineland, etc.) demanded the calling of a general strike. In Kiel and in Frankfurt-Hanau short demonstration-strikes had already taken place. At the beginning of March the Party Executive consulted with the General Commission of the trade unions on the proposal of a general demonstration-strike, but decided against calling one.

Rosa Luxemburg was well aware of the difficulties of the situation: a class which had never carried out a great common struggle, and which for years had been accustomed to receive all its slogans ready-made from the SPD, would find it difficult to make the leap from demonstrations to a political strike. She therefore demanded that the Party Executive work out a great plan of action which would, for the time being, include demonstration-strikes of limited duration. At the same time she proposed that the general strike should be put forward for discussion, to ascertain how militant the masses actually were.

It was clear that, despite its vigour, the movement for suffrage reform would be only a passing episode in the period of great mass struggles which Rosa Luxemburg saw facing the German working class. Up to now the party's left wing had been putting forward the slogan: socialism against imperialism. That was quite adequate for general anti-imperialist propaganda work, because it made clear the real significance of the whole historical epoch. However, as a slogan for immediate mass struggles, socialism, and even the seizure of political power, was too distant an aim. She therefore took yet another important tactical step and suggested the slogan of a republic to sum up the propaganda and action of the moment:

The *slogan of a republic* in Germany today represents something infinitely more than a beautiful dream of a democratic "people's state", something infinitely more than a demand of doctrinaires with their heads in the clouds. On the contrary, it is a practical war cry against militarism, navalism, colonialism, world politics, Junker domination, and the Prussianisation of Germany; it is the consequence and the drastic summary of our daily struggle against all these various phenomena of the ruling reaction.[85]

The slogan, in fact, meant even more for Rosa Luxemburg than she indicated. It was not only the 'password of class identity (*Klassenscheidung*), the watchword of the class struggle' for the whole of the everyday struggle. If her interpretation of the Russian Revolution were adapted to German conditions, it followed that the first decisive step in a German revolution would be the abolition of the dozen-and-one little monarchies throughout the country. Afterwards, of course, the revolution itself would be propelled beyond this first turning point towards the conquest of political power by the proletariat. Her slogan of a republic was thus not just something arbitrarily invented to fit the situation of the moment, not just a spontaneous brain-wave: it tied together all the great struggles of the day with the final aim, and it arose from her total conception of that particular historical epoch.

Even before the suffrage demonstrations had reached a high pitch, she summed up her ideas in a long article which she submitted to *Vorwärts*. It was returned to her at the beginning of March 1910 with the observation that party instructions forbade any propaganda in favour of a political strike. Kautsky, too, who had at first accepted the article for *Neue Zeit*, describing it as 'very fine and very important', finally yielded to the dictates of the Party Executive and refused to publish it. In the end the article was cut up and published in parts in various party dailies.[86]

Kautsky's behaviour was a personal affront to Rosa Luxemburg. She was the chief contributor to *Neue Zeit*, and had been his long-standing deputy-editor; in fact, the great respect which he enjoyed among radical socialists throughout the International was due in considerable measure to her intellectual collaboration. But Kautsky had not only bowed to party instructions: his action signified a political *volte-face* and the break-up of his intellectual alliance with Rosa Luxemburg. This was made quite clear when he published an article in *Neue Zeit* spitefully criticising the article he had rejected and advocating views which were in glaring contradiction to those he had previously favoured in the journal and in his most important tactical writings, the pamphlet *The Social Revolution* (2nd ed 1907) and the book *The Road to Power* (1909). In the latter he had proclaimed, in complete agreement with Rosa Luxemburg, that 'we have every reason to assume that we have now entered a period of struggles for the state institutions and for state power'. Now, however, he declared that such a view was senseless: the only possible position for the party was a defensive one, a policy of avoiding battle, an 'attrition strategy'–at least until the next Reichstag elections two years later, which would bring an overwhelming victory for Social Democracy, a 'catastrophe for the whole ruling-class system of government'. This alone would lead to conditions conducive to a final 'strategy of overthrow' (*Niederwerfungsstrategie*); already it put 'the key to this portentous historical situation' into the pocket of Social Democracy. Thus, according to Kautsky, the revolutionary situation was not supposed to develop out of the powerful activity of the working masses making itself manifest, but from a hypothetical catastrophe of the governing system brought about at the ballot-box. When Rosa Luxemburg wrote to Clara Zetkin about the party leaders who tried at every great turn of events 'to force everything back into the parliamentary mould' and who attacked everyone wanting to go beyond these limits as 'enemies of the people', she had mentioned Bebel, but had certainly hardly thought of Kautsky in this respect.

Subsequently the deep estrangement, both personal and political, between her and Kautsky became very evident. At first he advanced various transparent excuses for not publishing her reply to his action, and energetic pressure was necessary before he finally agreed to do so. Caught in his own contradictions, he then began a feud in which he maligned her, accusing her of falsification, and using all those literary subterfuges which are the invariable resource of renegades. In the dispute, which went on from May to August 1910, Rosa Luxemburg displayed all her brilliant polemical ability. Yet it was apparent that this time she was moved rather by embitterment at Kautsky's behaviour than by her usual delight in intellectual combat.

Franz Mehring also sided against Rosa in this particular episode, and even Lenin defended Kautsky against a 'wrong interpretation' of his attrition strategy, which the Mensheviks claimed as an endorsement of their own policy. Mehring soon came round to Rosa's position, however, and after the outbreak of the World War Lenin realised with a shock that the polemics between Kautsky and Rosa Luxemburg from 1910 onwards had not only been a matter of different opinions on the given political situation, but that Kautsky's attitude had signified his turning away from a real revolutionary policy. Indeed, it was not only the friendship between Kautsky and Luxemburg which broke up: the unity of the radical majority in the party fell to pieces too. The SPD divided into three clear tendencies: the reformists, who tended increasingly to espouse the ruling-class imperialist policy; the so-called Marxist Centre, which claimed to maintain the traditional policy, but in reality moved closer and closer to Bernstein's position; and the revolutionary wing, generally called the Left Radicals (*Linksradikale*), headed by Rosa Luxemburg alongside of Clara Zetkin, Franz Mehring, Karl Liebknecht, Karski (Julian Marchlewski), Karl Radek, and Anton Pannekoek.

The whole policy of the party in the pre-war period with its great international convulsions consisted in evasions and retreats, and in the creation of one illusion after another. In the summer of 1911, the German Foreign Minister, Kiderlen-Wächter, provoked a diplomatic crisis by sending the cruiser *Panther* to Agadir in Morocco (allegedly to protect German interests there) and brought Europe to the verge of war. The Bureau of the Second International thereupon appealed to all affiliated parties to organise a joint action against the danger of war. The SPD Executive refused, declaring that it had been informed by the Foreign Ministry that Germany did not intend war, and expressing the fear that the party would spoil its chances at the coming Reichstag elections if it took too strong an attitude against its country's colonial policies. Only when Rosa Luxemburg sounded the alarm at this monstrous line of argument was any action—and a rather lame one at that—organised against the Morocco adventure.

The Reichstag elections of 1912 brought the party a great increase in the number of votes (from 3,259,000 in January 1907 to 4,250,000 in January 1911) and seats (from 43 to 110). However, for the second stage of the elections the Party-Executive concluded a disgraceful compromise with the middle-class Progressives [the Progressive People's Party], which prescribed the 'toning down' (*Dämpfung*) of the election campaign and the abandonment of any independent propaganda in a large number of promising constituencies. It caused great confusion in the party ranks and was ignored in some of these constituencies. Kautsky justified this policy by asserting that a regeneration of the left bourgeoisie, brought on by a new liberalism based on the 'new middle classes', had taken place. Moreover, he acclaimed the winning of 110 parliamentary seats by Social Democracy as a turning point in world history and declared: 'Even though we have not won that commanding position for which we hoped (he had dreamed of at least 125 seats), still we have succeeded in condemning the government and the reaction to impotence.'

What actually happened was that, driven by their imperialist interests, the liberals veered more and more to the right, and neither government nor reaction had any further cause to fear real opposition from the bourgeoisie. There were now severe setbacks in German social policy, and the Prussian suffrage reform was buried. On the other hand, every year brought new armaments and accordingly new taxes to pay for them. After all the calculations involved in the scramble for parliamentary seats, the chickens had now come home to roost.

The official policy of German Social Democracy became more and more a flight from reality. Italy sent an expedition to raid Tripoli, the Balkan Wars presaged the World War, and Germany's foreign policy in the Balkans intensified the danger of war even further. Meanwhile, the party leaders still dreamt of peace, and the party members in the Reichstag congratulated the government on its foreign policy and lauded the 'peace mission' of the Triple Alliance. At the same time the imperialist wing of the party became increasingly outspoken, and in the *Sozialistische Monatshefte* it supported the bourgeois-press campaign stirring up nationalist feeling against Great Britain and Russia.

In the summer of 1913 the government introduced a military bill which had been worked out by Ludendorff, a bill without precedent in the history of armaments. It was supposed to cost a thousand million Reichmarks for both new and current expenditures. However, the SPD confined itself to mere parliamentary protests; its members in the Reichstag even voted for the financial measures necessary to meet the military demands, because this time these were to be covered by property taxes. Even members of the party's left wing (Radek and Pannekoek) advocated the passing of these measures. But knowing that nationalist and imperialist sentiments had moved many of the Reichstag members to vote in favour of the tax measures, Rosa Luxemburg underlined the principle that, in view of the rapidly approaching danger of war, the party should do nothing which might create even the appearance of expressing confidence in the government and consenting to its armaments policy.

Rosa's attacks on this whole policy evoked strong support from the party's rank and file, but for just this reason her opponents made even more furious attempts to justify their views. Kautsky inveighed against her and her friends as 'mass-actionists', 'anarcho-syndicalists', and 'Russians', and talked idly about 'coups-de-main', 'obstructionist intrigues', 'putschism', and 'revolutionary gymnastics'. In March 1913 a national press conference of the party made a decision, binding on all the editors, to refrain from criticising the Party Executive and the party's parliamentary members. It is true that most of the radical party editors did not abide by this undertaking, but when Paul Lensch resigned as editor of the Leipziger Volkszeitung in the summer of 1913 and Hans Block took his place, the paper (the most important organ of the radical opposition) submitted to the higher-ups in the party: after fifteen years of outstanding collaboration Rosa Luxemburg was pushed out of its pages. Mehring and Karski, who belonged to the editorial staff of the Leipziger Volkszeitung, declared their solidarity with Rosa, after having been encouraged to do so by Clara Zetkin. Naturally the breach took place with a great deal of personal friction. This was no literary squabble, however, but an episode of deep political significance. As Karski wrote to Block on 16 December 1913,

> The point is this: we three (Luxemburg, Mehring, Karski), and most particularly myself (which I would like to stress), are of the opinion that the party is undergoing an internal crisis much more serious than the one when revisionism first arose. These words may seem harsh, but it is my conviction that the party is threatening to waste away if matters go on like this. At such a time there is only one hope of redemption for a revolutionary party: the sharpest and most ruthless self-criticism conceivable.

In order to carry out this task and to secure wider publicity for their views, the three founded the Sozialdemokratische Korrespondenz in December 1913. It continued into the war-period, and then fell victim to the military censorship. Besides articles on tactical questions, Rosa Luxemburg wrote chiefly about militarism, and she increasingly concentrated her efforts on combating it. When the German generals in the fortress town of Zabern (Saverne) in Alsace-Lorraine proclaimed martial law and staged a little war—in order to protect the not exactly clean underwear of a minor lieutenant—Rosa led such a spirited campaign against the military clique that she incurred its undying hatred. It was not long before she was persecuted by the authorities.

The courts step into action

The first blow was struck on 20 February 1914 by the District Court (*Landgericht*) in Frankfurt am Main, which indicted Rosa Luxemburg for instigating soldiers to disobedience. The basis of the charge was a speech delivered in September 1913 in the Frankfurt area, in which she had cried out: 'If they expect us to lift the weapons of murder against our French or other foreign brothers, then let us tell them "No, we won't do it!" ' The charge was, of course, legally untenable, as the defence lawyers, Paul Levi and Kurt Rosenfeld, irrefutably argued. The Public Prosecutor asked for a one-year prison term and her immediate arrest. Such a sentence for an agitational speech had not been imposed since the days of the Anti-Socialist Laws. Rosa's behaviour was characteristic: she admitted having uttered the offending words, made no attempt to explain away their meaning, and, instead of defending herself, went over to the offensive. Lashing out at the Public Prosecutor, the officer caste, and Wilhelm II himself, she justified the struggle against militarism and war. She attacked the idea of militarism and utterly servile obedience on the part of the soldiers as the basis of state power, and she openly declared her own policy on war:

> We think that not only the army, "orders" from above and blind obedience from below will decide on the outbreak and the outcome of war, but that the great mass of the working people will decide and should decide. We are of the opinion that wars can be waged only so long as the working class takes part in them with enthusiasm, because it regards them as just and necessary; or at least patiently puts up with them. On the other hand, when the great majority of the working people come to the conclusion–and to bring them to this conclusion, to arouse this consciousness, is just the task we social democrats set for ourselves–when the majority of the people come to the conclusion that wars are a barbarous, deeply immoral, and reactionary phenomenon hostile to the interests of the people, then wars will become impossible–even if, for the moment, soldiers still obey the orders of their superiors! [87]

And in answer to the demand of the Public Prosecutor for her immediate arrest:

> In closing, just a word on the outrageous attack made on me, an attack which recoils on its originator. The Public Prosecutor said– and I have noted his exact words–that he is asking for my immediate arrest, because "it would be incomprehensible if the accused did not take to flight". In other words, he was saying: "If I, the Public Prosecutor, had to serve a year in prison, then I would try

to escape". Sir, I believe you; you would run away. A social democrat does not; he stands by his deeds and laughs at your punish-
ments. And now, sentence me![88]

She was sentenced to one year's imprisonment, but not arrested
on the spot. From the court-room she went directly to a mass meeting at which the workers of Frankfurt were awaiting the outcome of
the trial. In high spirits, Rosa took the floor as a triumphal warrior.
She scoffed at the verdict and sentence by boldly advocating the
same ideas which they were supposed to strike down, appealing for
an intensified struggle against militarism and imperialist war. The
repressive sentence roused deep indignation throughout the whole
German working class, and she was asked to address many meetings, which were attended by unusually large numbers of people. It
was the prelude to a great exciting propaganda campaign against the
class system of justice, militarism, and the violent world-storm whose
clouds were now massing threateningly.

Military questions were coming more and more to the fore: an
intimidatingly severe sentence pronounced by the Erfurt Military
Court, increasingly frequent cases of maltreatment of soldiers and
suicides among the troops intensified public interest. On one occasion, a Social Democrat in a Reichstag interpellation ('*Kleine
Anfrage*') enquired about certain abuses, and a government spokesman refused to reply, arguing with a cold and rude arrogance that
the representatives of the people were 'not authorised' to deal with
such cases. In strongly worded speeches and in writing in the *Sozialdemokratische Korrespondenz*, 4 May 1914, Rosa Luxemburg attacked
this "non-authorisation". A speech in Freiburg, in which she spoke
'of the dramas taking place day in and day out in Germany's
barracks, although the moanings of the aggrieved parties only seldom
reach our ears', brought the War Minister out into the open. He
charged her with insulting the army. The case created a storm. In
answer to an appeal issued by the defence, more than 30,000 victims
and witnesses of military maltreatment volunteered to give evidence.
Then when the trial was due to open (shortly before the war), the
representatives of the War Ministry had to beg humbly for its post-
ponement in order to prevent the thousands of accusers from parad-
ing to the witness-box. In the end the proceedings were shelved, but
the law's campaign against Rosa continued. In June 1914 she put
forward a resolution on the political mass strike at a party meeting
in Berlin. Although its tone was quite moderate and its content did
not go beyond what she herself and others had often said before, she
and all the signatories of the resolution were indicted, and an attempt
was even made to get hold of all those who had voted for the resolution. It was quite clear that the authorities intended to gag this revolutionary voice against imperialism. War came, and with it new

prosecutions. Since the days of Lassalle no political figure in Germany had been so systematically and persistently harried, and, like Lassalle, Rosa could boast that her escutcheon was studded with indictments.

Despite her poor health, which caused her much trouble, the prospect of a long term of imprisonment hardly depressed her at all. In fact, she regarded the persecution as a sure sign that she had done her duty well. What did depress her was the thought that the threatening storms ahead would find a spineless and cowardly generation in the leadership and officialdom of the party. She pinned her hopes on the younger generation, whose best forces she herself had schooled by her work and by her writings, the generation which looked on Karl Liebknecht as its fellow-comrade and leader.

Born on 13 August 1871, Karl was only a few years younger than Rosa. Because he had been compelled during his period of study and training as a lawyer outwardly to conform to Prussian legal restraints and to remain in the background, he had entered the political arena at a rather late date. But he had then thrown himself into the struggle with passionate intensity, displaying much independence and initiative which the party leaders tried to bridle, but in vain. He was one of the creators of the socialist youth movement, and was, in fact, the one who assigned it political tasks which went beyond purely educational objectives, namely the struggle against militarism. In 1906 he published a pamphlet, *Militarismus und Antimilitarismus unter besonderer Berücksichtigung der internationalen Jugendbewegung* (Militarism and Anti-militarism with Special Reference to the International Youth Movement), in which he imparted to German working-class youth the experiences particularly of the Belgian and the Swedish youth movements in the anti-militarist struggle, and drew up and justified a programme for this struggle in Germany. At the first International Youth Congress in Stuttgart (1907), he was elected, together with Hendrik de Man*, Director of the Youth International. Immediately afterwards, however, in October 1907, he was tried for high-treason on the basis of the

---

* At that time the young de Man was one of the hopes of the radical wing of the International. In the First World War, however, he became a Belgian nationalist. After the overthrow of the Tsar in February 1917 he went with Vandervelde to Petrograd for the purpose of urging Russia's troops to continue to fight on the side of the Entente. After the war he turned away from Marxism. For a while he was a professor in Frankfurt, but returned to Belgium after the Nazis came to power. He then became a strong proponent of planned economic policies, and became a Minister and President of the Belgian Workers Party. Although he remained a member of this party, he showed increasingly fascist tendencies, and collaborated with the Nazis after the occupation of his country. After the war he was sentenced *in absentia* to life imprisonment for high treason, but was later amnestied. In 1952 he was killed in an accident in Switzerland.

above-mentioned pamphlet, and sentenced to eighteen months' confinement in a fortress. This was a high distinction indeed, for high-treason trials against social democrats had become rare. From that time onwards Karl also occupied a special position in the party, whose members felt the vitality of his extraordinary intellect and strong revolutionary will, and put special trust in him. In 1908 the Berlin workers sent the fortress prisoner as their representative to that three-class parliament, the Prussian Diet. In 1912 he became Reichstag deputy for Potsdam-East Havelland.

Liebknecht developed a stronger international consciousness than did most of the party leaders, and this soon brought him into close contact with the Russian movement. He was one of the most important go-betweens of the Bolsheviks for their illegal work in Russia. In 1904, together with Hugo Hasse, he rendered a great service to the Russian revolution as one of the defending counsel in the so-called Königsberg Trial*, which the government of Herr von Bülow had planned as one of its henchman's services for Tsarism and which became, in effect, an exposé of absolutism to the world public. Already his achievements in the decade immediately preceding the First World War rose above the usual level of human endeavour. Rosa Luxemburg once described his life style in a letter to Hans Diefenbach [30 March 1917]:

> You probably know how he has lived for many years: practically only in parliament, meetings, commissions, conferences; running and rushing, always ready to jump from the commuter-train into the tram, and from the tram into a car; every pocket stuffed full of memo pads, his arms full of the latest newspapers which, of course, he never finds time to read; body and soul covered with street dust, and yet always with a kind and youthful smile on his face.

Indeed, he never seemed to get tired, for besides all this, besides speaking at meetings, doing office work, and acting as defence counsel in court, he could still spend whole nights debating and drinking merrily with the comrades. And even if the street dust did cover his soul at times, it could not stifle the genuine enthusiasm which imbued all his activities. It was this devotion to the cause, this passionate temperament and this capacity for enthusiasm that Rosa valued. She recognised the true revolutionary in him, even if they sometimes disagreed on details of party tactics. They worked together and complemented each other very well, especially in the

* The chief defendant at this trial was Otto Braun, the later Minister President of Prussia [during the Weimar Republic]. The indictment was for attempted high treason, insulting language against the Tsar, and association with illegal secret societies–crimes alleged to have been committed by smuggling revolutionaries' writings over the Russian border. The chief defendants were acquitted, and several co-defendants sentenced to short prison terms.

struggle against militarism and the danger of war. While Rosa gave the struggle its theoretical basis, Karl was undoubtedly the leader in action. Beginning with the last years before the war, they were to stand shoulder to shoulder—unto death.

10
Like a candle burning at both ends

The woman

The first of the great catastrophes prophesied by Rosa Luxemburg as early as the Bernstein debate was approaching. Ten years previously she had welcomed the revolution 'as joyfully as a hero on his way to victory'. Now, however, what lay ahead was not the final struggle for liberation which she so hoped and longed for, but a great blood-bath of peoples, for which she was prepared, but which she feared and loathed. And instead of the masses rising to the heights of heroism in the cause of their own emancipation, she saw them deluded, humiliated, and dragged to the slaughter-house for the most barbaric cause. A testing-time of severe physical and mental suffering began for Rosa, demanding the exertion of all her strength. She managed to defy misfortune. Although her health was poorer than ever, she was at the height of her intellectual powers. Her great talents had come to full maturity. Political work for her had never been the grind it was for some people, leaving them apathetic and indifferent. She had preserved her resilience. Far from tarnishing the precious stone of her character, her experiences had given it a fine polish, and it was now to shine out with the greatest brilliance.

For years her character was distorted in the public eye by hatred rather than flattered by favour. To her enemies she was 'Bloody Rosa', and she met with hostility from all quarters, from the out-and-out defenders of capitalist profit all the way to those who condescended to show their sympathy for their poor proletarian brothers by collecting on their behalf the crumbs which fell from the ruler's table, though at a pinch they could be revolutionary enough when it came to the remote past and far-off countries, while still regarding any disruption of the established order of things in their own time and country as nothing but criminal anarchy. Journalists and cartoonists drummed into their readers' heads a distorted picture of Rosa Luxemburg as a modern Fury, a shrew, a *petroleuse;* and in the critical revolutionary months of 1918-19 such mass suggestion was intensified to a pitch of hysteria, thus creating an atmosphere conducive to the murder of Rosa and Karl. There is not a word in anything Rosa ever wrote which could in the slightest justify the imputation of cruel heartlessness to her, unless one could reproach her for having expressed the simple truth that all great historical progress has had to be paid for at a high price.

When her letters from prison were published after her death, a reversal of public feeling occurred. There were many testimonials and self-accusations from men and women who now confessed their deep regret at having been accessories, however indirect, to her murder, for they had been gratified by the news of it at the time and now saw how deeply they had been misled. However, any judgment of her reached solely on the basis of these letters would be one-sided, and therefore wrong. In them the sensitive woman and artist almost conceals the revolutionary, but it is in this revolutionary side of her character that the full measure of her greatness is revealed.

Physically she was not cut out for the role of heroine. She was small, and not very well-proportioned. Because of her hip illness in childhood, her walk was ungainly. Her sharp facial features were pronouncedly Jewish—a face indicating unusual boldness and deter-mination. It provoked an immediate response, either repelling or fascinating people. Everyone felt the strength of her personality. In conversation her face reflected the range of her ever-changing im-pulses and feelings, from earnest meditation to unrestrained joy, from sympathy and kindliness to asperity and sarcasm. Her forehead was high and beautifully shaped, and around her eloquent lips there was sometimes a line of deep melancholy. Her large, dark and bright eyes dominated her whole face. They were very expressive, at times searching with a penetrating scrutiny, or thoughtful; at times merry or flashing with excitement. They reflected an ever-alert intellect and an indomitable soul. Her voice was fine-toned and resonant, and she spoke clearly, with pure vowels and well-articu-lated consonants. Her mastery of the German language was absolute, so that she could express the finest nuances of meaning. To the end of her life she retained a slight Polish accent, but it lent character to her voice and added a special zest to her humour. Because she was sensitive to the moods of others, she knew when to remain silent and to listen, as well as how to talk about the trivial things of life in a natural, down-to-earth, and spirited way. All this made every private moment with her a special gift.

However, she was not lavish with such gifts—except perhaps with children, towards whom she was very expansive. All the child-ren in the street where she lived knew and liked her as a special friend, and with Kautsky's sons she could frolic and romp almost as though she were one of them, applying herself to their games with solemn earnestness and zeal. But among people who did not belong to her close circle of friends she was usually cool and reserved, almost cold. Perhaps it was to safeguard her freedom of action in the case of political people with whom she might one day have dealings. Her aloofness certainly stemmed, at least in part, from the high value she placed on friendship. Not before she knew a person thoroughly did she consider him a friend; and her friendships were based not so much on a complete harmony of political views, as has been claimed, but on character. Any doubt that arose in this respect led inevitably to a breach. Thus, in the Polish movement, besides Leo Jogiches, she seems to have been really close only to Julian Karski and Adolf Warski. Although Karl Radek was perhaps the most gifted of her (and Leo's) pupils, she deliberately kept him at a distance because a certain rather ostentatious cynicism he adopted repelled her. In the most important questions concerning Russia she found herself in agreement with Trotsky, but she was not close to him personally. With Lenin, on the other hand, she often came to blows and had bitterly angry exchanges, but she always held him in the highest esteem. At the height of the Russian factional struggles, when she was boiling with rage at the Bolsheviks, she could still extol Lenin as a really strong-willed revolutionary, free of all affectation, and a man with whom it was always a pleasure to discuss. And then there was Jaurès, the French socialist leader: in the whole socialist camp one could hardly think of a sharper antagonism than that between his and her viewpoints, and yet she always felt attracted to his powerful personality. When she attacked him, even when she was mocking him, she always let her comradely feelings for him carry the day. What she valued in him once came out when writing to Sonja Liebknecht about Rodin: 'That must have been a splendid man: frank and natural, overflowing with warmth and intelligence; he reminds me forcibly of Jaurès.' Her judgment of human character was thus far from being narrow. She could be lenient and overlook personal weaknesses, even among her friends. From the latter, however, she did demand unconditional sincerity of character and political principle. Thus she was close to only a few people. In Germany these included, above all, Bebel, Mehring, Karl and Sonja Liebknecht, Mathilde Wurm, Marta Rosenbaum, and several artists; she had particularly intimate bonds of friendship with the Zetkin family, the young doctor Hans Diefenbach, and the Kautskys.

It was in this small circle that she loosened up completely. To each of her friends she offered much sympathetic understanding, responding to individual needs and giving of the richness of her character, whether consolation, inspiration, encouragement or joy. But she had a sharp tongue and a biting wit, and used them both unsparingly. On one occasion she was out for a walk with Clara Zetkin, and, deep in a discussion, they wandered into the danger zone of a military rifle-exercise. Later, they both went to the

Kautskys', where the 'Party Fathers' were assembled. The incident was recounted amid considerable amusement and speculation as to the tragic consequences the episode might have had if. . . . Bebel tried to draft an epitaph for the two women 'shot to death', but when he got tangled in all the superlatives, Rosa interrupted him with the dry comment that he should simply write, 'Here lie the last two men of German Social Democracy'. The old man reacted as if he had been punched in the nose. Generally, however, her caustic remarks were taken more lightheartedly, especially as she did not hold back from making them at her own expense. In such intimate company the atmosphere was mostly cheerful and sometimes high-spirited almost to excess. Politics were not her only interest: Rosa loved music, and she liked to sing, in particular the *Lieder* of Hugo Wolf and the arias of Mozart. She also liked to discuss literature. She could dream at times and give herself up to reverie, but whether she was serious or joking, intellectual or playful, she could create a sparkling and effervescent champagne-atmosphere which swept everyone around her.

At the same time, she was a serious scholar and an exacting worker, though with none of the pedantry often associated with ivory-tower academics who immerse themselves in the details of their subject and become blind to all else, to the realities of life itself. Her nature had nothing of the Faustianism exalted in German literature— at least, nothing in the sense that the spectres of the past did not haunt her, and she had no need to grapple with spiritual inhibitions and doubts. But she did have one thing in common with Faust: the imperative urge to grasp life, the quest for universal knowledge, and the elation of creative effort. 'One must at all times keep on becoming more of a human being!' And her talents enabled her to conquer far-flung fields. Politics and the sciences which offer themselves as its tools—economics and history—were not enough for her. Nevertheless, she worked unremittingly to master them, not merely out of a sense of duty, but with a desire to investigate the whole process of social development thoroughly. She also studied geology and ethnology, and her special favourites were botany and ornithology. She didn't nibble around the edges of these sciences, but plunged right into them and devoted herself to them with a genuine intellectual passion which made her forget all other things, sometimes for weeks and even months at a time. In the spring of 1917 [30 March] she wrote to her friend Hans Diefenbach:

> How glad I am that I threw myself into botany three years ago, and did it with my usual total ardour, with my usual total self, so that I lost all interest in the world, the party and my work, and one sole passion consumed me day and night: to roam about out-doors in the spring fields, to collect an armful of plants, and then

to sort them out at home, to identify them, and enter them in my notebooks. How I spent that whole spring as if in a fever! How much I suffered when I sat long in front of a new little plant and could not recognise and classify it! On several such occasions I almost fainted, so that Gertrud would get annoyed and threaten to "take away" the plants altogether. But now I am thoroughly at home in this green empire, which I conquered myself, by storm and with passion–and things you grasp with so much ardour strike firm roots in you.

Sometimes her artistic impulses took hold of her in the same passionately exclusive way. From childhood onwards she had done pen and pencil sketches of animals, landscapes, and portraits. Now she was suddenly seized with a desire to paint in oils; she therefore threw herself into oil-painting and overcame the technical difficulties without being taught by anyone. Professional painters were astonished at the talent and artistic instinct her work revealed. In 1909 she painted a self-portrait, and its stark realism shows great ability, even if her use of garish colours strikes one as a bit too unrestrained.

All her endeavours–like politics–were an outlet for her unruly energy and her eagerness to plunge into life, to live it to the utmost. She wanted to be creative, to urge forward the laggard and the lagging. Life resounded in her as it did in Victor Hugo:

Dans la tête un orchestre

Et dans l'âme une lyre.

If the road to politics had been barred to her, she would most probably have become a poet. Her childhood verses undoubtedly came from an inner urge for expression that sought a congenial outlet again and again, throughout her life. Her first article, an appeal for May Day, was rejected by Leo, because unconsciously she had turned it into well-scanned rhythm. It would not be surprising if, even today, unknown poems by her were still to be discovered somewhere, for the lyrical chords within her were quite powerful. Her letters prove it; many of them are pure poetry, particularly those written in prison, when, hungry for the pleasures of life, she sought and found them in her memories. She paints picture after picture; with a few lines she recreates a landscape before our eyes. She describes everyday and insignificant events with such colourful vitality that the drayman, the newspaper-seller, the old market-woman, the florist's shop across the way, and even the lottery tickets on display in the window of the tobacconist's speak to us in a familiar language; we breathe the dusty, hot sunny air of a summer's day, and experience in all this the pleasure of a poem joyously celebrating life. And she can graphically depict the suffering of every creature in deeply moving words. However, about her own suffering she cannot say anything; at most she manages to stammer a few words to her closest friends. She passes over her own pain in silence.

She could not develop some of her other talents fully, because political activity and scholarly research almost always demanded the commitment of her whole being. Thus, again and again it is her letters from prison, during the breaks in the struggle, that show her hidden strengths and resources. Ideas flash at every turn–ideas which deserve to have been worked on–historical parallels; characteristics of individual cultural periods; judgments on poetry and poets, music and composers, sketched in a few succinct lines, yet brilliant and profound. She wanted the historical and literary essay, whose masters were to be found in the English and the French literary traditions, to become an established form in German literature as well, and she was encouraged to try her hand in this field by her friend Diefenbach, a good literary connoisseur and an excellent stylist. Such an essay had to be 'a picture of life or of an age, lightly dashed off in a few lines ... which can be, at the same time, a really full and lovely experience'; it had to be imbued with 'intellectual gracefulness' and sketched 'in a few, artistically selected strokes which stimulate the reader's fantasy. . . . Just as when intelligent people commune privately with one another, gentle hints are more enjoyable than crudely blunt language'.[89]

Rosa Luxemburg did, in fact, produce such an essay–the preface to her translation of Wladimir Korolenko's memoirs. There she made Korolenko come alive:

> a sensitive poet, who is pursued his whole life by a childhood experience in a rustling wood, a boyhood walk on a dark evening across a desolate field, a landscape picture in all nuances of light and shade and of atmosphere; for whom political factionalism in reality always remains something strange and repulsive.

She went on to relate how he had to spend a decade in exile and how he finally devoted his life to the struggle against poverty and social injustice, against corruption and oppression. She then threw Korolenko into bold relief against the back-drop of a monumental sketch of Russian literature from Pushkin to Gorky. As was to be expected, she drew on her Marxist world-view even here, revealing how the contrast between Russian and contemporary Western literature rose out of the different social conditions. She exposed all the mystical ideas which had long been rampant in Western European critiques of Russian literature for what they were. Far from clouding the issue her essay is a clear presentation, which makes the artists, their works, and their social environment equally intelligible. This is proof that Marxism is in no way the crude model which its opponents make it out to be; in the hands of a master it becomes an instrument for uncovering the motive forces of artistic creativity and for producing an awareness of the moral power of art.

Moreover, for Rosa Luxemburg, æsthetic criticism was not a mere labelling or hasty judgment according to political criteria:

> Stereotyped terms like "reactionary" or "progressive" still mean little in art. Dostoevsky, especially in his later writings, is an avowed reactionary, a canting mystic and hater of socialists. His portraits of Russian revolutionaries are malicious caricatures. Tolstoy's mystic teachings at least only play around with reactionary tendencies. And yet the works of both these writers have a rousing, edifying, and liberating effect on us. The conclusion is: it is not that their starting-point is reactionary; it is not that social hate, narrow-mindedness, caste-conscious egoism, and adherence to the existing order dominate their thoughts and feelings; but rather the contrary: they are motivated by a boundless love of humanity and a deep-seated feeling of responsibility for social injustice. . . . Indeed, for a true artist the social medicine that he prescribes is of secondary importance: it is the source of his art, its animating spirit, not the aim which he consciously sets for himself, which is of paramount importance.[90]

According to her, the source of power for Russian art, which, armed like Athene, came out into the open and dominated the field for a century, was the struggle against darkness, barbarism, and oppression In her preface to Korolenko's autobiography, and in her writings on Tolstoy, Gorky and others, she analysed and presented the essence of this art in a masterly way.

There was much that was manly about Rosa Luxemburg, in her keen intellect, in her boundless energy, in her dauntlessness, in her confidence and assertiveness. Yet she had nothing of the bluestocking—that highly-strung creature that plays the man—about herself. In fact, because she could not be anything other than completely natural, she was all woman. She herself felt that a woman, as a personality, was not a so-called 'outstanding woman', but 'a heart full of goodness and inner strength'. And although this is not an exhaustive description of her character, this is what she was—completely. With all her forcefulness, she was tender and sympathetic, sensitive and helpful. And sometimes she was seized by a longing to abandon the hurly-burly of political struggle altogether. 'I must have someone who believes me when I say that I drifted into the whirlpool of world history by pure accident, and that I was really born to tend geese.'[91]

She also never felt it her destiny to stalk the stage as a 'great woman'. She could play and trifle with abandon. On one occasion she disguised herself as a geisha and attended a masked ball with good friends. She set great store by good literary taste, and yet she was not above devouring half a dozen trashy thrillers one after the other. In her moral views she was broad-minded and liberal, but sometimes harmless, old-fangled prejudices would reveal themselves. The younger generation would then be surprised, and delighted, too, at the opportunity to smile down on her for once.

The fighter

The letter from prison which has undoubtedly made the deepest impression is one in which she tells of the buffalo which was dragged off to Germany as war loot, broken to the yoke, and disgracefully maltreated before her very eyes: 'Oh, my poor buffalo, my poor beloved brother, we both stand here so powerless and reduced to apathy; we are united in our pain, impotence and yearning. . . .' Alongside this are experiences with other poor creatures: half-frozen butterflies she puts into the warm sunlight; and a dung-beetle under attack by ravening ants, which she has to free from its tormentors only to be tormented herself by the feeling that she has condemned it to a still slower and more painful death.

Again and again her sympathies for all suffering creatures, for man and beast, breaks through. It is more highly developed in her than in most people; it is a capacity for deep empathy with the pain of others, for direct and physical sharing of suffering with them, and it stirs her to the depths. Such compassion has produced the great philanthropists of all ages. She was always ready to help and, when necessary, to help quickly, but she knew only too well that the things she could do were just so many drops in the ocean. And in the distress of the individual she never forgot the misery of the world:

> Do you remember the Great General Staff report on the Trotha expedition* in the Kalahari Desert? ". . . And the rattle of the dying and the delirious shrieks of parched men resounded in the majestic stillness of infinity". Oh! that "majestic stillness of infinity", in which so many cries have echoed away *unheard!* It rings so loudly in me that I can have no special corner in my heart for the ghetto: I feel at home in the whole world, wherever there are clouds and birds and human tears.[92]

In her introduction to Korolenko's autobiography, Rosa Luxemburg spoke in great detail about the all-embracing feelings of 'solidarity with mass misery' and of 'social responsibility' which

* The General Staff report deals with the German campaign to exterminate the Herero people in German-Southwest Africa (1904-06). The Heroes were eventually driven into the Kalahari Desert, where all of them—men, women, and children—died of thirst.

always moved the great writers of Russia. And she might have been writing of herself when she said of Russian literature: 'With desperate strength it shook the social and political chains of the age, chafing itself raw, and honourably paying the price of the struggle with its heart's blood.' Perhaps she had the experience of her own inner-struggles in mind when she sought the origin of Leonid Andreyev's literary decadence in a 'super-abundance of social compassion under which the capacity for action and resistance inevitably breaks down'. Her own determination and energy were co-equal with her solidarity with the misfortunes of the masses; she was impelled by an imperative need to get to the bottom of social phenomena, and she never flinched from the final consequences of her discoveries. These were the elements of her militancy which made her into a revolutionary.

These elements were knotted together and could be descried not only in her origins and in her ideas, but also in all her revolutionary activities. In 1918, in the middle of the revolutionary storm, she did not forget to keep a promise made to her non-political fellow-prisoners, and called publicly for the alleviation of their sufferings and for the abolition of the death sentence (in *Rote Fahne*, December 1918), thereby laying down her guiding rule as a revolutionary fighter:

> Unrelenting revolutionary activity coupled with boundless human-ity–that alone is the real life-giving force of socialism. A world must be overturned, but every tear that has flowed and might have been wiped away is an indictment; and a man hurrying to perform a great deed who steps on even a worm out of unfeeling careless-ness commits a crime.

At the same time she knew very well–better than the party operators–that the stakes in political activity were human life and human happiness, and that the struggle would demand resolution. She never evaded any necessity arising out of a political task if it shortened the way to the final aim and spared still greater suffering. She was always very conscious of her own responsibility before his-tory, but she never attempted to shelter behind it, to flee from neces-sary struggles and persuade the enslaved masses that their customary yoke was lighter than the sacrifices they would have to make in order to shake it off. For her, responsibility was the imperative of action: it was the readiness to take necessary decisions; to look, but also to leap; and with iron self-control to demand sacrifices from others and to sacrifice oneself for the cause. The calm certainty that her sense of responsibility would never fail to guide her was one of the roots of that firm confidence which evoked wonder (and sometimes consterna-tion) in all those who were close to her.

This strong conviction of her own value spurred her on to still greater achievements. It was wedded to the passion with which she threw herself into every task and which pulsed through her political work from beginning to end. But despite the intensity of the fire glowing within her, Rosa Luxemburg was above all a woman of thought and will. Her heart was disciplined by her head: all her political decisions had to be defended before the tribunal of reason and justified in theory before being put into action. Thought and deed were an indissoluble unity. She never rested until she had been able to fit all the observations and experiences of the day into a coherent picture of social development as a whole. This compelled her again and again to delve into the confusing variety of phenomena and search for the simple and basic contradictions of society operating in history so that she could put all the apparently fortuitous factors of time and place in proper perspective. She was not bound to any dogma, simply because she had to grasp things which were in a state of flux, continual change and development, and she did not take any statement, judgment or tactical rule for granted, just because it had once been valid.

For Rosa Luxemburg, socialism was not only a hope, but the fixed object of a tremendous will to action. She was therefore prepared to accept any consequences, however extreme, once she recognised them as logical and inevitable. Even when these consequences might offend her, it never occurred to her that she should let the cup pass. There was no room for compromise in her thought, and no conflict between her theoretical work and her practical action.

This attitude alone, the result of iron self-discipline, was sufficient to make her far superior to most of her close comrades-in-arms. In addition, she possessed an unusual visionary power. This she placed at the service of Marxist thought, but at the same time she let it plunge forward with unrestrained boldness. It was the source of that creative realism she demonstrated again and again, and also the reason for her being regarded often enough as a dreamer. What she taught seemed frequently to contradict reality, because it did not tally with the tangible facts of the moment. Her theory of capitalist accumulation was vehemently attacked not so much because it led to unwelcome political conclusions, but because its opponents did not have sufficient reasoning power to think beyond the contemporary period of capitalist prosperity.

Political strategy on a large scale is impossible without insight into the future. Like the great strategists of the class struggle—Marx, Engels, Lenin, Trotsky—she found herself compelled to act as prophet again and again; and, like them, her predictions occasionally proved to be wrong, for no one can possibly grasp and correctly estimate all the elements of future development. At times, too, she was carried away by revolutionary impatience. However, when each case is examined on its merits, it usually turns out that from the higher ground of her knowledge she overlooked detours, and turns and twists in the path of development, and sighted the final objective nearer than it actually was. The expected phenomena, class conflicts, etc., sometimes failed to mature, because new factors brought about a change in the historical process; eventually, however, under new conditions, they did break out–and with greater force than could ever have been imagined. This happened often enough, thus demonstrating the triumph of her fundamental ideas on the motive forces of history.

Intellectual effort was both a pleasure and a vital necessity for her. She experienced the highest intensity of life in conflict–in intellectual conflict primarily. Almost everything she wrote was polemical. Even where she was investigating complicated problems she always had an eye on her opponent, ready to refute him, to cut him down. She certainly did not need the reminder, 'You must do things with joy. . . !' The joy of battle was always hers in the loud clang of polemical swordplay and in the testing of her moral superiority. When she had her opponent before the point of her sword, her intellect sparkled most brilliantly. Those stout souls of the socialist movement, who were themselves old hands at fighting, could not but admire her swordsmanship, even when they were the victims. A man like Plekhanov paid public homage to her–his sharpest opponent at the London Congress of Russian Social Democracy [1907]–for the passion, brilliance, and intellectual polish with which she had delivered an attack against him. Certain hidebound souls, however, were loud in their condemnation of her 'malice' and 'quarrelsomeness' and retaliated in kind. However, she only fought against opinions, and attacked her opponent in a personal way only when it seemed necessary to give tit for tat. Like Marx, she could state with resignation: 'Whoever criticises his opponent with insulting language has temperament; however, whoever insults his opponent with real criticism is a mean character.'

The strongest elements in her character–compassion, a thirst for knowledge, an iron will, a militant spirit–fused to a harmonious whole in her socialist ideas. In an obituary article Clara Zetkin declared:

> In Rosa Luxemburg the socialist idea was a dominating and powerful passion of both mind and heart, a consuming and creative passion. To prepare for the revolution, to pave the way for socialism–this was the task and the one great ambition of this exceptional woman. To experience the revolution, to fight in its battles–this was her highest happiness. With will-power, selflessness and devotion, for which words are too weak, she engaged her whole being and everything she had to offer for socialism. She sacrificed herself to the cause, not only in her death, but daily and hourly in

the work and the struggle of many years. . . . She was the sword, the flame of revolution.

As she herself admitted, the rendering of the confession of Ulrich von Hutten in Konrad Ferdinand Meyer's epic poem, *'Huttens letzte Tage'* (Hutten's last Days) reflected her own inner-most thoughts:

Mich reut die Stunde, die nicht Harnisch trug!
Mich reut der Tag, der keine Wunde schlug!
Mich reut–ich streu mir Asche auf das Haupt–
Dass ich nicht fester noch an Sieg geglaubt!
Mich reut, dass ich nur einmal ward gebannt!
Mich reut, dass oft ich Menschenfurcht gekannt!
Mich reut–ich beicht es mit zerknirschtem Sinn–
Dass ich nicht dreifach kühn gewesen bin!

I regret the hour in which I wore no armour!
I regret the day that struck no wound!
I regret–strewing ashes on my head–
That I did not believe more firmly in victory!
I regret that I was banished only once!
I regret that I have often known human fear!
I regret–and confess it with contrite feeling–
That I was not three times more daring!

These lines are engraved on the tombstone of her friend Bruno Schönlank. On one occasion, quoting them in a letter to her secretary, Mathilde Jacob, she expressed the wish that they might also be her own epitaph. Indeed, it was really her secret wish. Yet when she saw them again in black and white, she shrank back from their all too showy pathos, and brushed away the idea in a self-ironical tone:

You didn't take me seriously, Mathilde, did you? Yes, laugh about it. On my grave as in my life there will be no conceited phrases. My tombstone may have only two syllables on it: "tsvee-tsvee" (*zwi-zwi*). That's the call of the tom-tits, and I can imitate it so well that they come running here right away. It's usually a clear, fine sound, as sparkling as a steel needle. But imagine! For some days now there's been a very small warble in this tsvee-tsvee, a tiny chest-note. And do you know what that means? That is the first rustling of the coming spring. Despite snow and frost and loneliness, we–the tom-tits and I–believe in the coming of spring. And if I don't get to experience it because of my impatience, then don't forget: nothing should be on my tombstone except "tsvee-tsvee".[93]

The grand epitaph, her protest against it, and the way she formulated it are all Rosa Luxemburg. To lose herself in the gentle contemplation of Nature, to embrace mankind with ardour, to penetrate the world with her intellect, to live life to the full, and to accelerate its rhythm in a struggle ablaze with passion–that was her style of life. And her motto: 'Man must always live like a candle burning at both ends.'

In her devotion to scientific truth, in her scholarly urge, where her brilliant intuition and dogged will to gain knowledge joined forces, as well as in her humanitarian idealism, she resembles that other great Pole, Marie Curie. But she was inwardly freer, more relaxed, and without the asceticism of the great scientist. As a revolutionary she had the deep sensitiveness, the artistic nature, the enthusiasm, the passion, the burning militancy, and the boundless spirit of self-sacrifice of Louise Michel. However, her deep knowledge of the conditions of struggle, her scientifically based worldview, and her sure political instinct raise her above 'the Red Virgin'. The great talents of her heart and intellect and a flaming will to action united in her to a full-toned harmony. Our century will never see her like again.

The writer

Poles reading Rosa Luxemburg's Polish writings wax enthusiastic at her literary style, at its power and its shimmering beauty, and place her among the great masters of their language. Germans who are even only slightly acquainted with her work in German can well understand that. She herself, having shied away from writing in Russian because she believed she had not mastered it well enough, always felt faintly mistrustful of her German. She was plagued all the time by the fear that her Polish might creep in and affect its style. There was no need for her misgivings: she wrote a clear and masterly German. Apart from her earliest writings, only a certain very infrequent rigidity in sentence construction reminds us that German was not her mother-tongue. She had absorbed the spirit of the language, and its whole vocabulary was at her effortless command; even the earthy idioms of the people gave her no problems, and she knew how to use them to add colour and force to her argument.

As a hammer in the craftsman's hand becomes an extension of his arm, so language to her was a part of her being. Sometimes she wrote long and very complicated sentences, but she never succumbed to the danger that looms so large for German writers, namely of allowing the thread of ideas to get entangled in an underbrush of subordinate clauses. Her sentences grow out of her ideas; even when they are complicated, they run freely and naturally, and are therefore clear. Rosa's great talent as a propagandist is evident in her prose: she never forces her ideas upon her readers; she seeks to convince; she is above all teacher, rarely agitator. Her manner of looking at the world and its problems–always grasping the complex and interpenetrating phenomena of life, and in particular of social life, as a whole and as a continuing process–reveals itself in her writing. And yet her presentation is never pedantic. The echo of reality always resounds in it, and one can always feel the fiery and forceful temperament of the author.

The development of her style shows the self-discipline of the artist. In the beginning it is colourful, glittering; later the form becomes 'very simple, without any coquetry', as she herself once described her *Anti-critique*, written in 1915, to her friend Hans Diefenbach. In the same letter [8 March 1917], she wrote, with obvious pleasure at the 'heresy' which was now her taste and 'which valued the simple, the calm, and the grand in both scientific work and in art, and therefore, e.g. I now find the much-praised first volume of Marx's *Capital* a horror because of its overload of rococo ornaments in the Hegelian style'. It is probable that she herself always had to fight against the temptation to overload her style with ornamentation. Her lively intellect could easily make surprising and far-fetched associations, and evoke a stream of word-pictures, but it was held in check by artistic tact. Moreover, she often thought in pointed antitheses, but she never presented them in that antithetic form which has the effect of crackling fireworks, brilliant, but also blinding.

Like most great stylists, she loved the word-picture; it fitted into the flow of her ideas with the same ease with which it flashed into her mind as she was forming her ideas. Above all, it served her well in polemics, because she quickly discovered the weaknesses of her opponents, and always had the weapons of wit and irony at her command. Her writing was studded with them, for example, when she spoke of the bourgeois politician whose fate it was 'again and again to find himself clutching only the tassel of his nightcap whenever he thinks he is grasping at the brightest star'. Her images breathe life itself; they are well-polished and complete. They generally culminate in a point which either flares up like a dazzling exclamation mark, or tapers off like an ironic sigh fading away. Thus she once concluded a description of the outcome of the political tragicomedy of the Millerand episode with the sentence: 'And even the dying gas-lamps in the auditorium began to smell rather foul.' The whole atmosphere of the fiasco is there; and the picture becomes plastic and three-dimensional when, in her final words, she shows how Jaurès persisted in playing the old optimistic tunes from the early days of socialist ministerialism even though the flowering dreams had long since been pounded to bits by the hailstones of experience:

> Jaurès's melodies are already like the good old arias from Verdi's operas: once in sunny Italy these warbles were on the lips of every merry, dark-eyed cobbler's apprentice like the promise of a people's spring, but now they screech forth with dreadful monotony out of the dead mechanism of a barrel-organ: *Tempi passati!* The organ-grinder himself stares into space with an air of absent-minded boredom as he grinds. And we see that it is only the practised hand which is doing the grinding; the spirit is missing.[94]

Her metaphors and similes always have both feet firmly on the ground—or almost always. Occasionally an all-too-daring picture may misfire, but never does her writing plummet from the sublime to the ridiculous, as happened often enough to that other great literary artist, Lassalle. It was he who once shrieked about the 'Fury of the broken legal foundation' (*Erinnye des gebrochenen Rechtsbodens*)! She was immune from such absurdities. She not only had the tact that Lassalle so often lacked, but she also hated anything that smacked of pathos. Only the monumental nature of the recital of one shocking fact after the other imparts pathos and a profoundly stirring note to her style. And when events are so violent and the tragedy so crushing that pathos obtrudes itself, she then reaches out for the dissonance of irony. Her writings during the World War are particularly marked by it. Her *Juniusbroschüre* begins with this picture:

> Gone is the frenzy. Gone the patriotic uproar in the streets; the hunt after foreign gold transports; the stream of false telegrams; the wells poisoned with cholera germs; the Russian students throwing bombs at every railway bridge; the French airplanes flying over Nuremberg; the excesses of the spy-sniffing public in the streets; the surging crush of people in the cafés, where ear-splitting music and patriotic songs shook the air; whole town-populations transformed into rabble, prepared to denounce, to mishandle women, to shriek hurrah; a ritual-murder atmosphere, a Kishinev air, in which the policeman on the street-corner was the only representative of human dignity.[95]

She wrote regularly for newspapers, but she was not a journalist. She didn't allow herself to be harnessed to that yoke: day after day to grind out comments on ministerial speeches, parliamentary bills, diplomatic conflicts, and so on. It was almost always theoretical or tactical problems which moved her to write. Nevertheless, those few purely journalistic pieces she did write could find a place in any collection of journalistic masterpieces. These articles took events of the day out of their 'natural' setting and put them into a broad social context; they exposed the isolated phenomenon as a symptom of the social order, or they used a wound to illustrate the agony of humanity. When Mount Pelée on the island of Martinique erupted in 1902, she sketched an affecting picture of the eruptions of world politics which devastated not just an individual town but whole countries time and again with brutal regularity. When, after a lull of fifty years, new legislation in Germany gave slightly increased protection to child labour, she ripped the mask of hypocrisy from the face of society, which in the holy name of the family permitted and in fact legally bound workers in cottage industries to exploit the labour of their own children more than that of other children.[96] And during the Christmas festivities in 1911, over 150 unemployed and other social outcasts fell ill in Berlin's casual wards from drinking poisonous spirit, and more than half of them died. It inspired her to write an indictment in the incisive and crisp style of a Swift, but in it her deep sympathy with the utter misery of these pariahs and her hatred of and indignation at 'a social order which gives birth to such horrors' rose to heights of real pathos. And yet not one word in the whole essay is exaggerated.[97]

The orator

The renunciation of mere dazzle for its own sake is clearest where the temptation to indulge in it is greatest–in public speaking. Rosa Luxemburg was a fascinating speaker, but she never indulged in mere rhetoric. She was economical in the use of grand words and gestures; she achieved her effect purely by the content of her speeches, though in this she was assisted by a silver-toned, rich and melodious voice which could fill, without effort, a great hall. She never spoke from notes, and preferred to walk casually up and down the platform because she felt closer to her audience this way. She could establish contact within a few sentences, and from then onwards she kept her audience completely under her spell. As with all great speakers, inspiration had an almost visible effect on her, giving that final polish to her ideas and an added punch to her words.

She never sought to win an audience by appealing merely to its momentary mood; only seldom did she appeal to its feelings. Her aim was always to make it recognise the truth of what she was saying so that this recognition might lead to action. She held her listeners by the inescapable logic of her presentation and by her ability to express the essence of things in the simplest fashion. She never talked over their heads. A gripping picture, a striking simile, were often sufficient to enlighten an audience on a previously obscure point, or to fill with sudden new life an idea that had become a rigid formula. What her listeners had only dimly felt before became a certainty when she spoke. Relationships between things and new aspects now became clear, and wider horizons opened up. People felt themselves raised from the humdrum of everyday life into the higher realm of ideas. And what was really singular: the speaker faded almost completely into the background during the speech. Her ideas had such a strong riveting force that her listeners heard only the high, clear voice which expressed them, until some particularly elec-trifying remark snapped them out of the spell. Nevertheless, it was the person, the compact personality behind the speech; the intense vigour; the harmony of feeling, purpose, and thought; the clarity, boldness, and aptness of her ideas; and the well-disciplined tempera-ment which fascinated an audience.

This personality came suddenly to the fore, right into the lime-light, so to speak, when Rosa had the good fortune to find an opponent. Her polemical ardour fully aroused, she would use all her talents and determination to bring him down. She seized on her opponent's weaknesses immediately, at the point where his logic deserted him, and skilfully checkmated him. In his reminiscences of Rosa Luxemburg, published in *Der Kampf* (Vienna) in 1919, Max Adler spoke about the effect of such fighting speeches:

> An untamed revolutionary force was alive in this frail little woman; again and again, despite the many mockers and haters with whom she too had to contend, it brought listeners at party congresses under the spell of her fiery temperament, and moved even her op-ponents to join in the noisy applause. It was characteristic of her, however, that her intellect never lost control of her temperament, so that the revolutionary fire with which she always spoke was also mingled with cool-headed reflectiveness, and the effect of this fire was not destructive, but warming and illuminating.

The effect was, of course, even greater at public meetings than at party congresses, where the opposing camps were already more or less firmly established from the outset and the factional spirit strong.

Rosa's ready wit, her presence of mind, and her instinctive grasp of the psychological moment were displayed especially clearly in an incident which took place during the election campaign of 1907. She was speaking on colonialism and foreign policy in one of the great halls in the Hasenheide district of Berlin. It was jam-packed. A police lieutenant and an old constable ('*ein Blauer*'-lit. a man in blue) were present on the platform to watch the proceedings [in accordance with the prevailing laws of public assembly–so that if the officer thought fit he could declare the meeting closed at any time]. The young lieutenant was obviously very nervous, and on several occasions he started to reach for his helmet. [The donning of the helmet was the signal to break up.] Rosa grasped the situation, and each time she rapidly changed the subject, leaving the lieutenant in confusion. And when he finally seemed about to make a determined move, she addressed him directly, promising with a fine sense of irony to keep both the form and content of her speech within the limits permitted by the police regulations. She now proceeded to describe the dull life of those petit-bourgeois strata which oscillate in the great struggle between capital and labour, and are finally crushed. She pointed out their eternally disappointed hopes, their childish illusions, and their joyless existence. And then she touched on the narrowness of civil-service life, showing how a servant of the state was strangulated by rules, his whole being yoked to the cog-wheels of the repressive state machine—its tool and its victim at the same time. She explained the well-known saying of Marx that the bourgeoisie transformed the doctor, the lawyer, the priest, the poet, and the man of science into its hired labourers. 'And you, too', she turned to the police lieutenant, 'are nothing but a mere tool in the service of the bourgeoisie and its exploitation of the people, whether you know it or not.' Her words went straight to the hearts and minds of her listeners. The whole audience was tense with excitement. A particularly forceful and hard-hitting observation then triggered off an outburst of stormy applause, and it was seen that the old heavily-moustached policeman, the stout-hearted *Blauer*, was clapping along with the rest. When the speaker dealt with things which touched him so closely, the nothingness of his life, he forgot everything else, the fact that he was on duty, his task, his very self; he belonged to the masses in the hall, and he joined in the clapping with his big podgy hands—until he caught sight of the horrified and astounded face of his lieutenant. His arms dropped automatically to his side. Now, still obviously excited, he became an official again, but for a few minutes he had been a man of the people with the people.

In the days before the World War—a time which flowed by without any great upheavals, a time when the masses tended to regard the existing political conditions as a permanent state of affairs —Rosa Luxemburg made it clear that, in order to achieve the very high goals of socialism, great struggles were inevitable. She aroused enthusiasm among the masses for this coming period of revolt, and made them see the truth and the genuineness of her warning and exhortation: 'Be prepared to give to socialism not only your vote but also your life!'

11
War

The fourth of August

On 28 June 1914 a spark fell into the powder-keg of Europe. Crown Prince Franz Ferdinand, heir to the throne of Austria-Hungary, was murdered, together with his wife, in Sarajevo by Serbian nationalists. However, the tension unleashed by the event soon subsided. The storm-clouds seemed to pass, just as they had massed together and dispersed again in 1905-06 after the Morocco incident, in 1909 after the annexation of Bosnia, in 1911 after the Morocco and Tripoli incidents, and in 1912-13 after the Balkan Wars. The most dangerous knot of imperialist antagonism – that between Great Britain and Germany – seemed about to be unravelled; the two Powers were reaching an agreement covering a whole series of colonial questions. Then, on 23 July, the Hapsburg monarchy sent an ultimatum to Serbia, an ultimatum which had been re-drafted seven times in order to exclude any possibility of its acceptance and thus to force a war. On 25 July Austria-Hungary, supported and encouraged by the German government, declared war on Serbia. On 29 July partial mobilisation was ordered in Russia.

On 29 and 30 July the Bureau of the Workers' International met in Brussels to take a stand on the Austro-Serbian war and the general war danger. Most of the well-known leaders of the European socialist parties were present: Jaurès, Guesde, and Vaillant (France); Keir Hardie (Great Britain); Akselrod (Russia); Luxemburg (Poland); Haase and Kautsky (Germany); Morgari and Angelica Balabanoff (Italy); Victor and Friedrich Adler (Austria); Vandervelde (Belgium); Troelstra (Holland).

A report on the proceedings of this council at the highest level of the international working-class movement was never published. They were apparently treated as a dangerous diplomatic secret. Only a few indications of what happened were made public by some of the participants, and these add up to a depressing picture. The question of which line the socialist parties should adopt towards the war was obviously not treated in all its significant implications, but merely touched upon. Six years after the conference Kautsky wrote: 'It is curious that not one of us who was there got the idea of asking what was to be done if war really did break out beforehand [i.e. before the planned Congress of the International in August 1914 in Vienna–PF]; what attitude should the socialist parties adopt in this war?'[98]

That isn't completely correct. The debate was probably dominated by the question of how the Austrian party should behave in the Austro-Serbian war which had already broken out. And Victor Adler's attitude put the conference in an impasse. As recently as 1912, at the Peace Congress of the International in Basle, Adler had expressed the hope that any outbreak of the crime of war would automatically signify the beginning of the end of the rule of the criminals. Now, his spirit completely broken, he could only stammer:

> The war is already upon us. Up to now we have fought against war as well as we could. The workers also did their utmost against the war intrigues. But don't expect any further action from us. We are in a state of war. Our press is censored. We have a state of emergency and martial law as a back-drop.–I did not come here to address a public meeting, but to tell you the truth, that when hundreds of thousands are already marching to the borders and martial law holds sway at home, no action is possible here.[99]

When Friedrich Adler had to stand trial for his attempt on the life of Count Stürgkh*, he also described his impressions of the meeting of the International Bureau. At the time, he said, he felt for the first time that his views differed from those of his father. Before the meeting Victor Adler had had a discussion with Jules Guesde in which the former had emphasised that Austria-Hungary would have a front not only against Serbia, but also against Russia, Italy, Rumania, etc. 'Guesde said: *"Et la frontière ouvrière?"* (And the workers' front?), to which my father answered defensively: *"Non, non, non!"*–what that meant was that Austrian Social Democracy would not offer any resistance to the war-leadership of the ruling class.' Friedrich Adler also recounted that when Bruce Glasier of the Independent Labour Party (ILP) attacked the Austrians for their attitude, his father scoffed at him and pointed to the inactivity of the English proletariat during the Boer War. 'His speech made an extremely depressing impression on everyone, especially on the Germans and the French, and also on me. The report which Victor

---

* The shooting of the Austrian Minister Stürgkh, one of those chiefly responsible for the war provocation, by Friedrich Adler (1879-1960) on 21 October 1916 was intended to be a signal to the Austrian proletariat to wage a struggle against the war. Adler's initial death-sentence was commuted to 18 years imprisonment, and after the outbreak of revolution in Austria he was amnestied. His later political life was devoted especially to the re-erection of a socialist International.

Adler then gave to the conference breathed a spirit of absolute passiveness.'[100]

Even though these reports say very little about the proceedings of the conference itself, they nevertheless reveal its general mood. As we have seen, Victor Adler, the spokesman of a party which was already being put to the test–his authority within his own party far exceeded that of the leaders of other parties–declared that it would submit to the will of the instigators of the war without showing any will or fight of its own. The other party leaders, whom events had granted a short respite in which to make their decision, still clung to the ideas and resolutions of the International, and sought to wrench Adler out of his mood of capitulation. However, they did not try to do anything more than that, and some of them must have already felt that they themselves would be following Adler in a few days' time. The participants therefore evaded making any decision on the general war policy of the International. The resolutions of the conference prove how wrongly they estimated the tempo of history: the next Congress of the International, which was to have convened at the end of August in Vienna, was now rescheduled to begin on 9 August in Paris. In the meantime the proletarians of all countries were supposed 'not only to continue, but to intensify their demonstrations against the war, for peace, and for arbitration to settle the Austro-Serbian conflict'.

Nothing is known about the activities of Rosa Luxemburg at this conference. However, if we take into account everything we know about her, there can be no doubt about her basic position. But as to the arguments she used, the concrete demands she made–these we know nothing about. We can only conclude from one episode how badly the proceedings shook her confidence in the International.

Following the meeting of the International Bureau, a great rally against the war was held in Brussels. The *Cirque Royal* was filled to capacity, and thousands were standing outside the gates. The start of the assembly was delayed somewhat because the Bureau had not managed to finish its business on time. Meanwhile the workers in the hall were discussing the recent events. The mood was one of high spirits and optimism. 'They won't dare to do it; and even if they should, we have the International!' One worker struck up a revolutionary song, and the masses in the hall and outside joined in enthusiastically. Finally the members of the Bureau arrived, and the meeting began. Vandervelde and Hugo Haase spoke and were greeted with loud applause. With his flaming eloquence Jaurès enraptured the masses, who interrupted him with one storm of applause after the other. Among other things, he said: 'We Frenchmen have the duty to insist that the French government should energetically exhort Russia to keep out of the conflict. And if Russia doesn't do so, then it is our duty to say: "We know only one pact, the pact that binds us to humanity!" ' Jaurès then addressed Rosa Luxemburg directly: 'Allow me to greet that valiant woman, Rosa Luxemburg, who fills the hearts of the German proletariat with the flame of her ideas.' The whole audience was roused by his speech; it brought him an ovation that went on and on as if it would never end, 'an elevating and unforgettable *manifestation*', as *Le Peuple* in Brussels described it.

And Rosa Luxemburg? She arrived later than the other party representatives. Her face was pallid, and she was obviously trying to control a strong inner agitation. On the platform, where the members of the International Bureau were sitting, she remained standing for a long time and looked silently out at the crowd. She then sat down and hid her face in her hands. Members of the Bureau approached her twice, and spoke to her in pressing tones. She shook her head energetically and said only one word: 'No!'. It had been announced that she would speak, and Vandervelde, the chairman, said: 'I would gladly have given the floor to Rosa Luxemburg, but I would like to spare her the strain.' Jaurès interrupted: 'She will only get a rest in prison!' Vandervelde then continued: 'Nevertheless, I would like to greet the gallant German fighter who means so much for the German proletariat in the present situation. Since Rosa Luxemburg, that dangerous enemy of the state, will not take the floor, I shall give it to Troelstra.' Although Rosa was again and again besieged by the crowd, she just sat there, motionless and lost in thought, deep sorrow written on her face.*

This is a Rosa whom nobody knows. That she should be weary –she who usually had to shrug off frailty and illness to stand before the masses? That she should now not feel the urge or trust her strength to inspire and inflame others? At such a moment! That she who never broke down should break down in the face of a world catastrophe whose magnitude she grasped clearer than anyone else? Impossible! Her obstinate refusal to speak had other reasons, and these obtrude themselves with such force that there can be no mistaking them.

From the lessons of history, and especially from the experience of the Russo-Japanese War, she was familiar with the blinding and bewildering effects that nationalism had on the popular masses at

---

* In the first edition of this book, PF's account of the rally was based on the 'memories' of a member of the International Bureau at the time [a reference to Angelica Balabanoff's memoirs, published in German as *Erinnerungen und Erlebnisse*, Berlin 1927, and in English as *My Life as a Rebel*, London 1938]. With respect to Rosa Luxemburg's behaviour however, this source was inaccurate, and the present account is based on the report of *Le Peuple* (Brussels) and on the corroborative reports provided by several of the meeting's participants.

the beginning of a war. She knew that resistance to the slaughter of peoples would entail an arduous uphill struggle, exacting a heavy toll. She was aware of the enormity of the task which the International had set for itself in accepting her resolution against militarism at the Stuttgart Congress in 1907; she was aware of how much sense of responsibility, how much self-denial, and how much courage this task would demand from the parties and their leaders. During the proceedings of the International Bureau she had tried to look deeply into the hearts of the party leaders, and in the attitude of Victor Adler and Austrian Social Democracy she had recognised the symptom of an illness which had befallen the whole International. Even though she could not yet take in the full extent of the catastrophe, even though she might not believe that the socialist parties would, almost without exception, go over into the enemy camp, nevertheless one thing was perfectly clear to her: the majority of the parties would not pass the test, but would, at best, let the world-wide tempest rage about them without putting up any resistance or taking any action. This explains why she looked so searchingly into the mass of people in that hall, people who still turned to the International with hope and faith. Could she speak to these people? Could she tell them the awful truth, destroy their faith and produce a panic? This she could not bring herself to do–for both psychological and political reasons. Yet it would have been just as impossible for her to compromise with a lie, to feign optimism, to strengthen futile hopes among the masses, to deceive them. She therefore remained silent.

On 31 July both Austria-Hungary and Russia ordered full mobilisation, whereupon the German government sent an ultimatum with a twelve-hour time limit to St Petersburg. A state of war was proclaimed in Germany. In an atmosphere of oppressive anxiety, while expecting the arrest of all the party leaders at any moment, the Party Executive conferred with representatives of the social-democratic members of the Reichstag to discuss their position on the granting of war credits. Haase and Ledebour wanted to vote against the credits, but all the rest favoured their acceptance, although the prevailing opinion was that among the party members in the Reichstag the radicals would get the upper hand. It was decided to send Hermann Müller to Paris to discuss the possibility of joint action by the French and the German socialists. That very evening Jean Jaurès was assassinated in Paris.

The next day, 1 August, Hermann Müller met with the French party leaders. Neither the struggle against war, nor the continuation of the class struggle during the war if it came, was discussed, but merely the question of war credits. Müller declared that the German social-democratic deputies would probably vote against the credits;

there was a faint possibility that they might abstain, but under no circumstances would they vote in favour. The French socialist leaders cited the fact that the war was a defensive one for France, and they would therefore have to vote in favour of war credits. Müller retorted that by the time war broke out it would scarcely be possible to determine who was doing the attacking and who the defending, and that the deeper-lying causes of the war were to be found in the policy of imperialist expansion and the armaments race, which had been pursued by all the Powers with equal obstinacy for decades. He thus argued within the framework of the views accepted by the Socialist International; however, nobody, neither he nor anyone else, even mentioned the clear resolutions and policies prescribed by that body. The Belgian representative, Huysmans, even tried to persuade Müller that it would be better for the German socialists to abstain from voting on the war credits rather than to vote against them. The discussion clearly showed the embarrassment of the French socialist leaders at the idea that their German colleagues might take too-radical action. They were no longer able to think internationally, and were already lining up with their government and marching off to war, but they were still anxious to preserve some appearance of international unity.

While these discussions were proceeding, Germany declared war on Russia, and then followed in rapid succession the decisions which set the whole of Europe in flames. On 3 August the German social-democratic deputies in the Reichstag met to decide their stand regarding the war credits. Out of 111 deputies only 15, including Liebknecht, Haase, Ledebour, Rühle and Lensch, called for a 'no' vote. Their demand for special permission to register their minority vote was rejected. On 4 August the parliamentary membership closed ranks to vote in favour of the war credits. Even Karl Liebknecht bowed to party discipline.

This vote caused consternation in the international working-class movement, and at first the news was disbelieved in many places. The newspaper of the Rumanian socialist party declared it to be a monstrous lie, and even Lenin thought that the issue of *Vorwärts* containing the report of the Reichstag session was a forgery issued by the German General Staff. It was clear to all the left-wing radicals in the party that although the failure of other parties in the International would not necessarily spell complete disaster, the failure of the German party as the leading socialist party would mean the victory of nationalism all along the line and the utter collapse of the International. Such a thing was impossible to believe, impossible to grasp. But a rumour, spread around that same time, that Rosa Luxemburg and Karl Liebknecht had been court-martialled and shot to death, was believed. . . . This foreboding of the atrocious deeds of 15 January 1919 showed who were regarded by friend and foe alike in Germany as the real revolutionaries.

Under the banner of revolt

The decision of her party was a heavy blow to Rosa Luxemburg, much more so than the shock of the Brussels conference. The attitude of the Austrian Social Democracy was, at least for the time being, one of passive submissiveness, whereas the German Party Executive and the party's Reichstag deputies–whatever the alleged reason might have been–were indicating their consent to the war and their justification of it; they were swinging into line with the imperialist front. It is not true, as Kautsky claimed, that 'in the last few years before the war' she had 'held the view that the outbreak of war would be answered by the proletariat with revolution'. She knew from the experience of the Russo-Japanese war how difficult it was for the working class to take the great leap from war to revolution. Her emphatic rejection of the idea that the International should pledge itself to call a general strike upon the outbreak of war and the wording of the Stuttgart resolution demonstrate that she viewed matters more sensibly than Kautsky claimed. Besides, 'in the last few years before the war', Kautsky could hardly have had a chance to discuss this question with her. She did find it utterly incredible, however, that the German working class should let itself be driven to the slaughter-house without the slightest attempt at resistance, and that all the long years of work, of education and enlightenment, seemed to have been wiped out in the space of an hour. The capitulation of German Social Democracy, its desertion to the imperialist camp, the resultant collapse of the International, indeed the seeming collapse of her whole world, shattered her spirit.

For a moment–probably the only time in her life–she was seized by despair. But only for a moment! She immediately pulled herself together again, and by a sheer act of will, overcame her sudden sense of weakness. On the evening of that very day on which the social-democratic leadership concluded its alliance with the Kaiser and his General Staff–4 August–a small group of comrades gathered at Rosa Luxemburg's flat. Among them were the ageing Franz Mehring and Julian Marchlewski-Karski. They decided to take up the struggle against the war and against the war policy of their own party. That was the beginning of the rebellion which went into history under the banner of *Spartakus*. From Stuttgart Clara Zetkin declared her readiness to work with the group, and it was not long before Karl Liebknecht joined too. He had been quick to recognise how mistaken he had been to assume that the decision in favour of war credits had been only a temporary weak moment for the party, and he was now prepared to shoulder all the consequences of unpopular resistance. Throughout Germany, and particularly in the working-class quarters of Berlin, in Württemberg, in Saxony, in the Rhineland and the Ruhr, and in the industrial ports of the North, there were comrades who remained loyal to the party colours. Slowly, gropingly, they came together—grey-beards who had once fought in the days of the Anti-Socialist Laws, young people, and women—and thus began, both in public and underground, the struggle against the war.

For Rosa Luxemburg there now followed months when every single day brought new bad experiences. What had begun as a resigned submission to fate among the leaders of the International rapidly became a frenzy of patriotism. All socialist dignity was trodden under-foot in the press. Overnight editors forgot what they had known perfectly well before 1 August: that the war would not be a national war of defence, that all the Great Powers bore their share of responsibility for its outbreak, that it sprang from deep imperialist antagonisms and served predatory ends. These were the very men who had solemnly promised a hundred times and more, in word and writing, to fight against such a war without shunning the consequences. Now they poured forth a spate of lies, absolving their rulers of any blame, inciting their readers against foreign peoples, and heaping flattery on the state that had persecuted them only the day before and on the Kaiser who had reviled them. They concluded the *Burgfrieden* (intra-party truce), which handed over the working men and women, bound hand and foot, to the capitalists as wage-slaves and to the General Staff as cannon-fodder.

And daily came the news of new desertions from the international socialist camp. When Scheidemann, vain as a peacock, turned somersaults with his patriotic pathos; when Südekum became a propagandist for German imperialism in neutral countries; and when Rosa's old enemies from the trade unions fraternised at banquets with Stinnes and Thyssen—all this only strengthened her long-felt contempt for these so-called socialists. But Plekhanov, who had once preached a revolutionary rising against war, had now become the standard-bearer of Tsarism against Prussian barbarism. Guesde, the rigid Marxist, had entered the French War Cabinet. Even Rosa's old friend, Vaillant, had suffered a relapse into his former Blanquist nationalism and saw the France of 1914 with the halo of 1793, as the revolutionary nation *par excellence*. She had long parted from that other comrade-in-arms of her youth, Parvus, ever since the days of the Balkan wars when he had amassed a considerable fortune by speculation as a supporter of the Turks. Now he had become adviser to the German Foreign Office and organiser of Germany's trade with Scandinavia and the Balkans. At one point he dared to seek her out, but Rosa, feeling his visit to be a slap in the face, wordlessly showed him the door. Cunow, editor-in-chief of *Vorwarts*, and one of the '*kosher*' group with which she had taken over the editorship of the central organ of the party in 1905, now competed with the Austrian Karl Renner in pruning Marxism for imperialist ends. After wavering for a short while, Paul Lensch, the former editor-in-chief of the *Leipziger Volkszeitung*, who had always prided himself on being Rosa's pupil and shield-bearer, also deserted to the enemy camp; he praised the German war economy–that organised system of semi-starvation–as a victory for socialist ideas, and Germany's war against Great Britain–the 'despot of the world market'–as the revolution. Konrad Haenisch, once the enthusiastic trumpet of the Left Radicals, now sang '*Deutschland, Deutschland über alles!*' till he was blue in the face. And Karl Kautsky did his best to cover the shame of the socialist movement with a web of platitudes, sophisms, and misrepresentations. He asserted [in October 1914 in *Neue Zeit*] that it was impossible to determine the character of the war because it had not broken out in the normal way: 'Ordinarily, states formulate their demands, declare war, and then mobilise. This time mobilisation was not ordered because of war, but war was declared because of mobilisation, and not until the outcome of the war will the aims (for which the war was supposed to have been waged) be determined.' And he airily dismissed the collapse of the International with the brilliant statement: 'It [the International] is not an effective weapon in wartime; it is essentially an instrument of peace. Namely peace in a twofold sense: the struggle for peace, and the class struggle in peacetime!' Socialist theory thus abdicated voluntarily, and demanded that the working class as a political factor, should do likewise.

Rosa Luxemburg regarded it as her immediate task to organise resistance against the war policy of the SPD, and she worked harder than ever in the Berlin organisation, both among the rank and file and in its leading organs. The first successes were greater than might have been expected in view of the defection of most of the higher and middle-level party officials. There were seen to be at least strong oppositional minorities everywhere, and in the giant constituency of Niederbarnim a majority of the party members were in opposition. However, faced with the double oppression of military and party censorship, the oppositional tendencies could find hardly any public outlet for their views. The leaderless workers in the provinces who were opposed to the war, but still unclear about their position, were often forced to give way to the skilled proponents of the SPD Executive's policy. How were they to be encouraged and furnished with

effective arguments? There were still 15 members in the Reichstag
who had spoken out against the war credits; a public demonstration
by them would prove to the war-resisters that they were not alone.
Moreover, it would show foreign public opinion that a struggle
against the war within Germany was under way. Clara Zetkin later
described the efforts made in this direction in her preface to a new
edition of Rosa Luxemburg's *Juniusbroschüre*:

> The struggle was supposed to begin with a protest against the vot-
> ing of war credits by the social-democratic Reichstag deputies, but
> it had to be conducted in such a way that it would not be throttled
> by the cunning tricks of the military authorities and the censorship.
> Moreover, and above all, the significance of such a protest would
> doubtless be enhanced, if it were supported from the outset by a
> goodly number of well-known social-democratic militants. We
> therefore endeavoured to formulate it so that it would bring about
> the solidarity of as many as possible of the leading comrades who
> had sharply, even scathingly, criticised the policy of 4 August in
> the Reichstag and in small private circles. This consideration cost
> us much brain-racking, paper, many letters and telegrams, and
> precious time, and in the end all for nothing. Out of all those out-
> spoken critics of the social-democratic majority, only Karl Liebk-
> necht joined with Rosa Luxemburg, Franz Mehring, and myself in
> defying the soul-destroying and demoralising idol into which party
> discipline had developed.

The same game was played when the German government
again demanded additional credits from the Reichstag. At first, quite
a number of social-democratic deputies declared themselves prepared
to vote publicly against the war. However, as the date set for the
voting drew nearer, the little band of dissidents gradually dwindled.
In the innumerable discussions on the question, Rosa Luxemburg
and her friends had to struggle to extract every promise to speak out
against the credits and then to secure every 'no' vote. The excuses
with which the would-be heroes dissociated themselves from any
dissenting action went all the way to a downright admission of
personal cowardice, and it is understandable how Rosa Luxemburg's contempt for the weaknesses of human creatures grew. On
the day of the vote only one man was left: Karl Liebknecht. Perhaps that was a good thing. That only one man, one single person,
let it be known on a rostrum being watched by the whole world that
he was opposed to the general war madness and the omnipotence of
the state—this was a luminous demonstration of what really mattered
at the moment: the engagement of one's whole personality in the
struggle. Liebknecht's name became a symbol, a battle-cry heard
above the trenches, its echoes growing louder and louder above the
world-wide clash of arms and rousing many thousands of fighters

against the world slaughter. On that 2nd December 1914 a revolutionary front against the war arose in Germany, and from that day onwards the revolutionary alliance of Karl Liebknecht and Rosa Luxemburg became indissoluble.

Die Internationale

Rosa Luxemburg's political activity in the early months of the war was significantly different from Lenin's in Switzerland in the same period. The difference was due, not to any fundamental divergence in their general views about the war and socialist policies, but to the concrete conditions under which they had to work. Lenin was a political émigré, living in a neutral country, and thus almost completely cut off from the Russian masses. His work was for a small elite of men and women well versed in socialist theory, and he was therefore able to go straight to the heart of the chief problems raised by the war. He rejected the slogan of peace as too indefinite and too passive: it tended to turn the hopes of the working-class masses once again to the good-will of their rulers, the very people who had caused the slaughter. Even the demand for a 'democratic peace' did not attack those conditions which would inevitably give birth to war again and again. If socialists really wished to act in the spirit of the Stuttgart resolution of the International and strove 'to utilise the economic and political crisis brought about by the war to rouse the various social strata and to hasten the overthrow of capitalist class rule', then–as he explained in trenchant antithesis–their basic task was the 'transformation of the imperialist war into a civil war', the propagation, organisation, and preparation of civil war. He criticised Kautsky with a special vehemence, and it is clear that underlying the sharpness of his attacks was his bitterness at having once been deluded into defending Kautsky against Rosa Luxemburg. Writing to Shliapnikov in October 1914, he observed:

> Rosa Luxemburg was right; she realised long ago that Kautsky was a time-serving theorist, serving the majority of the party, serving opportunism in short. There is nothing in the world more pernicious and dangerous for the intellectual independence of the proletariat than the horrid self-satisfaction and base hypocrisy of Kautsky, who glosses over everything and attempts to lull the awakening conscience of the workers with sophistry and pseudo-scientific verbosity.

In contrast, Rosa Luxemburg's concern was to produce a direct effect on the masses and to secure some action, no matter how modest it might be at first. To do this she had to find the lines of approach and recognise the psychological conditions of the moment. What she wrote in these first months of the war (or what her friends wrote), and what she explained in innumerable discussions and at internal party meetings, were chiefly confined to an analysis of the causes of the war and its character, and to internal party questions, particularly the question of discipline:

> The discipline owed to the party as a whole, i.e. to its programme, by its members is more important than the direct discipline to a particular organisation within the party. In fact, it is this larger discipline alone which justifies the subordinate one and, at the same time, describes its natural limits.

Therefore, of all the social-democratic deputies, Liebknecht, by voting against the war credits, had been the only one to observe party discipline, and the fact remained that since the outbreak of war the most serious breaches of discipline were being committed all the time under the protective cover of martial law, 'breaches of discipline insofar as individual party organs, instead of serving the will of the party as a whole, i.e. the party programme, bend this will of their own accord'.

In the long run, however, such educational work based solely on the needs of the moment could not suffice. The problems had to be seized by the roots and brought before a larger public. Some sort of journal was necessary for this purpose, and, after great efforts and many disappointments, the insurgents succeeded in winning over the party publishing house in Düsseldorf for this bold undertaking. In the spring of 1915 *Die Internationale* appeared under the joint editorship of Rosa Luxemburg and Franz Mehring. Among its contributors were Clara Zetkin, August Thalheimer, Käte Duncker, Paul Lange, and Heinrich Ströbel. Its intellectual level was extraordinarily high. Mehring analysed the attitude of Marx and Engels to the problem of war and from it drew conclusions applicable to the current war. Zetkin dealt with the position of women in wartime, and Lange analysed the *Burgfrieden* politics of the trade unions. As in all the legal publications of the oppositional group, here, too, the struggle against the war was waged chiefly by criticising the official party's war policy, in order that the contributors would be at least somewhat protected from censorship and persecution. Under her own name, Rosa Luxemburg wrote an article entitled 'The Reconstruction of the International', and, under the pseudonym Mortimer, a second one entitled 'Perspectives and Projects', a critique of a book by Kautsky.[101]

In her first article, she noted the fact of the political abdication of German Social Democracy on 4 August and the simultaneous collapse of the International. For a decade the alternatives–socialism and imperialism–had adequately summed up the political orientation of Social Democracy. However, the moment the choice between these alternatives had become a political reality, Social Democracy had conceded victory to imperialism without putting up a fight. As the representative of the 'Marxist Centre', as the theoretician of a group stuck in a quagmire, Kautsky had contributed substantially to this collapse. When he declared that the International was not a weapon in wartime, when Friedrich Adler sadly observed that silence seemed to be the only behaviour befitting socialism during the war, then advocacy of such theories was a voluntary act of self-castration. In other words:

> In peacetime it is the class struggle which is all-important within each country, and international solidarity abroad; in wartime it is class collaboration which is all-important within, and the struggle between the workers of different countries abroad. In Kautsky's rendering, the world-historical appeal of the *Communist Manifesto* has been subjected to a substantial amendment, and now reads: "Proletarians of all countries, unite in peacetime, but slit one another's throats in war!" Thus today: "With every shot a Russian –with every blow a Frenchman!" And tomorrow, after the peace treaty: "Let's embrace all you millions and kiss the whole world!" –for the International is "essentially an instrument of peace", but "not an effective weapon in wartime".[102]

Thus did Rosa's deep bitterness vent itself with a sharp-edged terseness which marked all her writings during the war. However, at the same time she thought ahead: it was absurd to pretend that after the war the International could arise again as an organisaion of the class struggle unless the process of resurrecting it on that basis began now during the war. The International either had to revise completely its old peace tactics, proclaim class collaboration instead of class conflict, and work for the imperialist interests of the bourgeoisie, or it had to abandon the whole policy pursued since 4 August. The first step in the right direction was a struggle for peace, but it would have to be a real struggle, not solemn declarations in parliament 'against every policy of conquest' and simultaneous war-mongering. And by a struggle for peace, she did not in the least mean the setting up of fine programmes for the future such as disarmament, the abolition of secret diplomacy, general free-trade with the colonies and a League of Nations:

> If the collapse of 4 August has proved anything, it is the great historic lesson that the one and only effective guarantee of peace and the one and only bulwark against war is the vigorous will of the proletariat pursuing an unwavering class policy and loyally upholding its international solidarity throughout all the storms of imperialism; and not pious wishes, cleverly concocted prescriptions, and utopian demands addressed to the ruling classes. . . . This, too, is an either-or situation: either Bethmann-Hollweg or Liebknecht; either imperialism or socialism, socialism as Marx understood it.[103]

And, in conclusion, Rosa pointed to the deep-seated cause of the failure of Social Democracy, and at the same time to the one decisive hope for the rebirth of the International:

> Faced with its greatest historic test, which it had moreover fore-seen and foretold in all essential points with the certainty of a natural scientist, it [Social Democracy] proved to have nothing of the second vital element of the working-class movement: the vigor-ous will not only to *understand*, but also to *make* history. For all its exemplary knowledge and its organisational strength, Social Democracy was seized by the whirl of the historic stream of events, in no time spun around like a rudderless hulk and driven by the winds of imperialism, instead of steering a course against these winds and working its way forward to the safety of the island of socialism. . . . An historic collapse of the first order, which danger-ously complicated and retarded the liberation of humanity from the rule of capitalism. . . . The International can be reborn, and a peace corresponding to the interests of the proletarian class can be obtained–but only from the self-criticism of the proletariat and from its consciousness of its own power. . . . The way to this power –not paper resolutions–is simultaneously the way to peace and the way to the reconstruction of the International.[104]

This article is of extraordinary importance for an estimation of Rosa Luxemburg's tactical attitude at that time. Each political argu-ment is obviously carefully weighed, in order, first, to test the margin of expression still left by the military censorship, and, second, to say as much as the radical elements in the German working-class move-ment were still open to receive. The article is therefore by no means a full expression of Rosa's ideas. She registered the collapse of the International, and with a few hard blows she dismissed the majority of the party leaders, the social-imperialists. The brunt of her attack was directed against Kautsky. It is clear that she regarded the final split with the war-socialists as inevitable, both nationally and inter-nationally.

However, she was not prepared simply to race through the matter. She instructed those who were burning with impatience not to let themselves be guided by the mood of the moment. As long as there was still a certain amount of freedom of movement and pos-sibilities of working within the party, it was necessary to take advan-tage of them. Now the great task was to win back, by means of tire-less educational work, as much as possible of the membership for a policy guided by international considerations. Such educational work was significantly more effective if carried on from within than from outside the party. At that time Rosa believed that a showdown within the party would not occur until after the end of the war, after the return of comrades from the front. This expectation was soon dashed, because the SPD Executive answered the growing resistance of party members to its policy by suppressing party democracy step by step.

In those early years of the war the lines of demarcation even within the party leadership were not at all clear. Again and again Rosa found that Kautsky's behaviour confirmed the fact that he was irrevocably lost for the revolutionary party now being developed. Among the leading party officials and even among the deputies, however, there were people who were still undecided and who might be driven by events towards the left. Therefore, even though they were unwilling to draw the conclusions that she herself regarded as necessary, she held on to the alliance with the group around Georg Ledebour, Hugo Haase, and Adolf Hoffmann. This policy of postponing a showdown meant that she had to be prepared to make concessions in organisational questions and, under certain circumstances, to put off political actions. She set one unalterable condition, however: not to impose on herself any propaganda restraints; she would continue not only to wage a ruthless fight against the war policy of the Party Executive, but also to expose publicly every imperfection in the ranks of the opposition.

Although Lenin essentially agreed with her attitude, he and Luxemburg seemed to have differing opinions about the orientation of general propaganda.[105] Lenin decisively rejected the simple slogan of 'Peace', whereas Rosa made it the centre of her political agitation. However, she quite clearly opposed those who favoured an appeal to the ruling classes for peace, and it was in such an appeal that Lenin saw the great pitfall of a general peace slogan. Rosa spoke only of the class struggle, and not of revolution and not of civil war, both of which Lenin emphasised. Nevertheless, it is clear that she did hold the view that 'a peace corresponding to the interest of the proletarian class' could be obtained only by the seizure of power.

In 'Perspectives and Projects' (in *Die Internationale*, April 1915) Rosa just about tore Kautsky's new book to pieces, particularly his views on imperialism. It is interesting to note that she firmly rejected his attempt to equate 'modern democracy', as the aim of socialism, with the parliamentary regime:

> Has not Social Democracy always contended that "full democracy, not formal democracy, but real and effective democracy", is conceivable only when economic and social equality, i.e. a socialist economic order, has become a reality, and that, on the other hand, the "democracy" of a bourgeois national state is, in the last resort, always more or less humbug?

The first number of *Die Internationale* was designed to open up a systematic examination of all the problems of the working-class movement raised by the war, and it was certainly a spirited beginning. However, immediately after the publication of its first and only issue, the journal was banned, and the Public Prosecutor slapped an indictment for high treason on Mehring, Luxemburg, Zetkin, the publisher, and the printer.

A year in a women's prison

When *Die Internationale* appeared in April 1915, Rosa Luxemburg had already served two months of the sentence imposed on her in Frankfurt the previous year. Even before the outbreak of the war she had been in poor health, and the shock of events worsened her condition so much that she had to go into hospital. Owing to her illness the date on which she was to begin her sentence was postponed until 1 March 1915. On 19 February she was planning to leave for Holland with Clara Zetkin to make the final arrangements for an international women's conference aimed at establishing firmer international contacts. On the evening before her planned departure, however, she was suddenly arrested and brought to the women's prison in the Barnimstrasse in Berlin. As a dangerous revolutionary she was supposed to be buried alive for the duration of the war, and, in fact, her imprisonment was to last with short interruptions until she was released by the 1918 Revolution. In a letter to her friend and secretary, Mathilde Jacob, she described her first day in prison:

> Even the journey in the Black Maria didn't shake me up; after all, I had experienced exactly the same ride in Warsaw. Indeed, it was such a strikingly similar situation that it started a train of various cheerful thoughts. To be sure, there was one difference this time: the Russian gendarmes had escorted me with great respect as a "political", whereas the Berlin police declared they didn't give a damn (*'schnuppe'*) who I was, and stuck me into the car with my new "colleagues". Ah well, these are all piddling matters in the end; and never forget that life should be taken with serenity and cheerfulness. Incidentally, so that you don't get any exaggerated ideas about my heroism, I'll confess, repentently, that when I had to strip to my chemise and submit to a frisking for the second time that day, I could barely hold back the tears. Of course, deep inside, I was furious with myself at such weakness, and I still am. Also on that first evening, what really dismayed me was not the prison cell and my sudden exclusion from the land of the living, but–take a guess! –the fact that I had to go to bed without a night-dress and without having combed my hair. And, so as not to omit a quotation from the classics: do you remember the first scene in "Mary Stuart", when Mary's trinkets are taken away from her? "To do without life's little ornaments", says her nurse, Lady Kennedy, "is

harder than to brave great trials." (Do look it up; Schiller put it rather more beautifully than I have here.) But where are my errant thoughts leading me? *Gott strafe England** and may He forgive me for comparing myself with an English queen.[106]

This time Rosa went to prison rather reluctantly. In November she wrote to Diefenbach: 'Six months ago I was looking forward to it as if it were a feast, but now the honour falls as heavily on me as the Iron Cross on you.' She knew how badly she was needed outside. At first, as a political prisoner, she seems to have been treated with a certain amount of laxity, for she managed not only to write the *Juniusbroschüre* on the sly, but also to smuggle it out by April 1915. After that, however, it was apparently six months before she succeeded in getting any more political writings through to the outside world. It may be that she was subjected to more stringent regulations as the result of an encounter she had with a police detective whose insolence provoked her into throwing something at his head. For this incident, at any rate, extra punishment was meted out to her: ten more days in prison and four weeks of solitary confinement.

It is not difficult to imagine how heavily the deadening pressure of prison life weighed on her, how impatiently she tugged at her chains. Outside, the world-wide slaughter was dragging on, claiming victims and producing untold suffering; the hunger of the masses was growing, and morale breaking down. At the beginning of her imprisonment she had nourished the hope that by the time she was released the war would be over, but she soon had to give this up. Despite the reports of one German victory after the other, after each new battle no end to the slaughter was yet in sight. The official social-democratic leadership had long since given up its original scruples, and nationalism was rampant in the party. Already people were revelling in hopes of victory and conquest, and 1915 was the blackest year for the revolutionary movement. The opposition put up by Rosa's followers, who were still working together with representatives of the 'Marxist Centre', made no intellectual progress. She herself must have been deeply disappointed by the feebleness of the ideas expressed in the oppositional publications whenever she had the chance to read them in prison. It is true that in June 1915 a step forward was taken with the presentation of a protest petition signed by approximately 1,000 party officials to the SPD Executive. But it lacked inspiration and contained no great points of view; and, most important, it was not followed up by any action. The International Women's Conference in Berne (March 1915) organised by Clara Zetkin had met with no very great response. Not until September

* 'God punish England', a greeting used by German patriots during the war.

1915, when the International Socialist Conference in Zimmerwald paved the way for an international movement against war politics, did the opposition in Germany receive a new lease of life. In October housewives in Berlin and elsewhere demonstrated against the rising cost-of-living, and it was clear that the prospect of another war winter was greatly worrying the masses.

The whole opposition movement lacked people with fire and energy. Above all, it lacked Rosa Luxemburg herself. Even her closest comrades-in-arms had almost all been snatched away from the revolutionary to the war front. Karl Liebknecht was among those conscripted, and only when the Reichstag was in session could he leave the war area and intervene directly in the movement's activities. He bombarded the government with a rain of 'interpellations' (*Kleine Anfragen*), making use of the only parliamentary weapon left to him to expose the imperialist methods and aims of the war-lords so that the masses would prick up their ears. He also published several leaflets whose ruthless clarity and aggressive tone caused a sensation, particularly the one entitled 'The Main Enemy Is at Home!' Clara Zetkin was arrested in July 1915, and, when released in October, she was dangerously ill. In Berlin Wilhelm Pieck, Ernst Meyer, and Hugo Eberlein, and in Stuttgart Friedrich Westermeyer,* were arrested and not released for many months.

The reports reaching Rosa Luxemburg from the outside world were rarely encouraging, and the frequent bad tidings were terribly painful. Yet she stoically bore up against all these blows: 'I have trained myself to maintain such firm equanimity that I swallow everything with the most cheerful countenance without batting an eyelash.' Flinging herself into hard work, she wrote her *Anti-critique*, a settlement of accounts with her critics on the accumulation question, worked on her *Introduction to Economics*, and began to translate Korolenko's memoirs.

Not until the end of 1915 did her prison cell seem to open just wide enough to enable her to communicate with the outside world and the revolutionary movement: she managed to enter into a secret correspondence with Liebknecht, of which some fragments still exist.[107] She immediately took the political initiative. She and Karl agreed that the alliance with the 'tottering spooks' (*wankende Lemuren*) of the 'Marxist Centre' had become a hindrance to revolutionary enlightenment and action. At her instance a national conference of left-wing elements took place in Berlin on New Year's

---

* Westmeyer belonged to the close circle of friends around Clara Zetkin and Rosa Luxemburg. A man of political farsightedness and tireless activity, he was the leader of the party's radical wing in Württemberg. It was he who—even before the outbreak of the war—coined the saying, "The main enemy is at home!" He died during the war.

THE JUNIUSBROSCHURE | 217

Day, 1916. It was decided to form a tighter organisation, and the name *Spartakus*, which was adopted as a kind of imprint for their publications, subsequently became the name by which the new group was generally known. Rosa Luxemburg drew up a list of 'guiding principles' which succeeded in evading the suspicious eyes of the prison authorities and finding its way to the conference, where it became the basic programme of the organisation for the duration of the war.

In mid-February Rosa was finally restored to what freedom the military dictatorship had left in Prussia. However, the experience of breathing free air again proved almost too much for her at first. The year of imprisonment with its psychological torments, the pain of which she could never share or express, had weakened her considerably. She was seized by a *horror pleni*, a fear of crowds, but they surrounded her on the very first day in such overwhelming numbers that there was no way to ward them off. The women of Berlin among whom she had worked had stood by her during the war, and simply wanted to show her their admiration and love; full of joy at her release, sympathy with her in her sufferings, and gratitude for her efforts on their behalf, they prepared a reception for her. And then friend after friend came up to her, but all she could manage was torn sentences, as the effort of conversation was too much for her. Her first day of freedom thus became a sheer torture. And from then on there was no rest for her, and no peace. At once she was swept up in the whirl of active political life with its endless discussions and meetings, from which only her writing gave her a chance to recover. She had to summon up her whole energy to keep going, and to push her weakened strength to the utmost limits to carry out the most demanding tasks. Yet she continued to expend this strength without stint until the prison-gates once again closed behind her.

The *Juniusbroschüre*

On her release from prison she found the manuscript of her essay 'The Crisis of Social Democracy' untouched on her desk. The technical difficulties of publishing illegal material, and the arrest or conscription of most of the party officials close to her, had prevented its being printed. These obstacles were now quickly overcome, and in April 1916–a full year after it had been written–the work was published. Although it could only be distributed in secret, it became necessary to print several editions, one right after the other, because of the demand, and it became the intellectual armour of thousands of illegal militants.

Rosa had wanted to publish it under her own name. However,

friends persuaded her that such a courageous gesture would not, under any circumstances, be worth the privations of reimprisonment, and so she chose a pseudonym: Junius. The much-abused pen-name of the great English champion of liberty against the absolutist schemes of King George III thus acquired new lustre: here was the same intimate knowledge of political facts, the same polemical trenchancy, the same overwhelming weight of argument, and the same forceful and elegant language, though this time it was even more vehement and passionate, as befitted the monstrosity of events.

The pamphlet begins with a powerful chord, with indignation expressing itself in ice-cold sarcasm. Rosa describes a world in which the mass slaughter of human beings had become a tiresome everyday routine, in which business flourished in the ruins, and in which the vile hunt for profiteering opportunities was lauded as an expression of the same patriotism which led others to die a hero's death on the battlefield. She shows how the devastation of whole countries was accompanied by the rack-and-ruin of both the genuine cultural values and the idols of bourgeois society, and paints a picture of this society as it reveals its true face: 'not when, licked clean and respectable, it makes a mockery of culture, philosophy and ethics, law and order, peace and justice, but [when it appears] as a rapacious beast, as a witches' Sabbath of anarchy, as a pestilential stench for culture and humanity'. She scourges the treachery of international Social Democracy to the socialist cause, and does not spare even those enlightened workers who now abandoned their ideals to follow in blind faith the war-drums of their leaders. The essay is filled with sharp antitheses, and every sentence sounds like the crack of a whip.

However, the work is not a mere pamphlet. As in all her writings, her feelings are restrained, her indignation held under control. Her aim was to enlighten, to persuade, to solve the problems raised by the war. Thus the work becomes a guide to modern history and proletarian strategy. The imperialist drive of the Great Powers, which she had already described in rough outline in the historical chapters of *The Accumulation of Capital*, she now traced through all the foreign political entanglements of the last decades. She showed how each of the two imperialist camps were driven on a collision course as a result of events and of national interests, both antagonistic and entangling, until the knot created could no longer be undone but had to be cut with the sword. In so doing she laid bare the very essence of this war:

> The world war which began officially on 4 August was the same one . . . which social-democratic parliamentarians, newspapers, and pamphlets had branded a thousand-and-one times as a shameless imperialist crime that had nothing to do either with culture or

with national interests, but was on the contrary diametrically opposed to both.[108]

Only small states like Belgium and Serbia were formally waging a defensive war, but even they were only pawns in the great chess game of world politics. Plunged into the war, they immediately became members of one of the belligerent world consortia. Their situation could not be judged in isolation from the situation as a whole or according to formal considerations. It is 'the historic milieu of present-day imperialism which repeatedly determines the character of the war for each of the individual countries involved'.[109]

Thus she resolutely rejected the idea of copying in this war the attitude which democratic parties had adopted in nationalist wars of earlier times. Even the criterion which had been decisive for Marx and Engels up until the 1890s was no longer applicable. They had demanded that in all the great conflicts of their day the proletariat should side with the power whose victory would best serve both the cultural progress of humanity and the interests of the international proletariat as a whole. Rosa showed that both power-blocs were striving for conquest and subjugation, and that the victory of either of them would have pernicious consequences for the international working class. Therefore the working class should side with neither of these power-blocs, but should stand united internationally in the struggle against imperialism.

She even maintained that in the age of imperialism there could no longer be any national wars in the old and narrow sense, a statement which was very heatedly attacked by Lenin in a critique of the *Juniusbroschüre*.[110] He laid special emphasis on the great role which nationalist wars of defence waged by oppressed peoples against imperialist powers were destined to play in the era of proletarian world revolution. Lenin's idea broke new ground, and there is no doubt that Rosa Luxemburg would have agreed with it without reservation. What she had meant was that only nationalist wars within the imperialist camp were no longer possible, and not that nationalist wars were impossible altogether, and Lenin himself granted that this may have been what she meant.

However, it is another idea which causes more surprise at first. She was dealing with the question of national defence, and, seemingly contradicting her usual argumentation, she declared that it was in fact the duty of Social Democracy to defend the country in a great crisis, and reproached the German party for having 'left the fatherland in the lurch in the hour of greatest danger'–the very thing its leaders prided themselves on not having done. The apparent contradiction is easily resolved: Rosa was referring to the example of the Jacobin wars and the Paris Commune, and to a hypothetical non-imperialist Franco-Russian war against Germany as depicted by

Friedrich Engels in 1892, and she pointed out that 'when Engels spoke of national defence in line with social-democratic policy, he did not mean the support of the Prussian Junker militarist government and its General Staff, but a revolutionary action following the example of the French Jacobins'. It is clear that she was alluding to the defence of the fatherland after the seizure of power by the working class, and that she was reproaching Social Democracy for abandoning the class struggle and thus hindering any such seizure of power. As elsewhere in this work, she was not speaking with her usual explicitness about the revolutionary conquest of power, but the whole context shows clearly what she meant. While writing the work she probably still reckoned with its legal publication; hence the circumspection in her choice of words. But for this reason her readers, too, found it difficult to follow her train of thought, and they must have been even more confused when she connected her ideas with a programme of action which culminated in the 'slogan for a united great German republic'. She was reviving the idea she had propounded in 1910 as a possible lever of revolution. Although it was undoubtedly correct in 1910, under war conditions it could easily be used to justify the socialist war policy in the democratic countries. A German bourgeois republic would inevitably pursue an imperialist policy too, so that the slogan did not contain a truly socialist solution of the war problem.

Rosa Luxemburg did her utmost to smother any danger of confusion arising from this slogan by pulling apart the legend of the liberator mission with which both imperialist camps tried to win the support of the masses. Was it not the aim of the Entente to liberate the world from 'Kaiserism'? And was it not Hindenburg's task to carry the revolution into Russia at the point of German bayonets? With slashing blows she knocked the democratic banner out of the hands of the would-be world-conquerors and hacked to pieces the liberator legend of the German social-democratic leaders. In turn she pointed out the transformation in the foreign-political role of Tsarism and showed the fateful effect of the war on the reawakened revolution in Russia:

> The war was unleashed by Vienna and Berlin, and it buried the Russian revolution beneath the ruins–perhaps for years to come. "German rifle-butts" have not smashed Tsarism; they have smashed its adversaries. They have helped Tsarism by providing Russia with the most popular war she has had for a century. This time everything has had the effect of giving the Russian government the nimbus of moral justification: the provocation of the war by Vienna and Berlin, clearly visible to everyone outside Germany; the *Burgfrieden* in Germany and the nationalist delirium unleashed by it; the fate of Belgium; the necessity of running to the aid of the

French Republic–never has absolutism had such a shockingly favourable position in a European war. The hopefully fluttering banner of the revolution went under in the wild maelstrom–but it sank honourably, and it will rise out of the dreary slaughter to flutter again–despite "German rifle-butts" despite victory or defeat for Tsarism on the battlefields.[111]

And the prospects? With calm certainty, despite the daily reports of victories for the Central Powers, she predicted the collapse of Austria-Hungary and Turkey; and despite the proclaimed brotherhood of the 'Allied and Associated Powers', she prophesied rivalry between Japan on the one side and Great Britain and the USA on the other in the struggles over China. However, peace would be equally fateful for the workers of all countries, whether their governments were victorious or defeated–unless it was a peace dictated by the 'revolutionary intervention of the proletariat'. There was only one way to prepare for this intervention and to bring it about: the continuation and the intensification of the class struggle.

And she concluded the work with a presentation and interpretation of the monstrous events of the day in a passage of almost visionary power:

The present fury of imperialist bestiality in the fields of Europe has had yet another effect for which the "civilised world" has had no horror-stricken eyes, no shuddering heart: the *mass destruction of the European proletariat*. Never has a war killed off whole social strata to this extent; never within the last hundred years has it gripped in such a way all the great and old civilised countries of Europe. Millions of human lives have been wiped out in the Vosges, in the Ardennes, in Belgium, in Poland, in the Carpathians, on the Save; millions have been maimed. But nine-tenths of these millions are the working people from town and country. It is our strength, our hope, which is being mowed down in swathes like grass under the sickle. It is the finest, the most intelligent, the best-trained forces of international socialism, the bearers of the most sacred traditions and of the most daring heroism of the modern working-class movement, the vanguard of the whole world proletariat–the workers of England, France, Belgium, Germany, and Russia–who are now being gagged and butchered in heaps. . . . What is happening now is an unprecedented mass slaughter which is more and more reducing the adult working-class population of all the leading civilised countries to the women, the aged and the crippled–a blood-letting which threatens to cause the European working-class movement to bleed to death. . . . That is a crime even more vicious than the destruction of Louvain and of the Rheims Cathedral. That is . . . a deadly blow against the force which carries the future of mankind in its womb, the only force which can salvage the price-less treasures of the past and bring them and carry them on into a better society. Here capitalism reveals its death's-head; here it be-

trays to the world that it has forfeited its historic right to exist,
that its continued rule is no longer compatible with the progress of
mankind. . . .

"*Deutschland, Deutschland über alles!* Long live Democracy!
Long live the Tsar and Slavdom! Ten thousand tent-cloths guaranteed according to specifications! A hundred thousand kilos of
bacon, coffee-substitutes–immediate delivery!" Dividends are rising, and proletarians falling. And with each one sinks a fighter of
the future, a soldier of the revolution, a saviour of humanity from
the yoke of capitalism, into the grave.

The madness will cease and the bloody spectre of hell will disappear only when the workers of Germany and France, of England
and Russia finally awaken from their frenzy, extend to one another
the hand of brotherhood, and drown the bestial chorus of imperialist hyenas with the old, mighty, and thunderous battle-cry of
labour: "Workers of all countries, unite!"[112]

Spartakus

By virtue of its cogent line of argument and stirring language the
Juniusbroschüre is the most powerful document published against
war and war-politics. Its contents indicate that it was designed for
mass propaganda. Even today it is more than just a historical document: it is the thread of Ariadne in the labyrinth of our times. However, a year had passed between the day it was finished and the day
it was published, a year during which the anti-war movement had
ripened, so that concrete instructions for revolution action had
become necessary. These were given in the 'Guiding Principles concerning the Tasks of International Social Democracy', drawn up by
Rosa while she was still in prison and published as an appendix to
the *Juniusbroschüre*.

The 'Guiding Principles' served the conscious purpose of de-
taching the supporters of Luxemburg and Liebknecht from the hesitant and uncertain section of the German opposition. Their tactical
conclusions were especially emphatic in their rejection of 'utopian
and, at bottom, reactionary plans' of a purely pacifist nature (international courts of arbitration, disarmament, freedom of the seas, con-
federations, etc.) on which the supporters of Kautsky and Hugo
Haase set their hopes. The proclamation was perfectly clear:

> Imperialism, the last phase of life and the highest development of
> the political world-rule of capitalism, is the common deadly enemy
> of the proletariat of all countries. . . . For the international pro-
> letariat, the struggle against imperialism is at the same time a
> struggle for political power within the state, the decisive conflict
> between socialism and capitalism. The final aim of socialism will

be achieved only if the international proletariat opposes imperialism all along the line and elevates the slogan "war against war" to be the precept of its practical policy, summoning up all its strength and spirit of self-sacrifice to the utmost.[113]

Conclusions concerning the organisational form of the struggle were also drawn. The revolutionary movement had to be completely separated from those elements which had surrendered to imperialism. A new workers' international had to be erected, an organisation of a higher type than the one which had just collapsed, an organisation 'with a uniform conception of proletarian interests and tasks, and with uniform tactics and the capacity to take action in both war and peace'. The greatest importance was attached to international discipline:

> The centre of gravity of the organisation of the proletariat as a class lies in the International. In peacetime the International must decide on the tactics of its national sections on the questions of militarism, colonial policy, commercial policy, and the May-day celebrations; it must also decide on the general tactics to be followed in wartime.
>
> The obligation to carry out the resolutions of the International takes precedence over all organisational obligations. . . .
>
> The only means of defending all real national freedom today is the revolutionary class struggle against imperialism. The fatherland of the proletarians of all countries is the Socialist International, and everything must be subordinated to its defence.[114]

These 'Guiding Principles' set off violent discussions throughout the opposition. They were completely unacceptable to the right-wing tendency behind Kautsky, while the more leftist followers of Georg Ledebour objected above all to the strict commitment to international discipline contained in them. But this was precisely the point on which Rosa Luxemburg remained adamant: Social Democracy had failed because it had not developed an international spirit, and because the old international had not been a really united organisation, either in the consciousness or in the actions of its members. Among all the great socialist leaders she was the consummate internationalist, both in thought and feeling. What she wrote during the discussions at the time was not mere propaganda, but a genuine statement of her fundamental ideals: 'The world-wide fraternisation of the workers is the holiest and highest thing on earth; it is my guiding star, my ideal, my fatherland. I would sooner lose my life than be unfaithful to this ideal!'[115] She was often accused of interfering in the internal struggles of other parties, but in fact she regarded such intervention as a perfectly natural thing. In her consciousness the international proletariat was one body, acting unitedly, and now her resolute aim was to bring about this unity in reality. Whoever refused to work for this proved to her that he stood on altogether different ground.

In this way the line of demarcation was drawn within the opposition, and the extreme left wing rallied around Luxemburg and Liebknecht. A conference held in mid-March 1916 showed that quite impressive cadres had developed around those few individuals who had raised the banner of rebellion in German Social Democracy in the summer of 1914. Delegations were present from most of the industrial areas – from Berlin, Saxony, Thuringia, Central Germany, Frankfurt, Württemberg, the Rhineland. Declarations of solidarity came from North Germany, Bavaria and Upper Silesia. Above all, the Socialist Youth, which had held a secret conference in Jena at Easter 1916, stood overwhelmingly behind *Spartakus*. This upswing in the movement meant an increased work-load for Rosa, but she bore it cheerfully: extensive correspondence had to be carried on; discussions, even those most vital, seemed endless; and she had to do a lot of travelling, particularly in the provinces, to promote the work of organisation.

She also had the task – an unusual one for her – of curbing the impatient ones. Many now found it intolerable to remain within a party which had become a standard-bearer of the General Staff and whose leaders were now beginning to destroy the democratic rights of the members, depriving local organisations of their control over local newspapers, and expelling oppositional members from the party's representation in the Reichstag. These comrades pressed for a new and completely independent party, but Rosa was resolutely opposed to this. She granted that their aim should be to form a revolutionary party eventually, but as long as it was still possible for them to work within the old party without abandoning their principles they should do so; under no circumstances should they voluntarily leave the rank-and-file membership in the hands of apostate leaders. Thus for a long time she regarded it as her task to prevent the creation of sects, and, for the time being at least, to gather together her followers as an organised tendency within the party.

In addition, she felt that an attempt had to be made to mobilise the working masses themselves to act against the war, something which Liebknecht in particular was anxious to bring about. May Day 1916 was chosen for the first trial of strength, and *Spartakus* agitated in the factories of Berlin for a demonstration on Potsdamer Platz. It was a great success. At eight o'clock in the morning a dense throng of workers – almost ten thousand – assembled in the square, which the police had already occupied well ahead of time. Karl Liebknecht, in uniform, and Rosa Luxemburg were in the midst of

the demonstrators and greeted with cheers from all sides. Liebknecht's voice then rang out: 'Down with the war! Down with the
government!' The police immediately rushed at him and tore him
out of the crowd. Trying to shield him, Rosa flung herself in the
way, but was roughly thrust aside. Indignation rose among the
masses, and an attempt was made to free Karl, but it was ridden
down by mounted police. For two hours after Liebknecht's arrest
masses of people swirled around Potsdamer Platz and the neighbouring streets, and there were many scuffles with the police. For the
first time since the beginning of the war open resistance to it had
appeared on the streets of the capital. The ice was broken.

Liebknecht's demonstration again showed the great significance
of personal example. At a time of tremendous strain–when the SPD
was demoralised (which also meant the demoralisation of the working class), and the masses were powerless and had lost all confidence
in their leaders–individuals had to come forward and prove by their
self-sacrifice that with them, at least, words and deeds were identical,
and that deeds were still possible. It was their keen awareness of this
necessity to set an example which motivated Karl and Rosa to risk
every danger.

After Karl's arrest, the *Spartakusbund* (*Bund* = league) as it
was now called, embarked on a propaganda campaign of extraordinary intensity. Leaflet after leaflet was produced and distributed
throughout the Reich. Rosa herself wrote a whole series of them,
explaining Liebknecht's fight to the workers in stirring language and
calling upon them to follow his example. Liebknecht himself supported the campaign by using the only means open to him: he
bombarded the military judicial authorities with declarations which
all began with the formal wording, 'With respect to the investigation
against me . . .', and were ostensibly intended as self-defence statements. In reality he made no attempt to defend himself and turned
these pleas into an indictment of Germany's war policy. Each of
these documents somehow found its way out of prison into the open,
and was printed by the *Spartakusbund* and distributed in great numbers up and down the country. As a result many thousands were
won for the struggle against the war.

In addition, many thousands who, till then, had supported the
social-democratic leaders now turned away from them. In particular
the behaviour of the party members in the Reichstag contributed to
this development. When the military judicial authorities demanded
that the Reichstag lift Liebknecht's parliamentary immunity, the
bourgeois parties were, of course, quick to indicate their enthusiastic
agreement. It is true that the social-democratic deputies pleaded for
a continuation of his immunity, but not without slandering him at
the same time. They didn't even defend his parliamentary rights;

instead they declared him to be a harmless dreamer. The deputy
Eduard David added: 'A barking dog doesn't bite!' Whereupon
Rosa Luxemburg retorted that at least Liebknecht acted 'not like a
lawyer, not like a formalist, but like a real social democrat'. In a
handbill entitled 'Dog Politics' (summer of 1916) she wrote:

> A dog is someone who licks the boots of the master who has dealt
> him kicks for decades.
> A dog is someone who gaily wags his tail in the muzzle of martial
> law and looks straight into the eyes of the lords of the military dic-
> tatorship while softly whining for mercy.
> A dog is someone who barks raucously at a man in his absence,
> even a man in fetters, and thereby acts as a retriever for whoever is
> in power at the time.
> A dog is someone who, at his government's command, abjures,
> slobbers, and tramples down into the muck the whole history of his
> party and everything it has held sacred for a generation.

On 28 June 1916 Karl Liebknecht was sentenced to two years
and six months hard labour. On the day the trial started there were
tremendous demonstrations in Berlin, and on the day sentence was
pronounced 55,000 munitions workers there went on strike. At the
same time demonstrations took place in Stuttgart, and strikes in
Braunschweig and Bremen. The political strike, allegedly impossible
in peacetime with a strong and united organisation, and decried as
anarcho-syndicalism and revolutionary romanticism, became a reality
in war-time, even though the strikers were threatened with hard
labour or the trenches. Insofar as the spontaneous will and initiative
of the masses needed to be provided with an objective, the strikes
were the work of *Spartakus*. Although the organised supporters of
the *Spartakus* movement were still few in number, they were already
making themselves heard. The *Burgfrieden* had lost its taming force.
The nationalist frenzy was at an end. The awakening was beginning.

But German militarism took its revenge: many hundreds of
Spartakus militants were arrested. The factories were 'combed out',
and thousands conscripted in punishment, but as a result of this
move revolutionary ideas were carried to all parts of the front. Increasingly severe sentences were passed, and mass trials took place.
For the time being the military could credit itself with a victory.
Because the political movement in the factories was temporarily
robbed of its leaders, there were no protest actions when Liebknecht
was sentenced by a higher military court to four years hard labour.
However, his magnificent words, 'No general ever wore a uniform
with so much honour as I shall wear the convict's garb', made a deep
impression on people. The lonely man in Luckau gaol, set to cob-
bling shoes, thus became a symbol, the conscience of the nation.

Barnimstrasse, Wronke, Breslau

On 10 July 1916 Rosa Luxemburg, too, was re-arrested. Years later, a witness in a sensational political trial, General Ernst von Wrisberg, testified that her arrest had occurred at the direct request of a social-democratic deputy. Shortly afterwards the seventy-year-old Franz Mehring was also gaoled. Only recently released from prison, Ernst Meyer, too, was thrown back inside in August. Julian Karski was interned in a concentration camp. But all this did not paralyse *Spartakus:* Leo Jogiches now took over the reins. His political judgment, conspiratorial experience, energy, strict discipline, and his great gift for dealing with people brought new means and people into the service of the movement, and the work made steady progress. The *Spartakusbriefe* (*Briefe* = letters) now appeared with unfailing regularity, no longer typed, as in the beginning, but printed, for a larger circle of readers. They were no longer the mere information bulletin of a small political group, but a political journal, illuminating and dissecting world events–a weapon to rouse the masses. And, from prison, Rosa Luxemburg wrote regularly for each number, sometimes writing three-quarters of a whole issue. Somehow her manuscripts found their way outside, and fortress walls were unable to damp the sound of her voice.

This time Rosa had been arrested neither on the basis of a sentence nor because of a pending trial. 'Protective custody'–that was the name of this splendid device with which the traditions of the Bastille were revived in wartime Germany. Theoretically, as a political prisoner, an honoured guest of the state, she was allowed every personal freedom within the prison, but not that first right of every prisoner: to know when her time would be up. Under a 'protective custody' warrant no prisoner could be held for more than three months, but new arrest warrants, genuine *lettres de cachet*, arrived with Prussian punctuality every three months. The prisoner was permitted to occupy herself with whatever she wanted, but not with what she really wanted, namely politics. She was permitted to communicate unhampered with the outside world by means of letters, which were, however, censored; and by receiving visitors, who were, however, limited to one a month, namely someone whom the General Command considered worthy. She even had to pay for her stay in this hospitable place. This was all quite respectable, not like real punishment at all, yet in many ways worse than penal detention.

The first station was again the women's prison in Berlin, whose protective-custody department had been named the 'Barnimstrasse Military Women's Prison'. Here she was in familiar surroundings,

under familiar supervision. However, the military authorities must
have suspected that she was in contact with comrades outside, for
they decided to impose stricter isolation measures. Until they could
find a more secure place for her she was sent from the Barnimstrasse
to the Berlin Police Headquarters. This was pure hell—eleven cubic
metres, filthy, overrun with vermin, messy, and furnished in the most
primitive fashion—because the cells here were only temporary stop-
over places for prisoners awaiting transfer to regular prisons. No
artificial light was provided, and in the autumn weeks the cells became dark by five or six o'clock in the afternoon. All night long
heavy footsteps echoed through the corridors, keys rattled and iron
doors banged as new prisoners were delivered at all hours. On top of
that, there was the hellish music of the city-trains thundering by and
shaking the whole building. 'The month and a half I spent there
left grey hairs on my head and cracks in my nerves from which I
shall never recover,' wrote Rosa.[116]

At the end of October 1916 she was transferred to the fortress
prison of Wronke, situated in a far-off corner of the province of
Posen. At least there was peace and quiet, so that prison life here
was somewhat more bearable. The cell door was left open all day,
and in the prison-yard Rosa could tend her own flower-beds and
listen to the birds singing. It was almost idyllic, but in July 1917 she
was uprooted again, this time to Breslau (Wroclaw). The prison
there was a gloomy building. Except for short 'walks' she was locked
in her cell all day. In the narrow prison-yard she used to keep close
to the walls, where a little sun came in, and her eyes, craving a bit
of colour, would search out the green of the withered blades of grass
which managed to force their way up between the flagstones. This
was the world in which Rosa spent three years and four months of
the war (including the 1915 period), until the revolution of
November 1918 forced open the prison gates and set her free.

Outside, the world was in flames, and her mind and heart
glowed with a passionate determination to work, to teach, and to
urge others to action, in order to lay the basis for a new social order
in the midst of the chaos of this apparent *Götterdämmerung*. And
here she was, cast upon this island of death, living as though in the
rarefied air of a bell-jar, in oppressive loneliness and a leaden silence
in which for weeks on end she hardly heard the sound of her own
voice. With horrifying clarity she saw the mangled bodies in the
trenches, the fate of millions; she felt the growing misery of the
masses, the dying of children, the wasting away of a whole generation
the general brutalisation and the destruction of culture. But no privation, no force, no pain could break her will. Ever wide-awake and
outwardly relaxed, she remained unbowed.

She searched for joy in every bird-call, in every little blossom, among the ants building their tunnels between the stones, in the bumble-bee which once strayed into her cell, in the almost frozen butterfly which she was able to restore to life, and in the cumulus clouds piled high in the patch of azure visible to her. She lived in fantasy with her friends outside, and worried about them. Every letter she received she read searchingly, beween the lines, sensing the mental strain of the correspondent in each faint-hearted word. To everyone she managed to be a support. 'Calm down, I shall always remain your compass, because your straightforward nature tells you that I have the most imperturbable judgment', she wrote to Mathilde Wurm. And to Sonja Liebknecht: 'Dearest Sonjuscha, you must be calm and serene despite everything. That is life, and that is how we must take it, bravely, undauntedly and smilingly–despite everything.' She was able to put herself in the position of others and knew their individual needs. She even had a special style for each correspondent: to Sonja she was protectively tender, encouraging, and consoling; to Luise Kautsky she was comradely with a slight touch of cool irony; to Clara Zetkin she wrote in a tone of calm certainty indicative of their deep friendship, which grew out of the harmony of their ideas and their enduring partnership in the revolutionary struggle; to Diefenbach she chattered cheerfully, often playfully, and it is clear that she was simply trying to shower him with pleasant things to take his mind off the danger she knew he was in. And all her letters contain wonderful sketches of her memories and experiences.

In the loneliness and monotony of her prison life books were naturally a solace and a refuge. In this one point at least she was privileged in comparison with the ordinary convicts; she was allowed to read–whatever the censor permitted. She appeased her hunger for beautiful things by devouring both the classical and modern literature of France, England, Russia, and Germany. She immersed herself in the natural sciences. But, however passionately she might devote herself to any of this, it was all recreation only. The main thing was her work. In prison again she worked on her *Introduction to Economics*, on her translation of Korolenko, on a history of Poland, and later on her analysis of the Russian Revolution. At the same time she carefully followed world events and developments in the international working-class movement. On every 'post day' she had articles ready for publication, and they left the prison as contraband under the very eyes of the inspecting officials. She now found the right perspective, the right distance to things, and had time to think out problems thoroughly and formulate her ideas. Her articles thus became little masterpieces, whether she dealt with the intrigues of the Scheidemanns, the patching up of an 'independent Poland' as a new reservoir of cannon-fodder, or President Wilson's peace bluff.

And again and again she dwelt on the necessity of independent revolutionary action by the masses as in this *Spartakus* letter of April 1917:

> Socialist peace politics can be summed up today in the following simple words: Workers! Either the bourgeois governments will make peace just as they make war; but then, no matter what the outcome of the war, imperialism will remain the dominant power, and then there will inevitably be more and more new armaments, wars, ruin, reaction, and barbarism. Or you will pull yourselves together to make revolutionary mass uprisings and to struggle for political power, so that you will be able to dictate *your own* peace, both at home and abroad. Either imperialism and a decline (at times faster, at times slower) of society, or the struggle for socialism as the only salvation. There is no third possibility, no middle way.

Her hopes were fixed on such a rising of the people, and she clamoured for it with burning impatience. Meanwhile she showed the workers the fateful consequences their failure to act would have for the whole of humanity. But she was not pessimistic. Even now she was fully confident that history would take its course, knowing that even the German workers in uniform – 'the most robust, most intelligent, social-democratically educated, organisationally disciplined, theoretically schooled cannon-fodder' – would one day rise. And she continued to look forward to this day with impatience. To a woman friend she once wrote:

> World history seems to be like a tasteless cheap thriller in which lurid sensationalism and blood-curdling episodes outdo each other for the sake of effect. However, one shouldn't simply lay such a novel aside unread. I don't doubt for a moment the dialectic of history – and it moves!

She radiated cheerfulness 'in inexhaustible amounts', and was full of joy (although she hardly knew why); she looked for the reason in life itself: 'There is a beautiful little song of life in the harsh crunch of the wet sand under the slow heavy footsteps of the sentry – if one only knows how to listen for it correctly.'[117] However, this life took its toll on her; the slaughter, devastation and destruction outside, the triumph of barbarism, the brutalisation of life, the cowardice of men forced to be heroes on command, the trampling underfoot of everything she held sacred; in addition, her own helplessness, imprisonment and loneliness – blow after blow deranged her inner balance and sapped her energy. For seven months she maintained her usual robust disposition, but in the eighth her nerves gave way. She was tormented by depressive feelings. A shadow falling on her would make her shudder, and every little excitement, even a pleasurable one, shook her deeply. Then, when her will and hunger for life seemed to be triumphing once again, in autumn 1917 a terrible blow struck—a deep personal one this time: Hans Diefenbach was killed in action. The shock of the news left a gaping wound which never really completely healed. But when she managed to overcome the first sharp pain of grief, she found comfort in words she had written to Diefenbach at the beginning of the war, and now expressed these same thoughts to Sonja Liebknecht:

> You know, Sonitschka, the longer it lasts, and the more the base-ness and monstrousness of the things happening every day exceeds all limits and measure, the calmer and firmer I become. Just as one cannot apply moral standards to the elements—a storm, a flood, or an eclipse of the sun—here, too, one can only regard them as some-thing given, as an object of research and knowledge.

A year previously, in a letter to Luise Kautsky, she had affirmed with particular forcefulness this same life-principle had kept her going during the collapse of her whole world.

> Everyone who writes to me also moans and groans. I find nothing more ridiculous than that. Don't you understand that the general misfortune (Dalles) is much *too great* to moan about? But when the whole world goes out of joint, then I try simply to *understand* what and why it happened, and, having done my duty, I then feel calm and in good spirits again. *Ultra posse nemo obligatur* (one is not obliged to do the impossible). . . . To abandon oneself completely to the woes of the day is altogether incomprehensible and intoler-able. Look, e.g. at the cool composure with which Goethe managed to stay on top of things. And keep in mind what he had to go through: the great French Revolution, which, seen up close, must have looked like a bloody and utterly pointless farce; and then from 1793 to 1815 an uninterrupted chain of wars, when the world once again looked like a wide-open mad-house. And with what calmness and intellectual equanimity he pursued his studies all this while on the metamorphosis of plants, on chromatology, and on a thousand-and-one other things! I don't demand that you should write poetry like Goethe's, but surely everyone can adopt his con-ception of life—the universality of interests, the inner harmony—or at least strive to attain it. And if you say something like: but Goethe was no political fighter, then I say: a political fighter has even more need to try to be on top of things; otherwise, he will sink right up to his ears in every piddling matter—of course, I'm referring to a fighter of really high calibre.

12
Russia 1917

The first triumph

The outbreak of the war had cut Rosa Luxemburg off from the Polish and Russian working-class movements, though she probably had the satisfaction of hearing in time that her own party in Poland had not fallen victim to the general demoralisation, but remained loyal to the spirit of her ideas. Josef Pilsudski and Daszyński immediately attempted to put the Polish people under the command of the Austro-Hungarian war-machine, in the hope of receiving Polish 'independence' in fief from the Habsburgs and Hohenzollerns. On 2 August 1914, however, the SDKPiL, together with the left wing of the PPS and the *Bund*, issued a joint proclamation:

> The proletariat declares war on its governments and oppressors. . . .
> In its struggle for national rights the Polish proletariat will derive
> its demands from the class politics of Poland as a whole. . . . In
> order to bring about these demands the Polish proletariat must
> capture political power and take it into its own hands.

Rosa Luxemburg's old party remained unswervingly loyal to this programme, against both Russian absolutism and the German generals, and under the regime of the one as under the regime of the other, Pavillion X of the Warsaw Citadel, where she had been imprisoned in 1906, was the usual residence of Polish social-democratic leaders.

Among the Russian social democrats—both in Russia and abroad—the Bolsheviks proved to be the hard core of the Russian revolutionary movement. Only at the beginning was there a certain amount of vacillation, but it was on the periphery of the party and quickly overcome. In 1914 the Bolshevik members of the Duma were expelled on account of their revolutionary activity. Among the Mensheviks many shades of opinion were to be found—from the internationalists to those who now defended the Tsarist fatherland. After getting over the difficulties of the period of reaction which followed the Revolution of 1905, the revolutionary movement had made steady progress in Russia. In July 1914 barricades were once more erected on the streets of St Petersburg.

The war flung back the revolution for the moment. The bourgeoisie revelled in the hope of foreign conquest, the peasants believed that it meant new land under the plough, and the working masses were simply confused—but only for a while. By the beginning of 1915 there were new strikes and demonstrations, setting off, behind the long front-line, a process which was to wear down absolutism. The severe military defeats revealed the disorganised state of the Russian war-machine and the demoralisation of the state apparatus. The Court was being eaten up by intrigue. Privation increased rapidly throughout the country. As the workers became bolder in their activity, the bourgeoisie also went into action, hoping it could still secure victory by taking political power into its own hands. In its attempt to secure a large-scale reform, it unwittingly assisted at the birth of a social revolution. On 25 February 1917 (9 March, N S) the workers of Petrograd revolted successfully in alliance with the soldiers, and the Soviet (Council) of Workers' and Soldiers' Deputies was formed. It was actually already in possession of political power, but still lacked confidence in its own strength. In the exuberance of democratic hopes, it therefore handed executive power over to a bourgeois government headed by Prince Lvov.

The Russian Revolution was the first triumph of Rosa Luxemburg's ideas, the fulfilment of what she had spent a good deal of her life fighting for, and the promise, also, of revolution in Germany. Now she found it doubly difficult to be imprisoned and tied down. [On 27 May 1917] she wrote to Diefenbach:

> You can well imagine how deeply the news from Russia has stirred me. So many of my old friends who have been languishing in prison for years in Moscow, St Petersburg, Orel and Riga are now walking about free. How much easier that makes my own imprisonment here! A droll *change de places*, isn't it? But I am pleased and don't begrudge them their freedom, even if my chances have become so much the worse as a result.

At one time she thought of demanding her deportation to Russia, but whether she finally abandoned the idea, or whether she made the demand and it was rejected, we do not know.

From now on the Russian Revolution occupied the central place in all her thoughts, and she was seized by a growing impatience. Obsessed by the anxiety that the Russians might succumb in their isolation to their own internal difficulties and to the superior power of the foreign counter-revolution, she called for an insurrection of the German working class to save the Russian Revolution. The first visible effect of the Russian Revolution in Germany was very promising: in mid-April 1917 a wave of huge strikes by munitions-workers spread throughout the country. Over 300,000 workers went on strike in Berlin alone. The General Staff was ex-

ceedingly alarmed, and their contact-man with the SPD, the liberal
General Wilhelm Groener, coined the expression, 'He who strikes
is a low-down cur!', which was taken as an insult by the hungry and
enslaved workers. Once again, all those suspected of radical leanings
were hauled out of the factories and sent to the front. This again
paralysed the movement for a while, and the regular social-democratic fire-brigade was back at work quenching the flames of revolt.
Even the leaders of the newly formed Independent Social-Democratic Party of Germany (USPD) declared themselves against what
they termed 'revolutionary experiments': Germany was not Russia,
and the struggle for freedom at home had to be fought on parliamentary ground. In reply, Rosa lashed out at them with stinging
arguments, and the longer the depression and passivity of the
workers, the more vigorously and imploringly her voice rang out
with the appeal, 'Onward! Onward! Save the Russian Revolution
by ending the war and emancipating yourselves!'

She now did her utmost to study the events in Russia, but the
material at her disposal was scanty. Naturally, the German newspapers presented a distorted picture of the situation, and *Le Temps*
and *The Times*, copies of which she received occasionally, hardly
did any better. She sometimes made mistakes of detail, e.g. when she
overestimated the political strength of the Russian bourgeoisie. And,
just as Lenin had once had faith in Kautsky, she now had an un-
warranted confidence in the Mensheviks, who, she hoped, would
grow to greater stature with the revolution. Had not the French
Revolution forged great historic figures out of little men? However,
her general views on the character and aims of the revolution agreed
with those of the Bolsheviks. These she sketched in her first essay on
'The Revolution in Russia':

> The revolution in Russia has been victorious over bureaucratic ab-
> solutism in the first phase. However, this victory is not the end of
> the struggle, but only a weak beginning. On the one hand, the bour-
> geoisie will sooner or later retreat from its momentarily advanced
> post of resolute liberalism; this follows with inevitable logic from
> its general reactionary character and its class antagonism to the
> proletariat. On the other hand, the revolutionary energy of the
> Russian proletariat, now that it has been awakened, must–with the
> same inevitable logic–get back onto the road of extreme demo-
> cratic and social action, and revive the programme of 1905; the
> establishment of a democratic republic, the eight-hour work-day,
> the expropriation of large-landed property, etc. Above all, however,
> the most urgent task of the socialist proletariat of Russia, a task
> indissolubly bound up with all its other tasks, is to end the im-
> perialist war.
>
> At this point the programme of the Russian revolutionary pro-
> letariat changes into the most bitter opposition to the Russian im-

perialist bourgeoisie, which still dreams of Constantinople and profiteers from the war. The action for peace in Russia, as well as elsewhere, can be carried out in only one way: as a revolutionary class struggle against the native bourgeoisie, as a struggle for political power in the state. These are the unavoidable prospects for the further development of the Russian Revolution.[118]

She had full confidence in the inner historical logic of events in Russia, and the fact that Social-Revolutionaries and Mensheviks entered the bourgeois government did not make her waver in her conviction:

> The coalition ministry is a half-measure which burdens socialism with all the responsibility, without even beginning to allow it the full possibility of developing its programme. It is a compromise which, like all compromises, is finally doomed to fiasco.

The dictatorship of the proletariat was inevitable.

But it was this very fact which made the Russian Revolution a burning international problem:

> Unless it receives backing from an international proletarian revolution in time, the dictatorship of the proletariat in Russia is doomed to suffer a stunning defeat, compared with which the fate of the Paris Commune will probably seem like child's play.

However, she did not regard this prospect as a reason for putting a brake on the revolution in Russia. The law of revolution was ceaseless progress. Any hesitation, any stagnation would guarantee the victory of the counter-revolution, paving the way for a period of bloody vengeance wreaked by the ruling classes. Only if the international proletariat joined the fighting front of their Russian brethren could the revolution be saved. Until then the Russian workers would to continue their struggle for power irrespective of the outcome.

In dealing with the tragic dilemma of the Russian Revolution, Rosa laid particular stress on the central problem of the day: the peace-question. In a long article entitled 'Burning Questions of the Day', published in *Spartakusbriefe* in August 1917, she exposed the desperate contradictions resulting from Kerensky's July offensive:

> ... any further active prosecution of the war, every new military offensive by the Russians, does not–according to the logic of the objective state of affairs at the moment–serve the defence of the Russian Revolution, but rather the interests of Entente imperialism. No peace formulae, however radical and democratic they may be, can obliterate the conspicuous fact that every military action undertaken by Russia benefits the war aims of England, France and Italy, i.e. although the Russian Republic professes to be fighting a purely defensive war, in reality it is participating in an imperialist

one, and, while it appeals to the right of nations to self-determination, in practice it is aiding and abetting the rule of imperialism over foreign nations.

However, what is the situation now that Russia refuses to undertake any offensive and limits herself militarily . . . to a passive, wait-and-see attitude, merely remaining on stand-by alert just to ward off possible German attacks? By this passivity, which is in itself only a half-measure, a way of avoiding the war problem and not of ending it, she has rendered incalculable services to German imperialism by permitting it to concentrate its main forces against the Western front, and, to a certain extent, covering its rear in the East. Thus the Russian Republic finds itself between Scylla and Charybdis. . . .

By reason of its historical character and its objective causes, the present world war is an international contest between the imperialist powers, and the best will in the world cannot turn it into its opposite in any one corner of the world or in any one country, namely into a democratic war of national defence. Caught by the wheel of the world imperialist catastrophe, the Russian Republic cannot evade the consequences of this catastrophe on its own; not only can it not extricate itself from the wheel on its own, but also even the wheel cannot come to a standstill by itself. Only a proletarian world revolution can liquidate the imperialist world war. The contradictions in which the Russian Revolution is inextricably involved are nothing but the practical expression of the fundamental antithesis between the revolutionary policy of the Russian proletariat and the grovelling policies (*Kadaverpolitik*) of the European proletariat, between the class-conscious action of the masses of the people in Russia and the treachery of the German, English, and French working masses to their own class interests and to socialism.[119]

It is clear that Rosa Luxemburg did not apply herself to studying the Russian Revolution with mere self-complacent enthusiasm. She analysed the situation with merciless trenchancy, took careful note of the threatening dangers, and never for one moment allowed herself to take comfort in the cowardly hope that a miracle might solve the cruel contradictions. She saw clearly that only the action of the masses elsewhere could sever the knot, yet in every word one feels how she was torn by the agonising thought that the insurrection of the workers in other countries might come too late to be effective.

She regarded all the sanctimonious peace speeches and peace resolutions, intended to lure the proletariat into continuing to put up with the slaughter, as one of the greatest obstacles to the development of its forces, and it appeared to her that even the international peace conference called in the summer of 1917 by the Petrograd Soviet of Workers' and Soldiers' Deputies in Stockholm, would develop into yet another attempt to dupe the masses into continuing the war. She felt that if this conference took place—a conference which would be monopolised by the social-imperialists of all the warring countries—any attempt to clarify the situation would be drowned in the hopeless confusion of political concepts and aims:

> What is really being prepared in all this muddle is not peace, but mutual reconciliation between the "neutral" and the "belligerent" socialists, mutual absolution and a general amnesty for past sins, and the restoration of the old International as a *maison de tolérance* for socialist treachery.[120]

The Stockholm farce would prove to be preliminary spadework for a future diplomatic congress of the belligerent powers. The socialists preparing the way for an agreement between the capitalist governments were totally blind to the obvious fact that any negotiated peace between the existing governments would inevitably be a peace negotiated against the proletariat and at its expense; it would be a deal endangering its very existence. The official slogan of the conference—peace without annexations and indemnities—was the formula of an abortive undecided test of strength between the warring imperialist powers, the formula for a breathing-space in which to prepare for the next round. Above all, it accorded with the interests of German imperialism, whereas the Entente governments still hoped for a decisive military victory. It was the formula for the restoration of the *status quo ante,* 'and this *status quo* includes all the old borders and all the old power relations externally, and of course all the old power relations internally as well: bourgeois class rule, the capitalist state, and imperialism as the predominant power and the general foundation'.

Thus the Stockholm peace preparations were nothing but a continuation of the 4th August policy, the abdication of the proletariat as a class with its own policies and strategy for action, the continuation of its lackey services to the ruling classes and to imperialism. Since 4 August the socialist parties had been the most effective means of paralysing the masses, i.e. a counter-revolutionary factor; and they were merely faithfully carrying on this function when they endeavoured to bring about an agreement between the belligerent governments and the re-establishment of imperialism in its pre-war power-position.[121]

Here again, hard on the heels of her prophecy came its confirmation. The German Junker government promoted the attempt to explore peace possibilities in Stockholm by granting the German social-democratic delegation every possible facility. However, the Western democratic powers (England and France) forbade their socialists from attending the conference, and the enterprise then collapsed. This article on the 'Burning Questions of the Day' is an especially clear example of the impressive consistency of Luxemburg's policy against the war. Any haggling over her own ideas, any attempt to outwit history, any hope of a miracle–she rejected them all. Only a very few of even the great revolutionaries have had such strength.

The October Revolution

From her prison-tomb Rosa Luxemburg followed the violent class struggle taking place in Russia with great suspense. However, she soon felt her hopes dwindling away. At first she had believed that sheer revolutionary will would drive the Mensheviks to break very quickly with the bourgeoisie and take over all power for themselves, but she was then forced to realise that the socialists in the government were increasingly becoming the prisoners of their own class enemies. They were stemming the promised tide of urgent large-scale reforms, carrying on the imperialist war policies, and subjecting the Bolsheviks to a campaign of terror–which is to say that they were steering an anti-revolutionary course. For Rosa there could be no doubt that this policy would lead straight to the restoration of Tsarism. Already the generals were starting a civil war. However, the workers and soldiers advanced against General Kornilov's troops, and, by dint of their arms and propaganda, smashed his army, the hope of the counter-revolution. Thus Rosa's strong faith in the masses was not misplaced. She expressed her unreserved approval of the Bolsheviks, who in the hour of crisis put aside all their indignation at the governmental persecutions and concentrated solely on the task of saving the revolution. The victory before the gates of Petrograd set free the energies of the masses throughout the country. Peasants revolted against their landlords, and in far-away industrial centres Soviets took power. The decisive hour was approaching. Would there be a force capable of directing the chaotic mass movement into one channel towards the correct aim?

On 25 October 1917 (7 November, N S) the Bolsheviks, with the aid of the workers' militia and the Petrograd troops, seized power from the Provisional Government. The dictatorship of the proletariat, which Rosa Luxemburg had viewed as the aim of the revolution from the outset, was now a reality. But her own jubilation was quickly smothered, for almost simultaneously with the news of the victory she learned of the death of Hans Diefenbach.

There is nothing from her pen to show us what effect the first news of the successful Bolshevik revolution had on her. Despite the shock of her friend's death she probably managed to pull herself together sufficiently to write about the great event for one of the *Spartakusbriefe*. Just at that time, however, the paper was appearing less frequently, owing to technical difficulties and further arrests, and when it finally did appear again, great problems arising from the October Revolution had to be dealt with. Certainly Rosa welcomed the revolution with enthusiasm; she felt herself raised above the humiliations of the day by the magnitude of this event and by the daring heroism with which the Bolsheviks had intervened in world history. However, she recognised at the same time the monstrous dangers in which the proletarian dictatorship, because of its isolation, would inevitably be enmeshed. A letter to Luise Kautsky on 24 November confirms this:

> Are you glad about the Russians? Of course, they won't be able to maintain themselves in this witches' Sabbath–not because statistics show that their economic development is too backward, as your clever husband has worked out, but because Social Democracy in the highly developed West consists of a pack of piteous cowards who are prepared to look on quietly and let the Russians bleed to death. But such an end is better than "living on for the fatherland"; it is an act of world-historical significance whose traces will not be extinguished for æons.

The first difficult decision facing the Bolsheviks was the one concerning peace with Germany. Their expectation that the great example of the Russian Revolution would bring the closed ranks of the international proletariat into the arena had been disappointed, and the utter demoralisation of the Russian army made further resistance impossible. Germany's military power threatened to crush the revolution, but a peace, even one lasting only for a very short time, would grant it a much-needed breathing space. For the Russians the alternatives were: Brest-Litovsk or downfall.*

Rosa Luxemburg was aware of the historical compulsion under which the Bolsheviks acted. However, she obviously had the impression that they were giving way too easily under the pressures of the situation, an impression which she was also to have of them on some later occasions. If she were right, the morale of the revolution would inevitably be undermined, its leaders lose their political grip, and the revolution itself sink into opportunism. Her fears in this respect were so strong that in the summer of 1918, on the basis of press reports, she even believed in the possibility of a Russo-German war alliance. She could not know how seriously the Bolsheviks were wrestling with the tricky problem; while submitting to the overwhelming pressure of the moment, they were, at the same time, preparing for a new

---

* 'The discussions concerning the attitude to be adopted towards the peace question led to the most serious crisis in the Bolshevist Party, which was on the verge of bringing itself and the Revolution to grief.' (Lenin, speech on 'War and Peace', delivered on 7 March 1918 at the Seventh Party Congress of the Communist Party of the Soviet Union, reprinted in Lenin, *Collected Works*.)

revolutionary thrust. Above all, she feared that the Bolsheviks might play the German diplomatic game and recognise a peace dictated by armed force as a 'democratic peace without annexations and indemnities', in order to curry favour with the German General Staff. The revolutionaries would then have degenerated into mere politicians, and the dissolving acid of mistrust would spread throughout the movement. However, it was not long before she recognised her error and stated: 'Lenin and his friends made no attempt to deceive either themselves or others about the facts; they admitted the capitulation quite frankly.'

Thus she publicly declared her approval of Lenin's peace policy, though not without inner reluctance. The consequences of Brest-Litovsk seemed much too fateful to her. At least since the end of 1915 she had been certain of Germany's defeat, though, of course, such an outcome of the war was not her aim: she fought for the smashing of *all* imperialisms by the international proletariat. However, she realised that if the working class of the European Great Powers could not summon up sufficient strength to end the war by revolution, then Germany's defeat was the next best solution. A military victory for ravenous German imperialism under the barbarous regime of Prussian Junkerdom would only lead to the most wanton excesses of the mania for conquest, casting all of Europe and other continents as well into chains, and throwing humanity far back in its quest for progress. At the same time a German victory would be the victory of imperialist thought in the international working-class movement; it would complete the demoralisation of the working class, and finish off the Russian Revolution. It now seemed to Rosa Luxemburg that the peace of Brest-Litovsk made such a victory possible once again, and the prospect obsessed her nightmarishly. More furiously than ever before she scourged the leaders of the German working class for having brought about this situation, and she sought all the more vehemently to drive the German workers forward on the road to revolution:

> . . . it was only the pertinaciously slavish attitude of the German proletariat which compelled the Russian revolutionaries to make peace with German imperialism as the sole ruling power in Germany. And it was only this slavish attitude which *made it possible* for German imperialism to exploit the Russian Revolution for its own interests. . . . General peace cannot be obtained without the overthrow of the ruling power in Germany. Only by lighting the torch of revolution, only by launching an open mass struggle for political power, democracy, and a republic in Germany can a renewed burst of genocide and the triumph of the German annexationists in the East and in the West now be prevented. The German workers are now called upon by history to take the message of

revolution and of peace from East to West. No mere pursing of the lips will help here; real whistling is needed![122]

Not only the decision of the Bolsheviks to sign the Brest-Litovsk Treaty, but also some of their other political measures caused Rosa Luxemburg to be torn by grave doubts and worries about the fate of the Russian Revolution, a concern which she expressed in quite a few of the *Spartakusbriefe*. Her views often differed from those of her closest friends, particularly Paul Levi, who had taken over the running of *Spartakus* after Leo Jogiches's arrest in March 1918. In order to convince these comrades and to come to a thorough understanding of the problems involved herself, she began to write a comprehensive critique of Bolshevik policy in the autumn of 1918. The outbreak of the German Revolution prevented the completion of the work, and the torso was not published by Paul Levi until 1922.[123]

Legends have surrounded this work. In his preface Paul Levi said the suggestion had come from a certain quarter (meaning Leo Jogiches) that it should be put in the fire, but Clara Zetkin, in her work *Um Rosa Luxemburgs Stellung zur russischen Revolution* (On Rosa Luxemburg's Attitude towards the Russian Revolution) (Hamburg 1922), has given very good reasons for discounting Levi's assertion. As a matter of fact, Leo Jogiches was against the publication of the work because he knew that in certain fundamental points Rosa had subsequently changed her views, and that she was thinking of writing a whole book on the Russian Revolution. However, he was undoubtedly in favour of including the pamphlet in a collected edition, if only for the sake of completeness. In addition, it would have been difficult to destroy the work, because the manuscript was, so to speak, non-existent: no one knew where it was – not even Leo had it. In the end Levi published the work from an inaccurate and incomplete copy, and not from the original. The original manuscript had been taken by a comrade for safe-keeping in the January days of 1919 and then forgotten. It was not unearthed until almost a decade later, and Felix Weil then published the necessary corrections, and also very important and extensive additions to the Levi edition in the *Archiv für die Geschichte des Sozialismus und der Arbeiterbewegung* in 1928.*

Revolutionaries in Germany were naturally carried away by the tremendous happenings in Russia, and, out of sheer spite against the fierce baiting which now began against the Bolsheviks, they tended to accept Bolshevik policies too uncritically. However, Rosa, who always came to grips with every great historical phenomenon without

* 'Archives for the History of Socialism and of the Working-class Movement', the so-called *Grünbergarchiv*, edited by Dr Carl Grünberg a member of the *Institut für Sozialforschung* in Frankfurt am Main–Tr.

shying away from the results of her analysis, insisted that, instead of being unreflectively apologetic, active comrades should be constantly alert and critical so that they could learn to make effective use of the experiences of history for their own struggle. She feared (prophetically) that in their enthusiasm the German workers would blindly accept the Russian example as an 'unblemished authority'; and she laughed at the anxious suggestion that a critical examination of Bolshevik policies would 'undermine the prestige and the fascinating power of the example of the Russian proletariat, the only things which could overcome the fatal inertia of the German masses':

> Not by the creation of a revolutionary hurrah-spirit, but rather the reverse: only by insight into the whole frightful seriousness of the situation and into the whole complexity of the tasks entailed; only by political maturity and intellectual independence; only by the development of the capacity for critical judgment among the masses, a capacity which, under the most varied pretexts, was smothered by German Social Democracy for years–only thus can the capacity for historical action be created in the German proletariat.[124]

Never at any time did she have the intention of launching a campaign against the Bolsheviks. She was always sparing with her hymns of praise, but she never spoke of people or of a party with so much enthusiastic approval as she did of the Bolsheviks in this work. It is a myth, and one which has been sedulously spread by the reformists, to say that she condemned the whole Bolshevik policy, including the October Revolution, and that she rejected the idea of the proletarian dictatorship, and thereby justified the policy of the Mensheviks. Her pamphlet leaves no room for doubt. At the very beginning she asked whether Kautsky and the Mensheviks were right in declaring that Russia was ripe enough only for a bourgeois revolution, and she answered by showing how in the revolutionary camp the struggle had begun immediately around the two focal points of peace and land, and how, on both these questions, the bourgeoisie had gone over to the counter-revolution. If the bourgeoisie had been successful, their victory would have sealed the fate of democracy and the republic:

> Military dictatorship with a reign of terror against the proletariat followed by a return to monarchy would have been the inevitable consequences.
>
> From this one can judge how utopian, and fundamentally reactionary, too, was the tactic by which the Russian socialists of the Kautskyite tendency, the Mensheviks, let themselves be guided. Obstinately insisting on the fiction of the bourgeois character of the Russian Revolution–because, for the time being, you know, Russia is not supposed to be ripe for revolution–they clung desperately to their coalition with the Liberals. . . .

In this situation then we are indebted to the Bolshevist tendency for the historic service of having proclaimed, from the very beginning, and of having followed with iron consistency the only tactic which could save democracy and spur on the revolution. All power exclusively in the hands of the worker and peasant masses, in the hands of the Soviets–this was indeed the only way out of the difficulties which the Revolution had got into; it was the sword which cut the Gordian knot and let the Revolution out of the impasse into the free and open fields where it could continue to develop without restraints.

The party of Lenin was thus the only one in Russia which grasped the true interests of the Revolution in that first period; it was the element which drove the Revolution forward, and thus, in this sense, the only party which pursued a really socialist policy. . . . The real situation of the Russian Revolution boiled down within a few months to the alternatives: victory of the counter-revolution or dictatorship of the proletariat; Kaledin *oder* Lenin. . . .

The determination with which, at the decisive moment, Lenin and his comrades offered the only slogan that could drive the Revolution forward . . . transformed them almost overnight from a persecuted, vilified, and outlawed minority whose leaders were forced to hide, like Marat, in cellars, into the absolute masters of the situation. . . . Whatever a party in an historic hour could muster of courage, energy, revolutionary far-sightedness, and consistency–all these things Lenin, Trotsky and their comrades have achieved in abundance. All the revolutionary honour and capacity for action which Social Democracy in the West was lacking was represented in the Bolsheviks. The October insurrection not only saved the Russian Revolution in actual fact, but it also saved the honour of international socialism.[125]

Criticism of the Bolsheviks

Thus Rosa Luxemburg took up the cudgels on behalf of the October Revolution, praising its basic principles in the most glowing terms, but at the same time she took a critical look at Bolshevik policy on the questions of agrarian reform, national self-determination, democracy and terror.

The old agrarian programme of the Bolsheviks provided for the nationalisation of landed estates as one of the first measures of socialism. The Social-Revolutionaries were in favour of distributing the confiscated land among the peasants, but Lenin had declared as early as 1905 that this would lead to the ascendancy of a new village bourgeoisie. However, when the peasants took the initiative in carrying out a revolutionary distribution of land, the Bolsheviks shelved their own programme and adopted that of the Social-Revolutionaries.

Thus it came about that almost all the large estates were distributed among the peasants.

Rosa Luxemburg was aware of the tremendous difficulties connected with the solution of the agrarian question, and knew it would be impossible to find an ideal solution right at the beginning of the revolution. But she demanded that it should be the general principle of a socialist government 'to take measures which point the way towards providing the basic preliminary conditions for a later socialist reform of agrarian relations'. At the very least, anything barring the road to such measures should be avoided. Unfortunately, what the Bolsheviks were doing was bound to point in the opposite direction, for the distribution of land by the peasants cut off the way to socialist reforms: 'it piles up insurmountable obstacles to the transformation of agrarian relations.' According to her, this transformation depended on two things:

> In the first place, only the nationalisation of the large-landed estates, as the technically most advanced concentration of the means and methods of agrarian production, can serve as the point of departure for a socialist agricultural economy. . . . Only this offers the possibility of organising agricultural production in accordance with great, coherent socialist principles.
>
> In the second place, it is one of the prerequisites of this transformation that the separation of agriculture from industry (a characteristic feature of bourgeois society) should be done away with, so as to bring about a mutual interpenetration and fusion of both, to make way for a working out of both agrarian and industrial production according to unified points of view. . . . The nationalisation of the large and medium-sized estates, the union of industry and agriculture – these are the two fundamental principles of every socialist economic reform, without which there is no socialism.[126]

The Bolsheviks' policy of land distribution, she stated, far from eliminating property distinctions, tended in fact to sharpen them in certain respects. It would bring the greatest benefits to the rich peasants and usurers, who made up the village bourgeoisie and held the reins of local power in every Russian village. Thus, its effect would be a shift of power damaging to proletarian interests:

> Formerly a socialist land reform would have had to face at most the opposition of a small caste of aristocratic and capitalist large-landed proprietors as well as that of a small minority of the rich village bourgeoisie, whose expropriation by the revolutionary popular masses is mere child's play. Now, however, after the "squatting", the enemy of all attempts to carry out the nationalisation of agriculture is the enormously grown and powerful mass of land-owning peasants, who will fight tooth and nail to defend their newly acquired property against every socialist attack. The question of the future nationalisation of agriculture – and thus of produc-

tion in general in Russia–has become the question of the antagonism and struggle between the urban proletariat and the peasant
masses.[127]

As abstracted above, the principles set out here are irrefutable. They
can and should serve as the bearings for every nationalisation policy.
In Russia their soundness was proved in the course of bitter and,
indeed, tragic experiences. The attempts made by the Bolsheviks in
1917 to solve the agrarian question kept resulting in new social and
economic crises which, one-and-a-half decades after the October
Revolution, led to the creation of a situation resembling civil war,
in which the Soviet government suppressed, with appalling cruelty,
those peasants still clinging to private property. Today, the dictatorship in Russia has not been overturned by a real democracy of the
working people, but has degenerated into a totalitarian regime, and
we must look to the regulation of agrarian relations in 1917 as one of
the most decisive causes.

Certainly, in autumn 1917, the Bolsheviks did not foresee such
a development. However, their action was not determined by any
failure on their part to recognise the prerequisites of a socialist
economy. Rosa Luxemburg herself pointed to the determinant factor
in a few key-words, which, however, need further explanation–'the
slogan [of land distribution] taken over from the much maligned
Social-Revolutionaries, or more correctly, from the spontaneous
movement of the peasantry'. Apparently Rosa did not grasp the full
significance of what was involved in this peasant movement. She
appeared to have believed that the Bolsheviks were capable of resisting the spontaneous activity of the peasants or of guiding it towards
an historically higher aim. But this the Bolsheviks could not do.
Their agrarian policy was something they pursued not of their own
accord but because of inescapable pressures. If they had tried to
oppose the distribution of land instead of sanctioning and regulating
it, they would have had to wage civil-war against the peasants. That
would have been the downfall of the revolution. It was precisely in
this dilemma that the deep contradiction inherent in the nature of
the October Revolution revealed itself–namely that it was both a
bourgeois (peasant) and a proletarian revolution.

As the Bolsheviks were compelled at the very outset of the
revolution to make a great and dangerous concession to the millions
of revolutionary peasants for the sake of the revolution itself, they
could not let themselves be affected by Rosa's clearly-aimed criticism of their peasant policies. However, her criticism completely
served the main purpose of her pamphlet–as a warning against the
uncritical acceptance and taking-over of Bolshevik practice as the
model for every socialist revolution. And the whole weight of her
argument hit home again when, after the Second World War, the

Russian occupation forces enforced land-distribution policies in East Germany.

In one point, however, Rosa Luxemburg seems to have missed the mark completely, namely in her spirited attack on the slogan concerning the right of national self-determination. She had always opposed this part of the Russian social-democratic programme with the irrefutable theoretical argument that real self-determination could never be realised in a capitalist world, but only under socialism. But now it was being proclaimed in a revolution which set socialism as its goal, and Lenin was right in practice when he declared that a revolutionary party in a country which oppressed other nations had to put forward this principle if it wanted to obtain the revolutionary unity of all the peoples involved. And when the Russian working class seized power, it had to proclaim this slogan within the framework of the revolution, because it was the only means of preventing the falling away of Soviet areas, and of winning back at least a part of the territory lost in the war (e.g. the Ukraine). It was precisely the national policy of the Bolsheviks under Lenin's leadership which won millions and millions of people for the revolution and flung open for them the gates of culture.

The central point of Luxemburg's criticism referred to democracy and a constituent assembly. As in the agrarian question, she argued from the old standpoint of the Bolsheviks, who issued the slogan 'All power to the Soviets!' and at the same time demanded the convening of a constituent assembly. She was unable to understand the about-face the Bolsheviks made in dissolving parliament [6 January 1918]. To the excuse that this body no longer represented the revolutionary mood of the people since the elections [held in mid-November] she retorted with the argument she had advanced back in 1905 for this eventuality: that it could have been dissolved and re-elected on a new basis. It almost seems, at least to judge from some of Trotsky's remarks at the time, that even the Bolsheviks themselves were not quite clear at the time about the fundamental import of the step they had taken. The idea which determined their policy prior to the seizure of power and to which Rosa Luxemburg still held–Soviets and parliament at the same time–would have led, in practice, to a dualism which would have inevitably led to the break-up of the Soviet power. A choice had to be made: either one thing or the other! And there is no doubt that a fundamental historical law asserted itself here in the Russian Revolution: just as representation based on the 'estates of the realm' was an expression of feudalism, and parliament an expression of the rule of the bourgeoisie, so Soviets (workers' and soldiers' councils) were an expression of a state founded not on any particular form of private property, but on collective ownership and on the achievements of labour. During the German Revolution Rosa Luxemburg completely corrected her views on this point and rejected the slogan upheld by the Independents: Workers' Councils *and* a Parliament.

It is more than likely that even when Rosa Luxemburg wrote her critique she did not attach such great importance to the institution of parliament as it might seem, and certain reservations indicate this. The main point of her criticism concerned not just a particular historical outward form of democracy, but democracy in general, democracy in its widest sense. As in 1904, when she had opposed Lenin's idea of an over-centralised party organisation in which all initiative, all wisdom, and all power would lie in the hands of a Central Committee, so in the early autumn of 1918 she opposed the concentration of power in the government and in the top ranks of the party, as well as the elimination of any initiative and control on the part of the popular masses. At that time these developments were far from being as pronounced as they were later. The popular masses through their Soviets still had enormous room for action and a tremendous determination to make use of it which far exceeded what goes under the name of democracy in countries governed by parliaments. However, the concentration of power had already reached the stage where an alert and critical observer could clearly see the future trend of developments, and Rosa regarded this concentration as the greatest threat to the Revolution. Above all, she feared that the spokesmen of the Bolsheviks would make a virtue out of necessity and fashion a dubious theory to justify a development which had been forced into being by the sheer hard pressure of events.

In her criticism she placed particular stress – and this seems to us to be the most important (and too little noticed) point of the whole discussion – on what she called the cardinal error of the Lenin-Trotsky theory. Like Kautsky, the Bolsheviks also posed the question: democracy *or* dictatorship? But they arrived at 'opposite' answers, Kautsky opting for bourgeois democracy and the Bolsheviks for dictatorship in its bourgeois sense, i.e. the rule of a handful of people. Rosa explained the inevitability of dictatorship:

> Yes, indeed! Dictatorship! But this dictatorship consists in a particular *manner of applying democracy* and *not* in *doing away with* it, in energetic and determined encroachments on the well-entrenched rights and economic relations of bourgeois society; without such intervention a socialist transformation cannot be brought about.[128]

> When the proletariat seizes power, it can never again follow Kautsky's good advice to dispense with a socialist transformation of a country on the ground that "the country is unripe". . . . It should and must in fact immediately embark on socialist measures in the most energetic, the most unyielding, and the most ruthless

way; in other words, it must exercise a dictatorship, but a dictatorship *of the class*, not of a party or of a clique—and dictatorship of
the class means: in full view of the broadest public, with the
most active, uninhibited participation of the popular masses in an
unlimited democracy.[129]

To a remark made by Trotsky, 'As Marxists, we have never
been idol-worshippers of formal democracy', she replied:

Indeed, we have never been idol-worshippers of formal democracy.
Nor have we ever been idol-worshippers of socialism or Marxism
either. Does it perhaps follow from this that we, too, may dump
socialism or Marxism on the rubbish heap à la Cunow, Lensch, and
Parvus, if it becomes uncomfortable for us? Trotsky and Lenin are
the living negation of this question. We have never been idol-
worshippers of formal democracy—that only means: we have
always distinguished the social kernel from the political form of
bourgeois democracy; we have always exposed the bitter kernel of
social inequality and lack of freedom under the sweet shell of
formal equality and freedom—not in order to reject the latter, but
to spur the working class not to be satisfied with the shell, but
rather to conquer political power and fill it with a new social content. It is the historic task of the proletariat, once it has attained
power, to create socialist democracy in place of bourgeois democracy, not to do away with democracy altogether.[130]

For Rosa this meant not the restriction, but the broadening of
democracy. It meant a democracy of a higher order which does not
wear itself out in occasional elections, but is the direct activity of
the masses. Such a democracy is 'the active, unrestrained, and energetic political life of the broadest masses of the people'. Rosa regarded this mighty display of popular activity as the essence of
socialism, in fact, as both the instrument and the aim of socialism.
Only by educating itself in creative democratic activity could the
working class raise itself to the high cultural level it needed to accomplish its task and cast off the weaknesses and vices characteristic
of an oppressed class:

Socialist practice demands a total spiritual transformation in the
masses degraded by centuries of bourgeois class rule. Social instincts
in place of egoistic ones, mass initiative in place of inertia, idealism
which overcomes all suffering, etc. etc. . . . The only way to a rebirth is the school of public life itself, the broadest and the most
unlimited democracy, and public opinion. It is rule by terror which
demoralises.[131]

Only this active and operative democracy, this resolution of
the masses to take matters into their own hands, could secure the
carrying out of revolutionary measures, the way to socialism:

If this is the case, however, then it is clear that socialism by its very nature cannot be imposed from above or introduced by ukase. . . . The negative, the tearing down, can be decreed; but not the positive, the building up. New territory. A thousand-and-one problems. Only experience is capable of correcting and of opening up new ways. Only uninhibited, effervescent life falls into a thousand new forms and improvisations, illuminates creative forces, and corrects all blunders itself. The public life of states with limited freedom is so inadequate, so poverty-stricken, so schematic, so unfruitful, precisely because, in excluding democracy, it seals off the living sources of all spiritual wealth and progress.[132]

Rosa was in favour of an unrelenting campaign to crush counter-revolutionary resistance and any attempts to sabotage socialist measures, but she was unwilling to see criticism suppressed, even hostile criticism. She regarded unrestricted criticism as the only means of preventing the ossification of the state apparatus into a downright bureaucracy. Permament public control, and freedom of the press and of assembly were therefore necessary:

> Freedom for supporters of the government only, for members of one party only–no matter how numerous they might be–is no freedom at all. Freedom is always freedom for those who think differently. Not because of any fanaticism about "justice", but because all that is instructive, wholesome, and purifying in political freedom depends on this essential characteristic, and "freedom" effectively loses all meaning once it becomes a privilege.[133]

She described the consequences which the break-down of democracy would inevitably have:

> But with the suppression of political life throughout the country, life in the Soviets must become more and more crippled. Without general elections, without unrestricted freedom of the press and of assembly, without the free struggle of opinion, life in every public institution dies down and becomes a mere semblance of itself in which the bureaucracy remains as the only active element. Public life gradually falls asleep. A few dozen party leaders with inexhaustible energy and boundless idealism direct and rule. Among these, a dozen outstanding minds manage things in reality, and an elite of the working class is summoned to meetings from time to time so that they can applaud the speeches of the leaders, and give unanimous . approval to proposed resolutions, thus at bottom a cliquish set-up–a dictatorship, to be sure, but not the dictatorship of the proletariat: rather the dictatorship of a handful of politicians, i.e., a dictatorship in the bourgeois sense, in the sense of a Jacobin rule. . . .
>
> . . . every long-lasting regime based on martial law leads without fail to arbitrariness, and all arbitrary power tends to deprave society.[134]

When Rosa Luxemburg penned these thoughts, democracy in

Russia had not by any means died down. In the broad Russian empire it enabled tremendous achievements to take place: in the creation of the rudiments of a new organisation of society, in the defence of the Revolution and in the struggle against unimaginable difficulties resulting from the war and the social upheaval. However, in the actual restrictions put on democratic procedures; in the growth of party rule, already well under way; and in the lack of democratic controls on the state leadership, Rosa recognised the colossal dangers to the future development of the revolution. These did indeed set in, and even worse things happened than she had ever foreseen. Moreover, she was also well aware that, in view of the enormous tasks facing the Bolsheviks, who had to wrestle daily with hostile forces simply to hang on to the power they had seized, they would be under an almost irresistible pressure to concentrate all their power, to reduce the dangers of the moment by restricting freedoms and dictating necessary measures from above. After depicting the effects of democratic activity by the masses, she observed:

> No doubt, this is exactly how the Bolsheviks would have proceeded had they not suffered under the terrible pressures of the World War, the German occupation and all the attendant abnormal difficulties–circumstances which were bound to have distorted any socialist policy, however imbued it might have been with the best intentions and the finest principles.[135]

In the first years of the revolution, the Bolsheviks–given that they were unwilling to capitulate–could hardly have acted any differently under the pressure and strain of their circumstances. Their really serious mistake was to bend over backwards in justifying their measures, elevate what they had done to a generally valid principle, and–despite their many reassurances to the contrary–deny and act against the fundamentals of democracy. They suppressed democratic ideas in the consciousness of the masses and of the leading cadres, and thus threw out the stopper that could have kept the state machine from slipping down into totalitarianism. Rosa intended her critique to sound the alarm against this danger.

She also understood that the 'abundant use of terror'–although it cut her to the quick with a burning pain and caused her sleepless nights–was the result of this same terrible pressure. Far from condemning the Bolsheviks, she remarked:

> Everything happening in Russia is understandable as an inevitable chain of cause and effect, the starting-point and corner-stone of which are: the failure of the German proletariat to rise to the occasion and the occupation of Russia by German imperialism. . . . By their determined revolutionary attitude, their exemplary energy and their unswerving loyalty to international socialism they [the

Bolsheviks] have truly accomplished everything possible under confoundedly difficult conditions.[186]

Rosa's aim was simply to warn the Bolsheviks against making a virtue of necessity, against laying down a detailed theory about tactics forced on them by fateful circumstances and then recommending them to the international proletariat as model socialist tactics, worthy of emulation. The point at issue at the moment was not this or that tactical detail, but the capacity for action and the will to power of the proletariat:

> This is what is essential and enduring in the policy of the Bolsheviks. In this sense they have renderd the immortal historic service of having led the way by conquering political power and by posing the problem of making socialism a practical reality. . . . In Russia the problem could only be posed; it could not be solved there. And in *this* sense the future everywhere belongs to "Bolshevism".[187]

That statement is clear and unambiguous, and in a fragment found with the same manuscript there is the following passage:

> "Bolshevism" has become the catchword of practical revolutionary socialism, for all working-class efforts to seize power. The historic service of Bolshevism lies in the tearing asunder of the social chasm in the bosom of bourgeois society, and in the deepening and sharpening of class contradictions on an international scale. And in this work–as is always the case with great historical events–all the specific mistakes and errors of Bolshevism sink into insignificance.[188]

Rosa Luxemburg's work on the Russian Revolution remained unfinished. Was it only because she had no time? Perhaps it was also because, while writing it, she found that her opinion on important points was a bit shaky. In any case, we know that a few weeks afterwards she revised several important details. Adolf Warski, her Polish comrade-in-arms, has published a letter written to him by Rosa Luxemburg around the end of November or the beginning of December 1918 in answer to certain misgivings he himself had expressed about the policy of the Bolsheviks:

> Our party [in Poland–PF] is full of enthusiasm for Bolshevism; yet at the same time it has come out in opposition to both the Brest-Litovsk Peace and the Bolshevik propagation of the slogan of "national self-determination". That is enthusiasm coupled with a critical spirit–what more could we wish? I, too, shared all your reservations and misgivings, but have dropped them in the most important questions, and in others I have not gone as far as you have done. Terrorism certainly indicates great weakness, but it is directed against internal enemies who build their hopes on the existence of capitalism outside Russia, and receive support and encouragement from it. If the European revolution comes, the Russian counter-revolutionaries will lose not only this support, but–what is

more important—their courage as well. In short, the terror in Russia is above all an expression of the weakness of the European proletariat. It is true that the new agrarian relations which have been created represent the sorest and most dangerous point of the Russian Revolution. But here, too, the truth holds good that even the greatest revolution can bring about only what is historically ready for fulfilment. This sore point, too, can be healed only by the European revolution. And this is coming! ...[189]

Like Lenin and all the leading Bolsheviks of the day, Rosa Luxemburg was convinced that the Russian Revolution was doomed to destruction unless the proletariat elsewhere came to its aid by seizing power in other countries, i.e. that 'socialism in one country alone' was impossible. The saving world revolution did not materialise. Nevertheless, international capitalism had been weakened by the war, and the revolutionary solidarity shown by the working class in other countries was strong enough to enable the Bolsheviks to come off victorious in the terrible civil war, to consolidate state power, and to discover the great possibilities of manœuvring in their domestic policy.

This development seemed to nullify Rosa Luxemburg's misgivings with regard to Bolshevik policy. However, although her criticism did not hit the bull's-eye every time, in the long run it did turn out to be correct, and today (1939) her pamphlet reads like one great prophecy. Things have come to pass just as she predicted: the life of the Soviets has become crippled, 'a mere semblance of itself in which the bureaucracy remains as the only active element', a bureaucracy which has in fact developed into a special dominating social stratum. The ruling group in the Soviet Union has appointed itself the 'unblemished authority' in the international communist movement, demanding blind faith and stifling any attempt at criticism. The bloody persecution of the Old Bolshevik Guard and countless communists and Soviet citizens on the pretext of the most absurd accusations went far beyond Rosa's worst apprehensions. To think that at one time she shuddered at the mere thought that the Bolsheviks might enter into an alliance with German imperialism! And now, in 1939, with the signing of the Stalin-Hitler pact, we are experiencing a Russian domestic and foreign policy that no longer has anything in common with the principles of socialism.

Thus in this work Rosa Luxemburg again proved herself to be a great revolutionary by her refusal to accept things uncritically and evade the precepts of history. She exposed the difficulties of Russian isolation and sought to overcome them by extending the revolutionary front. Like her articles on the Russian Revolution, this pamphlet was primarily intended to spur the German proletariat into action.

13
The German revolution

Prelude

The year 1918 was the worst of all the years Rosa Luxemburg spent in prison. Despite the plucky resistance she put up, the enforced loneliness, and the privations and disappointments frayed her nerves. She had already fallen seriously ill in Wronke, and wrote bitterly of the 'treatment' recommended by the doctor. It reduced itself to the advice given by the vicar of Ufenau to the dying Hutten:

Vergesset, Hutten dass ihr Hutten seid!

Forget, Hutten, that your name is Hutten!

To which Hutten could only answer:

Dein Rat, mein teurer Freund, ist wundervoll:
Nicht leben soll ich, wenn ich leben soll.

Your advice, my dear friend, is wonderful:
I should not live any more, if I am to live at all.

In Breslau her condition was made worse by complete isolation, a stricter prison regime, and the progressive restriction of her correspondence (obviously the flower of the nation who were controlling her letters did not have sufficiently developed taste to enjoy these works of art). Protests against the arbitrary detainment were of no avail. A judicial body set up to examine protective-custody warrants for the purpose of appeasing public opinion turned out to be a fig-leaf for the military dictatorship. In March 1918 Rosa wrote to Sonja Liebknecht: 'My complaint has been dismissed with a thorough description of my wickedness and incorrigibility, and so has my application requesting leave, at the least. No doubt I'll have to wait until we've defeated the whole world.'

She could still brush aside the malice and chicanery of the authorities with humour, and she could still find the strength to cheer up Sonja and help her bear her heavy burden. But in 1918 one can almost hear the snap–like that of glass cracking–in the tone of the few letters she was still permitted to write. At times she could not suppress an anguished cry: 'My nerves, my nerves! I can no longer sleep.' Suddenly, and without any real reason, she would be tormented by a feeling of absolute certainty that some calamity or other had befallen someone dear to her. This happened, for example, when she failed to receive any sign of life from Clara Zetkin for a long time, and she became very anxious about the fate of her friend's sons, who were at the front. As she explained in a letter to Luise Kautsky [25 July 1918]: 'I have enough courage to cope with whatever may happen to me. But to bear the sorrows of *others*, and Clara's too, if "God forbid! " anything should happen–for that I lack courage and strength.'

Her thoughts were constantly revolving around tricky problems: the threatening victory of German imperialism, the mortal dangers facing the Russian Revolution, and the deathly silence with which the international and, above all, the German proletariat seemed to put up with everything and go on doing all the bloody work of its masters. To be sure, inflamed by the glorious example of the Viennese workers, a new wave of mass strikes rolled over Germany at the end of January 1918 in protest against the coercive peace of Brest-Litovsk and against the growing hunger at home, and in favour of democratic reforms. It was a mighty action which embraced about twenty large towns; in Berlin alone half a million workers went out on strike. However, as mighty as the charge of the workers was, the reaction of the military dictatorship was swift and brutal. Once again the 'hydras of the revolution' had their 'heads' cut off. Military courts were set up to deal with those civilians accused of political offences. Formidable sentences were imposed up and down the country, and the gates of hard-labour prisons clanked shut behind many a *Spartakus* militant. In March those in charge of military propaganda for the *Spartakusbund*, together with its main organiser, Leo Jogiches, were arrested. The national leadership had dwindled down to two or three people forced to work under the most difficult conditions. While Ludendorff was conducting his desperate offensive on the Western front, the working class seemed to be in a torpor, and all activity stifled. In the *Spartakusbrief* of June 1918 Rosa Luxemburg cried out with pained bitterness:

> Having failed to halt the storming chariot of imperialism, the German proletariat is now being dragged behind it to overpower socialism and democracy all over Europe. Over the bones of the Russian, Ukrainian, Baltic, and Finnish proletarians; over the national existence of the Belgians, Poles, Lithuanians, Rumanians; over the economic ruin of France, the German worker is tramping, wading over knee-deep in blood, onward, to plant the victorious banner of German imperialism everywhere.

But each military victory which Germany's cannon-fodder helps to win on foreign soil means a new political and social triumph for reaction inside the Reich. Every storming of the Red Guards in Finland and in South Russia increases the power of East-Elbian Junkerdom and of Pan-German capitalism. Every Flanders town riddled with bullets means the fall of a position of German democracy.

Rosa's most gnawing anxiety was that the German Revolution would come too late to save the Russian Revolution. Her absolute conviction was that it would come. But however much she strained to listen, she heard nothing of the elementary process going on without fanfare in the depths of German society. The fury over the wholesale slaughter and the hatred of the ruling power remained unspoken, but could be seen in the eyes of the masses. Rebellion against the semi-starvation rationing had not yet erupted, but resentment was certainly growing. The ground was beginning to tremble under the feet of the upper social classes so that they were gripped by fear; panic was constantly threatening to break out, and the number of those who bolted from the front of 'bitter-enders' (*Durchhalter*) grew larger and larger.

For German militarism, the Brest-Litovsk peace of conquest was beginning to prove a treacherous advantage. Although it urgently needed the troops stationed in the East for the Western front, it had to draw a *cordon sanitaire* around them. The very soldiers who had defeated the remnants of the Russian armies in the Baltic provinces and in the Ukraine had themselves become infected with the Bolshevik bacillus, and carried it to the West. Ludendorff sent cripples and half-grown children to battle under the sickle of death, but behind the lines there were hundreds of thousands of deserters. Such mass desertion was the fruit of the progressive disintegration of the whole of German society, and the deserters in their turn furthered the process of disintegration.

A mass rising was brewing. The factories became nests of conspirators. The radical elements propagated revolutionary ideas, but at the same time they put on the brakes, for they didn't want the action to fizzle out before it really had a chance to get under way. They wanted it to go the whole hog from the outset.

On 1 October two events occurring at the opposite poles of German society indicated that the hour had struck. Hindenburg and Ludendorff, who, for a week, had been making frantic appeals for help to the government, now demanded that an immediate peace offer be made to the Entente. At the same time a joint national conference was held by the *Spartakusbund* and the group associated with it, the Left Radicals, whose centre was in Bremen, where their organ, *Arbeiterpolitik* (Workers' Politics), appeared legally. It was the war council of the approaching revolution. Agreement was reached on a programme of political action culminating in a rallying cry for a united republic, not as a final aim but as a 'criterion of the genuineness of the democratic claims with which the ruling classes and their agents try to swindle you'. It was also decided to intensify the agitation among the troops as much as possible and to set about immediately to form workers' and soldiers councils everywhere.

The death-agony of Wilhelmine rule began. As usual in such instances, the up-and-down fever which had seized the old order produced a panic-stricken mood among the authorities, who hastily enacted the most contradictory measures in an attempt to save the regime by reforms. A 'parliamentary' government was formed with the future Grand-Duke of Baden, Prince Max, at its head (to safeguard the monarchy), and among its ministers was the social democrat Philipp Scheidemann (to appease the popular masses). As the victory symbolised by the Brest-Litovsk peace had now become impossible, the Kaiser made it incumbent on parliament to conclude a peace of defeat. The General Staff pressed for surrender, but at the same time it was preparing last-ditch actions and seeking to incite the people against the very peace negotiations it was categorically demanding. The prisons opened to release some of the oppositional leaders, but at the same time masses of 'politicals' from the army and the factories were being flung into them. The democratisation of the whole of political life was announced, but at the same time troops were being concentrated in the capital to crush any rising of the people. Freedom of assembly was proclaimed, but the volley of police prohibitions made this a farce, and demonstrations were fired upon. Each new measure, each act of violence, and each concession led to the further disintegration of the old power. The ice was broken. No more holding back!

For Rosa Luxemburg, too, there was now no more holding back. Gripped by fever and unrest, she could no longer bear the narrowness of her cell and demanded her immediate release from the Chancellor, Prince Max. She yearned to be caught up in the tide of events: to urge the people on, to direct, to act. On 18 October she wrote to Sonja Liebknecht:

> But, in any case, one thing is certain: my mood is already such that a visit of my friends under surveillance has become impossible. I have stood everything quite patiently for years and, under other circumstances, would have remained just as patient for years more. But when the general swing in the situation occurred, something psychological in me also snapped. The conversations under surveillance, with no possibility of talking about the things which really interest me, have now become such a burden that I would prefer to do without any visits at all, until we can see each other as free people.

Anyway, it can't last much longer. When Dittmann and Kurt Eisner are released, they won't be able to keep me any longer in prison, and Karl, too, will soon be free.

On 20 October an amnesty was issued for convicted political prisoners, and on 23 October Karl Liebknecht was freed and welcomed in triumph by the Berlin workers. The amnesty did not apply to Rosa, however. She had not been convicted and was not serving a sentence; she was 'only' sitting in protective custody–and there she remained. In fact, the protective-custody warrant against her was renewed just at that time. Was this because, in the era of democratisation, the bankrupt military was still proving to be stronger than the government? Or was it because the government thought it had enough on its hands with the one enemy Liebknecht? Whatever the reason, Rosa was kept cooped up in her cage for another two weeks. She was bursting with impatience, and it was only by the greatest exertion of will-power that she forced herself to maintain her usual outward calm so that no one could have the triumph of gloating over her helplessness.

November

Events now moved at the double. The fronts collapsed. On 26 October Ludendorff, who had been the real ruler of Germany, was forced to flee abroad with a false passport. On 28 October the German Admiralty, seized by a fit of raving madness, resolved to risk the lives of 80,000 men in a 'decisive' naval battle on the North Sea in order to save the 'honour of the navy'. This provoked the final blow.

The fleet was caught up in the revolutionary ferment even more strongly than the army. As early as August 1917 a large and well-organised anti-war action had occurred at the naval base in Kiel, yielding the first martyrs of the revolution. Two sailors, Reichpietsch and Köbis, were sentenced to death for mutiny and high treason, and were shot on 5 September 1917; more than fifty of their co-defendants were thrown into prison with intimidating hard-labour sentences. Nevertheless, secret sailors' councils existed on almost all the vessels, and they kept a mistrustful watch on the officers. The sailors were still ready to go into action to fend off an enemy attack, but they were not prepared to take part in senseless adventures.

When the fleet was gathered on the high sea and the signal given to stand by for action, the stokers put out the fires in the boiler-rooms and forced the ships to return to port. On board, the officers had already lost control, but on land they tried to reassert their authority by arresting 600 sailors. Full-scale rebellion then broke out: the sailors joined forces with the workers of Kiel. Within a few days the movement had grown into a general strike in ships and factories. On 4 November the Governor of Kiel was forced to resign, and a Workers' and Sailors' Council made itself master of the town. The government still believed it was dealing with an isolated mutiny, and sent the social democrat Gustav Noske to restore order. But it was Revolution which now, like a conflagration fanned by the wind, proceeded to conquer one town after another.

In the two weeks following his release, Karl Liebknecht had been working feverishly: carefully observing the mood of the workers and soldiers, speaking at one factory meeting after another to inflame his listeners into action. He was co-opted into the Revolutionary Shop Stewards (*Revolutionäre Obleute*), an organisation which had existed since the big January strike, and consisted of trade-union representatives in the factories. It was the embryo of a workers' council, and at the same time a revolutionary committee of action. This body met almost daily to prepare for the rising. Its members were being hunted by the police, who were after Liebknecht in particular. He could no longer go home, sleeping sometimes on a bench in a workers' pub, sometimes in a furniture-van; forced to make his way at night through the Treptow Woods [Berlin] to evade the pursuers always on his heels. He had differences of opinion with the Shop Stewards' leaders. He wanted a greater mobilisation of the masses, demonstrations of workers on the streets to win the soldiers, and intensive propaganda in factories and barracks. The most daring elements in the Shop Stewards' organisation had conspiratorial ideas: they thought in terms of an insurrection which was to follow a meticulously worked out plan. They counted their revolvers and engaged in endless technical preparations. Their slogan was 'All or nothing!', and the hesitant joined them–precisely because it meant 'nothing'! Again and again a date for the rising was fixed, and again and again it was postponed. In the end these 'leaders' had just enough time to place themselves at the head of the Berlin workers–something which called for no special revolutionary technique, since the workers could no longer be restrained anyway. It was new confirmation of Rosa Luxemburg's theory that revolutions cannot be 'made', that revolutions spring from the will of the masses when the situation is ripe.

On 9 November the hour struck for Berlin, already surrounded by the revolutionary waves in a great semicircle, on the north, west, and south. Events there were decisive for the whole country. On that morning, hundreds of thousands of workers poured out of the factories. All idea of resistance was abandoned, and even the special detachments of officers who had been prepared for civil war capitulated. Wilhelm II fled to the Netherlands. Prince Max of Baden announced the abdication of the Kaiser and that the Crown Prince had renounced the succession. By taking this step, he still hoped—with the assistance of the social-democratic leaders—to save the crown for some other Hohenzollern. He then handed over the office of Reich's Chancellor to the SPD chief, Friedrich Ebert, who accepted it with the assurance: 'I hate revolution like mortal sin.'

While this was going on, the cries of the vast crowds in the streets calling for the abdication of the Kaiser became more and more stormy. Scheidemann was called out of a meeting by his supporters and asked to speak to the masses. From a window of the Reichstag he delivered a short speech, finishing with the shout, 'Long live the German Republic!' He was immediately attacked, in a most furious manner, by Ebert, who was still endeavouring to save the monarchy. The masses moved on to the Imperial Palace, where, from the balcony, Karl Liebknecht proclaimed the Socialist Republic. On that same evening the catchword was taken up by the Provisional Workers' and Soldiers' Council, which was meeting in the Assembly Hall of the Reichstag.

Councils were elected in factories and barracks, and an Executive Committee of Workers' and Soldiers' Councils was formed which claimed full power throughout the Reich. All government buildings were occupied by representatives of the working class. The prisons were stormed and thousands released, among them Leo Jogiches.

Now the overthrow of the old order spread almost automatically to all other big towns. In Breslau, too, the prison gates were opened, and on 8 November Rosa Luxemburg was free at last.* She went straight from prison to Cathedral Square, in the centre of the city, where she was cheered by a mass demonstration. On 10 November she arrived in Berlin, and was greeted with great joy by her friends from the *Spartakusbund*—but with deep inner sadness as well, for they now saw what the years in prison had done to her. She had aged, and was a sick woman. Her hair, once deep black, had now gone quite grey. Yet her eyes shone with the old fire and energy. She urgently needed peace and quiet to recuperate, but from that moment on there was to be no more rest for her. She had two months left to live, months of almost superhuman effort

---

* According to Mathilde Jacob's account, published in the *Leipziger Volkszeitung* on 15 January 1929, Rosa Luxemburg was officially released late in the evening of 7 November. However as she did not know where to spend the night she remained in prison until the following morning. She then telephoned Mathilde Jacob, requesting that she be fetched by car since no trains were running. Twice her friends tried and failed to make it to Breslau, and it was not until 10 November, when the trains began to operate again, that she was able to travel to Berlin.

and strain, both physical and mental. Without a thought for her own health and safety, without any consideration for her own personal wishes, she threw herself with passion and energy into the struggle and participated in 'the colourful, fascinating, thrilling and tremendous spectacle of revolution'.

Such a display of flaming passion and an immense will to action filled many observers with deep misgivings, even many who admired her personality though they did not stand on the barricades with her. It seemed to them that she had lost all sense of proportion and had completely misjudged the reality of things. Blind to the limits of the attainable, she was gropingly tempting fate itself. They claimed that she was uncritically copying the Russian example without showing any understanding of the very different conditions prevailing in Germany. If such objections are examined in detail, however, then the complete failure of these people to understand revolutionary politics at all becomes evident. Not that the policy of the *Spartakusbund*, or of Rosa Luxemburg herself, in those stormy days was faultless. Whoever is called upon to take decisions of far-reaching significance in such a chaotic struggle of great mass forces must inevitably make mistakes from time to time, even if he has a genius for perceiving the objective factors in a situation. And whoever has the courage to take bold decisions, and is not willing to let himself be dragged along in the wake of events, will often enough have to keep ahead of existing power relations in order to shape them favourably. A revolution storming ahead with ever-growing momentum will bury the mistakes of the revolutionary party under the ruins of the old society, and bring about in reality what only a moment before seemed like an optimistic illusion of the vanguard taking the initiative.

Rosa Luxemburg's fundamental attitude was determined by the vital law of all great revolutions, which she formulated as follows:

> Either it must storm ahead with great speed and determination, overcome all hindrances with an iron hand, and keep setting its aims further and further ahead, or it will very soon be flung back beyond its weaker starting-point and crushed by the counter-revolution.[140]

But even in the rush of events of those days, her revolutionary temperament, impetuous though it was, was still curbed and controlled by her reason. The fact that the first revolutionary period nevertheless ended in a serious and, in the long run, decisive defeat of the working class was due not so much to the many errors committed by the revolutionary forces, but to the incredible difficulty of the situation which led to these errors.

The gathering of forces

Outwardly the course of the German November Revolution bore such an amazing resemblance to that of the French February Revolution of 1848 that the question inevitably arises: how was it possible that a period of development from a predominantly manufacturing economy of small workshops to modern large-scale industry, a period characterised by cataclysmic changes in the social composition of the nation, did not produce entirely different results, did not lead to a smooth victory of the proletarian revolution? The truth is that the German Revolution took place under conditions which could hardly have been more unfavourable. Like the Russian Revolution of February 1917, the German November Revolution drove the last remnants of feudalism out of power, and brought about the flowering of all the illusions attendant on modern democracy–above all, the idea of achieving socialism through parliament. The revolution found scarcely an echo in the countryside: the German peasant still believed that the tremendous sacrifices that he, too, had made during the war would be covered, materially at least, by the war-bond stored away in his cupboard. Apart from hoping for the repeal of the war-economy restrictions, he had no urgent wants.

On the other hand, the German capitalist class was incomparably more powerful and more class-conscious than its Russian counterpart. Also, the Russian Revolution, which seemed destined to be the strong support of every revolutionary movement and did, in fact, play this role a long time for the international working class, had very contradictory effects just during the decisive period of the German Revolution. By its example it clearly demonstrated the character and aims of revolution to all classes, and the bourgeoisie grasped its implications even more quickly than the proletariat. The capitalist class with its petit-bourgeois and feudal appendages immediately drew conclusions from the situation, and made political and economic concessions to the working class with the idea at the back of its mind of regaining the surrendered terrain at a later date. At the same time, realising that its very existence was at stake, it was ruthlessly and cruelly determined to defend its power position and crush its enemies. It therefore grouped all its forces around the banner of orthodox Social Democracy: Stinnes came to an understanding with Legien, the leader of the trade unions; Hindenburg, the head of the army, placed himself at the disposal of Ebert. The leading representative of the East-Elbian Junkers, Herr von Heydebrand, once known as the 'uncrowned king of Prussia', assured

Ebert of his loyalty and sympathy; and the high-ranking representative of Pan-German officialdom, *Landschaftsdirektor* Kapp, later the 'hero' of the abortive Kapp Putsch, did the same.

The confidence of the German capitalist class in Ebert and his friends was well-placed. Here, too, a fundamental difference from the Russian Revolution became evident. It is a fact that the Mensheviks and the right-wing Social-Revolutionaries allied themselves with the bourgeoisie and that they opposed any conquest of power by the proletariat. Nevertheless, they did, at least, have revolutionary pretensions, however naïve these may have been (which explains their vacillating policies). Even when the Bolsheviks were already securely in power, many Mensheviks continued to serve the revolution, although they held fast to their own views. Not until later did certain Menshevik leaders go over individually to the counter-revolutionary camp. In Germany, on the other hand, the General Staff of old Social Democracy—Ebert, Noske, Legien, Scheidemann, Landsberg, etc.—were conscious opponents of the revolution from the very beginning. Determined to take up the power that the November storm had blown into their lap, they opposed every socialist policy, every initiative of the masses to transform society. On 10 November Ebert was made head of the revolutionary government by the Berlin Workers' and Soldiers' Council; on the same day he concluded a pact with the army's General Staff (Groener and Hindenburg) with the aim of suppressing the Berlin workers by force of arms. The old SPD was still a strong power even though its influence on the organised working class had waned during the war. It could still feed on the trust stored up by the party of August Bebel, and was the chief beneficiary of the deep political excitement churned up among the popular masses by the revolution. Its ranks were joined by previously apolitical working-class elements, clerical employees, masses of petit-bourgeois, and, above all, the grey mass of soldiers returning from the front—a strong, but blindly trusting contingent which was, for a long time to come, easy to manipulate.

Even where the example of the Russian Revolution had been most effective, it proved to be of doubtful value. The Workers' and Soldiers' Councils, the natural child of any modern revolution, arose directly from the initiative of the masses, only where the latter themselves had taken the bastions of power by storm. However, in large areas of Germany where the council idea, as a product of the 9th November in Berlin, was simply adopted and mechanically repeated, the Councils were more of a decorative appendage than anything else, as they were merely the result of a compromise between the leaders of the old party and of the USDP, and often even with bourgeois parties. In short, they were not real organs of mass power. Furthermore, even when the lower officials of the SPD voiced their support of the Revolution, they let their actions be determined by the party leadership. The USDP was deeply split. Its followers in the large towns were revolutionary enough, but hampered by their leaders–Haase, Kautsky, Hilferding, and Bernstein–who wanted a revolution without the unavoidable social upheaval any revolution must bring with it. With its leaders unwilling to bear the costs of revolution, the USDP in its character and action resembled the Mensheviks after February 1917. The *Spartakusbund* was the only organisation in Germany which showed any revolutionary determination and unity of purpose.

Thus the working-class movement was extraordinarily divided, and the various groups were at quite different stages of theoretical development. In addition, the power-centre of the counter-revolution was located right within its own ranks. And to top it off, there was another fact of the greatest significance: history provided the movement with no direct or imperative objective that could be brought about only by revolution. Peace and land were the two great slogans which had carried the Russian Revolution to victory, but in 1918 peace was already a fact, and defeated German imperialism was prepared to pay anything for it, providing it could retain power at home; and although a broad section of the small-hold peasants made a rather precarious living, land-hunger was not strong enough to rouse the rural areas into revolt. Having been kept until then in complete servitude by Junkers and rich land-owning peasants, the agricultural labourers made only hesitant use of the 'coalition right' and their new-found political freedom. The working class was certainly in favour of the socialisation of the economy, but the greater part of the masses came to realise what this demand meant and how it could be carried out only after all chance of doing so was irrevocably lost.

However, there was one factor which forced matters to a fateful showdown: sections of the working class were armed. Now, it is a law of history that no class is prepared to let itself be disarmed without a struggle, just as power in a society can only be in the hands of a ruling class which has the undisputed monopoly of arms. This factor made a struggle for power, i.e. civil war, inevitable.

The most important factors determining the relation of forces in war are well known, but still it is the practical test which finally decides which side prevails. In revolution, however, which is an elementary process of a very different order, inestimable intellectual and psychological factors play a much greater role: revolution disturbs the basis of society much more deeply than does war, and changes in the understanding and energy of the masses tend to be sudden and full of surprises.

As far as it was at all possible to recognise the character of the main actors in the drama, the significance of their actions, and the relation of forces in the revolutionary period, Rosa Luxemburg succeeded with great acumen. She grasped intuitively the difficulties of the situation, but, far from capitulating to them, she set herself the task of overcoming them. She accepted the dictum of Saint-Just: *'Oser, c'est toute la politique de l'heure actuelle'*–that to dare is the first precept of revolution–and yet she never lost her head. She did not want ephemeral successes, nor did she want to harvest unripe fruit. Her actions immediately upon her arrival in Berlin bear witness to this. In the first days of the revolution the Independents had occupied the offices of three bourgeois newspapers and were issuing the newspapers on their own account. A group of *Spartakus* supporters did the same with the *Berliner Lokalanzeiger*, a nationalist mass-circulation paper loyal to the Kaiser, and turned it into *Rote Fahne* (Red Flag). Rosa was opposed to this move–not because she respected the old regime's laws or the big capitalist interests behind the *Lokalanzeiger*, but because she recognised that the *Spartakusbund* was still not strong enough to hold on to the position it had seized. And so it happened: the premises had to be evacuated at the first sign of trouble.

However, both a revolutionary organ and a revolutionary organisation were urgently necessary. The *Spartakusbund* was still rudimentary, and consisted chiefly of innumerable small and almost autonomous groups. Liebknecht continued to agitate tirelessly among the masses on street-corners, on public squares, in factories and barracks, explaining the aims of the *Spartakusbund* and the tasks of the day, and was ably supported by other prominent speakers of the organisation–Paul Levi, Hermann Duncker, Wilhelm Pieck, and others. Meanwhile Leo Jogiches took the tasks of organisation in hand. Serious difficulties stood in the way of setting up a newspaper. The new power-holders used the war-time restrictions on the use of paper as a political weapon against the left. Nevertheless, on 18 November 1918, the first number of the new *Rote Fahne* finally appeared, bearing the names of Karl Liebknecht and Rosa Luxemburg as editors. Rosa was the real leading light of the paper. In directing a group of select contributors, including Paul Levi, August Thalheimer, and Paul Lange, she used equal measures of forcefulness and tact, backed up by the absolute authority and respect she enjoyed among all her collaborators. She determined the contents of each issue, and, in articles aglow with her passionate spirit and resounding with the blustering storms of those times, she illuminated current events, interpreted their significance and laid bare their consequences. As though from a great height, her eye ranged over the whole battle-field of the revolution. She kept a sharp watch on its enemies: like Marat before her, she revealed a flair for recognising, from even slight hints, counter-revolutionary conspiracies and intentions–and this with a certitude which unshakeable documentary evidence coming to light only much later has vindicated. At the same time she studied the actions and reactions of the masses, critically examined their weaknesses, welcomed their gains with great enthusiasm, and sought to guide them to the great objective: the seizure of power. Under her editorship *Rote Fahne* became part and parcel of the history of the revolution –its torch, its whip, and its tocsin. It proved to be, above all, Rosa Luxemburg's last and decisive profession of faith, her political testament.

The programme of the revolution

Her very first article in *Rote Fahne* showed how far her ideas had developed since the writing of her pamphlet on the Russian Revolution. After a few brief sentences summing up the results of the first week of the revolution, she laid down the chief points of a revolutionary programme:

> The abolition of capitalist rule and the realisation of a socialist order of society–this and nothing less is the historical theme of the present revolution. It is a tremendous work which cannot be accomplished instantaneously with a few decrees from above, but can only be started by the conscious action of the toiling masses in town and country, and can only be brought through all the storms safely into port by the highest degree of intellectual maturity and inexhaustible idealism of the popular masses.
>
> The road of the revolution follows clearly from its aim; its method follows from its task. *All power in the hands of the working masses, in the hands of the Workers' and Soldiers' Councils, and the safeguarding of the revolutionary work from lurking enemies*–that is the guiding principle for all the measures of a revolutionary government.
>
> Every step, every action of the government should point like a compass in this direction:
>
> The extension and re-election of local Workers' and Soldiers' Councils in order that the first chaotic and impulsive gesture which brought them into being may be replaced by a conscious process of understanding the aims, tasks, and methods of the revolution; . . .
>
> the speediest possible convening of the Reich's parliament of workers and soldiers in order to constitute the proletarians of all Germany as a class, as a compact political power, and to rally them behind the work of the revolution as its bulwark and driving force;

the immediate organisation–not of the "peasants"–but of the rural proletarians and small peasants, social strata which up to now have remained outside the revolution;

the formation of a proletarian Red Guard for the permanent defence of the Revolution, and the training of a workers' militia in order to fashion the whole of the proletariat into an alert force ever-prepared for action;

the ousting of the old organs of the absolutist and militarist police-state from the new administration, judiciary, and army;

the immediate confiscation of all dynastic wealth and property, and of all large-scale landed property as a first provisional measure to secure the feeding of the people, for hunger is one of the most dangerous allies of the counter-revolution;

the immediate convening of a world congress of workers in Germany to stress sharply and clearly the socialist and international character of the revolution, because the future of the German Revolution can be anchored only in the International, in the world revolution of the proletariat.[141]

She then compared this programme with the actions of the 'Revolutionary Government' of Ebert and Haase: the preservation of the old state apparatus, the sanctification of private property, the securing of capitalist conditions, the giving of a free hand to the counter-revolution. And in this political indictment occurs the following sentence:

The present government is calling a constituent assembly in order to create a bourgeois counter-weight to the Workers' and Soldiers' Councils, thereby shunting the Revolution onto the track of a mere bourgeois revolution and conjuring away its socialist aims.

Only a little while before she had criticised the Bolshevik policy for refusing to permit the existence of parliament side by side with Soviets, but she now put forward a clear-cut alternative: *either* parliament *or* Workers' and Soldiers' Councils. Was this a revision of her original criticism of the Russian Revolution? Indeed it was, but was this a mere copying of the Russian example? Not at all, for it was the reality of the German situation which led her to recognise the necessity of developments in Russia. What Friedrich Engels had prophesied in a letter to August Bebel (11 December 1884) had come to pass: 'In any case, our only opponent on the day of the crisis and on the day afterwards will be the whole reaction grouped around the standard of pure democracy.'

All the elements in Germany who were opposed to the intro-duction of socialism and opposed to working-class power–from the extreme Right to the very leadership of the USDP–were in favour of a national assembly. The fiercest opponents of general suffrage, those people who, even during the war period characterised by the most senseless national sacrifice, had refused to surrender an iota of their class privileges, were now full of enthusiasm for the principle of 'equal rights for all'. And those who only a few weeks before had been imperial 'Marxists', who had wanted to save the monarchy even in its last days, and who were now working to establish a bloody bourgeois dictatorship, came out in favour of democracy over everything else: not the democracy advocated by all great revolutionaries from Robespierre to Babeuf and Blanqui, and from Marx to Lenin—i.e. the real 'rule of the people'—but the banal pseudo-democracy of a bourgeois parliament, which simultaneously 'represents and tramples on' the popular will. Thus the alternatives, National Assembly and Workers' Councils, became the two opposite poles of German society, pointing either back to capitalism or forward to socialism. Again and again Rosa Luxemburg insisted on the fundamental importance of this issue. In the *Rote Fahne* issue of 20 November she vigorously attacked the USPD leaders, who were in favour of a national assembly, but who wanted to have the elections postponed in the hope of avoiding civil war.

> The National Assembly is an obsolete heirloom of bourgeois revolutions, a husk without content, a stage-prop from the period of petit-bourgeois illusions about a "united people", about the "freedom, equality, and brotherhood" of the bourgeois state.
>
> Whoever reaches for the idea of a National Assembly is consciously or unconsciously pushing the revolution back to the historical level of a bourgeois revolution; he is either a disguised agent of the bourgeoisie or an unconscious spokesman of the petit-bourgeoisie. . . .
>
> Today the alternatives are not democracy and dictatorship. The question placed on the agenda by history is: bourgeois democracy or socialist democracy. The dictatorship of the proletariat is democracy in a socialist sense. The dictatorship of the proletariat does not mean bombs, putsches, riots, and "anarchy", as the agents of capitalist profit deliberately allege; it means the use of all instruments of political power to bring about socialism and to expropriate the capitalist class in accordance with and through the will of the revolutionary majority of the proletariat, i.e. in the spirit of socialist democracy.
>
> Without the conscious will and the conscious action of the majority of the proletariat there can be no socialism. In order to sharpen this consciousness, steel this will, and organise this action, a class instrument is necessary: the Reich's parliament of the proletarians in town and country.[142]

National Assembly or Workers' and Soldiers' Councils? The answer to this question was also the chief plank of the programme of the *Spartakusbund*, published on 14 December in *Rote Fahne*.

In strong words Rosa Luxemburg defined the alternatives put before society by the World War: 'Either the continuation of capitalism, new wars and a very early decline into chaos and anarchy, or the abolition of capitalist exploitation.' Socialism was the only salvation of humanity, and socialism could be brought about only by the action of the working masses:

> The proletarian masses must therefore replace the traditional organs of bourgeois class rule, the federal councils, parliaments, municipal councils, etc., from the supreme leadership of the state down to the smallest community, with their own class organs: Workers' and Soldiers' Councils; they must occupy all public posts, superintend all public activity, and measure all the needs of the state by their own class interests and socialist tasks. The state can be imbued with a socialist spirit only if there is constant and vital reciprocity between the popular masses and their organs, the Workers' and Soldiers' Councils. . . .
>
> The proletarian masses must learn how to develop from being dead machines, placed by capitalists in the productive process, into thinking, free, and independent managers of this process. They must acquire a feeling of responsibility as active members of the general public, which is the sole owner of social wealth. They must become industrious without the entrepreneur's whip, attain the highest achievements without the capitalist slave-driver, learn to be disciplined without the yoke, and establish order without domination. The highest idealism in the interests of the general public, the strictest self-discipline, and a genuine civic sense on the part of the masses are the moral foundation of socialist society, just as stupidity, egoism, and corruption are the moral foundation of capitalist society.[148]

During these weeks a flood of calumny poured over the *Spartakusbund*. Its leaders as well as its supporters were represented as lecherous and sadistic beasts planning terrorism and blood-shed. Newspapers, leaflets, and posters alleged in screaming headlines that various bloody crimes (for which the authorities themselves were already making the final preparations) were the deliberate acts of the *Spartakusbund*. Rosa Luxemburg replied to these imputations in the above-mentioned programme:

> In bourgeois revolutions bloodshed, terrorism, and political murder have always been indispensable weapons in the hands of the rising classes. However, the proletarian revolution needs no terrorism to attain its ends; it hates and abhors murder. It needs none of these weapons because it is fighting against institutions, not against individuals. Because it doesn't enter the arena with naïve illusions, it needs no bloody terror to avenge any disappointments it might suffer. The proletarian revolution is not the desperate attempt of a minority to shape the world by violence according to its own ideals; it is the action of the great millions of people called upon to fulfil

a historic mission and to transform historical necessity into historical reality.[144]

This statement of the aims and methods of proletarian revolution came from the heart, and behind it one can sense the pain Rosa Luxemburg felt at the use of terror in the Russian Revolution, though she recognised it to be the extreme defensive weapon in the dangerous back-to-the-wall situation of the Revolution. At the same time it was an appeal to the German workers to arm themselves morally against those excesses of rage which are never completely avoidable in life-and-death struggles, but which must be counteracted as far as possible by an awareness of deep responsibility. This attitude had nothing in common, however, with the self-abnegation theories of Tolstoy or Gandhi. Rosa knew too well that 'one doesn't heal a great illness with attar or musk'. She knew too well that 'it is stark raving madness to believe that capitalists would ever submit willingly to the verdict of a socialist parliament and quietly abandon their property, their profits, and their privilege of exploiting others'. She looked ahead and saw already the first indications that the imperialist capitalist class, as the last scion of the exploiting caste, would outdo all its predecessors in baseness, unconcealed cynicism, and brutality; and that it would sooner see the country turned into a heap of smouldering ruins than it would renounce wage-slavery. For the working class there should therefore be no question of hesitation:

All this resistance must be broken step by step with a mailed fist and with ruthless energy. The violence of the bourgeois counter-revolution must be met by the revolutionary violence of the proletariat. The attacks, intrigues, and plots of the bourgeoisie must be foiled by unwavering resoluteness, watchfulness, and constant readiness for action on the part of the proletarian masses. The threatening counter-revolutionary dangers must be met by arming the people and disarming the ruling class. The parliamentary obstructionist manœuvres of the bourgeoisie must be met by the active organisation of the masses of workers and soldiers. The omnipresence and the thousand-and-one instruments of power used by bourgeois society must be met by the concentrated, massed, and most highly intensified power of the working class. Only the solid front of the whole German proletariat, of the South German with the North German proletariat, of the urban with the rural proletariat, of the workers with the soldiers; the living spiritual contact of the German Revolution with the International; the enlargement of the German Revolution into the world revolution of the proletariat—only this can create the granite base on which the building of the future can be erected.

The struggle for socialism is the most tremendous civil war that world history has ever seen, and the proletariat must prepare itself for this civil war with the necessary arms; it must learn how to use them, to fight and be victorious.

This equipment of the compact masses of the working people with full political power for the tasks of the revolution—this is the dictatorship of the proletariat and therefore true democracy. Not where the wage-slave sits next to the capitalist, and the rural proletarian next to the Junker in sham equality in order to debate their vital questions in a parliamentary way; but there where the mass of proletarian millions seizes total state power with calloused hands in order to use it, like the god Thor his hammer, to smash the ruling classes—only there can one find democracy which is not a swindling of the people.[145]

After drawing up these general guiding principles of revolutionary action, the *Spartakus* programme enumerated the tasks to be accomplished in the struggle to conquer and secure power, prepare for a socialist economic order, increase the living standards of the popular masses, and raise the level of mass culture. Finally the programme proclaimed the general rules for the behaviour of the *Spartakusbund* in the struggle for power. The organisation regarded itself only as the most conscious section of the proletariat, drawing the attention of the workers to their historic tasks at every step, and standing up for the final aim of socialism at each stage of the revolution, and for the interests of the world revolution in all international questions. It refused to share governmental power with enemies of the revolution, or to take up the reins of government ahead of time merely because they were slack in other hands. The programme was thus a determined rejection of any policy of rashness, adventurism or putschism:

> The *Spartakusbund* will never take over governmental power except in accordance with the clear and explicit will of the great majority of the proletarian masses throughout Germany, except in accordance with their conscious approval of its views, aims, and fighting methods.[146]

Two weeks later, when Rosa Luxemburg presented this programme to the inaugural Congress of the Communist Party of Germany (KPD), she declared it to be the resuscitation of the fundamental principles of the *Communist Manifesto*. And it is certainly true that the same ideas concerning the character of the revolutionary struggle, the same aims, the same fighting methods, and the same determined measures are presented in the birth certificate of modern socialism and in this last important document drawn up by Rosa Luxemburg. The same spirit informs both works. This vast common ground had its origins in the very similar political situations in which both documents were conceived. In February 1848 Germany was on the eve of a bourgeois revolution, which Marx regarded as the immediate precursor of a proletarian revolution. In November 1918 a quick onslaught removed the last rubble of feudalism, and the bourgeois revolution was completed. Bourgeoisie and proletariat now faced each other for a decisive struggle. After seventy years of tremendous social development, the curve of revolution ran once again alongside that of the days of the March Revolution, though in a much wider arc and on a much higher level. However, the programme of the *Spartakusbund* did not simply copy the programmatic instructions of the *Communist Manifesto*; it summed up the immediate political situation in Germany, and thereby proved to be yet another example of the harmony of ideas existing between Karl Marx and Rosa Luxemburg, and–at the same time–of her independence in the application of his methods.

The counter-revolution strikes back

When *Rote Fahne* published the programme of the *Spartakusbund*, revolution and counter-revolution in Germany were already locked in combat. The enemies of the revolution had worked circumspectly and cunningly. On 10 November Ebert and the General Army Headquarters concluded a pact whose preliminary aim was to defeat the Berlin workers. During that month there were bloody clashes between workers and returning front-line soldiers who had been stirred up by the authorities. On military drill-grounds special troops, in strict isolation from the civilian population, were being 'ideologically' and militarily trained for civil war. Photographs show the typical composition of such groups: officers, old war veterans for whom war had become a trade, and young recruits who had been flung into the slaughter at the last minute and were now being incited against the 'enemy at home'.

On 30 November an Iron Division was set up under the political leadership of Reich's Commissar August Winnig, a former trade-union leader, for the struggle against Bolshevik Russia and for the protection of the Baltic barons. An immense number of *Freikorps*, allegedly intended for a war against Poland, were also founded. Ten elite divisions marched into Berlin, but they of course quickly melted away in the fire of the Revolution. The social-democratic Commandant of Berlin, Otto Wels, then founded a Republican Soldiers' Defence Corps (*Republikanische Soldatenwehr*), which in time grew to 15,000 men and was financed directly by capitalist groups.

The military forces on the side of the revolution were weak. The Berlin Police President, Emil Eichhorn, a USPD member, had formed a security force, composed of workers organised in trade unions, which patrolled the streets. Stationed in the Imperial Palace was the so-called People's Naval Division (*Volksmarinedivision*), totalling about 3,000 men. Politically it was wavery, and for a while it was under the command of Wilhelm II's old friend Count Wolff-Metternich. There was also a small force of *Spartakus* supporters, the Red Soldiers' League (*Roter Soldatenbund*). In addition, however, many thousands of workers were armed–when their military units had been disbanded, they had simply taken their weapons home–and were quite willing to defend the revolution.

On 6 December the counter-revolution ventured its first open thrust. In Hamburg and in the Rhineland counter-revolutionary conspiracies were uncovered. In Berlin a group of soldiers 'loyal to the government' proclaimed Ebert President of the Republic and demanded that he should launch a *coup d'état*. Meanwhile another group of troops arrested the Executive Committee of the Workers' and Soldiers' Councils, and 200 men occupied the editorial offices of *Rote Fahne*. In the north of Berlin a demonstration organised by the Red Soldiers' League with the knowledge and permission of the authorities was fired on under the pretext that a Spartakist putsch was being planned. Eighteen demonstrators were killed and thirty wounded. An investigation directed by Police President Eichhorn revealed that all these incidents had their origin in a coordinated plan: all the threads converged on the office of Berlin Commandant Wels, on the War Ministry, and on the Foreign Office. The happenings of this day seriously shook the prestige of the government. Following an appeal by the *Spartakusbund*, hundreds of thousands demonstrated on the streets of Berlin against the machinations of the counter-revolution. However, no direct measures were taken to protect the revolution.

A campaign of hysterical incitement against *Spartakus* now set in. Spartakist putsches were announced every day. 'Bolshevism' and '*Spartakismus*' became the bogies of frightened bourgeois everywhere. 'Bolshevism nationalises women!' Every crime was put down to the account of *Spartakus*. Liebknecht, Luxemburg, and their followers were represented as a horde of dangerous incendiaries. With wanton fantasy the Anti-Bolshevik League, well supplied with government money, kept inventing new monstrosities which screamed out from posters plastered on walls and boardings in towns and villages up and down the country. Spies and *agents provocateurs* were trained according to special orders, an atmosphere of murder and pogrom was deliberately fomented, and the killing of *Spartakus* leaders was advocated in public meetings and in the press. 'When the *Spartakus* cronies make outlaws of ourselves and our future, then Karl Liebknecht and company will find themselves outlawed!' Under the nose of the social-democratic government, giant placards

–paid for by that centre of corruption serving the old imperial government, the *Heimatdienst*–were put up:

> Workers! Citizens!
> The downfall of the Fatherland is imminent.
> Save it!
> It is not being threatened from without, but from within:
> By the *Spartakus* group.
> Strike its leaders dead!
> Kill Liebknecht!
> You will then have peace, work and bread!
>
> Soldiers from the Front

On 7 December Karl Liebknecht was seized in the offices of *Rote Fahne*, but before he could be carried off, someone managed to alert Eichhorn, who saw to it that he was freed. Later it was discovered that the attempted kidnapping had been part of a murder plan. The Berlin Commandant, the social democrat Wels, organised a mercenary band of down-and-outs, who were under instructions 'to ferret out and hunt down [the leaders of the *Spartakusbund*] by day and by night to prevent them from carrying out either agitational or organisational work'.[147] Even more sinister intentions were concealed behind this formula, and life became very dangerous for the *Spartakus* leaders, who were forced to be constantly on the run. Overwhelmed with work, Rosa Luxemburg had visited her home in the quiet suburb of Südende only very rarely, and now it became quite impossible. Her enemies lay in wait there, and the area was under the dictatorship of the local *Bürgerrat*.* Every night she had to stay at a different hotel under a false name, and to leave early in the morning to avoid unpleasant surprises. Thus she seldom managed to get enough sleep. Even the editorial offices of *Rote Fahne* were not safe; hardly a day passed without the threat of raids by misled and incited bands of soldiers.

Rosa maintained her unshakeable poise and intellectual freshness in the midst of all these dangers, in the rapid whirl of events, and in the hurly-burly of the editorial offices, which were not only constantly visited by hosts of people–workers, soldiers, and comrades–seeking advice and instructions, but were also harassed by all sorts of doubtful characters. She thrust aside the 'minor inconveniences' of such a life. Her body had no right to complain of being overtired and overstrained; it had to obey the dictates of her will. And in those critical days, when work had to be interrupted again and again, and the editorial programme had to be revised repeatedly as the result of fresh news demanding further discussions and decisions, she would not allow her nerves to give way. Her mind–sus-

---

* *Bürgerrat*, the bourgeois or middle-class counterpiece to the Workers' and Soldiers' Councils–EF.

tained by the 'fascinating spectacle of revolution' – succeeded again and again in squeezing new reserves of energy from her body.

Despite all the efforts, all the lies, incitement, conspiracies, provocations, and bloody raids of the reaction, the revolution won new ground every day. The naïve trust in promises and sacred oaths gave way to a critical examination of deeds. More and more social strata were swept into the whirlpool. Stuffed with devilishly inflammatory propaganda, and often boiling with rage at the universal enemy, *Spartakus*, whole troop units returning to the large towns were transformed within a short time into pillars of the revolution. Above all, however, workers were making more and more frequent use of their own traditional weapon – the strike. From Upper Silesia and the Rhineland-Westphalia industrial area a vast wave of strikes rolled over the country. New forms of strike organisation and leadership developed, and the elementary force of these strikes, in which hundreds of thousands took part, spread alarm in the camp of 'law and order'. The so-called socialist government prepared to crush the strikes by military force, and even the most left-wing member of the government, Emil Barth, complained furiously that the 'glorious revolution' was threatening to degenerate into a mere wage movement.

Well-meaning historians later cursed the German workers for having failed to show sufficient idealism in the days of revolution, and for having thought only of their own miserable existence instead of the great tasks of the revolution. What a lack of historical understanding! After long years of naked hunger, was it not inevitable that the workers should utilise the power-position they had won in the revolution to improve their material conditions at least a little? In any case, the strikes were not mere wage movements: they were part and parcel of the revolution. The prize at stake, not only historically and objectively, but also openly proclaimed by the strikers themselves was power in the factories and a real socialisation of production.

From the revolution of 1905 Rosa Luxemburg was familiar with the role played by economic struggles in times of social upheaval, and she had therefore expected such a flood of strikes to start. In her work *The Mass Strike, the Party and the Trade Unions* she had prophesied:

> In Germany, too, a revolutionary period would very much alter the character of the trade-union struggle and would intensify it to such an extent that the present guerrilla warfare of the trade unions would be child's play in comparison. And, on the other hand, the political struggle would also repeatedly derive new impetus and fresh strength from this elementary economic storm of mass strikes. The reciprocal relationship between the economic and the political

struggle . . .–so to speak, the regulating mechanism of the revolutionary action of the proletariat–would result just as naturally [as in Russia] from the given conditions in Germany, too.[148]

This prophecy was hardly listened to in Germany at the time, but during the revolution it was even outdone by reality, because the conscious will of the workers to fight for the highest aim, to fight for a socialist economy itself, was expressed in this storm of elementary mass-strikes. In an article entitled 'Acheron on the Move' (*Acheron in Bewegung*),* published in *Rote Fahne* on 27 November 1918, she rejoiced:

> Instead of waiting for the benevolent decrees of the government or the resolutions of the wonderful National Assembly, the masses are instinctively adopting the only real method which leads to socialism: the struggle against capital! . . . The strike movement now beginning is proof that the political revolution has driven a wedge into the basic structure of society. The revolution is recalling its own original basis: it is brushing aside the paper scenery of ministerial changes and decrees, which have not produced the least bit of change in the social relationship between capital and labour, and stepping on to the stage of events in person. . . .
>
> In the present revolution the strikes which have broken out are not a mere "trade-union conflict" about trivia, about matters connected simply with the wage relationship. They are the natural answer of the masses to the tremendous upheaval which took place in capital relations as a result of the collapse of German imperialism and the short political revolution of the workers and soldiers. They are the first beginnings of the general contest between capital and labour in Germany; they signal the start of the violent class struggle, the outcome of which can be nothing less than the elimination of the wage relationship and the introduction of a socialist economy. They unleash the living social force of the present revolution: the revolutionary class-energy of the revolutionary masses. They open up a period of direct activity on the part of the broadest masses, and the socialisation decrees and measures of any representative body or the government can only provide the accompaniment to such activity.

She was full of optimism; there was no doubt that the working masses were marching rapidly to the left. However, this advance took place on an elementary level, under the pressure of direct experiences, and all its political consequences were not immediately realised. The effects of the reciprocal relationship between the economic and the political struggle were not felt one right after the other. In particular, the composition of the Workers' and Soldiers' Councils lagged behind the increasing militancy of the masses. This

---

*   Acheron is the mythological river of woe of the underworld. Frölich takes up the allusion in the final sentence of the book.–Tr.

was a matter of very great importance, because in this initial period of revolutionary fermentation the Councils were in such a position that they could either exercise public functions according to their revolutionary rights, or renounce this power in favour of the old governing and administrative institutions. But everywhere the official Social Democrats were urging the Councils to abandon their powers, and working to rebuild the old state apparatus of imperial Germany. This put a strong weapon into the hands of the counter-revolution and facilitated the superior organisational set-up of the forces hostile to the working class.

The glaring contradiction between the mood of the masses and the political will of the old parties expressed itself at the first national Congress of the Workers' and Soldiers' Councils in Berlin from 16-20 December 1918. The delegates were not elected directly, but appointed by the local Councils. The Congress represented the attitude of the masses in the first days of the revolution, but that was all, and it lacked even the great-hearted illusions of those first days. It represented the past, not the present; the backward small and middle-sized towns rather than the big towns and the most important industrial areas. In political character it was more an Upper House than a People's Parliament of the working class. There were 489 delegates present, of whom 288 were Social Democrats, 80 Independents, and only 10 *Spartakus* followers. Social reality outside the Congress was very different.

When the Congress met, its character was still shrouded in mystery, but everywhere great hopes were placed on it. Rosa Luxemburg wrote in *Rote Fahne* that it should accomplish the following tasks: the removal of the Ebert-Scheidemann-Haase Cabinet; the disarming of all troops which did not unconditionally recognise the authority of the Workers' and Soldiers' Councils; the disarming of the reactionary White Guards formed by the government and the creation of a Red Guard; and the rejection of the National Assembly as an attempt to divert the revolution and as an attack on the Workers' and Soldiers' Councils. With these demands in mind the *Spartakusbund* called upon the Berlin workers to welcome the Congress. Hundreds of thousands answered the call; it was the biggest demonstration Berlin had ever seen. Referring to the moment when a deputation of these masses presented the demands to the Congress, a large bourgeois paper commented: 'The impression was similar to the one King Belshazzar must have had when watching the mysterious hand write on the wall of his palace.'

Those directing the Congress understood this sign too well, and they hastened to isolate the Congress from the masses. They did allow several platonic and nebulous resolutions to be passed, behind which they could take good cover, such as the one 'to take all immediate measures to disarm the counter-revolution'. The chief resolution was actually directed against the revolution: 'The Reich's Congress of Workers' and Soldiers' Councils in Germany, representing total political power, hereby transfers legislative and executive power to the Council of People's Commissars until such time as the National Assembly may make other arrangements.' A Central Council was set up ostensibly to control the national and the Prussian governments, but in reality it was merely the fig-leaf for their dictatorial policies. The elections for the National Assembly were fixed for 19 January 1919. With this the Workers' and Soldiers' Councils committed political suicide and surrendered the keys to power.

Rosa Luxemburg recognised that the Congress had dealt a heavy blow to the revolution and had revealed the fatal weakness of the revolutionary wing. She also recognised, no doubt, that the demands advocated by the *Spartakusbund* had gone too far, and explained the surrender of the Councils (*Rote Fahne*, 21 December 1918) as follows:

> This is an expression not merely of the general inadequacy of the first unripe stage of the revolution, but also of the particular difficulties attending this proletarian revolution and the peculiarities of its historical situation. In all former revolutions the combatants entered the lists with their visors up: class against class, programme against programme, shield against shield. In the present revolution the defenders of the old order enter the lists not with the shields and coats-of-arms of the ruling classes, but under the banner of a "Social-Democratic Party". If the cardinal question of the revolution was openly and honestly: capitalism or socialism, the great mass of the proletariat today would not have any doubts or hesitation about the answer.

She remained convinced that time was working for the revolution, for the soldiers were gradually taking off the livery of imperialism, putting on overalls, and regaining their contact with the native soil in which their class consciousness was rooted. In addition, enormous problems were arising: unemployment, the economic struggle between capital and labour, and the bankruptcy of the state. As a result class differentiation would inevitably grow clearer and sharper, and revolutionary tension increase.

She set two tasks for her own party and the working class: the utilisation of the election campaign to mobilise the revolutionary masses and to educate them as to the aims and character of the revolution, and the machinations of its enemies; and the defence, consolidation, and gradual extension of the positions held by the revolution. As she put it (*Rote Fahne*, 23 December 1918): 'The future belongs to the proletarian revolution; everything must serve it—even the National Assembly elections.' But no premature attacks, no struggling for aims not yet accepted by the overwhelming majority of the working class, and no putsches!

She had already, a month before (*Rote Fahne*, 24 November 1918), laid open the hidden background of the baiting campaign of lies being spread about the alleged putschism of the *Spartakusbund:*

> There are others who urgently need terrorism, a reign of terror and anarchy today, and I mean the gentlemen of the bourgeoisie and all the parasites of the capitalist economy who are quaking in their boots for their property, their privileges, their profits and their ruling prerogatives. These are the people who are trying to saddle the socialist proletariat with the responsibility for anarchy and putsches fabricated by themselves so that they can unleash real anarchy at an opportune moment with the help of their agents, throttle the proletarian revolution, and erect on its ruins a class dictatorship of capital to last for all time. . . . From our historical vantage point we can look upon the spectacle with a cool smile. We can see through their game – the actors, their managers and their roles.

Time was working for the revolution. Above all, the managers of the counter-revolution and the Generals knew it. They knew that their political success at the Congress of Workers' and Soldiers' Councils would be worth nothing unless they quickly succeeded in destroying the power of the revolution. They soon chose their first target. Quartered in the heart of Berlin – in the old Imperial Palace – and therefore dominating the governmental-office district was the People's Naval Division. After the counter-revolutionary putsch of 6 December, it had deposed its commander, Count Wolff-Metternich, and elected an ordinary sailor as its leader. At the same time it had announced that, if the government should break up, it would support the Independents. Most of the men were not *Spartakus* followers, but they were sincerely in favour of the revolution. Thus it happened that the authorities took advantage of the first opportunity after the Congress to pick a quarrel with them. A flood of slanderous accusations, the untruth of which was later frankly admitted, gushed forth over the Division, and provocative demands which would have meant its dissolution were made. After a demonstration of sailors was fired upon, they took Berlin Commandant Wels as a hostage to secure their rights.

This provided the authorities with the excuse they were looking for to attack. The sailors had not expected fighting, and had only the usual number of sentries on duty in the Palace, scarcely a hundred men. Nevertheless, they rejected the ultimatum to surrender with its attendant hypocritical promises, and on the morning of 24 December, the holy-day of Christmas Eve, artillery fire was opened on the Palace and the Imperial Stables. The bombardment lasted four hours, but in vain! The sailors held out, and Eichhorn's security force and numerous workers came to their assistance. Women mingled with the attackers, hindering them from proceeding with their murderous work against their brothers, and inducing them to lay down their weapons. By evening it was evident that the attack had failed, and negotiations began. Concessions were made to the sailors, and Wels, who had remained unharmed throughout the battle despite its many casualties, was compelled to resign.

This was the first victory for the revolution. As a result, however, the gulf between revolution and counter-revolution had widened. If there had ever existed any possibility of class conciliation, it was clear that this had now become impossible.

The founding of the German Communist Party

What was this *Spartakusbund* which Rosa Luxemburg and Karl Liebknecht headed? It was a loose organisation numbering several thousand members during the war. Its core was the old left-wing of Social Democracy, an elite well-grounded in Marxism and schooled in the tactical ideas of Rosa Luxemburg. After activists in the socialist youth movement joined forces with this group, its ranks were swollen by additional elements coming from varied social and political backgrounds who had been driven to the extreme left wing of the working-class movement as a result of their militant opposition to the war. During the war years all these people had incurred dangers quite new to the working-class movement in Western Europe. They were all enthusiastically in favour of revolution, though many of them still had very romantic ideas about it. The enormous difficulties of illegal work during the war had prevented any tight and closely-knit organisation, and when the revolution came the *Spartakusbund* was only a federation of local groups existing in almost all the larger towns, and not yet a political party. When the USPD was formed as a break-away from the old party at Easter 1917, the *Spartakusbund* joined it as an affiliated body, maintaining, however, its own organisation, discipline, and programme. It wanted to take advantage of being part of a strong organisation to propagate its own views. In *Der Kampf*, the official paper of left-wing Social Democracy published in Duisburg, Rosa Luxemburg justified this practice by saying that it was easy to talk about planting the 'pure banner' of an ideal, but the task was to bring it to the masses, to win them over to it. However, only a few of the groups were flexible enough to make the most of the great chances which affiliation offered.

Apart from the *Spartakusbund* there was a group of Left Radicals with its centre in Bremen, and branches in North Germany,

Saxony, and the Rhineland. It published a legal weekly paper, *Arbeiterpolitik* (Workers' Politics), and was in general agreement with the *Spartakusbund* on fundamental principles, but from the beginning it was more closely associated with the Bolsheviks. Chance factors connected with the origins of both groups, old differences stemming from the Russian and Polish movements, and minor disagreements on tactical matters had prevented organisational amalgamation. In the end what separated the Left Radicals and *Spartakus* was hardly more than the question of affiliation to the Independents, which the Left Radicals had rejected.

The left wing of the German working-class movement was thus not organisationally prepared for the great tasks of the revolutionary period, and, before long, amalgamation and the formation of a centrally-organised political party became urgently necessary as the only means of giving the spontaneous revolutionary movement throughout the country an organisational backbone and a common direction. An important prerequisite was the clarification of the situation within the deeply divided USPD. As members of the government, together with Ebert and Scheidemann, the party's leaders bore a joint responsibility for·all the official acts of the government. Although it is very unlikely that they knew anything definite about its unofficial counter-revolutionary machinations, nevertheless they were misused and they let themselves be misused. They shied away from working together with the bourgeois parties, preferring to look backward, and longing for the day when their party could again play the role of a parliamentary opposition which would not be disloyal to the 'class struggle'. Meanwhile they had to contend with steadily growing opposition within their own party ranks. Although completely unorganised and not very clear about its political attitude, this opposition was quite firm in its rejection of the policy of its own leaders in the government. Since the counter-revolutionary putsches of 6 December at least, it could count on the support of the majority of the party members in the most important centres: Berlin, Saxony, and the Rhineland.

The *Spartakusbund* did its best to win over this instinctively revolutionary wing of the USDP, and demanded the immediate convening of a party congress. Rosa Luxemburg forcefully advocated this demand at a general meeting of the USPD in Berlin (15 December 1918), but the party leaders opposed this left-wing pressure with an obstinacy they had never managed to display against the compromising demands of the right-wing socialists. A resolution put forward by Rosa Luxemburg was defeated, winning 195 votes against 485 in favour of a resolution put forward by Rudolf Hilferding.

In the meantime the struggle between revolution and counter-revolution was approaching its climax, and the creation of an efficient party became the need of the hour. Towards the end of the year the *Spartakusbund* therefore convened its own national conference, whose first act was the founding of the 'Communist Party of Germany (*Spartakusbund*)' (KPD). The Left Radicals held a simultaneous conference and decided to join the new party.

The most important question to be decided was whether the new party should take part in the National Assembly elections or not. In *Rote Fahne* (23 December 1918) Rosa Luxemburg indicated her stand in favour of participation. Although the purpose of the National Assembly would be to consolidate the power of the new bourgeois regime, she maintained that the work of the socialists within it now could not have the same character as their earlier parliamentary activity and could therefore not aim at mere reforms within the capitalist system:

> We are now in the midst of revolution, and the National Assembly is a counter-revolutionary fortress erected *against* the revolutionary proletariat. Our task is thus to take this fortress by storm and raze it to the ground. In order to mobilise the masses *against* the National Assembly and appeal to them to wage a very intensive struggle against it, we must utilise the elections and the platform of the National Assembly itself. . . . To denounce mercilessly and loudly all the wily tricks of this worthy Assembly, to expose its counter-revolutionary work step by step to the masses, and to appeal to the masses to intervene and force a decision–these are the tasks of participation in the National Assembly.

The other leaders of the *Spartakusbund* were in complete agreement with Rosa Luxemburg, though Liebknecht admittedly gave only grudging support to the idea of participation. However, the great majority of the delegates to the conference and of the members they represented regarded it as a contradiction to reject the National Assembly on principle and yet to participate in the elections to it. They had the Russian example all too clearly in mind, but they saw only the final October victory and not the long period of preparation involving careful and often very complicated manœuvring. This majority was so certain of the victory of the German Revolution that participation in parliamentary elections appeared as a highly doubtful detour–or even worse. In vain did Rosa Luxemburg warn the delegates against underestimating the difficulties ahead, against counting on a quick and easy victory, and against neglecting any means of winning adherents. The inaugural Congress of the KPD rejected the proposal to participate in the National Assembly elections by 62 to 23 votes. Leo Jogiches was deeply shocked at this result, and took it as a sign that the decision to form a Communist Party had been premature. However, Rosa simply declared that a new-born child always squalled at first. In a letter to Clara Zetkin, who was also deeply perturbed by the negative vote, she expressed her firm conviction that the new party would eventually find the right path despite all its errors, because it embraced the best core of the German proletariat.

The tension which developed at the Congress between the leadership and the impetuously impatient younger elements was quickly reduced by Rosa Luxemburg's speech on the party programme. The delegates had anxiously observed what a great effort of will she needed to pull together her exhausted body, but no sooner had she begun to speak than inspiration worked wonders. All her physical weakness fell away from her, and all her usual energy and intellectual spiritedness returned. For the last time the magic of her oratory held her audience spellbound: convincing, gripping, inspiring, and stirring–an unforgettable experience for all who were present. For the last time they felt themselves to be borne aloft by her intellectual flights of genius.

The speech exuded her spirit of readiness for action and will to victory. Yet at the same time it was meant to damp exuberant expectations, bring the reality of the situation into sharp focus, and emphasise to the party the necessity of maintaining its flexibility. Rosa foresaw a long road ahead, a road with many twists and turns; as she had noted in the Spartakus programme, the proletarian revolution could fight its way forward only by stages, step by step, along a road to Calvary paved with bitter experiences, through defeat after defeat–to final victory:

> We can no longer afford to foster and repeat the illusions of the first phase of the revolution, the idea of 9 November that the overthrow of one capitalist government and its replacement by another would be entirely sufficient to ensure the continued progress of the socialist revolution. . . . I would also like to remind you here of some deficiencies of the German Revolution which have not been overcome in the first phase and which clearly show that unfortunately we are not yet in a position to secure the victory of socialism simply through the overthrow of a government. I have tried to explain to you that the revolution of 9 November was above all a political revolution, whereas on the whole a revolution has to be an economic one. Moreover, this revolution was only an urban one; the rural areas have up to now remained practically untouched. . . . If we are serious about wanting a socialist transformation, we must pay attention to the rural areas as well as to the industrial centres, and in this regard we have unfortunately not yet even begun to make a beginning. . . .
>
> History is not making things as easy for us as it did for bourgeois revolutions; then it was sufficient to overthrow the official power and replace it by a couple or a couple of dozen new men. But we

must work from below to the top, and that is in exact accordance with the mass character of our revolution and its aims, which involve the fundamental nature of our present social order. . . .

As I describe it, the process probably appears more protracted than you feel inclined to believe at the moment. I believe, however, that it is very healthy for us to realise fully and clearly all the difficulties and complications of our revolution. . . . I shall not venture to prophesy how long the whole process will take. But who expects that from us, to whom does it matter, so long as our lives are long enough to bring it about?[149]

14
The road to death

The January struggle

Rosa Luxemburg delivered this speech on 30 December 1918; its peroration was an exhortation to revolutionary socialists to judge the situation realistically, and to get down to the tough work of preparing for the revolution so that social conditions would be ripe for the decisive struggle. A few days later street-fighting broke out in Berlin and led to the defeat of the working class. The event went into history as the *Spartakus* uprising, and the defeat paved the way for the counter-revolution. What brought about this sudden change in the situation?

Was it the result of the unfortunate decision to boycott the National Assembly elections? Did that decision inevitably lead to an attempt to prevent the elections by force? Nothing of the sort: none of the delegates who voted against participation ever considered such a possibility, and the leadership of the *Spartakusbund*, i.e. the new Communist Party (KPD), certainly had no intention of abandoning the tactical policy developed by Rosa Luxemburg in agreement with all the leading comrades. Or did the Russian Embassy in Berlin drive *Spartakus* into a senseless offensive to relieve pressure on the Bolsheviks (as has been claimed in certain history books)? But there was no Russian Embassy: the government of Prince Max of Baden had expelled the Russian diplomats on 4 November as the result of a frame-up organised by Philipp Scheidemann–a Reichstag-fire affair in miniature. Karl Radek was the only official 'Russian' in Berlin at the time, and a letter written by him to the Central Committee of the new party during the January fighting–a letter in which he urgently advised the party to withdraw from the fighting as soon as possible–is the strongest refutation of this fairy-tale.[150] In any case, the idea that either Rosa or Leo would let themselves be thrust into an adventure by 'advisers' is an absurdity. A final explanation is that Rosa and her friends suddenly, and for no apparent reason, launched a general putsch for which no preparations of any kind had been made, i.e. that they lost their heads. There are otherwise thoughtful people who believe something of the sort simply because they do not dare to see the truth of the matter.

The truth is: there was no Spartakus uprising. Irrefutable proof of this is contained in the leading articles in *Rote Fahne*, which faithfully mirrored the policy of the *Spartakusbund* during those critical days: 1 January, 'Behind the Scenes of the Counter-Revolution' (dealing with the official documents relating to the war resumed against Russia by the German counter-revolution); 2 January, 'Slave-Traders' (the same subject); 3 January, 'The First Party Congress'; 4 January, 'The Prospects of Revolution in Italy'; 5 January, 'Henchmen of Mining Capital' (the economic struggle in the Ruhr area); and 6 January, 'Unemployment'. The titles clearly show that the leaders of the KPD were, for the foreseeable future, reckoning on a steady development of the revolution and not in the least with an armed struggle on the streets of Berlin.

The truth is that the January fighting was cautiously and deliberately prepared and cunningly provoked by the leaders of the counter-revolution. It originated in a diabolical plan which at the time was without parallel in modern history, but which has since found its match in the political practices of fascism. Let the facts speak.

During the so-called '*Dolchstoss* Trial'* in Munich (October 1925), General Groener described under oath Reich President Ebert's arrangement with the General Staff. With regard to the January fighting he testified: 'On 29 December Ebert summoned Noske to lead the troops against *Spartakus*. On that same day the volunteer corps assembled, and everything was now ready for the opening of hostilities.' The decision to launch the decisive action in Berlin was therefore taken on the opening day of the inaugural congress of the Communist Party by the heads of the provisional government and the military. The preparations, of course, went further back. For weeks previously volunteer corps had been mobilised under the pretext of defending the borders against the Poles. On 27 December they began to be concentrated around Berlin. Since it was impossible to conceal these preparations entirely, Ebert obtained the consent of the USPD members of his Cabinet by misrepresentation. As they would never have been willing to accept responsibility for open civil war, it became necessary to exclude them from the government altogether. On the same day they were brazenly called upon to agree to the reinstatement of the old Hohenzollern generals and to the raising of a new army for war against Poland and Russia. (War against Russia was already being

---

* *Dolchstoss:* 'stab-in-the-back'. The theory held in patriotic circles to explain away Germany's defeat in the World War–EF.

waged in the Baltic provinces; 'Poland', for the time being, was also the code-name for Berlin.) The brazen demand led to the break-up of the Cabinet. At the end of the year the Independents resigned, and a right-wing socialist government, consisting of Ebert, Scheidemann, Landsberg, Wissel, and Noske, was formed. Noske then took supreme command of the civil-war troops with the notorious observation: 'Someone must be the bloodhound!'

In his memoirs General Georg Maercker reported: 'In the very first days of January, a meeting attended by Noske, who had just returned from Kiel, took place at General-Staff Headquarters in Berlin with the *Freikorps* leaders concerning the details of the march [into Berlin].' The strength of the troops can be gauged from the enumeration given by General Maercker: the Volunteer Rural-Police Corps, the *Garde-Kavallerie-Schützen-Division* (Division of Horse Guards and Riflemen), the 17th and 31st Infantry Divisions, the *Landesschützenkorps* (State Riflemen's Corps), and the Hülsen *Freikorps*. [These six Volunteer Corps consisted of trained soldiers picked for their reliability from the ranks of the old army and had a very high proportion of officers.] In order to conceal their strength, they were known collectively as the Lüttwitz Detachment. Maercker called them an 'extended General Command'. They were armed for war conditions; they even had flame-throwers.

Alongside the military prepartions for civil war were the 'moral' preparations. After the bloody 24th December, a frenzied campaign of incitement against *Spartakus* flared up again in the press, and, with the social-democratic *Vorwärts* leading the way, it reached new heights every day. The victims of the Christmas Eve attack on the People's Naval Division were buried on 29 December, and untold masses followed the coffins to the cemetery. The SPD chose just this day for a counter-demonstration, and the leaflet issued for the occasion read as follows:

> The shameless doings of Liebknecht and Rosa Luxemburg besmirch the revolution and endanger all its achievements. The masses cannot afford to wait a minute longer and quietly look on while these brutes and their hangers-on cripple the activity of the republican authorities, incite the people deeper and deeper into a civil war, and strangle the right of free speech with their dirty hands. With lies, slander, and violence they want to tear down everything that dares to stand in their way. With an insolence exceeding all bounds they act as though they were masters of Berlin. . . .

At this same demonstration the *Bürgerrat* distributed leaflets containing a further scarcely veiled instigation to murder Liebknecht:

> The Christmas pranks of the *Spartakus* group [!–PF] will lead

directly into the abyss. .... The raw violence of the band of criminals can be met only by counter-violence. ... Do you want peace? Then see to it, every man of you, that the violent rule of the *Spartakus* people is ended. Do you want freedom? Then see that the armed loafers who follow Liebknecht do no more damage! ...

A few days later the Anti-Bolshevik League put up public notices with a price of 10,000 Marks on the head of Karl Radek. Tremendous sums were poured into this civil-war propaganda, but there was as yet no excuse to open fire.

Then on 1 January the *Politisch-Parlamentarische Nachrichten* (Political and Parliamentary News), a social-democratic publication, opened up a slander-campaign against the Police President of Berlin, Emil Eichhorn, a USPD member. This man, whose integrity was known to be beyond doubt by all the social-democratic leaders, was accused of embezzling public funds. At the same time, the men who were already concentrating counter-revolutionary troops around Berlin charged Eichhorn with preparing to launch civil war, although they knew very well that he did not have even sufficient arms to equip his own police force. On 3 January he was called to the Ministry of the Interior, overwhelmed with a confusion of charges, and asked to resign. He demanded a 24-hour reprieve so that he could refute all the charges in writing. Although this request was granted to his face, the government was in a hurry and feared the publication of such a document. Thus it happened that on the morning of 4 January, before his time was up, Eichhorn was relieved of his post. The social democrat Eugen Ernst, later to be a supporter of the Kapp Putsch, was appointed in his stead. Eichhorn refused to accept his dismissal; such a step would have been an acknowledgement of guilt, and he had to preserve his honour. Anyway, he was subordinate, not to the Minister of the Interior, but to the Berlin Executive of the Workers' and Soldiers' Councils, and he stoutly maintained that he could neither break the law created by the November Revolution nor abandon his important position.

When the dismissal order arrived, the Berlin Executive of the USPD was in joint session with the Revolutionary Shop Stewards, and a resolution supporting Eichhorn was adopted. With a view to giving the government one last chance to settle the conflict, Eichhorn said he would comply with any decision made by the National Central Council of the Workers' and Soldiers' Councils, in which the right-wing socialists had a majority. However, the government rejected even this offer; it wanted an intensification of the conflict as an excuse for military intervention. The USPD Executive and the Revolutionary Shop Stewards then called for a demonstration on 5 January. The KPD joined in, and hundreds of thousands of people marched in tremendous processions to Police Headquarters. They arrived just as Eichhorn was about to be forced out, and implored him to remain, declaring their intention to defend this stronghold of the revolution.

Under the impression created by this enormous demonstration, the Berlin Executive of the USPD and the Revolutionary Shop Stewards met again, together with two representatives of the KPD, Karl Liebknecht and Wilhelm Pieck. They believed the reports of Heinrich Dorrenbach, an officer of the People's Naval Division, that the Berlin garrison was behind them and that they could reckon on strong military assistance from Spandau and Frankfurt a. d. Oder. The meeting therefore decided to resist Eichhorn's dismissal and to undertake an attempt to overthrow the Ebert-Scheidemann government. A 'Revolutionary Committee' was set up, headed by Georg Ledebour, Karl Liebknecht, and Paul Scholze (representing the USPD, the KPD, and the Revolutionary Shop Stewards, respectively).

Was this resolution well thought out? Did it correspond to the real power situation? Were those responsible for it capable of leading men in such an undertaking? This remained to be seen. In any case, while the discussion was still proceeding, things were happening which made an armed conflict inevitable. Already on 25 December groups of revolutionary workers–in retaliation for the bombardment on the People's Naval Division in the Imperial Palace –had spontaneously occupied the editorial offices of *Vorwärts*. Their action grew out of their indignation at the attitude of a paper which had at one time belonged to the Berlin workers, but which had been wrested from them as a result of a *coup de main* by the SPD Executive during the war. Because of the objections of Däumig and other left-wing Independents they had been compelled to evacuate the premises, but now at the end of the great demonstration on 5 January a suggestion was made to occupy *Vorwärts* again. The slogan caught on, and a group of workers then occupied the headquarters of the right-wing socialists together with the *Vorwärts* printing-office. That same evening all other important newspaper printing-offices were occupied, followed the next day by the Reich Printing Office (where paper money was printed).

There is no doubt that these actions coincided with the spirit of the masses, but this time they were acting not without outside instigation, instigation in fact from the enemy camp. Later on a reliable tribunal, the Committee of Investigation appointed by the Prussian Diet, established that all these newspaper occupations had been carried out under the leadership of agents in the pay of the Berlin Commandant's office or, at any rate, by highly dubious elements. At the head of the group occupying *Vorwärts* was the waiter Alfred Roland, who was later exposed as a dangerous *agent provoca-*

teur. In the big conspiracy to inflict a military defeat on the Berlin working class nothing had been forgotten. Now, after the build-up of troops, the final resolution to take action, the appointment of Noske as commander-in-chief, and the provocative dismissal of Eichhorn, came the 'democratic' pretext: freedom of the press had to be saved.

Spartakus and the January rising

The initiative for this showdown thus lay completely in the hands of the counter-revolution. Nevertheless, the workers held some very good cards. They still had weapons and were determined to fight. Resolute action would in all probability have brought out the Berlin regiments, which had declared themselves neutral, on the side of the revolution. Energetically and skilfully conducted street-fighting would have posed serious problems for the military. Thus victory for the workers in Berlin was not impossible, but in the event of victory there were great dangers lurking in the rear—in the backwardness of the movement in the rural areas.

The defeat of the workers in Berlin was sealed by the complete failure of their leadership. The Revolutionary Committee, the body which had so boldly proclaimed the intention to seize power, was incapable of undertaking anything to achieve this aim. It issued an appeal for another demonstration on 6 January, distributed some weapons to the forces in the Imperial Stables, and made an attempt to occupy the War Ministry. That was all. It did not bother about the armed workers who had occupied the newspaper offices; it assigned them no tasks and left them in buildings of no strategic importance whatsoever. The only measure of reasonable military value was taken by the workers themselves at their own initiative when they occupied the railway stations. Meanwhile the Revolutionary Committee spent days and nights in endless, but unfruitful discussions, the upshot of which was that it grasped at the straw of negotiations with the enemy—a step which only led to confusion and demoralisation within the ranks of the armed workers.

But what stand did the KPD take on the struggle? Liebknecht and Pieck had voted for the action, and Liebknecht's prestige was certainly instrumental in bringing about the decision. Liebknecht had always been a man in a tearing hurry, a daredevil, not a political strategist accustomed to reflect quietly about things, and now his impetuousness carried him away again. He and Pieck had acted on their own initiative and without the knowledge of their party leadership, which did not agree in the slightest with the idea of staking the revolution on such a showdown. Rosa Luxemburg quarrelled very violently with Liebknecht about his arbitrary action. Amazed and reproachful, she is reported to have said (according to Liebknecht himself): 'Karl, is that our programme?'[151]

And what stand did Rosa take? She did not completely reject the idea of armed struggle, but she insisted that its defensive character should be stressed. She regarded the situation as still not nearly ripe enough to justify an attempt to seize political power. The young Communist Party enjoyed a great amount of sympathy among the active masses of Berlin, but it was not yet the undisputed leader of the working class, and it was still too immature and not capable of solving the tremendous organisational problems of a struggle for power as yet, much less of exercising power. For these reasons Rosa was in favour of resistance to the counter-revolutionary attack, but with aims which would not frighten off the vacillating sections of the masses of workers and soldiers, but would lead them a substantial step forward in the long-range struggle. Throughout the fighting, therefore, *Rote Fahne* was consistent in standing up for the following demands: the disarming of the counter-revolution, the arming of the proletariat, the unification of all troops loyal to the revolution, and new elections for the Workers' and Soldiers' Councils. The aim of the latter demand was to defeat the Ebert-Scheidemann clique in the key structures of the revolution, and make the Councils into real centres of action. Victory in Berlin was the prerequisite to the fulfilment of this programme; it would also have given a mighty impetus to the movement in the rest of the country. Rosa therefore pressed for the energetic continuation of the struggle once it had begun; day after day she tried to get the leaders of the movement to act.

She regarded the negotiations between the Revolutionary Committee and the other side as a trap, and again and again she appealed for action, not negotiations. She was absolutely right. The men around Ebert were using the negotiations to wear down their opponents so that the government could then break its promises and the truce it had agreed upon, and launch a counter-revolutionary offensive with the utmost brutality.

Clara Zetkin has left an authentic account of Rosa Luxemburg's attitude during that period based on one of Leo Jogiches's letters:

> As significant and hopeful as they were, Rosa Luxemburg did not look at the events from the perspective of a Berlin ivory tower. She grasped their implications in the given situation and especially in the light of the level of political consciousness of broad sectors of the population throughout Germany. In consequence her demand for the overthrow of the Ebert government was for the time being primarily only a propaganda catch-all slogan to rally

the revolutionary proletariat rather than a tangible object of revolutionary fighting. Under given conditions, confined chiefly to Berlin, such fighting would have led, in the best case, to a "Berlin Commune", and probably on a smaller historical scale to boot. For her the only immediate aim of armed struggle was the vigorous repulse of counter-revolutionary coups, i.e. the reinstatement of Eichhorn, the withdrawal of the troops who were supposed to crush the Berlin proletariat, the arming of the workers, and the transfer of all military executive power to the revolutionary political representatives of the proletariat. But these demands had to be won by action and not by negotiation.

Because of this situation the young Communist Party led by Rosa Luxemburg was faced with a difficult task involving many conflicts. It could not accept the aim of the mass action–the overthrow of the government–as its own; it had to reject it. But at the same time it could not let itself be separated from the masses who had taken up the struggle. Despite their contrary attitudes the party had to stand by the masses and to remain among them in order to strengthen them in their struggle against the counter-revolution and to further the process of their revolutionary maturation during the action by making them aware of the conditions enabling them to move forward. For this purpose the Communist Party had to show its own face, to define and work out clearly its own evaluation of the situation without breaching the proletarian, the revolutionary solidarity it owed to the fighting workers. Its role in the fighting had to be at once negative and critical on the one hand, and positive and encouraging on the other.[152]

There was another essential factor which supported this argument for Rosa Luxemburg. As she repeatedly pointed out, in times of very high revolutionary tension the intellectual development of the masses takes gigantic strides forward as soon as they are really in movement: 'In world history the hours of the revolution count as months and their days as years.'

In the meantime action was spreading throughout the Reich. In the Rhineland counter-revolutionary troops were defeated in a pitched battle, and in Düsseldorf and in Bremen the local Workers' and Soldiers' Councils took power. An energetically waged struggle in Berlin would have compelled the enemy to make big concessions and have won new ground for the revolution. For all these reasons Rosa Luxemburg, and with her the leadership of the KPD, did not accept Karl Radek's demand (put forward at the very beginning of the fighting) that the party should take the initiative and call on the workers to break off the struggle and beat a retreat. There was an additional reason: in January 1919 the cadres of the young KDP were by no means as firmly organised and consolidated as those of the Bolshevik Party in July 1917 when they carried out a dangerous but successful retreat from a similarly precarious position. The KPD was not in a position to take over the undisputed leadership either in attack or in retreat.

All these considerations justify the general policy pursued by the party under Rosa Luxemburg's leadership in those critical weeks. However, there is something which causes serious misgivings. The party tactics consisted in a political defence of the revolution, which was threatened and under attack, but the defence should have been conducted actively and not passively; it should have consisted of mobilising every possible resource of the revolutionary proletariat and striking out on the offensive to compel the enemy to retreat both politically and militarily. And when it became only too clear that this mobilisation and organisation of the masses could not be effected, that therefore a military offensive was also impossible, and that thousands of fighting workers had fought their way into strategically unfavourable positions—was it not the party's imperative duty to put energetic pressure on the Revolutionary Committee to secure a safe retreat for the fighters?

In *Rote Fahne* Rosa Luxemburg could act only as a critic of the Revolutionary Committee, and this is what her role there should have been. But the KPD was actively engaged in the struggle and its representatives were directing it. It bore joint responsibility together with the other organisations involved. It is not known what direct influence the party's central committee exercised on the leadership of the movement, or even if it exercised any at all, and we know nothing of other views which may have been expressed at the meetings of the central committee apart from those of Rosa Luxemburg. We also know nothing of any party resolutions or what if anything was done to carry them out.

Throughout the fighting Karl Liebknecht was always with the workers: at the risk of his life and in constant danger he hurried from position to position during the skirmishes, giving the fighters advice and moral support. However, he was almost out of touch with the party leadership the whole time, and neither the available documentary material nor the memoirs published by the members provide us with more of a close-up of the views, intentions, and measures of the central committee during that time than that obtained in Jogiches's letter to Clara Zetkin.

According to the statements of the women who worked most closely with Rosa Luxemburg in the critical days, a great change took place in her, both physical and mental. During the first months of the revolution, which were an unprecedented strain, she had given confidence and strength to everyone through her energy and composure, simply through the glowing and cheerful radiance of her personality. She always found time to concern herself with other people. With a smile of recognition or even an ironical remark (made with so much tact that the sting was lost in a feeling of personal warmth and affection) she encouraged others to exert themselves even more for the cause. For the movement as a whole and for the smaller circle of her enthusiastically devoted collaborators Rosa Luxemburg was a living flame, and she remained sanguine in the midst of all the hustle and bustle of the revolution with its great moments and problems alike.

In the January days, however, those who were close to her felt that she, too, was torn by internal conflicts. She became taciturn, and at times avoided others. The principle of 'mind over matter' had always applied to her life: her indomitable spirit and will-power had always commanded her body, enabling her to overcome her physical infirmities. But now it seemed that the point had come when even her will began to sag. The merciless pace of the last two months, during which she expended all her energy without stint, seemed to be completing the destructive work of the war years in prison. She became subject to sudden fainting fits which happened almost every day. Advice to take rest, to place herself in the hands of a doctor, was rejected as almost treachery in the given situation, and if she noticed anyone about to broach the subject a glance was sufficient to make the words stick in his throat. A last great struggle was proceeding between her iron will and her failing body. Bordering on the miraculous, the triumphs of her will-power can be seen in the issues of *Rote Fahne*, in articles whose tremendously forceful language betrays nothing of her terrible struggle to keep going.

But these were only partial victories. At times it seemed that she could no longer fashion policies in a coherent and consistent way without anguished conflicts. The painful question thus arises: did her physical strength simply not suffice for the necessary tasks, or did this great leader, who as a theoretician and as a strategist of class struggle moved ahead with such unshakeable inner strength and tenacity, lack that crowning touch of the party leader who can make realistically sound judgments at critical moments irrespective of his mood and who knows how to see to it that his decisions are carried out–that crowning touch which became Lenin's second nature. This question, of course, can never be answered. . . .

The man-hunt

In the night of 8 January machine-guns opened fire on the building in the Wilhelmstrasse which housed the *Rote Fahne* editorial offices. This was followed by an abortive attempt to take the place by storm. The attackers probably feared an ambush, for it was, after all, 'generally known' that the *Spartakisten* had turned the house into a 'fortress'. As a matter of fact, there was only one comrade, a woman, in the editorial offices at the time. Fortunately, she was more frightened than hurt. There were never any arms in the building and never any guard; at any time a group of armed men could have arrested everybody in the building. However, the incident was a warning which needed to be taken seriously. Located three minutes from *Vorwärts* and the centre of the fighting, and only two minutes from Belle-Alliance-Platz, the most important assembly-point of the enemy troops, *Rote Fahne* could expect an attack at any time. Thus, on 9 January the editorial offices were evacuated. A patrol of government troops was already before the door. As usual, Rosa seemed to ignore the danger completely. As she left the house, she took one scrutinising look at the men, and, having decided that only hunger could have driven them into the enemy camp, she immediately began to show them how they were letting themselves be misused against their own real interests. It was only with difficulty that her woman companion managed to whisk her away from an imminently dangerous situation. Soon afterwards Hugo Eberlein found her involved in heated discussion amid a crowd right in the heart of the fighting area, and had to drag her away almost by force. Rosa was contemptuous of danger, and, in fact, she was rather inclined to seek it from a romantic sense of responsibility, a feeling that she simply had to share every danger with the ordinary fighters of the revolution.

For a few days she found lodgings in the house of a friend, a doctor, near Hallesches Tor, also located in the fighting area. It was the first station on the road that was to lead to her death. One wonders whether Rosa and Leo had to try very hard to repress all thought of danger. Experienced conspirators though they were, they ignored the most elementary precautions. They met with other comrades and with the leaders of the various groups of fighting workers in public eating places, always in and around the comparatively small area in which the chief fighting was going on. They seemed not to notice that a net was being drawn more and more tightly around them. On the evening of 10 January the Berlin Commandant's office carried out a series of raids with a view to seizing leaders of the USPD and the KPD. Georg Ledebour and Ernst Meyer were arrested in their homes and treated in a way that indicated clearly that their murder was being planned.

Ledebour's arrest came as quite a surprise, especially since he had been taking part in the negotiations between the right-wing socialists and the Independents which were scheduled to be concluded the next morning (11 January). Even an appeal to the government failed to bring about his release. The reason was soon to become all too apparent—and bloody. There was a 'danger' (from the government's point of view) that an evacuation of the buildings occupied by the workers might be decided upon, and this had to be hindered at all costs if the counter-revolution was to secure the striking victory it needed. This was later borne out before a court of inquiry by the evidence of Major Franz von Stephani, one of the commanders of the government's troops. According to his testimony, he was ordered on 9 January to take the *Vorwärts* building by storm, but he considered the undertaking too risky without previous artillery preparation, and proposed that negotiations should be opened up with the occupying workers to obtain their evacuation of the premises. However, Brutus Molkenbuhr, the son of a well-known member of the SPD Executive, declared that *Vorwärts* had to be taken by force of arms. In the early morning hours of 11 January the bombardment of the building began with heavy artillery and mortar fire which did considerable damage and cost many lives. Nevertheless, this full military attack was repulsed by the workers. The bombardment was resumed and continued for two hours before it finally rendered the position untenable. The workers now sent intermediaries bearing a truce flag and led by the worker-poet Werner Möller and the writer Wolfgang Fernbach to negotiate with the besiegers. One of the deputation was sent back with a demand for unconditional surrender. The 300 workers remaining in the *Vorwärts* building surrendered, but in the meantime all the other intermediaries, together with two captured couriers, had been brutally murdered in cold blood. The White Terror had begun.

After the re-capture of *Vorwärts* the undefended office of the KPD in the Friedrichstrasse was seized and demolished. Leo Jogiches and Hugo Eberlein were arrested, but the latter managed to escape, and Leo had just enough time to tell him to advise the leadership of the party to leave Berlin for Frankfurt am Main, where it could work in safety. Indeed, an incident which occurred at about the same time heavily underscored his advice: a woman comrade, sent out to discover what was happening in the *Rote Fahne* offices, was seized on the street by the soldiery, who mistook her for Rosa Luxemburg and subjected her to long hours of frightful treatment before she finally managed to escape. It left no doubt as to Rosa's fate if she were caught. But when her 'double' described the death threats and warned her to flee, she emphatically rejected the idea, explaining that she and Karl had to remain in Berlin to prevent the defeat of the workers from leading to their demoralisation.*

---

* The attitude of Rosa Luxemburg and Karl Liebknecht has occasionally been contrasted with that of Lenin during the July days of 1917, when after coolly reflecting on the realities of the situation, he decided to elude his pursuers by going into hiding. However, we now know from Krupskaya's memoirs that both Lenin and Zinoviev were prepared to give themselves up for trial, and that they finally fled only at the insistence of Bolshevik workers.

On 11 January, in the evening, a meeting took place in Rosa Luxemburg's refuge at Hallesches Tor, and Liebknecht was also present. It was clear that the place was no longer safe, and Karl and Rosa were then quartered with a working-class family in Neukölln, certainly the safest place for them, because the enemy hardly dared to show its face in that outlying working-class district. However, on 13 January, they were forced to leave, owing to a warning which was in all probability a false alarm, and friends in Wilmersdorf, a middle-class suburb in the southwest of Berlin, gave them shelter.

It was here that they wrote their last articles. 'Even in the midst of battle, amid the triumphant screams of the counter-revolution, the revolutionary proletariat has to account for what has happened, and to measure events and their results on the great scale of history.' To bring about such an understanding of the causes of the defeat was the aim of Rosa's article entitled 'Order Reigns in Berlin', published in *Rote Fahne* on 14 January 1919. She pointed out the weakness of the revolution: the political unripeness of the masses of soldiers who still allowed themselves to be misused by their officers for purposes inimical to the interests of the people. She regarded the backwardness of the soldiers as an expression of the immaturity of the German Revolution. The rural areas were still hardly touched by the revolution; and even though the workers in the most important industrial centres sided heart and soul with the Berlin proletariat, they failed to keep abreast of its advance, they failed to act directly in concert with it. Above all, the economic struggles were just beginning to develop. One could therefore not reckon with a final, lasting victory at this point. Moreover, it would be a mistake to view the fighting as a deliberate thrust forward, for the workers were really defending themselves against a provocation:

> From this contradiction between the sharpening of the problem and the lack of prerequisites to its solution in the initial stage of revolutionary development it follows that the individual skirmishes of the revolution may end in *defeat*. But revolution is the sole form of "war"–and this is its special law of life–where the final victory can be prepared only by a series of "defeats"! [153]

Rosa cautiously laid bare the weaknesses of the armed action. A detailed self-criticism, something she regarded as indispensable for the self-education of the masses, was supposed to follow. In the hour of defeat she was concerned with counteracting the danger of panic and with raising the confidence and victory hopes of the beaten fighters. More strongly than most of the comrades she felt and recognised the severity of the defeat. Nevertheless she maintained her firm belief in the final victory of the revolution. And her own fate? She knew that death was lurking, but she was prepared for all eventualities. Her thoughts, however, were concentrated on the morrow's work.

In contrast, Karl Liebknecht's last work was a fiery glorification of the militant *Spartakus* idea: 'For *Spartakus*—that means the fire and spirit, the heart and soul, the will and deed of the proletarian revolution!'—punctuated at the end by a premonition of death proudly acknowledged: *Trotzalledem!*—Despite everything!

The murders

When Rosa Luxemburg and Karl Liebknecht arrived in Wilmersdorf, the noose had already tightened around them. Innumerable spies, paid by various counter-revolutionary institutions, were hunting them down. The Anti-Bolshevik League, founded by Russian aristocrats, started the murder propaganda against the two leaders of the working class. It had a network of agents all over Germany, and set prices on the heads of Liebknecht, Luxemburg, and Radek. It was one of their agents, von Tyszka, also in the pay of the Berlin Commandant's office, who had attempted to seize Karl Liebknecht on 7 December. And it was von Tyszka and a First Lieutenant Gürgen—again on the instructions on the Commandant's office—who undertook to arrest Georg Ledebour and Ernst Meyer. The *Bürgerrat* of Berlin also had its own spy organisation, with branches in the various suburbs, as did the *Garde-Kavallerie-Schützen-Division*, quartered in the Eden Hotel.

Finally, there was the spy office of the so-called Reichstag Regiment, founded by the SPD. The true colours of this institution, officially known as the 'Auxiliary Service of the SPD, Section 14', were later exposed in the libel proceedings conducted against a certain Herr Prinz. According to the findings of the court, this Section 14 of the Reichstag Regiment, in the names of Philipp Scheidemann and the regiment's financial backer, Georg Sklarz (an evil grafter and speculator), set a price of 100,000 Marks on the heads of Karl Liebknecht and Rosa Luxemburg. Hesel, the officer in charge of Section 14; Ernst Sonnenfeld, the regiment's paymaster; and Krasnik, an officer in the regiment, all declared under oath that Fritz Henck, Scheidemann's son-in-law, had expressly confirmed to them that the offer of the reward was serious and that money was available for such a purpose. A host of other members of the regiment confirmed this testimony, reiterating that an order to murder Liebknecht and Luxemburg had been given though it had never been put into writing, and that whoever brought in the two, dead or alive, was to receive a reward of 100,000 Marks. By acquitting Prinz of the libel charge, the court was in effect condemning

Scheidemann and Sklarz. Neither of them ever dared to try and clear themselves of this incriminatory verdict.

Bourgeois and social-democratic organisations alike set their henchmen to track down the two revolutionary leaders; in fact, they cooperated and competed with each other at the same time. Their liaison-man, who sat in the Berlin Commandant's office, was Public Prosecutor Weissmann, a jack-of-all-trades who, for his services in the January days, was promoted to the post of State Secretary for Public Order under Friedrich Ebert.

But as if it were not enough to set loose a pack of volunteer and mercenary head-hunters, the incitement against *Spartakus*, which had begun in the very first days of the revolution amid the ecstatic declarations of brotherhood, had become by January the chorus of raving sadists. The press accompanied the murders committed by the soldiery in the working-class districts with hymns to the 'Liberators' which sang of the walls spattered by the brains of those 'shot to death in accordance with martial law'. The campaign turned the whole bourgeoisie into a blood-thirsty mob seized by a denunciation-craze to drive all 'suspects'–revolutionaries and perfectly harmless and innocent people alike–before the rifles of the execution commandos. And all this shreiking culminated in the baiting-cry: 'Liebknecht! Luxemburg!' The heights of unabashed shamelessness, never mind of brutal frankness, were scaled by *Vorwärts* on 13 January with its publication of a poem by Artur Zickler, a regular contributor–he later wrote an apology in the paper –which ended with the verse:

Vielhundert Tote in einer Reih–

Proletarier!

Karl, Radek, Rosa und Kumpanei–

Es ist keiner dabei, es ist keiner dabei!

Proletarier!

Many hundred corpses in a row–

Proletarians!

Karl, Radek, Rosa and Co.–

Not one of them is there, not one of them is there!

Proletarians!

Vorwärts was the first paper to bring the news on Thursday, 16 January, that Liebknecht and Luxemburg had been arrested. No mention of the murder. Not until midday did the papers carry the screaming headlines: 'Liebknecht shot to death while trying to escape!' (*auf der Flucht erschossen*) and 'Luxemburg beaten to death by the multitude!' (*von der Menge erschlagen*).

What had happened?

On 15 January, around 9 o'clock in the evening, Karl and Rosa, together with Wilhelm Pieck, were arrested at their last place of refuge, 53 Mannheimer Strasse in Wilmersdorf, by a group of soldiers led by a Lieutenant Lindner and an innkeeper named Mehring from the Wilmersdorf *Bürgerrat*. At first the arrested leaders gave false names, but in vain, for they had apparently been clearly described by a spy who had wormed his way into Liebknecht's confidence. Karl was first taken to the *Bürgerrat's* headquarters, and from there to the Eden Hotel. Shortly thereafter Rosa Luxemburg and Pieck followed, accompanied by a strong military guard.

At the Eden Hotel, arrangements had already been made, under the direction of a Captain Pabst of the *Garde-Kavallerie-Schützen-Division* to murder Karl and Rosa. The moment Liebknecht was brought in, he was struck twice over the head with a rifle-butt. His wounds were not allowed to be dressed. Rosa Luxemburg and Pieck were then received with wild shouts and a torrent of disgusting abuse. While Pieck was held under guard at one end of the corridor,* Rosa and Karl were hauled into Captain Pabst's room for 'interrogation'. Shortly afterwards Liebknecht was led away. On leaving the building he was struck down by rifle-butt blows at the hands of the rifleman Otto Runge, and then dragged into a car by First Lieutenant (*Kapitänleutnant*) Horst von Pflugk-Hartung; Captain Heinz von Pflugk-Hartung; Lieutenants Liepmann, von Ritgen, Stiege, Schultz; and a rifleman–all members of Pabst's staff. They all got into the car, as they had a sham order to transport the captives to the prison (normally reserved for those awaiting trial) in Moabit. By the lake in the Tiergarten (Zoological Gardens), in a dimly-lit area, the car came to a halt, owing to alleged motor trouble. Half-conscious, Liebknecht was pulled out of the car and dragged several yards under the cover of six of the captors, all armed with pistols (with the safety-catches off) and hand-grenades. After being forced to take a few steps, he was shot to death allegedly while trying to escape, i.e. murdered. The car was now, of course, ready to go again, and the corpse was driven to a first-aid station and delivered as that of an 'unknown man'.

A short while after Liebknecht had been taken away, Rosa Luxemburg was led out of the hotel by a First Lieutenant Vogel. Awaiting her before the door was Runge, who had received an order from First Lieutenants Vogel and Pflugk-Hartung to strike her to the ground. With two blows of his rifle-butt he smashed her skull.

* Runge had been ordered to shoot Pieck to death. To ward off this immediate threat, Pieck requested to be allowed to make a further statement. What he said was utter humbug, but he was thereupon taken into military custody, whence he managed to escape.

Her almost lifeless body was flung into a waiting car, and several officers jumped in. One of them struck Rosa on the head with a revolver-butt, and First Lieutenant Vogel finished her off with a shot in the head. The corpse was then driven to the Tiergarten and, on Vogel's orders, thrown from the Liechtenstein Bridge into the Landwehr Canal, where it was not washed up until 31 May 1919.[154]

Afterwards

> As though lashed on by invisible spirits, the horses of the sun-god career forward with the frail chariot of our destiny; and nothing remains for us but to hold the reins with calm courage. . . . If I am to fall, then a clap of thunder, a high wind, or even a false step might hurl me into the depths–and there I would lie with many thousands of others. I have never scorned to cast the bloody dice for small gain with my good comrades-in-arms, and should I haggle now when all the freedom and worth of life are at stake?
>
> (Goethe, *Egmont*)

There is something of Rosa Luxemburg's philosophy of life in these words. She knew the personal risks she would be taking in the revolutionary struggle, for many had taken them before her and paid the supreme price. She knew that the great historical advances for which she was striving would be achieved only when many thousands had sprung into the breach. The sacrifice of her life was thus the fulfilment of a destiny freely embraced. She was not striking a pose when she wrote to Sonja Liebknecht: 'You know, I hope nevertheless to die at my post, in a street-battle or in a hard-labour prison.'

No one can say what effect her work would have had on the history of the past twenty years [i.e. 1919-39, Tr.], whether it could have given the course of events a different twist, had she lived. But as she could hardly have survived to see the victory of her cause, her death–met at the hands of the enemy during the height of the struggle–seems significant because it marked the end of the life of a revolutionary militant. This significance raises her death above its attendant horror. Her death became a symbol. Acting on orders, a ruffian, showing all the marks of a degenerate, and brutalised in war, smashed a magnificent vessel of genius without realising what he was doing. Thus it happened that during those January days murderous hate, savageness, and servility, harnessed in the service of capitalist barbarousness, struck down the proletariat's longing for freedom.

The news of the murders shattered the last remnants of strength in the aged Franz Mehring, and he died on 29 January. Leo Jogiches, broken by the heavy blow and only a shadow of his former self, worked hard to expose the crime and managed to publish not only accounts of eye-witnesses, but also a really searing document: a photo of the drinking-bout at which the murderers celebrated the deaths of the two *Spartakusbund* leaders. He thereby signed his own death warrant. On 10 March 1919 he was arrested, taken to the prison attached to the Police Headquarters, and murdered–'shot to death while trying to escape'–by a detective named Tamshik. And, as their leaders had done, thousands of revolutionary workers sealed their loyalty to the *Spartakus* cause by laying down their lives, either killed in action or treacherously murdered in the subsequent White Terror.

The counter-revolution danced a jig over their graves, believing that the social revolution had been struck down once and for all. What exultation! Justice–that blindfolded whore–and *raison d'état* banded together to hush up the crimes. Public Prosecutor Jorns piled one perversion of justice on top of another in an effort to blot out all traces of the murders.[155] However, *Rote Fahne* blared the truth up and down the country, and roused the public conscience to such an extent that the authorities were compelled to arrest at least some of the assassins. The prison now became transformed into a perjurer's forge, a counterfeiters' workshop, a clip-joint, a brothel. Nevertheless, when the cynical travesty of justice was finally staged before the court, the truth managed to cut through the web of intimidation and bribery. The court, in cahoots with the *Garde-Kavallerie-Schützen-Division*, acquitted all the aristocratic murderers without exception. Lieutenant Liepmann was sentenced to be confined to quarters. First Lieutenant Vogel received two years and four months imprisonment for committing a misdemeanour while on guard duty and for disposing illegally of a corpse. The soldier Runge was sentenced to two years imprisonment for attempted manslaughter.*[156] While still in detention awaiting the outcome of the trial, Vogel managed to plan his escape;[157] he provided himself with a false passport and visa, and, the day after his sentence was passed, got away to Holland. Pabst and Jorns were told of the preparations for the escape, but did nothing to prevent their being carried out.

Detective Tamschik (the one who had murdered Jogiches) then shot and killed Dorrenbach, one of the leaders of the People's Naval Division, because the victim was allegedly 'trying to escape'. In recognition of his services he was later promoted to be an officer in

---

* Runge made two confessions, the first during his imprisonment and the second subsequently in *Vorwärts* on 29 and 30 May 1922. See *Illustriete Geschichte der Deutschen Revolution* (Illustrated History of the German Revolution), Berlin 1929.

the Prussian security police by the social-democratic minister Carl Severing.

The January fighting was followed by a campaign of Noske's civil-war army from town to town, and the bourgeois republic was saved. But not forever. The victory of the counter-revolution in January 1919 paved the way for Hitler's victory in January 1933. The murderers were now on top: Captain Pabst, who had organised the murders, could now boast of his deeds;* Runge, who had been convicted of attempted manslaughter, begged for and received a special award for his genuinely national-socialist acts; Vogel was granted special leave on grounds of health; and Jorns, who had already been promoted to be Reich's Attorney (*Reichsanwalt*) during the Weimar Republic, could glitter as the incarnation of fascist justice, the President of Hitler's 'People's Court'.

Many of the old *Spartakus* fighters were thrown into concentration camps, where a large number of them were murdered; many old social democrats, trade unionists, and honest democrats suffered the same fate. Rosa Luxemburg's possessions were plundered by the soldiery, and irreplaceable manuscripts stolen, scattered, and destroyed. In 1933 her writings were publicly burned, together with other works of cultural value belonging to the German people. The memorial dedicated to her and those who fell with her in the January fighting was razed to the ground.

But worse than this desecration of her grave was the desecration of her political heritage, committed by the very people who should have felt the call to preserve and add to it. They were the ones who insulted her memory by distorting her ideas, slandering her name, falsifying her political work, and outlawing her followers. The names of Luxemburg and Liebknecht were abused as red rags with which to cover up a policy which was incompatible with the aims of these two great socialists. Many of her comrades-in-arms and pupils, both German and Polish, paid for their faithfulness to her ideas in Stalin's prison-camps, and many were shot to death after having been robbed of their revolutionary honour.

The icy breath of a long period of reaction has swept over the flowering field of great and fruitful ideas.

Nevertheless! ...

When Rosa Luxemburg's body sank into the Landwehr Canal, it was rumoured in the proletarian districts of Germany that the

---

* In January 1962 Pabst felt that the time had come to represent his role in the murders of Liebknecht and Luxemburg as a deed to save the 'Christian West from collapse', and thus 'thoroughly justifiable (*vertretbar*) even from a moral standpoint'. His version, namely that the two had been executed in accordance with martial law, was taken up by the *Bulletin* of the Press and Information Office of the German Federal Government on 8 February 1962.

news of her murder were not true, that she was still alive, that she had managed to escape and would again place herself at the head of the revolutionary movement when the time came. People did not want to believe that so much will-power, enthusiasm, and intellectual strength could have been wiped out by a rifle-butt.

There is a grain of truth in this belief. The law of conservation of energy is valid not only for the physical world. In the long run, no bonfire and no dictatorial order can destroy ideas that have once lived in the minds of great masses of people. Forces which strive to stem and turn back the course of history will perish in the end, no matter how much havoc they may have wreaked for a time. The intellectual seed has been sown, and will bear fruit in the future. Who knows the names of the men of the Thermidor? But Babeuf's ideas helped the revolutionary movement of the French proletariat to new life thirty years after his execution in 1797.

When the triumphal procession of barbarism reaches its limits –and it will do so–the Acheron will begin to move again, and victors will spring from the spirit of Rosa Luxemburg.

Postscript

Rosa Luxemburg belongs neither to the victorious revolutionaries nor to those who finally accommodated themselves to reality. Her death at the hands of murderers almost fifty years ago forcibly interrupted strivings which would have led neither to acceptance of the Stalinism of the Soviet Union nor to a taking-over of social-democratic reformism. Therefore, wherever uneasiness at the sterile alternatives of Soviet bureaucratism and reformist adaptation is voiced, Rosa Luxemburg and her work should be remembered. It is true that her violent end and the discovery of her sensitive letters have intensified the interest in her person even further, but her work and her aspirations are still–in both East and West–misinterpreted and attacked, distorted or hushed up.

Three years after Rosa Luxemburg's murder–on the occasion of the publication by Paul Levi of her fragmentary work on the Russian Revolution–Lenin noted:

> To this we reply with two lines from a good old Russian fable: an eagle can indeed sometimes fly lower than a chicken, but a chicken can never rise to the same heights as an eagle. Rosa Luxemburg erred on the question of Polish independence; she erred in 1903 in her evaluation of Menshevism . . . [a series of further "errors" follows]. . . . But despite all these mistakes she was and remains an eagle. And not only will she always be dear to the memory of communists throughout the world, but her *biography* and the *complete edition of her works* (a matter in which the German communists have delayed intolerably, and the incredibly enormous sacrifices in their difficult struggle can only partly excuse their negligence) will provide a very useful lesson in the education of many generations of communists throughout the world. [Written in February 1922, first published in *Pravda*, 16 April 1924.]

Commissioned by the KPD leadership to edit the *Gesammelte Werke* (Collected Works) of Rosa Luxemburg, Paul Frölich built up an extensive collection of material which included Polish writings in German translation, the greatest part of which–it is presumed–is now located in East Berlin and Moscow. Of the nine planned volumes, however, only three (Vol. VI, *The Accumulation of Capital and What the Epigoni Have Done with Marxist Theory. An Anticritique*; Vol. III, *Against Reformism*; and Vol. IV, *Trade-Union Struggle and Mass Strike*) had been published by 1928. In that same year Frölich was expelled from the party for 'right-wing deviationism', and the work on the Rosa Luxemburg collection was quietly shelved. However, because he had been expressly designated by Rosa Luxemburg's heirs to be the editor of the planned edition of her works, the material remained in his possession. He also managed to safeguard the precious documents from the clutches of the Nazis. But, during his imprisonment, acquaintances to whom he had entrusted the material for safekeeping thought that it could be stored most safely in a Moscow archive. And thus it landed in the Marx-Engels-Lenin-Institute. Since then more than thirty years have passed, and not one further volume of the *Gesammelte Werke* has been brought out by either the Soviet or the East German Communists.

When Josef Goebbels arranged for the 'spontaneous' burning of thousands of books throughout Germany on 10 May 1933, the writings of Rosa Luxemburg were naturally included. The memory of her works was supposed to be extinguished just as she herself had been fourteen years earlier. In the whole international communist movement, however, the Stalinist line had been victorious since the late 1920s. An erroneous doctrine dubbed 'Luxemburgism' had been distilled from Rosa Luxemburg's teachings and attributed to a 'theory of spontaneity', which she was alleged to have advocated. In certain circles of the revolutionary working-class movement, however, her spirit and her teachings had not been completely forgotten, and, particularly in view of the defeat of the working-class movement in Germany and the development of Stalin's autocracy in the Soviet Union, the need arose to recall her personality to the minds of the up-and-coming generations by means of an authentic biography. At a time when many models had become questionable–Stalin was letting an unflattering light fall even on Lenin–Rosa Luxemburg must have seemed all the more attractive both as a thinker and as a political figure.

Having succeeded in emigrating to France after being confined in the concentration camp at Lichtenburg, Paul Frölich was besieged by many friends requesting that he write a book which would fulfil this function. Despite the total inaccessibility of his extensive archive materials and under unfavourable research conditions, he managed to complete his book on Rosa Luxemburg's thought and activities in 1938-39. Shortly before the outbreak of the war, in 1939, the first German edition appeared in Paris, and the first English translation appeared in 1940. Thanks, above all, to the

English publisher, Victor Gollancz, who enabled Frölich to work relatively undisturbed for one year on the book, the English-speaking world was informed in a comprehensive and thorough-going way for the first time about Rosa Luxemburg. The book, published in the 'Left Book Club' series, became a surprising success: within a short time more than 20,000 copies were sold–and this at a time when the war was already claiming everyone's attention. The second German edition appeared in 1949, while Frölich was still living in exile. He returned to Germany in 1951, but not for long–he died in Frankfurt am Main on 16 March 1953. In the course of time the book was translated and published in Hebrew (1949), in Serbo-Croat and Slovenian (1955), and in French (1965); a US edition is now in preparation. J P Nettl, who devoted an extensive two-volume biography to Rosa Luxemburg in 1966, was indebted, like numerous other members of his generation, to Frölich's book–the only serious publication on Rosa Luxemburg for over a decade–for the impulse to concern himself with this great revolutionary theoretician and practitioner.

Not until 1951 did a two-volume selection of her *Writings and Speeches* appear in East Berlin. It was prefaced by the detailed polemics of both Lenin and Stalin, and was put in the proper framework and 'made safe' for consumption by the simultaneous publication of a 'critical biographical sketch' by Fred Oelssner. In fact, the editors responsible for the selection exercised such great caution that they even left out texts which were referred to at length by her critics. In the Soviet Union it appears that only her *Introduction to Economics* (during the 1920s) and a volume containing her writings 'on literature' (1961) have been published. In contrast, in Poland a number of historical studies, showing a more worthy appreciation of Rosa Luxemburg, have appeared in recent years, and Feliks Tych is preparing a three-volume edition of *all* of Rosa Luxemburg's surviving letters to Leo Jogiches (Vol I: 1893-1900, Vol II: 1901-1905, Vol III: 1906-1914), to be published in Warsaw in 1967 or 1968). There is no doubt that here, too, the Polish communists have displayed more self-reliance and independence in confronting Stalinist relics than any other communist party.

Does Rosa Luxemburg still have something to say to our own times? It seems to me that–irrespective of whether her political-economy theories and political decisions still have 'topical value'– the question can only be answered in the affirmative. Rosa Luxemburg herself would have been the last person to have allowed a dogma or binding canon to be fashioned for later generations from her theories and acts. What one can still learn from her, however, is the deliberately responsible thoroughness with which she studied social and political relations before deciding upon any course of political action. One can also learn from the close and consciously reflected link between theory and practice in her work, a link which did not involve the application of a schematised theory to any and all conditions, but rather the illumination of a specific situation in the light of theory in order to enable successful political action to take place. And finally Rosa Luxemburg showed that realistic politics does not necessarily mean doing without far-reaching perspectives and aims, and that accommodation to existing conditions merely represents a form of capitulation to the supposed invariability of the *status quo* passing itself off as statesmanlike wisdom.

In his essay 'Rosa Luxemburg as a Marxist' (1921) Georg Lukács showed that she differed from the Marxist epigoni in the Second International in that she was able to grasp *reality as a totality*. She did not divide reality into two halves, the one governed by 'objective laws' which have to be accepted fatalistically while the other can only be changed by individual moral endeavour. She sought to grasp the whole of the dynamics of the capitalist world economy, too, in her main economic work, *The Accumulation of Capitalism*, and Lukács is certainly right in pointing out the inability of her ideological opponents in the Austrian Social-Democratic Party even to recognise the problem at issue. Regardless of whether her suggested solution of the problem was correct, her opponents ought at least to have recognised and acknowledged the relevance of the *question*. Rosa Luxemburg analysed the imperialist phase of capitalism as a whole, not–as in vulgar Marxism–in its individual aspects, but as a *total process*.

In this respect, the decisive question concerning the real possibilities of the extended reproduction (i.e. accumulation) of capital under contemporary conditions was one which could not be solved simply by referring to the model drawn up by Marx in the second volume of *Capital*. In his main work Marx–as is well-known–starts with the fiction of a purely capitalist economy whose inner laws of movement he reconstructs dialectically. But vulgar Marxist epigoni have overlooked the fact that he was dealing only with a *methodological hypothesis* which does not in the least suppose the 'real possibility' of such an economy let alone its unlimited duration. In fact, the isolated model was incorporated by Marx himself into the context of the totality of historical reality on numerous occasions–for example, when he was describing primitive accumulation. This fragmentary method of observation in *Capital*, which itself has been handed down only as a torso, was applied by Rosa Luxemburg to the problem of accumulation as it presented itself to the highly developed industrial nations of her day. She was consequently driven to draw conclusions which were far more radical and critical than those reached by her opponents, whose 'identification of Marx's abstractions with the totality of society' was termed 'a "rational" means of self-defence for a capitalism in decline' by Lukács in his *History and Class Consciousness*.

But it was not only because of the start she made towards working on a total analysis of socio-economic relations within the world economy of her period that Rosa Luxemburg stood head and shoulders above the other Marxist theoreticians of the Second International: the link between theoretical analysis and revolutionary practice in her work was also dialectically reflected, even if it was not fully and consciously transparent. Only the low level of the scientific research into her work is to blame for the fact that even today the mistaken idea is still being peddled around that there is an antithesis between the 'necessity of socio-economic development' exhibited in her main work and her tendency to favour revolutionary activism. In reality, her analysis of the immanent laws of the development of capitalist relations between industrial states and 'developing countries' was supposed to exhibit not the superfluousness, but precisely the *urgency* of revolutionary actions. The prospect of internecine struggles among the great industrialised powers for the distribution of non-capitalist areas—indispensable for the sheer survival of a capitalist economy dependent on economic expansion—did not lend itself at all to the calming down of revolutionary tendencies, but rather the opposite: it intensified them. The reduction to a primitive state and the brutalisation of the population which Rosa Luxemburg feared would result from the World War, whose coming she predicted, came to pass, and proved to be the decisive brake operating against revolutionary progress. It was not by chance, but quite in line with her theoretical insights that she emphatically opposed war preparations and nationalism in the hope of being able to halt the course of development and lead the working-class movement to victory before such a 'reversion to barbarism' occurred.

Here again Rosa Luxemburg saw the historical process as a dialectical unity and thereby overcame the dilemma of choosing between the poor alternatives of passively accepting an allegedly inevitable evolutionary process and Blanquist activism. She conceived of revolutionary action as an integral part of the historical process itself, a part which could nevertheless manage to revolutionise the whole order if it seized the objective possibilities available.

Rosa Luxemburg knew that there is no such thing as infallibility in grasping the nature of objective and subjective revolutionary situations, and certainly she herself must have committed decisive errors on more than one occasion. Nonetheless, the correctness of her insight into the necessity of consciously seeking to grasp a situation and of consciously taking *action*, was based on this understanding.

Perhaps even more important than her scientific approach to possible revolutionary forms of action, in maintaining Rosa Luxemburg as a model for the working-class movement, has been the fact that she–perhaps alone among the great Marxists–never ceased to be both a democrat and a social democrat. It is true that in her criticism of the German party bureaucracy she kept an eye on its reformist vacillation and tried to play off the revolutionary spirit of the masses against it, but this is only one aspect of her attitude. She would never have been satisfied with any revolution made against the interests or the declared intentions of the majority of the population. The programme of the *Spartakusbund* expressly states:

> The *Spartakusbund* will never take over governmental power except in accordance with the clear and explicit will of the great majority of the proletarian masses throughout Germany, except in accordance with their conscious approval of its views, aims, and fighting methods.

Here again Rosa Luxemburg did not subordinate the one aim–revolution–to the other value–democracy. In contrast to the reformist socialists, who shrank back from socialist revolution if it was to take place in extra-parliamentary channels, she did not opt for bourgeois democracy as a natural right, but considered democracy to be the decisive and indispensable means of effecting a revolutionary transformation. She knew that education for freedom can only take place in freedom and that happiness cannot be forced on people. Without even being familiar perhaps with modern pedagogy, she carried over its insights into the areas of popular political education and democracy, whereas Lenin–probably not merely by accident–advocated conservative views in both these areas; or at least he promoted the idea that just as minors need leadership and guidance, the proletarian masses need a theoretically educated elitist party. Not that Rosa Luxemburg would have denied the necessity of such education and leadership, but she preferred that both should only assist the *self-education and the self-formation* of the democratic will of the working class. Just as the aim of modern pedagogy since Rousseau and Pestalozzi has been above all to help the potential forces of growth in children to develop smoothly, so Rosa Luxemburg wanted her revolutionary theory and practice to serve the creative development of the masses awakening (and to be awakened) to democratic self-consciousness. What later–in compliance with Lenin's criticism–became known as Luxemburg's 'theory of spontaneity' was simply an erroneous and misleading extrapolation from her theories dealing with the need of the masses to learn from their own personal experiences.

We should not isolate Rosa Luxemburg's now famous (and prophetic) critique of the October Revolution from her other writings. The work set out in the first instance to warn against merely adopting the methods used in Russia, which were perhaps unavoidable there, but nevertheless not exemplary–even if they did lead to victory in 1917 and help to secure it afterwards. She maintained that the Central and West European working-class movement had to move in its own channels, seek its own way. However, this way could only be a free and democratic one, and should in no way exclude the possibility of hard and bitter struggles with capitalists wrestling for the preservation of their privileges. On the contrary!

Rosa Luxemburg's prognosis for the development of revolutionary Russia was bleak. She could not assume that the Red Power would last, but then, too, she could hardly suppose that a bureaucratic state capitalism with the fictitious label of 'socialism' would come into the inheritance of the great October Revolution. It is true that the massive increase of petit-bourgeois peasant property-owners has not led to the counter-revolution predicted by Rosa Luxemburg, but it has led to the complete destruction of democracy and to the administrative transformation of rural private property (through a 'revolution from above', as Stalin himself called it). Although this, in turn, has helped to maintain and consolidate the power of the Communist Party of the Soviet Union, or rather of its top leadership, it has led the party even further away from the ideal of socialist democracy than was the case in 1917-18. It seemed such a matter of course to Rosa Luxemburg that freedom and democracy should accompany the formation of a future socialist society that she did not even think of the possibility of Stalin's 'solution' to the problem, even though as early as 1918 she was able to foresee the beginnings of a 'bureaucratic degeneration'. Even today–fifty years after October–Rosa Luxemburg would doubtless place a considerable portion of the blame for this development on the socialists in the industrially developed West and Central European countries.

It is difficult to judge today whether she could have markedly changed the course of events. Because of her violent death she has grown to legendary size in the consciousness of revolutionary workers throughout the world. As early as 1921 Georg Lukács glorified her death as 'logically, the crowning pinnacle of her thought and life'. The individual events of her life, however, do not constitute a legendary destiny. One can speculate about what would have become of the German communists under Rosa Luxemburg's leadership. It is, of course, inconceivable that she would have played a leading role under the tutelage of the Stalinist Third International, but one can just as little assume that she alone could have succeeded in preventing the International from developing into an instrument of Soviet power politics.

Here we must break off our speculations. It would be idle and would invariably lead to false edification, to prefer to imagine that nothing more than disappointment and fraternal quarrels in her own party would have awaited Rosa Luxemburg had she lived. Her murder and the murder of Karl Liebknecht, Leo Jogiches, and many lesser known German socialist revolutionaries should not and ought not to be either glossed over or extenuated. They belong to that oft cited *'unbewältigte Vergangenheit'* – that past with which we have not yet come to terms – that past which did not simply begin in 1933, but in fact culminated in the years of Nazi rule. Whatever standpoint the reader might adopt towards Rosa Luxemburg's theory and practice, the integrity and the pure, courageous and sensitive personality of this revolutionary will fascinates everyone who concerns himself with her life and work.

Paul Frölich's monograph on Rosa Luxemburg has the great advantage of having been written by an author who was not only thoroughly acquainted with her works, but was also an active comrade-in-arms. We can therefore be certain that the political background and milieu of the revolutionary working-class movement are portrayed exactly. Although particular details in his evaluation can be criticised, the work as a whole remains the first comprehensive presentation of what Rosa Luxemburg wanted to achieve and how she worked. It cannot nor does it aim to make an impartial analysis and reconstruction of her life from a distant historical vantage-point, but aims to make a dynamic contribution towards representing and bringing to life Rosa Luxemburg's 'thought and action'.

This great fighter for a better social order, for understanding among peoples, and against imperialism and war, sought to bear and to shape the fate of the Jewish, the Polish, and the German peoples. Her work is part and parcel of the history of socialism and of the international working-class movement. Polish and German socialists, in particular, are greatly indebted to this woman who belonged to neither of their peoples, yet felt herself bound at the same time to both of them and to the whole of mankind.

IRING FETSCHER

References

1   Rosa Luxemburg, *Briefe an Karl und Luise Kautsky*, (Letters to Karl and Luise Kautsky), Berlin 1923, p 61 *et seq.*
2   Rosa Luxemburg, *Die Akkumulation des Kapitals. Ein Beitrag zur ökonomischen Erklärung des Kapitalismus* (The Accumulation of Capital. A contribution to the Economic Explanation of Capitalism), Berlin 1923.
Rosa Luxemburg, *Die Akkumulation des Kapitals oder Was die Epigonen aus der Marxschen Theorie gemacht haben. Eine Antikritik* (The Accumulation of Capital or What the Epigoni have done with Marxist Theory. An Anticritique), Berlin 1919: both works appear in Vol IV of the *Gesammelte Werke* (Collected Works) Berlin 1923. Quote is from pp 203-4.
3   Rosa Luxemburg, Introduction to Wladimir Korolenko, *Geschichte meines Zeitgenossen* (History of my Contemporary). Originally published by Paul Cassirer Verlag, Berlin 1919. Republished Berlin (East) 1947, p 32.
4   Rosa Luxemburg, *Gesammelte Werke* III, Berlin 1925, p 249.
5   Autobiography of Julius Wolf, in *Die volkswirtschaftliche Lehre der Gegenwart* (National Economic Teaching of the Present), Leipzig 1924, p 12.
6   Franz Mehring, *Aus dem Literarischen Nachlass von Karl Marx* (From the literary papers of Karl Marx) III, Stuttgart 1902.
7   Rosa Luxemburg, *Die industrielle Entwicklung Polens* (The Industrial Development of Poland), Doctoral dissertation, Leipzig, 1898.
8   Karl Marx-Friedrich Engels, *Werke* (Works) XVI, Berlin (East) 1962, p 198.
9   Rosa Luxemburg, *Neue Strömungen in der polnischen sozialistischen Bewegung in Deutschland und Österreich* (New Tendencies in the Polish socialist movement in Germany and Austria), *Neue Zeit*, Year 14, 2 vols, pp 176, 206.
10   Karl Kautsky, 'Finis Poloniae?', *Neue Zeit*, Year 14, 2 vols, p 519.
11   Rosa Luxemburg, *Die industrielle Entwicklung Polens*, p 69.
12   Rosa Luxemburg, *Die russische Revolution* (The Russian Revolution), Europäische Verlagsanstalt, Frankfurt am Main 1963, p 83.
13   N Lenin and G Zinoviev, *Gegen den Strom* (Against the Stream), 1921, pp 407-9.
14   *Internationaler Sozialistischer Arbeiter- und Gewerkschaftskongress*, (International Socialist Workers' and Trade-union Congress), London 1898, Minutes, p 18.
15   *Z Pola Walki*, No 1, Warsaw 1959.
16   'Einige Briefe Rosa Luxemburgs' (Some letters of Rosa Luxemburg), *Bulletin of the International Institute of Social History*, Leiden 1952, No 1. Letter of 11 October 1902.
17   *Die Krise der Sozialdemokratie (Juniusbroschüre)* (The Crisis in Social Democracy–The Junius Pamphlet), in Rosa Luxemburg, *Politische Schriften* II, Europäische Verlagsanstalt, Frankfurt am Main 1966.
18   Marx-Engels, *Studienausgabe* III, Fischer-Bücherei, Frankfurt am Main 1966, p 238.

19   Karl Marx, *Der 18 Brumaire des Louis Bonaparte* (The 18th Brumaire of Louis Bonaparte), Insel-Verlag, Frankfurt am Main 1965, p 9.

20   *Juniusbroschüre*, in Rosa Luxemburg, *Politische Schriften* II, p 30.

21   Rosa Luxemburg, *Gesammelte Werke* III, p 269.

22   *Sozialreform oder Revolution?* (Social Reform or Revolution), in Rosa Luxemburg, *Politische Schriften* I, pp 113-19.

23   Rosa Luxemburg, *Gesammelte Werke* III, p 281.

24   Rosa Luxemburg, 'Rede auf dem Stuttgarter Parteitag 1898' (Speech at the Stuttgart Party Congress 1898), *Gesammelte Werke* III, p 127.

25   *Sozialreform oder Revolution?* in Rosa Luxemburg, *Politische Schriften* I, p 59.

26   *ibid*, p 60 *et seq*.

27   *ibid*, p 64 *et seq*.

28   *ibid*, p 71 *et seq*.

29   *ibid*, p 104.

30   Rosa Luxemburg, *Politische Schriften* I, p 107.

31   Rosa Luxemburg, *Gesammelte Werke* III, p 390 *et seq*.

32   *ibid*, p 273.

33   *ibid*, p 336.

34   *ibid*, p 326 *et seq*.

35   *ibid*, p 355.

36   Rosa Luxemburg, *Gesammelte Werke* IV, Berlin 1928, p 361 *et seq*.

37   *ibid*, p 366.

38   *ibid*.

39   Bulletin no 1 of the International Institute of Social History, Amsterdam 1952.

40   Rosa Luxemburg, *Briefe an Freunde* (Letters to Friends), p 81 *et seq*.

41   Rosa Luxemburg, *Die russische Revolution*, p 28 (q.v. note 12 above).

42   *ibid*, p 32.

43   *ibid*, p 33.

44   *ibid*, p 44.

45   *Lenin Digest*, 36 vols, Leningrad/Moscow 1925-59. Reprinted in Rosa Luxemburg, *Ausgewählte Reden und Schriften* (Selected Speeches and Writings), Dietz Verlag, Berlin (East) 1951.

46   Friedrich Engels, *Der Deutsche Bauernkrieg* (The Peasant War in Germany), Berlin 1908, p 106.

47   Rosa Luxemburg, *Ausgewählte Reden und Schriften* II, p 244.

48   Ladislaus Gumplowicz in *Sozialistische Monatshefte* (Socialist Monthly), March 1905.

49   Rosa Luxemburg, 'Co Dalej?', No 1, (What Next?), *Czerwony Sztandar*, April 1905.

50   *ibid*.

51   *ibid*.

52   'Co Dalej?', No 3, Warsaw 1906.

53   V I Lenin, *Two Tactics of Social Democracy*, July 1905.

54   'Co Dalej?', No 2, 1905.

55   Rosa Luxemburg, 'Pomnik hánby' (A Monument of Shame), *Przeglad Socjaldemokratyczny* (Social-Democratic Review), July 1909.

56   *Juniusbroschüre* in Rosa Luxemburg, *Politische Schriften* II, p 93 *et seq*.

57   N Cherevanin, *Das Proletariat und die russische Revolution* (The Proletariat and the Russian Revolution), Stuttgart 1908.

58   Letter to Emmanuel and Mathilde Wurm, Warsaw 18 July 1906, in Rosa Luxemburg, *Briefe an Freunde*, p 43.

59   *Illustrierte Geschichte der Deutschen Revolution* (Illustrated History of the German Revolution), Berlin 1929, p 62.

60   Marx-Engels, *Studienausgabe* III, 1966, p 160.

61   *ibid.*

62   Rosa Luxemburg, *Gesammelte Werke* IV, p 341 *et seq.*

63   Henriette Roland-Holst, *Rosa Luxemburg, ihr Leben und Wirken,* (Rosa Luxemburg, her life and work), Zürich 1937, p 218.

64   Rosa Luxemburg, *Massenstreik, Partei und Gewerkschaften* (Mass Strike, Political Party and Trade Unions), in *Politische Schriften* I, p 172.

65   *ibid,* p 180 *et seq.*

66   *ibid,* p 182.

67   *ibid,* p 199.

68   *ibid,* p 183 *et seq.*

69   Rosa Luxemburg, *Gesammelte Werke* III, p 391.

70   Rosa Luxemburg, *Gesammelte Werke* IV, p 380.

71   *ibid,* p 669.

72   *Einführung in die Nationalökonomie* (Introduction to Economics), in Rosa Luxemburg *Ausgewählte Reden und Schriften* I, Berlin, (East) 1951.

73   See footnote 2 above.

74   N Bukharin, 'Der Imperialismus und die Akkumulation des Kapitals' (Imperialism and the Accumulation of Capital) in *Unter dem Banner des Marxismus,* 1925.

75   Fritz Sternberg, *Der Imperialismus* (Imperialism), Berlin 1926.

76   Rosa Luxemburg, *Gesammelte Werke* VI, pp 334-5.

77   *ibid,* p 361.

78   *ibid,* p 380.

79   N Bukharin, *op cit* I, p 254.

80   *Sozialreform oder Revolution?* in Rosa Luxemburg, *Politische Schriften* I, p 86.

81   Rosa Luxemburg, *Gesammelte Werke* VI, p 479.

82   Rosa Luxemburg, *Gesammelte Werke* VI, p 397.

83   *ibid,* p 480 *et seq.*

84   *ibid* IV, p 511.

85   *ibid,* p 559.

86   *ibid,* p 509 *et seq.*

87   Speech delivered 20 February 1914, in Rosa Luxemburg, *Politische Schriften* II, p 10.

88   *ibid,* p 17.

89   Rosa Luxemburg, *Briefe an Freunde,* p 103.

90   Rosa Luxemburg, Introduction to Wladimir Korolenko, *op cit,* p 9 *et seq.* (q.v. note 3 above).

91   Rosa Luxemburg, *Briefe an Karl und Luise Kautsky, op cit,* p 156.

92   Rosa Luxemburg, *Briefe an Freunde, op cit,* p 49. From a letter to Mathilde Wurm.

93   Letters to Mathilde Jacob, previously published.

94   Rosa Luxemburg, *Gesammelte Werke* III, p 375.

95   *Juniusbroschüre* in Rosa Luxemburg, *Politische Schriften* II, p 19.

96   Rosa Luxemburg, *Gesammelte Werke* IV, p 157.

97   *ibid,* p 160.

98   Karl Kautsky, *Vergangenheit und Zukunft der Internationale* (Past and Future of the International), Vienna 1920.

99   According to Friedrich Adler's account, related to Max Ermers, *Victor Adler,* Vienna 1932.

100 Friedrich Adler, *Vor dem Ausnahmegericht* (Before the Special Court), Jena 1923.

101 Karl Kautsky, *Nationalstaat, imperialischer Staat und Staatenbund* (National State, Imperial State and League of States), Nürnberg 1914.

102 Rosa Luxemburg, *Ausgewählte Reden und Schriften* 11, Berlin (East) 1951, p 522 *et seq.*

103 *ibid,* pp 528 and 530.

104 *ibid,* p 530 *et seq.*

105 N Lenin and G Zinoviev, *Gegen den Strom,* Hamburg 1921, p 24.

106 From an unpublished letter to Mathilde Jacob.

107 Published in *Unter dem Banner des Marxismus,* Heft 2, 1925.

108 *Juniusbroschüre* in Rosa Luxemburg, *Politische Schriften* 11, p 84 *et seq.*

109 *ibid,* p 125.

110 N Lenin and G Zinoviev, *Gegen den Strom,* p 415 *et seq.*

111 *Juniusbroschüre* in Rosa Luxemburg, *Politische Schriften* 11, p 96 *et seq.*

112 *ibid,* p 149 *et seq.*

113 *ibid,* p 154 *et seq.*

114 *ibid,* p 156 *et seq.*

115 *Entweder-Oder* (Either-Or), illegal leaflet produced during the war.

116 *Briefe an Freunde,* p 120.

117 *Briefe aus dem Gefängnis* (Letters from Prison), p 56.

118 *Spartakusbriefe,* Berlin (East) 1958, p 303 *et seq.*

119 *ibid,* p 353 *et seq.*

120 *ibid,* p 359.

121 *ibid,* p 366 *et seq.*

122 *ibid,* pp 409-10.

123 *Die russische Revolution. Eine kritische Würdigung aus dem Nachlass von Rosa Luxemburg.* (The Russian Revolution. A Critical Appreciation from the papers of Rosa Luxemburg) edited and introduced by Paul Levi, Berlin 1922. The most recent (German) edition is that edited and introduced by Ossip K Flechtheim, 1963 (Europäische Verlagsanstalt, Frankfurt am Main) from which we cite.

124 *ibid,* p 48.

125 *ibid,* p 50 *et seq.*

126 *ibid,* p 55 *et seq.*

127 *ibid,* p 58.

128 *ibid,* p 78.

129 *ibid,* p 77.

130 *ibid,* p 78.

131 *ibid,* p 74 *et seq.*

132 *ibid,* p 74.

133 *ibid,* p 73.

134 *ibid,* pp 75, 76.

135 *ibid,* p 78.

136 *ibid,* p 79.

137 *ibid,* p 80.

138 *ibid,* p 86.

139 A Warski, *Rosa Luxemburgs Stellung zu den taktischen Problemen der Revolution* (Rosa Luxemburg's Position on the Tactical Problems of Revolution), Hamburg 1922, p 7-Warski cites from memory.

140 Rosa Luxemburg, *Die russische Revolution,* p 52.

141 *Der Anfang* (The Beginning), in Rosa Luxemburg, *Ausgewählte Reden und Schriften* 11, p 594 *et seq.*

142   *ibid*, p 606.

143   *Was will der Spartakusbund?* (What does the Spartakusbund want?), in Rosa Luxemburg, *Politische Schriften* II, p 161 *et seq*.

144   *ibid*, p 163.

145   *ibid*, p 164 *et seq*.

146   *ibid*, p 169.

147   Anton Fischer *Die Revolutionskommandantur in Berlin* (The Revolutionary Commandant in Berlin), Berlin 1920.

148   *Massenstreik, Partei und Gewerkschaften*, in Rosa Luxemburg, *Politische Schriften* I, p 192.

149   *Unser Programm und die politische Situation. Rede auf dem Gründungs parteitag der* KPD *(Spartakusbund)* (Our Programme and the Political Situation. Speech to the Founding Conference of the KPD), in Rosa Luxemburg, *Politische Schriften* II, pp 197 *et seq*, 200 *et seq*.

150   See, *Illustriete Geschichte der Deutschen Revolution* (Illustrated History of the German Revolution), Berlin 1929. Fotomechaniser Nachdruck, Frankfurt 1968.

151   Paul Levi, in the *Leipziger Volkszeitung*, 15 January 1929.

152   Clara Zetkin, *Um Rosa Luxemburgs Stellung zur russischen Revolution* (Rosa Luxemburg's Position on the Russian Revolution), Hamburg 1922.

153   *Ordnung Herrscht in Berlin* (Order Reigns in Berlin), in Rosa Luxemburg, *Politische Schriften* II, p 207.

154   On the murder see: *Der Mord an Karl Liebknecht und Rosa Luxemburg. Zusammenfassende Darstellung des gesamtem Untersuchungsmaterials mit ausführlichem Prozessbericht* (The Murder of Karl Liebknecht and Rosa Luxemburg. A Comprehensive Presentation of the Total Investigation Material with a detailed Report of the Trial), Berlin 1920: E J Gumbel, *Vier Jahre politischer Mord* (Four Years of Political Murder), Berlin 1922: Paul Levi, *Der Jorns-Prozess, Rede des Verteidigers Paul Levi nebst Einleitung* (The Jorns Trial, Speech of the Defence Attorney Paul Levi plus an Introduction), Berlin 1929.

155   Paul Levi, *op cit*.

156   See *Illustriete Geschichte der Deutschen Revolution*, p 298.

157   Elisabeth Hannover-Druck u. H. Hannover, *Dokumentation eines politischen Verbrechens* (Documentation of a Political Crime), p 179 *et seq*.

Supplementary Works by Rosa Luxemburg

1 *Briefe an Leon Jogiches* (Letters to Leon Jogiches), 1894-1914, a selection edited by Dr. Feliks Tych, Frankfurt/M. 1971.

2 *Gesammelte Werke* (Collected Works), 1893-1905, edited by the Marx-Engels-Lenin Institute, 2 vols, Berlin (East) 1970.

3 *Internationalismus und Klassenkampf* (Internationalism and class struggle), works from the Polish (1893-1908), edited by Jürgen Hentze, Neuwied 1971.

4 *Letters to Mathilde Jacob*, 1913-1918, edited by Nahiriko Ito, Tokyo 1972.

Bibliography

1   Works by Rosa Luxemburg

The fullest bibliography available is that given by J P Nettl in his biography *Rosa Luxemburg*, 2 vols, Oxford University Press, London 1966, pp 863-917. Listed below are the standard collections of Rosa's works available in German, and all the material available in English translation. It must be pointed out that the quality of the English translations is in general very poor (but q.v. B 2 and B 3 below).

A   STANDARD COLLECTIONS IN GERMAN
   1 *Gesammelte Werke* (Collected Works), edited by Clara Zetkin and Adolf Warski, editor-in-chief Paul Frölich, Berlin 1923-1928.
   Planned in 9 volumes:
      Vol I   *Polen* (Poland)
      Vol II   *Die russische Revolution* (The Russian Revolution)
      Vol III *Gegen den Reformismus* (Against Reformism)
      Vol IV   *Gewerkschaftskampf und Massenstreik* (Trade Union Struggle and Mass Strike)
      Vol V   *Der Imperialismus* (Imperialism)
      Vol VI   *Die Akkumulation des Kapitals* (The Accumulation of Capital)
      Vol VII *Nationalökonomie* (Economics)
      Vol VIII *Krieg und Revolution* (War and Revolution)
      Vol IX   *Briefe, Gedenkartikel, historische Aufsätze* (Letters, Occasional pieces, historical works etc)
   Only Vols III, IV, and VI were published.
   2 *Ausgewählte Reden und Schriften* (Selected Speeches and Writings), edited by the Marx-Engels-Lenin-Institute, Central Committee of the German Democratic Republic, 2 vols, Berlin (East) 1951.
   3 *Politische Schriften* (Political Writings), edited and introduced by Ossip K Flechtheim, 3 vols, Frankfurt am Main 1966, 1968.
   4 *Briefe aus dem Gefängnis* (Letters from Prison–to Sonja Liebknecht), Berlin 1919.
   5 *Briefe an Karl und Luise Kautsky* (Letters to Karl and Luise Kautsky), 1896-1918, Berlin 1923.
   6 *Briefe an Freunde* (Letters to Friends), Hamburg 1950.

B   WORKS IN ENGLISH TRANSLATION

1 *Rosa Luxemburg Speaks*, edited with an introduction by Mary-Alice Waters, Pathfinder Press 1970.

A collection which includes the traditional translations of most of the material which has been or still is available in pamphlet or article form in English translation. It contains the following texts:

Social Reform or Revolution (1898-99)

Socialist Crisis in France (1900-01). Incomplete.

Stagnation and Progress of Marxism (1903)

Organisational Questions of Russian Social Democracy (1904) (Sometimes called 'Leninism or Marxism')

Socialism and the Churches (1905)

The Mass Strike, the Political Party and the Trade Unions (1906)

What is Economics? (1907 onwards; 1st publ after Rosa's death)

Peace Utopias (1911). Incomplete.

The Crisis in German Social Democracy (The Junius Pamphlet) (1915)

Introduction to Korolenko's 'A History of My Contemporary' (1918)

The Russian Revolution (1918)

Against Capital Punishment (1918)

Speech to the Founding Conference of the KPD (1918) (Sometimes called 'Spartacus', 'Our Programme and the Political Situation')

This collection also includes a handful of Rosa's letters from prison to Sonja Liebknecht, and appraisals of Rosa by Lenin and Trotsky.

2 *Selected Political Writings*, edited and introduced by Dick Howard, Monthly Review Press, New York and London 1971.

All the writings in this collection have been newly translated, and much has been made available in English for the first time. An excellent compilation, containing

Speeches to the Stuttgart Congress (1898)

Speech to the Hanover Congress (1899)

Social Reform or Revolution (1898-99)

Militia and Militarism (1899)

from: In Memory of the Proletariat Party (1903)

The Eight Hour Day at the Party Congress (1902)

Women's Suffrage and Class Struggle (1912)

from: Mass Strike, Party and Trade Unions (1906)

Speech to the Nürnberg Congress (1908)

Organisational Questions of Russian Social Democracy (1904)

What are the Origins of May Day? (1894)

The Idea of May Day on the March (1913)

The Crisis in German Social Democracy (The Junius Pamphlet): Part I (1915)

Either-Or (1916)

To the Proletarians of all Countries (1918)

What does the Spartacus League want? (1918)
Our Programme and the Political Situation (Speech to the Founding Congress of the KPD) (1918)
Order Reigns in Berlin (1919)

3 *Rosa Luxemburg: Selected Political Writings*, edited and introduced by Robert Looker, London 1972.
This collection includes a wide range of material, mostly fairly short newspaper articles made available in English for the first time, as well as short extracts from *Social Reform or Revolution, The Mass Strike* etc. The *new* material made available (or only otherwise available in the *Selected Political Writings* edited by Dick Howard, entry B 2 above) is as follows:

Opportunism and the Art of the Possible (1898)
Militia and Militarism (1899)
Social Democracy and Parliamentarianism (1904)
The Revolution in Russia (1905)
The Two Methods of Trade-Union Policy (1906)
The Next Step (1910)
Concerning Morocco (1911)
What Now? (1912)
The Political Mass Strike (1913)
Rebuilding the International (1915)
Either-Or (1916)
The Old Mole (1917)
The Russian Tragedy (1918)

Also included are 10 pieces from the period of revolution, November 1918–January 1919, viz:

The Beginning (18 Nov)
A Duty of Honour (18 Nov)
The National Assembly (20 Nov)
To the Proletariat of all Lands (25 Nov)
The Acheron in Motion (27 Nov)
What does the Spartakusbund want? (nd, 1918)
The Elections to the National Assembly (23 Dec)
What are the Leaders Doing? (7 Jan)
House of Cards (13 Jan)
Order Reigns in Berlin (14 Jan)

4 *The Accumulation of Capital*, Routledge and Kegan Paul 1951. Translated by Agnes Schwartzschild, with an introduction by Joan Robinson.
A fine translation of Rosa's major treatise on Marxian economic theory.

5 *The Accumulation of Capital or What the Epigoni have done with Marxist Theory. An Anticritique.*
Forthcoming 1972 from Allen Lane the Penguin Press.

6 *The Second and Third Volumes of 'Capital'*, being Chapter 12

section 3 of Franz Mehring, *Karl Marx: the Story of his Life*, London 1936.

7 *Letters from Prison*, translated by Eden and Cedar Paul. Most recent edition by the Socialist Book Centre Ltd, London 1946.
Rosa's letters from prison to Sonja Liebknecht.

8 *Letters to Karl and Luise Kautsky from 1896 to 1918*, ed Luise Kautsky, trans Louis P Lochner, New York 1925.

9 Pamphlets. Various. Published by Sydney Wanasinghe, Ceylon and Merlin Press, London. These all appear to be some of the same texts which are collected together in B 1 above.

10 *The Russian Revolution* and *Leninism or Marxism?*, introduced by Bertram D Wolfe, Michigan 1961. The same translations as in B 1 above.

11 Miscellaneous fragments
'On the 20th Anniversary of Marx's Death', *Fourth International*, December 1941.
'The Fallen Women of Liberalism', *New International*, NY July 1942.
'Introduction of Capitalism in South Africa', *Fourth International*, Amsterdam 1960 no 9.

2 Works in English on Rosa Luxemburg and the International background and movement.

This list is highly selective, containing both Marxist and non-Marxist works. They have all been chosen because of the light they throw on the subject matter which this book deals with, but with many of them it is vitally necessary to maintain one's critical distance.

Anderson, Evelyn, *Hammer or Anvil: The Story of the German Working Class Movement*, London 1945.
Balabanoff, Angelica, *My Life as a Rebel*, London 1938.
Beer, Max. *Fifty Years of International Socialism*, London 1935.
Berlau, A Joseph, *The German Social Democratic Party, 1914-21*, New York 1950.
Bernstein, Eduard, *Evolutionary Socialism*, New York 1961.
Bevan, Edwyn, *German Social Democracy during the War*, London 1918.
Böhm-Bawerk, Eugen von, *Karl Marx and the Close of his System*, New York 1949 (This volume includes R Hilferding's reply 'Böhm-Bawerk's Criticism of Marx', and L von Bortkiewicz's essay 'On the Correction of Marx's Fundamental Theoretical Construction in the Third Volume of *Capital*').
Borkenau, Franz, *European Communism*, Berne 1952.
Borkenau, Franz, *World Communism. A History of the Communist International*, New York 1939.

Braunthal, Julius, *History of the International 1864-1943*, 2 vols, London 1966 and 1967.

Burdick, Charles B, and Lutz, Ralph H (eds), *The Political Institutions of the German Revolution 1918-1919*, New York 1966.

Cecil, Lamar, *Albert Ballin: Business and Politics in Imperial Germany 1888-1918*, Princeton 1967.

Cliff, Tony, *Rosa Luxemburg*, London 1959.

Cole, G D H, *The Second International, 1889-1914*, 2 vols, London 1956 (Vol III Parts I and II of a series entitled *A History of Socialist Thought*).

Cole, G D H, *Communism and Social Democracy*, London 1958 (Vol IV of *A History of Socialist Thought*).

Comfort, Richard A, *Revolutionary Hamburg: Labour Politics in the Early Weimar Republic*, Stanford 1966.

Davis, Horace B, *Nationalism and Socialism*, New York 1962.

Degras, Jane (ed), *The Communist International 1919-1943, Documents*, Vol 1, London 1956.

Deutscher, Issac, *The Prophet Armed, Trotsky: 1879-1921*, London 1954.

Dunayevskaya, Raya, *Marxism and Freedom*, 3rd rev ed, London 1971.

Dziewanowski, M K, *The Communist Party of Poland*, Cambridge Mass 1959.

Eyck, Erich, *A History of the Weimar Republic*, Vol 1, Cambridge Mass 1962.

Feldman, Gerald D, *Army, Industry and Labor in Germany 1914-1918*, Princeton 1966.

Fischer, Fritz, *Germany's Aims in the First World War*, London 1967.

Fischer, Ruth, *Stalin and German Communism*, London 1948.

Gankin, O H and Fisher, H H (eds), *The Bolsheviks and the World War: The Origins of the Third International*, Stanford 1940.

Gay, Peter, *The Dilemma of Democratic Socialism: Eduard Bernstein's Challenge to Marx*, New York 1952.

Gerschenkron, Alexander, *Bread and Democracy in Germany*, Berkeley and Los Angeles 1943. Reprinted with a new introduction, New York 1966.

Goldberg, Harvey, *The Life of Jean Jaurès*, Madison 1962.

Jackson, J Hampden, *Jean Jaurès*, London 1943.

Joll, James, *The Second International 1889-1914*, London 1955.

Kautsky, Karl, *The Class Struggle*, Chicago 1910.

Kautsky, Karl, *The Erfurt Program*, Chicago 1910.

Kautsky, Karl, *The Road to Power*, Chicago 1909.

Krupskaya, Nadezhda K, *Memories of Lenin, 1893-1917*, London 1942.

Kuczynski, Jürgen, *A Short History of Labour Conditions under Industrial Capitalism*, London 1945.

Lenin, Vladimir Illich, *What is to be Done?* Collected Works Vol 5, Moscow.

Lenin, Vladimir Illich, *The Right of Nations to Self-determination,* Collected Works Vol 20, Moscow.

Lenin, Vladimir Illich, *Two Tactics of Social Democracy,* Collected Works Vol 9, Moscow.

Lenin, Vladimir Illich, *State and Revolution,* Collected Works Vol 25, Moscow.

Lorwin, Val R, *The French Labor Movement,* Harvard 1954.

Lukács, Georg, *History and Class Consciousness,* London 1971.

Lutz, R H (ed), Fall of the German Empire 1914-1918. Documents of the German Revolution, 2 vols, Stanford 1932.

Mehring, Karl, *Karl Marx: the Story of his Life,* London 1936.

Michels, Robert, *Political Parties* (1911), 2nd edition New York 1959.

Miliband, Ralph, *Parliamentary Socialism,* London 1961.

Mitchell, Allan, *Revolution in Bavaria 1918-1919. The Eisner Régime and the Soviet Republic,* Princeton 1965.

Nettl, J P, *Rosa Luxemburg,* 2 vols, London 1966.

Neumann, Franz, *Behemoth: The Structure and Practice of National Socialism,* London 1942.

Neumann, Franz, *European Trade Unionism and Politics,* New York 1936.

Rosenberg, Arthur, *The Birth of the German Republic,* London 1931; reprinted as *Imperial Germany: The Birth of the German Republic 1871-1918,* New York 1967.

Rosenberg, Arthur, *A History of Bolshevism from Marx to the First Five Years' Plan,* London 1934.

Rosenberg, Arthur, *The History of the German Republic,* London 1936.

Rossi, A, *The Rise of Italian Fascism 1918-1922,* London 1938.

Ryder, A J, *The German Revolution of 1918,* Cambridge 1967.

Scheidemann, Philipp, *The Making of New Germany: The Memoirs of Philipp Scheidemann,* 2 vols, New York 1929.

Schorske, Karl, *German Social Democracy 1905-1917: The Development of the Great Schism,* Cambridge Mass 1955.

Schweitzer, Arthur, *Big Business in the Third Reich,* London 1964.

Serge, Victor, *Memoirs of a Revolutionary 1901-1941,* London 1963.

Strobel, Heinrich, *The German Revolution and After,* New York 1923.

Trotsky, Leon, *History of the Russian Revolution,* 3 vols, London 1932.

Trotsky, Leon, *My Life,* London 1930.

Waite, Robert G L, *Vanguard of Nazism: The Free Corps Movement in Post-War Germany. 1918-1923,* Cambridge Mass 1952.

Waldman, Eric, *The Spartacist Uprising of 1919,* Milwaukee 1958.

Zetkin, Clara, *Reminiscences of Lenin,* London 1929.

Index

Accumulation of Capital, 58, 156f, 158f, 218; quoted from, 6, 56, 157, 158
Accumulation of Capital: an Anti-critique, 160, 216; quoted from 165-6
'Acheron on the Move'; quoted from, 275
Adler, Friedrich, 199, 200, 211
Adler, Max; on RL, 197
Adler, Victor, 199, 200, 201
Agrarian question, 122-3; in Russian Revolution, 243-6
Akselrod, Pavel, 12, 14, 81, 117, 199
Algemener Yiddisher Arbeter Bund; see the *Bund*
Allemane, 37
Anti-Bolshevik League, 272, 287
Arbeiterpolitik, 255, 280
Armed uprising, 102f, 296
Association of Polish Socialists Abroad, 32, 34
Aussem, 113

Balabanoff, Angelica, 199, 202
Bardowski, Pjotr, 16
Barth, Emil, 274
Bauer, Otto, 160
Bax, Belfort, 48
Bebel, August, 20, 40, 41, 48, 98-9, 125, 126, 132, 168, 183, 184, 262; letter to, 71
'The Beginning'; quoted from, 265, 266, 267
Bernstein, Eduard, 47, 67, 131, 154, 166, 263; and reformism, 47f, 51, 54f, 57, 58f; RL on, 51f, 54f, 58f, 70f, 72, 126, 153
Bethmann-Hollweg, Theobald von, 169f, 213
Blanquism, 18, 19, 84, 89, 110, 278
Block, Hans, 17
Bolsheviks, 81-3, 90, 129; and the war, 232; in power, 238f; RL's criticism of, 241-52
Braun, Otto, 179n

Brest-Litovsk, 239-40, 255
Brodowski, 113
Bukharin, Nicolai, 156, 161-2
The *Bund*, 13, 231
Burgfrieden, 206, 220, 226
'Burning Questions of the Day'; quoted from, 235-7

Capitalist development, 6, 43f, 55-7, 218f; and crisis, 150f; *see* imperialism
Cherevanin, A, 119
Chernyshevski, 2
Communist Party of Germany (KPD); foundation, 270, 279f; in January 'uprising', 284f, 289f, 294
Cunow, Heinrich, 207, 248
Czerwony Sztander, 101, 102, 116

Daszyński, Ignaz, 21, 33, 34, 110, 111, 232
David, Eduard, 126, 166, 226
'In Defence of Nationality', 76
Democracy; dictatorship and, 247-50
Dickstein, Simon, 16
Dictatorship and democracy, 247-50
Diefenbach, Hans, 231, 238; letters to, 8, 74-5, 159, 179, 184-5, 194, 215, 229
Dietz, IHW, 148
Dluski, Kasimir, 16
'Dog Politics'; quoted from, 226
Domski, Henryk, 113
Dorrenbach, Heinrich, 288, 301
Dual power, 246f
Duncker, Hermann, 146, 264
Duncker, Käte, 210
Dzierzyński, Feliks, 36 and n, 113

Eberlein, Hugo, 216, 295
Ebert, Friedrich, 259, 261, 262, 266, 271, 272, 280, 285, 286, 290, 298
Eckstein, Gustav, 146
Economics; RL on, 11, 146f
Economism, 19-20, 53
see also reformism

Eichhorn, Emil, 271, 272, 273, 278, 287, 289
Eisner, Kurt, 99, 131, 257
Engels, Friedrich, 34, 47, 92, 265; and Polish independence, 21, 23; and general strike, 128-9; on war, 219-20; introduction to *Class Struggles in France*, 45-6, 52, 68
Ernst, Eugen, 287

Figner, Vera, 17
France; parliamentarism in, 62f

German Revolution, 255f; fleet mutinies, 257f; Berlin uprising, 258f; programme of *Spartakus*, 265f; January 1919 'uprising', 283f; strength and weaknesses, 261-3
Germany; situation in 1890s, 38f, trade unions in, 138-40; parliament and elections in, 169, 173-4; *see also* German Revolution, SPD
Glasier, Bruce, 200
Gordon, A, 13
Gorter, Hermann, 30
Gradnauer, Georg, 42, 73, 99
Guesde, Jules, 37, 48, 63, 199, 200, 206

Haase, Hugo, 179, 199, 201, 203, 204, 213, 222, 263, 266
Haenisch, Konrad, 207
Hanecki, Jakob, 113, 118
Hardie, Keir, 199
Hebbel, Friedrich, 75
Heine, Wolfgang, 54, 131
Heinemann, Hugo, 146
Herzen, Alexander, 2
Hilferding, Rudolf, 131, 146, 263, 280
History; RL on, 50, 51, 71, 141, 144
Hoffmann, Adolf, 213
Hutten, Ulrich von, 25, 141; quotes from Konrad Meyer's epic poem about, 192, 253
Huysmans, Camille, 203

Imperialism, 45, 163; and capital accumulation, 156-8; and capitalist politics, 164f; and war, 218f
Independent Social Democratic Party of Germany (USPD): formation, 234, 279-80; in 1918 revolution, 262-3, 266, 267, 278, 285; withdrawal from Government, 286
Industrial Development of Poland, 19, 27, 36
Die Internationale, 209f, 214
Introduction to Economics, 148f, 152, 156, 216

Jacob, Mathilde, 299n; letters to, 192-3, 214-5
Jagow, Traugott von, 169
Jankowska, 21, 34
Jaurès, Jean, 48, 199, 201-2, 203; and parliamentarism, 63-8; RL and, 75-6, 183, 195
Jogiches, Leo 12-15, 19, 34, 73; and RL, 14-15, 39, 73-4, 183; in Poland, 113, 114, 117-18; on the Bolsheviks (1908), 121-2; and *Spartakusbund*, 227, 241, 254, 264, 281; and KPD, 295, 300-1; letter to, 99
Juniusbroschüre, 143, 215, 217; quoted from, 20, 43, 119-20, 195, 218-19; Lenin on, 219

Karski, *see* Marchlewski-Karski, Julian
Kasprzak, Martin, 6, 9, 33
Kautsky, Karl, 37, 40, 41, 48, 60, 71, 90, 98, 116, 143; on imperialism, 45, 165; on the mass strike, 132; breaks with RL, 172-4; and the war, 199, 200-1, 205, 207, 209, 211, 212-13, 222; in 1918 revolution, 262
Kautsky, Luise; letters to, 3, 229, 231, 239, 254
Kerensky, Alexander, 235
Kiderlin-Wächter, Alfred von, 166, 173
Kilbalshitch, Nicolai, 17
Köbis, Albin, 257
Korolenko, Wladimir; RL's introduction to, 7, 186-7, 188-9, 216; quoted from 7, 186, 187
KPD; *see* Communist Party of Germany
Krichevskii, 20, 81
Kunicki, Stanislaus, 16

Labriola, Antonio, 48
Landsberg, Otto, 262, 286
Lange, Paul, 219, 264
Lassalle, Ferdinand, 71, 149, 195
Lavrov, Peter, 2, 10
Ledebour, Georg, 203, 204, 213, 288, 294, 297
Leder, Josef, 113
Left Radicals, 255, 279-80, 281
Legality, 68-70
Legien, Carl, 261, 262
Lenin, Vladimir Ilych, 77, 81, 168, 173, 183, 204, 209; on the national question, 30-1, 219; on organisation, 81f, 86f, 106-7; on the coming Russian Revolution, 93-4; against the war, 213, 219
Lensch, Paul, 175, 204, 248
Leuthner, Karl, 164
Levi, Paul, 148, 176, 264; edits RL's *Russian Revolution*, 241

Liebknecht, Karl, 98, 173, 178-80, 183; and war credits, 204, 208; conscripted, 216; imprisonment, 224-6; release, 257; role in 1918 revolution, 258, 264, 281, 288, 298-90; murder of, 297f

Liebknecht, Sonja; letters to, 114-15, 183, 229, 231, 253, 256-7, 300

Liebknecht, Wilhelm, 36, 45, 48, 68, 73

Luxemburg, Rosa; and literature; 4-5, 39, 186-7; as a speaker; 39, 41, 97, 171, 196f; as a debater, 48-9, 75-6, 191; as a fighter; 70, 187f; as a writer, 193f; as a teacher, 146f; as a person, 181f, see also entries under Zetkin and Jogiches in particular; as a journalist, 37, 39f, 175; as an editor, 42, 74, 99, 210, 264; in prison, 76, 113f, 214f, 227f, 253-4; method of analysis, 49-51, 70-1, 149f; for her writings, see under each title; see separate entries for her political views (e.g. armed uprising, organisation, etc.)

Malecki, 113
Man, Hendrik de, 178
Marchlewski-Karski, Julian, 11-12, 34, 38, 41, 113, 159, 173, 175, 183, 205, 227
Martov, Julius, 81, 82, 83, 168
Martynov, AS, 89
Marx, Karl; and the national question, 21, 23, 28-9, 30, 32; and capitalist collapse, 50, 152f
'Marxist Centre', see SPD
Mass strike, 98, 101, 108f 119f, 127f, 133f, 177; Hilferding on, 121; Kautsky on, 132; German trade unions and, 130, 137-40
The Mass Strike, the Party, and the Trade Unions, 117, 127f, 133f, 139-40; quoted from, 129-30, 134-5, 136-7, 137-8, 274-5
Maurenbrecher, Max, 164
Mehring, Franz, 4, 22, 41, 48, 71, 74, 75, 98, 140, 146, 159, 173, 175, 183, 205, 208, 210, 214, 227, 300
Mendelsohn, Stanislaus, 16, 21, 34
Mensheviks, 81-3, 89, 92, 120, 173, 238
Meyer, Ernst, 216, 227, 294, 297
Mickiewicz, Adam, 4
Millerand, Alexandre, 62-7
Ministerialism, 92; see parliament
Morgari, Odino, 199
Müller, Hermann, 203, 204

Narodnaya Volya, 7, 13, 16-17, 18, 24, 34-5
National question, 21f, 35, Proletariat party and, 17-18; PPS and, 111-13; Bolsheviks and, 246
Naumann, Friedrich, 74, 100
Noske, Gustav, 262, 285, 286, 289
'Order Reigns in Berlin'; quoted from, 296
Organisation, 79f; RL and Lenin on, 84f, 106f, 247; and discipline, 84, 210; and spontaneity, 108, 133-7, 138f, 140f
Organisational Questions in Russian Social Democracy; quoted from, 84-85, 86
Ossowski, Michael, 16

Pannekock, Anton, 173, 174
Parliament, 61-2; Spartakus and boycott of, 281-2, 284; participation in p. in France, 62f; and soviets, 246f
Parvus-Helphand, Alexander, 12, 38, 40, 41, 45, 48, 58, 90, 93, 122, 206, 248
'Peace Utopias'; quoted from, 167
People's Naval Division, 272, 278, 286, 288
Peretz, Leon, 2
Permanent revolution, 90f, 121-2
'Perspectives and Projects'; quoted from, 213
Perl (Bundist), 34
Perovskaya, Sophie, 17
Pieck, Wilhelm, 216, 264, 288, 289, 299
Pietrusiński, 16
Pilsudski, 13, 31, 103, 111-12, 232
Plekhanov, Georgii, 7, 12, 14, 34-5, 77, 81, 122, 124, 190, 206
Poland; Jews in, 1-2, 5; schools in, 5; economic development of, 7-8; early socialist movements in, 15f; national question and, 17-18, 21f; 1905 revolution in, 101f, 118f; the left and the war, 232; code-name for Berlin, 286. see also: Proletariat party, PPS, SDKPiL
Polish Socialist Party (PPS), 102, 103; formation, 19; early split, 34-5; and SDKPiL, 107f; 1906 split, 111-12; 'Revolutionary Fraction' of, 112
Polish Workers League, 9
PPS; see Polish Socialist Party
Proletariat party, 6, 7-9, 15-18, 34-5; reorganised (1888), 18-19; and national self-determination, 17-18, 21, 32

'The Proletariat's Pilgrimage of Supplication'; quoted from, 79-80

Quessel, Ludwig, 164-166

Radek, Karl, 30, 113, 173, 174, 183, 284, 287, 291
Rappaport, Charles, 13
Red Soldiers' League, 272
Reform and revolution; relationship of, 19-21, 51-4, 65-7, 108-10, 274-5
Reformism, 45-8, 51f, 53f, 58f, 61f
Reichpietsch, Max, 257
Renner, Karl, 207
Revolution; relationship of reform and, 19-21, 51-4, 65-7, 108-10, 274-5; international character of, 250, 251, 252
'Revolutionary Committee', 288, 289, 290, 292
'Revolutionary Fraction'; see Polish Socialist Party
Revolutionary Shop Stewards (Revolutionäre Obleute), 258, 288
Revolutionary-Socialist Party Proletariat; see Proletariat Party
Roland, Alfred, 288
Roland-Holst, Henriette, 30; letter to, 132-3
Rote Fahne, 264-5; RL's articles quoted, 189, 265-6, 267, 268-9, 269-70, 275, 277, 278, 296; in January 'uprising', 285, 290, 292
Rühle, Otto, 204
Russia, capitalist development in, 5-6, 24-5, 26-7, 90-1; Tsarism and reaction, 22f; 1905 revolution 77-80, 100-101, 118-20; character of the revolution, 89f, 120-3
Russian Revolution; February 232f; October, 238f; RL on, 233-6, 239f, 243f; agrarian question, 243-6; national question, 246; constituent assembly, 246-7; democracy and, 247f
The Russian Revolution, 241-252; quoted from, 85-6, 242, 243, 244-5, 247-52, 260
Russian Social Democracy; early years, 80-1; 1903 split, 82-3; organisation of, 84-8; and 1905 revolution, 89f, 120f; 1907 Congress, 121-2, 191; see also Russian Revolution, Bolsheviks, Mensheviks
Ryazanov, David, 47

Scheidemann, Philipp, 206, 256, 262, 280, 284, 286, 297, 298
Schippel, Max, 48, 164
Schmidt, Julian, 149

Schmoller, Gustav, 72
Scholze, Paul, 288
Schönlank, Bruno, 40f, 43, 48, 74, 192
SDKPiL; see Social Democratic Party of the Kingdom of Poland and Lithuania
Second International; Zetkin at founding congress, 40; Zürich congress (1893), 34-5, 53; Amsterdam congress (1904), 92; Stuttgart congress, 168-9; and war, 168-9, 173, 199f; RL on collapse of, 211-12, 217f
Seidel, Robert and Mathilde; letter to, 39-40
Semkowska, Irene, 113
Shliapnikov, AG, 209
Singer, Paul, 40
Social Democratic Party of Germany (SPD), 38, 45-6, 124; reformism of, 45-6, 98, 173f; tendencies in, 45-6, 73-154, 166f, 173f, 216, 222; 'Marxist Centre', 131, 165-6, 173, 211, 215, 216; Bernstein and, 47-8, 72, 73; and 1905 revolution, 98-9, 125; leadership of, 85, 138f, 173; Party school, 146f; and imperialism, 166f, 173f; and the vote, 169f; support for the war, 214f; and 1918 revolution, 261-2, 275-6, 285-6; see also Spartakusbund, Independent Social Democratic Party of Germany
Social Democratic Party of the Kingdom of Poland, 35
Social Democratic Party of the Kingdom of Poland and Lithuania (SDKPiL), 36, 103, 113; and PPS, 107f; and the war, 232
Social Reform or Revolution, 51-60, 70-126; quoted from, 52-3, 56-7, 58-9, 162
Sombart, Werner, 70, 150
Soviets; in Russia, 96, 108, 233; and parliament, 246f; in Germany, 262-3, 265-6, 268, 275-6, 287-8, 290; Congress of workers' and soldiers' councils, 276-7
Spartakusbriefe, 227, 238-9, 241; quoted from, 230, 234-5, 235-6, 237, 240-1, 254-5
Spartakusbund, 216-17, 254, 279; 'Guiding Principles', 222-3; 1916 conference, 224; 1916 demonstrations, 224-5, 226; 1918 conference with Left Radicals, 255; in 1918 revolution, 264, 272-3, 276, 284f; programme of, 265f; and USPD, 279, 80
SPD; see Social Democratic Party of Germany

'Speech to the Founding Congress of the KPD'; quoted from, 282-3
Spontaneity; and organisation, 108, 133-7, 138f, 140f
Sprawa Robotnicza (Workers' Cause), 19, 34, 36
Stadthagen, Arthur, 146
Stampfer, Friedrich, 131
Sternberg, Fritz, 156
Stockholm conference (1917), 236-7
Ströbel, Heinrich, 210
Suffrage, 169f

'A Tactical Question', 64
Thalheimer, August, 210, 264
Trade Unions, 58-60; mass strike and, 130, 137-40; war and, 206, 220
Troelstra, Piter, 199
Trotsky, Leon, 81, 90, 93, 121, 122, 126, 246

Unszlict, J., 113
USPD: *see* Independent Social Democratic Party of Germany

Vaillant, Edouard, 37, 199, 206
Vandervelde, Emile, 34, 67, 68, 199, 201, 202
Violence, 68-70, 250, 268-270
Vollmar, Georg von, 68, 72, 126

War, 166f, 199f, 205f; RL on, 210-13, 235-7; on strategy against, 217f, 222f; Lenin on, 213 34, 38, 113, 183, 251
Warszawski-Warski, Adolft, 12, 19, Waryński, Ludwig, 16, 18, 21
Weil, Felix, 241
Wels, Otto, 271, 278
Westermeyer, Friedrich, 216
'What does the *Spartakusbund* want?'; quoted from, 268-70
What Next?, 102f; quoted from, 104, 105, 106
Winnig, August, 164, 271
Wissel, Rudolf, 286
Wolf, Julius, 11-12
Working class; leading role of, 17-18, 26, 91-2, 93, 94f, 109, 230; *see also* reform and revolution
Wurm, Emmanuel, 146
Wurm, Mathilde; letters to, 143-4, 229

Zasulich, Vera, 12, 81
Zetkin, Clara, 45, 48, 98, 173, 205, 208, 210, 214, 215, 216; and RL, 14, 40, 97, 175, 183, 254, 290
Zheliabov, 17
Zimmerwald, 216
Zinoviev, Grigori, 140

NB Material in the introduction, preface and postscript has *not* been indexed.

About Haymarket Books

Haymarket Books is a nonprofit, progressive book distributor and publisher, a project of the Center for Economic Research and Social Change. We believe that activists need to take ideas, history, and politics into the many struggles for social justice today. Learning the lessons of past victories, as well as defeats, can arm a new generation of fighters for a better world. As Karl Marx said, "The philosophers have merely interpreted the world; the point, however, is to change it."

We take inspiration and courage from our namesakes, the Haymarket Martyrs, who gave their lives fighting for a better world. Their 1886 struggle for the eight-hour day, which gave us May Day, the international workers' holiday, reminds workers around the world that ordinary people can organize and struggle for their own liberation. These struggles continue today across the globe—struggles against oppression, exploitation, hunger, and poverty.

It was August Spies, one of the Martyrs targeted for being an immigrant and an anarchist, who predicted the battles being fought to this day. "If you think that by hanging us you can stamp out the labor movement," Spies told the judge, "then hang us. Here you will tread upon a spark, but here, and there, and behind you, and in front of you, and everywhere, the flames will blaze up. It is a subterranean fire. You cannot put it out. The ground is on fire upon which you stand."

We could not succeed in our publishing efforts without the generous financial support of our readers. Many people contribute to our project through the Haymarket Sustainers program, where donors receive free books in return for their monetary support. If you would like to be a part of this program, please contact us at info@haymarketbooks.org.

Order these titles and more online at www.haymarketbooks.org or call 773-583-7884.

CPSIA information can be obtained
at www.ICGtesting.com
Printed in the USA
JSHW020148021122
32462JS00002B/3

9 781608 460748